Reluctant Warriors

STUDIES IN CANADIAN MILITARY HISTORY
Series editor: Andrew Burtch, Canadian War Museum

The Canadian War Museum, Canada's national museum of military history, has a threefold mandate: to remember, to preserve, and to educate. Studies in Canadian Military History, published by UBC Press in association with the Museum, extends this mandate by presenting the best of contemporary scholarship to provide new insights into all aspects of Canadian military history, from earliest times to recent events. The work of a new generation of scholars is especially encouraged, and the books employ a variety of approaches – cultural, social, intellectual, economic, political, and comparative – to investigate gaps in the existing historiography. The books in the series feed immediately into future exhibitions, programs, and outreach efforts by the Canadian War Museum. A list of the titles in the series appears at the end of the book.

CANADIAN WAR MUSEUM
MUSÉE CANADIEN DE LA GUERRE

Reluctant Warriors
Canadian Conscripts and the Great War

Patrick M. Dennis

UBCPress · Vancouver · Toronto

26 25 24 23 22 21 20 19 18   5 4 3 2

Printed in Canada on FSC-certified ancient-forest-free paper
(100% post-consumer recycled) that is processed chlorine- and acid-free.

Library and Archives Canada Cataloguing in Publication

Dennis, Patrick M., author
  Reluctant warriors : Canadian conscripts and the Great War / Patrick M. Dennis.

(Studies in Canadian military history)
Includes bibliographical references and index.
Issued in print and electronic formats.
ISBN 978-0-7748-3597-8 (hardcover). – ISBN 978-0-7748-3599-2 (PDF)
ISBN 978-0-7748-3600-5 (EPUB). – ISBN 978-0-7748-3601-2 (Kindle)

  1. Draft – Canada – History – 20th century. 2. Draftees – Canada – History – 20th century. 3. World War, 1914–1918 – Casualties – Canada. 4. Canada. Canadian Army – Recruiting, enlistment, etc. – World War, 1914–1918. 5. Canada – Armed Forces – Recruiting, enlistment, etc. – World War, 1914–1918. 6. Canada. Canadian Army – History. 7. Canada – Armed Forces – History – 20th century. 8. World War, 1914–1918 Canada. 9. Canada – History, Military – 20th century. 10. Soldiers – Canada – History – 20th century. I. Title. II. Series: Studies in Canadian military history

D547.C2D36 2017   940.4'1271   C2017-903777-3
                                                     C2017-903778-1

Canada

UBC Press gratefully acknowledges the financial support for our publishing program of the Government of Canada (through the Canada Book Fund), the Canada Council for the Arts, and the British Columbia Arts Council.

This book has been published with the help of a grant from the Canadian Federation for the Humanities and Social Sciences, through the Awards to Scholarly Publications Program, using funds provided by the Social Sciences and Humanities Research Council of Canada.

Publication of this book has been financially supported by the Canadian War Museum.

Printed and bound in Canada by Friesens
Set in Helvetica Condensed and Minion by Artegraphica Design Co. Ltd.
Copy editor: Matthew Kudelka
Proofreader: Alison Strobel
Indexer: Judy Dunlop
Cover designer: George Kirkpatrick

UBC Press
The University of British Columbia
2029 West Mall
Vancouver, BC V6T 1Z2
www.ubcpress.ca

For Leo, Denny, and Theodore,

and for all the other reluctant warriors who

made the ultimate sacrifice in the Great War

Honour and shame from no condition rise;
Act well your part; there all the honour lies.

—ALEXANDER POPE, "ESSAY ON MAN" EPISTLE IV

Contents

Illustrations

Maps

Photographs and Illustrations

Foreword

By J.L. Granatstein

MANY YEARS AGO WHEN I was teaching courses on the history of Post-Confederation Canada to third-year students at York University, I would devote four or five lectures to the Great War of 1914–18. One of my sessions invariably focused on conscription and how Sir Robert Borden, the Prime Minister, parlayed the Military Service Act, the Wartime Elections Act, and the Military Voters Act into helping him form a Union Government of Conservatives and pro-conscription Liberals. Once the Union took shape, Sir Wilfrid Laurier and the anti-conscriptionist Liberals were doomed, however loudly francophones, farmers, and labour protested against compulsory service; the results of the general election of December 17, 1917, confirmed Borden's victory.

The first call-ups under the Military Service Act came in January, 1918, and before long, unhappy recruits were in training. In May the first soldiers reached the front in France and Flanders, and soon there were casualties. But there were some 620,000 men in all enlisted in the Canadian Expeditionary Force, there were 425,000 volunteers serving overseas and more in Canada, and 345,000 men and nurses served in France and Flanders, and of those 236,618 officers and other ranks served in the 50 infantry battalions in the Canadian Corps. Yet, as the charts in Colonel G.W.L. Nicholson's official history of the army in the 1914–18 War demonstrate, of the hundred thousand men conscripted in Canada, only 24,132 served in the field with the Corps before the Armistice on November 11, 1918. Only 24,132 soldiers, I told my students, and for that paltry number, French and English Canada, rural and urban Canada, labour and capital, were divided in 1917–18 as they had never been before.

I am now forced to admit that I was flatly wrong to argue as I did. In the first place, 24,132 reinforcements numbered more men than were found in any one of the four divisions of the Canadian Corps. That was a substantial number, almost one quarter of the strength of the Corps' ranks. Then too, the war had been expected by the Allied generals and politicians to continue well into 1919; if that had occurred, the full hundred thousand conscripts – and perhaps more, if necessary – would have reached the front. And those conscripts were essential if the Canadian Corps' forty-eight infantry battalions were to keep their ranks at full strength. Understrength battalions suffered more casualties in trying to take their objectives. Full strength units, their firepower and man-oeuverability maximized, simply did better on the battlefield.

And there was one final point. When on August 8, 1918, the Canadians, Australians, and British struck the German lines at Amiens and punched a huge hole in them, the war for the Allies shifted from trench warfare to open warfare. The Canadian Corps were the "shock troops of the British Empire," and they would be used as such for the next Hundred Days, or so the campaign that ended the war was labelled. After Amiens, the Canadians moved north to Arras, cracked the Drocourt-Quéant Line, crossed the Canal du Nord, liberated Cambrai and Valenciennes, and pursued the retreating enemy to Mons in Belgium. These battles were the most important ever fought by Canadian troops, and they might truly be said to have won the war. But they were costly, with forty-five thousand killed, wounded, and taken prisoner in the period from Amiens to the Armistice, some 20 percent of all Canadian casualties in the Great War. Without those 24,132 conscripts, without the conscripts still en route overseas, the Canadian Corps might have ceased operations for want of men.

I should have understood these facts and explained them to my students. What I did not know was who the conscripts were, why they had not volunteered for military service, and what they did – how they performed – in action in the critical battles of 1918. No one had looked at the conscripts en masse, a great gap in our historical knowledge.

Now that gap has been filled in this very fine book by Patrick Dennis, a retired Canadian Air Force colonel. Dennis answers these questions completely, and he does so in part by focusing on members of his family who, he discovered, had been called up under the Military Service Act and served at the front. His grandfather was conscripted as was his first cousin and two more distant relatives. Three of Dennis' family had been killed in action and his grandfather suffered serious wounds. Of course, this was "a very small sample," Dennis writes, but it "was not entirely consistent with ... Canadian historiography" that dismissed the conscripts as inconsequential (as I had) and, because they were "reluctant warriors," of little value in action.

With his fine research and careful analysis, Patrick Dennis has corrected the story that I and others told for so long. Some conscripts may have been shirkers – so were some volunteers – but most did their duty in a succession of great and terrible battles that broke the German Army. Many sacrificed their lives for their comrades and their country, and Dennis' important book definitively sets the record straight.

– J.L. GRANATSTEIN is the author of several books on the Great War including *Broken Promises,* a history of conscription, *Canada's Army,* and *The Greatest Victory.* He is Distinguished Research Professor of History Emeritus at York University.

Acknowledgments

THIS HAS BEEN AN extraordinary journey. A decade ago and just shortly before his death, my father (a volunteer who flew a tour of bomber operations with the Royal Air Force in the Second World War) handed over to me for safekeeping a handful of letters that his own father, a conscript, had written from France and England nearly ninety years earlier. The gift of letters was an unexpected surprise. Although I knew of these treasured heirlooms, written in French and English, at the time I still had no idea what a rich and important story they told, i.e., that my grandfather's experience during the Great War had embraced a much larger narrative, one that involved tens of thousands of other conscripts, and one that in time has touched hundreds of thousands of Canadian lives – in short, an important and genuine piece of undocumented Canadian history.

Resolving to more fully explore this fascinating story, I subsequently published "A Canadian Conscript Goes to War – August 1918," *Canadian Military History* 18, 1 (Winter 2009) which, as it turned out, raised more questions than it answered. Principal among these was the great contradiction revealed regarding the apparent importance of conscripts in the final campaign of the Great War, and the lack of documented history supporting that observation. Nevertheless, this story might have ended there had my research not revealed two more important facts of which my own father may not have been aware. First, the day that my grandfather was conscripted so too was his first cousin, Leo Dennis, who later served with the 1st Battalion, Canadian Expeditionary Force (CEF), and was killed in action. Second, in a somewhat more stunning revelation, I learned that I had two other distant cousins who had met similar fates – the Caza brothers, William and Theodore. Suddenly I realized that I had four blood relatives, all conscripts and all of whom had been in action at some critical point during the Hundred Days. Three had been killed in action and a fourth had nearly died after sustaining a severe bullet wound. Needless to say, this was a very small sample size, but it certainly confirmed one preliminary finding – four conscripts and four casualties was a curious statistic that was not entirely consistent with what appeared to be the great majority of Canadian historiography on this subject. And so began my own journey, a search to answer two fundamental questions: what did Canadian conscripts really contribute to the Hundred Days, and what price did they ultimately pay? Thus was born *Reluctant Warriors*.

Throughout this journey my search was sustained by the interest and support of Canadians coast-to-coast, by many historians who welcomed my research and offered encouragement, by ordinary Canadians seeking to learn more about the sacrifice made by members of their own families, and by countless small museums and historical organizations, which provided important clues about the fate of so many conscripts. For all their help I am most appreciative, but take this opportunity nonetheless to offer special thanks to a number of friends, colleagues and interested acquaintances, without whom *Reluctant Warriors* would not have been possible.

I am indebted first of all to Tim Cook, who was the first to encourage me to turn, what he called, this "new page in Canadian military history," and to Terry Copp, who offered very helpful advice early on, as well as strong counsel regarding the framing of my analysis and central arguments. These scholars, along with Dean Oliver, Stephen Harris, Yves Tremblay, Andrew Iarocci, James Wood, Mike Bechthold and Doug Delaney, all provided equally strong support for this project right from the beginning.

Subsequently my research was significantly enhanced, thanks to generous advice and support from Jonathan Vance, Andrew Godefroy, Bill Stewart, Mark Humphries, Andrew Burtch and Dan Byers, and especially from the late Richard Holt, whose knowledge of the CEF's system of reinforcement had no peer.

Notably the writing of such a history posed a number of technical challenges, not least of which was the requirement to stay within prescribed word limitations, while still preserving the essential components of the narrative. For his exceptional patience and his very professional editorial assistance in this regard, I am particularly grateful to Roger Sarty. In addition, for sharing his encyclopaedic knowledge of the Western Front and the employment of Canadian infantry in 1918, my sincere thanks goes as well to Keith Maxwell.

To those Canadians across the country who responded positively to my many requests for support, I am equally grateful. Among them I wish to specially thank Carol Reid (Canadian War Museum), Al Lloyd (historian, 21st Battalion CEF), Jane Rumble (Blenheim District Museum), David Willis (Fort Frontenac Library), Michael O'Leary (the *Regimental Rogue*), Jerry Hind (Chatham-Kent's *Gathering Our Heroes*), Jeff Outhit (*Waterloo Region Record*), Jeffrey Booth (Elgin Military Museum), Eileen Wejr and Georgie Hay (Lumby and District Historical Society), Stephen Davies (Canadian Letters and Images Project), Brian Tennyson (Cape Breton University), Matt Baker (Laurier Centre for Military, Strategic and Disarmament Studies), Major Mathias Joost (Directorate of History and Heritage at National Defence Headquarters) and Marika Pirie, whose daily internet contributions on soldiers of the First World War have become a national resource. Countless others have also made important contributions, large and small, and I have done my best to recognise their generous support in the endnotes.

In addition, I wish to acknowledge the sterling efforts of the team at UBC Press, who have nurtured *Reluctant Warriors* over the past six years. To Emily Andrew, who kept the faith and provided strong encouragement for the first five years, and to Randy Schmidt, who saw the manuscript through its final battles, thank you both. To the peer review team, who offered so many helpful suggestions for change, thank you. And to the production team, led by Megan Brand, whose skilful labours turned *Reluctant Warriors* into the fine volume you see before you, thank you as well. Any errors of omission or commission are mine alone.

Lastly, I should like to acknowledge two others who have greatly affected the outcome of this daunting project in a most positive way. To Dr. Jack Granatstein, whose lifelong study of conscription has been a major inspiration for this work, and who has honoured me with his very thoughtful foreword to the text, I am most grateful. And to my wife, Wendy, whose enormous patience, constant support and encouragement has no limit, and without whom *Reluctant Warriors* could not have been written, I tender my biggest thank you of all. After the long dark night, it is morning, and the sun shines brightly once again.

Abbreviations

ADS	advanced dressing station
BCR	British Columbia Regiment
BCRM	British–Canadian Recruiting Mission
BEF	British Expeditionary Force
BGGS	Brigadier-General, General Staff
CCRC	Canadian Corps Reinforcement Camp
CCS	casualty clearing station
CDR	Circumstances of Death Report
CE	Canadian Engineers
CEF	Canadian Expeditionary Force
CFA	Canadian Field Artillery
CGS	Chief of the General Staff
CIB	Canadian Infantry Brigade
CIBD	Canadian Infantry Base Depot
CMGC	Canadian Machine Gun Corps
CMMG	Canadian Motor Machine Gun (Brigade)
CMR	Canadian Mounted Rifles
CO	commanding officer
CSEF	Canadian Siberian Expeditionary Force
CVWM	Canadian Virtual War Museum
DCM	Distinguished Conduct Medal
DCO	deputy commanding officer
DHH	Directorate of History and Heritage (National Defence Headquarters)
DND	Department of National Defence
DOW	died of wounds
D-Q	Drocourt-Quéant
GHQ	general headquarters
GOC	general officer commanding
GSO	general staff officer
HQ	headquarters
JOL	jumping-off line
KIA	killed in action
LAC	Library and Archives Canada

LOB	left out of battle
MM	Military Medal
MSA	Military Service Act
NCO	non-commissioned officer
OC	officer commanding
OMFC	Overseas Military Forces of Canada
OR	other ranks
PC	Privy Council
PPCLI	Princess Patricia's Canadian Light Infantry
RCR	Royal Canadian Regiment
WD	war diary
WIA	wounded in action
WO	War Office (Great Britain)

Reluctant Warriors

Introduction:
Slackers, Shirkers, and Malingerers

There are three types of men:
Those who hear the call and obey,
Those who delay, and – the others.
To which do you belong?

       – ILANA R. BET-EL, *CONSCRIPTS:*
       LOST LEGIONS OF THE GREAT WAR

The Men Who Weren't There

PRIVATE GEORGE LAWRENCE PRICE of the 28th North West Battalion, Canadian Expeditionary Force (CEF), was shot and killed by a German sniper in the Belgian hamlet of Ville-sur-Haine only minutes before the Armistice went into effect at 11:00 a.m. on 11 November 1918; he thus became the last Canadian to fall in battle during the Great War. Less well known is that Price, originally from Falmouth, Nova Scotia, was a conscript, having been drafted into the Canadian army on 4 December 1917, while working as a farm labourer in Saskatchewan. Price had completed his basic training with the 15th Reserve Battalion at Bramshott, England, before being dispatched to France on 2 May 1918. Then, after nearly three weeks' additional training and indoctrination, he had begun his combat service on 24 May. Four days later he was sent into the front line, where his time in the trenches at Mercatel and Neuville-Vitasse was relatively brief. Nonetheless, he subsequently fought in the epic summer battles at Amiens and Arras before being wounded and hospitalized as a gas casualty on 9 September.[1] Afterwards, his recovery and convalescence were understandably slow. But by 15 October he was back with his unit in the Canadian Corps' famous pursuit of the German army to Mons and, in his case, for a fateful rendezvous with an enemy sniper.

At first glance, and given that more than 50,000 Canadian soldiers had been killed in combat in France and Belgium up to this point in the war, Price's story appears noteworthy only insofar as he was the last Canadian to die in combat. However, beyond this poignant and tragic footnote to history lies a larger and much more compelling narrative, one that speaks to us not only from Private Price's simple grave in the St Symphorien Military Cemetery just a few kilometres east of Mons, Belgium, but from the voices of thousands of other

Figure 1.1 Private George Lawrence Price, last soldier in the CEF to be killed in action, 11 November 1918. *Source:* Courtesy of George Barkhouse and Parks Canada.

conscripts, now forever silenced, who also served honourably at the front and whose stories remain largely untold.

In this context Price's story is most remarkable, especially when one considers that the prevailing wisdom of Canadian historiography on the subject of conscripts in the Canadian Expeditionary Force, both generally and specifically, frequently suggests that these so-called slackers arrived too late and in insufficient numbers to make any significant contribution to the Canadian Corps during the final campaign of the war – the Hundred Days.[2] In fact historian Kathryn Bindon once wrote that "in the end, the numbers were less than significant." More recently David Bercuson has made a passing reference to "the few thousand conscripts who had reached the front" by the end of the war, while Andrew Theobald has flatly declared that "few conscripts played a role in the final fighting."[3] Still others might well argue that this is a quite valid analysis, since one will search largely in vain for evidence to the contrary among most histories that have been written about the Canadian Corps. But one doubts very much that Private Price's mother, Mrs. Annie Price, or indeed his beloved sister Florence, would have embraced this view, particularly when so many other facts seem to contradict such harsh judgments.[4] To use Price's case as an example, he served in the trenches at the front from the late spring of 1918 onwards; indeed, apart from the Canadian action at Cambrai when he was still recovering from a poison gas wound, he fought in all of his unit's major engagements throughout the Hundred Days, thus qualifying him as a veteran soldier in every sense of the word. If Price's story is not unique, and if his journey to war was repeated by a significant number of his fellow conscripts, then many of the myths that are typically attached to the role of Canadian conscripts during this period of the war must be called into question.

What, then, would constitute a *significant* number? In his official history of the CEF, Colonel G.W.L. Nicholson estimated that 24,132 conscripts had "served in the field" with Canadian units in France by the time hostilities ceased.[5] While some may understandably dispute this precise number, especially for reasons Nicholson himself identified, it is still a reasonable "approximation," the significance of which will be borne out by this study. Others, including J.L. Granatstein and J. Mackay Hitsman, suggested at one time that this figure of roughly 24,000 hardly constituted a significant percentage of the total 619,636 Canadians who were enlisted in the CEF, and therefore that the Military Service Act (MSA) "can be considered only a partial military success."[6] At first glance then it would appear that such skepticism was perhaps warranted. But Tim Cook notes that when we look at these statistics a bit more closely, we find that of "the roughly 425,000 Canadians serving overseas," about "345,000" all ranks actually served in France.[7] Of this latter number, one is further struck by the fact that of all troops dispatched overseas, just "236,618 passed through the 50 Canadian battalions which served in France and Belgium."[8]

In assessing the relative importance of 24,000 conscripts at war, one is next drawn to the Canadian Corps in France, itself numbering approximately 100,000-plus soldiers in the field at that time, and thence to a primary focus of this study – the four Canadian infantry divisions and their complement of forty-eight infantry battalions, numbering in the early summer of 1918 about 50,000 men. In this regard, as will be shown, most conscripts were sent to the infantry, where they were needed most. Moreover, since the infantry sustained the highest number of casualties in the CEF and equally had the highest demand for reinforcements, the actual results of this symbiotic relationship – that is, between conscripts as reinforcements and infantry requirements at the sharp end of the spear – clearly warrant a closer analysis.[9]

Reluctant Warriors, however, is neither an extended study of conscription per se (since the politics of conscription have long been the subject of scholarly analysis), nor a detailed examination of the much larger issue of reinforcements in the CEF (which has recently been accomplished), although it will be necessary to explore key elements of both.[10] Similarly, the link between conscripts as infantry reinforcements and the origins and implementation of the MSA must be examined, especially in order to better understand the core issue of military necessity.[11] In this respect, conscripts did provide the crucial manpower necessary for Lieutenant-General Sir Arthur Currie (Canadian Corps Commander) to execute an aggressive and continuous series of offensives, which led to successive triumphs in the Hundred Days and ultimately to what historian J.L. Granatstein has described as Canada's "greatest victory."[12] Currie came to utterly depend on his conscripts in this history-making advance; indeed, it is quite evident that this timely infusion of manpower provided an additional fighting margin, one that led him to take a number of tactical risks, many of which paid off brilliantly. Others, as will be shown, had costly and near disastrous results, the consequences of which were mitigated only by the ready availability of replacements. Hence the impact of conscripts on Currie's battlefield decision-making is also an important element of this story.

Key military events at both the strategic and operational level also merit consideration, at least insofar as they helped give birth to the Canadian Corps and were instrumental in creating the severe troop shortages that eventually provided the impetus for conscription itself. In this context, to gain a better appreciation of how ordinary citizen-soldiers came to find themselves at war without their consent, it will also be necessary to consider the essential political, military, and social factors that put them there.

Myth and the Canadian Conscript

This is not the first study to challenge the received wisdom on this controversial subject. In 1956 the Canadian historian A.M. Willms wrote that "most historians seem to have accepted the thesis that conscription was a failure, that it did not produce worthwhile results. But this is not true." Willms argued that conscription was "militarily necessary" and that the MSA was largely successful in satisfying the specific manpower goals identified by Prime Minister Robert Borden in June 1917.[13] Other scholars, however, have questioned whether the MSA was a success, although mainly within the framework of the deep and fundamental political, social, and cultural divides that conscription either created or deepened. In most of these analyses, the issue of military necessity has not been the principal focus and the actual contributions of conscripts in the field have been addressed inaccurately or not at all. This analytical weakness, coupled with the unproven theory that conscripts arrived at the front too little and too late, has fostered several historical myths, all of which collectively have reduced the combat role of Canadian conscripts to a passing footnote. For example, in responding to the rhetorical question "Was their journey necessary?," historian Desmond Morton once observed that "the MSA men filled the ranks only when the worst fighting was over." Indeed, a decade later he wrote: "Most of the so-called MSA men never actually experienced battle."[14]

In a similar vein, there are anecdotes that disparage the performance of conscripts in the field, including the remarkable charge by General Currie that conscripts were key suspects in fomenting one of the more infamous postwar riots that took place in England.[15] Moreover, as we will see, the fact that volunteers frequently praised conscripts does not appear to have diminished the impact that the myth of their poor performance has had on Canadian military historiography. Actually, the portrayal of the conscript as a disloyal soldier – or worse, a mutineer and rioter who deliberately defamed the hard-earned reputation of the Canadian Corps – has a very dubious foundation. Similarly, some scholars have asserted that those draftees who did make it to the front were insufficiently trained.[16] The evidence presented here, however, strongly suggests otherwise – that conscripts in general appear to have performed remarkably well during the most intensive and sustained fighting of the entire war.

The most common calumny visited upon non-volunteers is that many Canadians, civilians and soldiers alike, viewed these men as "slackers," or as shirkers and malingerers.[17] Although such negative stereotypes have made for popular and convenient labelling, they could have been equally applied to those thousands of "volunteers" who had similarly delayed joining up for a year or two or three. Yet it was the non-volunteers and later the conscripts who were the real targets of the public's opprobrium. Considered by many pro-conscriptionists to be unpatriotic and anti-democratic, by the end of the war some draftees were even suspected of having Bolshevik sympathies.[18] These slanderous allegations would collectively give birth to the myth of the conscript as anti-hero. And in an era when social norms permitted widespread and often unsettling displays of intolerance and public incivility, a whole generation of young men would be subjected to intense psychological pressures and often to physical abuse. Such coercive recruiting methods would manifest themselves in Toronto, where, for example, as historian Ian Miller has noted, recruiting sergeants conducted door-to-door "canvassing," newspaper editorials "attempted to shame local men into joining up," citizens were openly encouraged to report their neighbours in a "GIVE US HIS NAME" campaign, and in one documented case an eligible recruit was accosted in the street.[19]

Integral to this defamatory campaign was the myth of the "majority." As Colonel A.F. Duguid pointed out in the preface to his incomplete *Official History*, Canada in 1914 was very much "a young country, as yet imperfectly knit by bonds of mutual danger, of joint interest or of common origin." In other words, a great many Canadians did not see this "European War" as any affair of Canada's, and certainly they did not perceive any direct threat to Canada from the Central Powers. Not surprisingly then, by mid-1916, as casualty lists grew ever longer, support for the war had begun to erode across all segments of Canadian society. So when Duguid remarked on the contribution made "by that third of the adult male population which served in the armed forces," he inadvertently underscored a most salient point in this discussion.[20] Conscripted men were in fact part of that larger *majority* of draft-age Canadian men who had freely chosen not to step forward to offer their services until, in some cases, their country legally demanded that they do so. Yet the myth of the "volunteer" as the majority endures.

Canadians Are Entitled to Know Their Own History

With respect to Canadian conscripts, this thoughtful declaration by Desmond Morton seems to beg at least one pertinent question: Why has their story not been more fully told? This is a reasonable enquiry for which there appears to be no simple answer.[21] Tim Cook has pointed out that conscripts were enlisted men and that most unit histories were written by officers. An unsurprising result is the paucity of information in those histories about deeds performed by individuals in the ranks, be they conscripts or volunteers.[22] Nevertheless, there is an abundance of Great War literature about the Canadians and in particular about ordinary Canadian combat soldiers during the Hundred Days. Likewise, the subject of conscription in Canada has attracted deep and widespread analysis. However, only one book has ever been written specifically about the conscripts themselves: Ilana Bet-El's account of the British experience, *Conscripts: Lost Legions of the Great War.* And even this important work does not focus explicitly on the conscripts' overall contribution to the British war effort; instead, it goes to extraordinary lengths to describe how British conscripts were systematically purged from Britain's memory of the Great War, thus helping create a central myth of the conflict – the virtual "non-existence of the conscripts."[23] The lack of even one book in Canada that addresses the role conscripts played on the battlefield suggests that a similar phenomenon has also occurred here. With few exceptions, the Canadian historical narrative appears to have largely overlooked the contribution that conscripts made to the triumph of the Canadian Corps during the Hundred Days.[24]

One of the biggest challenges facing any attempt to sharpen the focus on the battlefield exploits of Canadian conscripts is the belief – at least in some people's minds – that to do so would be to somehow diminish the great sacrifice of all those volunteers who came before them. At the time, for some Canadians, the mere possibility that the conscripts' narrative might usurp in any way that of the volunteers was an emotionally charged issue (and for some Canadians it still is).[25] Thus for politicians, regimental historians, the Militia, the Overseas Ministry, and the Canadian Corps itself, it would have been politically risky to document the achievements of conscripts on the battlefield in a timely and fulsome manner. But it seems that not doing so came with a far higher price – the false and politicized assumptions of succeeding generations that this extraordinary national effort did not deliver on its original promise to provide up to 100,000 soldiers for the CEF. Indeed, official records reveal that tens of thousands of conscripts faithfully served their country, and that many of them displayed on the battlefield levels of courage and tenacity the equal of their volunteer comrades.

Canadian Conscripts and the Hundred Days

A close analysis of the large number of conscripts who did flow to the Canadian Corps in the late spring, summer, and early fall of 1918, coupled with an in-depth examination of their role as critical reinforcements for the line infantry battalions, reveals a number of surprising and sometimes startling facts. Principal among these revelations are the numbers of conscripts killed and wounded in battle and, as will be seen, the important contributions of conscripts to Canadian success in the Hundred Days. Yet it was Sir Arthur Currie's own surprising postwar impression that "very few conscripted men reached France before September, 1918," and that furthermore, among the "five or six thousand" Canadians "killed or died of wounds" in the last two months of the war, only "a very small proportion must have been conscripted men."[26] Moreover, Currie's inaccurate recollection of these troops has been buttressed for decades by what appear to be other similarly ill-informed impressions. Hence the precise role that conscripts did play in the final Canadian offensives of the war remains at best a mystery and wholly obscure. At worst, the historiography is misleading.

Reluctant Warriors seeks to fill this gap and to correct these misconceptions. The focus is on the conscripts themselves, on the key events that shaped their long and troubled journey from Canada's farms, factories, forests, and sea coasts to all the major battlefields of the Canadian Corps in 1918, and finally on new evidence that has come to light that challenges the reader to confront enduring myths, both about these conscripts and about their senior commanders. In this key respect, the story of the Canadian conscripts is not just about the draftees themselves but to a certain extent about the men who determined their fate and who directly employed them in battle. Implicit in this latter analysis is one overarching fact: had the lifeblood of the Canadian Corps not been continuously infused with conscripts during the Hundred Days, "Canada's greatest victory" simply would not have been possible.[27]

This analysis seeks to better define the precise nature of the conscripts' battlefield contribution during the Hundred Days, building on statistical data derived in part from Edward Wigney's seminal work *The C.E.F. Roll of Honour*, from a

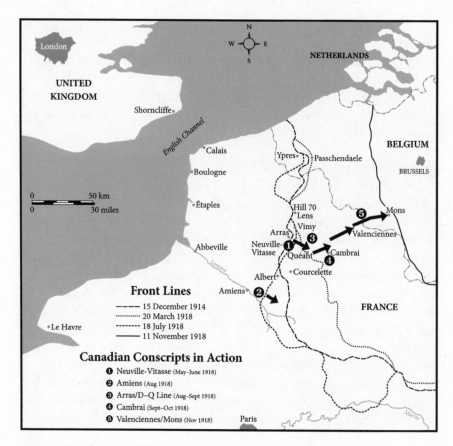

Map 1 Canadian conscripts at war, 18 April–11 November 1918. Map by Mike Bechthold.

comprehensive review of relevant war diaries and official histories, and from the nominal rolls of numerous regimental histories. Further evidence is drawn from more than 7,000 conscript attestation papers and hundreds of digitized personnel files, as well as wartime letters, private diaries, newspapers, and postwar personal accounts, and of course from a broad spectrum of secondary sources, including the corporate and private histories that are most germane to Canada's combat operations on the Western Front during 1918.[28] Finally, raw data have been drawn from official Circumstances of Death Reports, which include the casualty's name, rank, unit, and grave location. These chillingly brief accounts do not spare the brutal details of the violent deaths that many of these men suffered. To do otherwise would obscure their great sacrifice.

This is the story then of men from towns and villages across the nation and from all walks of life who lawfully exercised their rights as citizens in the face of exhortations by the press, the churches, and a good part of the enraged Canadian citizenry (most of them beyond the age eligible for military service). Some of these men were genuinely opposed to compulsory military service; others simply waited their time to be called. But then, having stepped forward to discharge their civil responsibilities as loyal citizens, they embarked on the same perilous journey as had their volunteer comrades before them. Thousands of these men ultimately fell in battle for a cause in which many of them did not believe, but for a country they loved and, most importantly, in defence of cherished principles – Canada's *Reluctant Warriors*.

1
"The Blood Dimmed Tide"

The chronicle of mass conscription in modern democracies is the story of the changing relationship between the state and its citizens, and the Great War is one of the major turning points, especially in the Anglo-Saxon democracies.

– MARGARET LEVI

THE DRAFTING OF CITIZEN-SOLDIERS has been practised for millennia around the world, and Canada's early history is no exception to this. From the time of New France and the comte de Frontenac in the late seventeenth century, through to British colonial times in the eighteenth and nineteenth centuries, ordinary citizens were periodically compelled to serve the Crown in response to various threats to the regime. Resident governors secured legislative approval for successive Militia Acts that, in principle, could have conscripted "almost all the fit men in the Canadas" but that in practice were subordinated to volunteer militias, thus avoiding the high costs of maintaining a large standing army as well as any nascent political objections to such a scheme. With Confederation a new Militia Act conferred upon "all physically fit males between 18 and 60" a compulsory requirement to serve, absent any overriding exemptions or legal disqualifications.[1] However, while this feudal-like decree retained its overarching powers of compulsion, it was considerably narrowed in scope, allowing "conscription by ballot if necessary" but continuing the tradition of a voluntary militia, which would effectively meet all of the young Dominion's military needs for the next fifty years.[2]

For Europeans, by contrast, conscription had long been *the* principal method for raising land forces. In *The Western Front*, Richard Holmes underscores that both France and Prussia successfully employed conscript armies in the nineteenth century, the latter having done so against Austria (1866) and then against France in the Franco-Prussian War (1870–71). Thus conscription in peace and war, as an integral element in a much broader national mobilization strategy, was the norm for most European governments.[3]

Such was the case in the early summer of 1914 when a young Bosnian Serb gunman named Gavrilo Princip assassinated the Austrian Archduke Franz Ferdinand, heir to the throne of Austria-Hungary, along with his wife Sophie during a state visit to the Bosnian provincial capital of Sarajevo. Less than five weeks later, Russia, France, Germany, and Austria-Hungary had all mobilized large armies of conscripts. Austria-Hungary declared war on Serbia on 25 July. Then on Sunday, 2 August, Germany (which had declared war on Russia only the day before) issued an ultimatum demanding that German forces be permitted to cross Belgian territory in response to a perceived threat from France – a subterfuge wholly rejected by Belgium. On 3 August, Germany declared war on France; the very next day, it invaded Belgium.

For Canada and the rest of the British Empire, it was a fateful moment. On 4 August, Britain demanded that Germany respect Belgium's neutrality. By then, German forces had already crossed the Belgian frontier. Later that evening, when the time limit for the British ultimatum had passed (at 11:00 p.m. London time), Britain found itself at war with Germany. In fact, the entire empire found itself equally at war – a tragic *fait accompli*. There had been no "parliamentary debate and no public discussion of war aims."[4]

Two days later, on 6 August, Prime Minister Herbert Asquith dramatically ended his first wartime address to Parliament with the following exhortation: "Let us now make sure that all the resources, not only of this United Kingdom, but of the vast Empire of which it is the centre, shall be thrown into the scale."[5] For Canada, this urgent summons was well understood and received with considerable popular and political support. But Canadians, like the British and the Europeans, firmly believed that this would be a short war; the general public expected that one and all would be safely home by Christmas. In fact, what Michael Neiberg calls this "nearly universal belief in a short war" was echoed by the eminent French historian Marc Ferro, who wrote: "It was reckoned absurdly out of date to suppose that war could last more than a season ... life would be intolerably disrupted."[6]

Such was the genesis of the world's first man-made global cataclysm. Less than three years later, young Canadian men who had neither the slightest interest in European affairs, nor any inclination to don a military uniform, found themselves faced with an extraordinary decision: *go or be fetched*. Indeed, how ordinary law-abiding citizens throughout the Dominion could eventually be compelled to fight against their individual will, simply because an Austrian prince had been murdered in the Balkans, is at the very heart of this story, one that would also witness the prime minister renege on a solemn promise and, more remarkably, see a large force of Canadian conscripts deployed overseas.

Canada: Ready Aye Ready?
In the summer of 1914, Canadians in general were unprepared for the rapidly developing crisis in Europe. Meanwhile, the militia minister, Colonel Sam Hughes, and the military staff were totally seized by the situation. On 30 July

"the country was informed by press despatch that preparations were being made for calling out and equipping a first contingent of 20,000 or 25,000 men to join the Imperial forces without delay."[7] The following day Prime Minister Borden cut short his summer holiday and returned to Ottawa, where on 1 August he cabled the Secretary of State for the Colonies: "If unhappily war should ensue the Canadian people will be united in a common resolve to put forth every effort and to make every sacrifice necessary to ensure the integrity and maintain the honour of our Empire."[8]

Such a firm commitment reflected a high level of resolve, although perhaps not nearly as strong as imagined by the drafters of this text. Moreover, this solemn pledge would later be put to some very severe tests and would ultimately underpin efforts to legitimize compulsory military service.

A great many Canadians greeted the news of war and of so-called German and Austrian aggression with enthusiastic support for the empire, and from Montreal to Victoria the streets saw singing, dancing, and "spontaneous parades."[9] Fifty years later, historian G.R. Stevens, a veteran of the Great War, would remark: "If ever a country wanted war it was Canada in that week." Still, there is considerable evidence to suggest that there was not quite the national consensus perceived by Stevens or imagined by the prime minister, who boldly affirmed at a special session of Parliament that Canadians "all are agreed; we stand shoulder to shoulder with Britain and the other British dominions in this quarrel."[10]

Borden could be forgiven for his words, though, inasmuch as his speech had been preceded by one by Sir Wilfrid Laurier, who had confidently affirmed: "There is in Canada but one mind and one heart ... all Canadians stand behind the mother country ... We have long said that when Great Britain is at war we are at war."[11]

Parliament rapidly passed eight key bills, including the notorious War Measures Act (WMA), which together constituted the first steps towards preparing the country for mobilization. In particular, the WMA provided the government with unlimited powers involving the "censorship of publications and communication, arrest, detention, exclusion and deportation, control of harbours ... transportation ... trade and manufacture." The impact of all this legislation would be subtle at first, but in some respects it endures to this day.[12] Soon all would witness the erosion of personal freedoms – including the once-unimaginable suspension of civil liberties – as well as ever-increasing government control of the economy, and, ultimately, the heart-rending aftermath of death and wounds that would directly affect hundreds of thousands of Canadians and indirectly millions more. For many young men, though, there was a more practical dimension to the whole affair. The prospect of a modest but steady wage, coupled with free food, clothing, and shelter, prompted a positive response from many of them to the nation's first call to the Colours.[13] Indeed, as Robert Rutherdale notes in *Hometown Horizons*, "peer pressure and economic necessity may, as often as not, have been greater inducements" to join this "great adventure" than "the patriotic reasons they gave voice to."[14] Conversely, for a great many other Canadians, there were a number of good reasons even then for harbouring more sober views, not least of which was that Canada itself had not yet been directly threatened by any of the belligerents.

For those Canadians, the decision to forgo any direct participation in this "European War" was, however briefly, an acceptable one. It was also the choice made by most as they struggled to understand the rapidly expanding conflict and the role that each might inevitably play in it. Moreover, such personal (and later unpopular) judgments were obscured by the fact that tens of thousands of volunteers had quickly stepped forward to secure coveted places in what many feared might be Canada's only overseas contingent.[15] Thus the silent majority were safe for the time being to go about their own business and to do so without physical threats from misguided zealots or harassment in the street – a welcome respite that would last less than a year.

Early Volunteers and Others

On the day the "European War" began, King George V expressed his thanks to Canada and to its ministers for the "spontaneous assurances of their fullest support."[16] Meanwhile the young nation moved quickly forward with the formation and dispatch of an expeditionary force, which would be composed entirely of volunteers. "Not a man will be accepted or leave Canada on this service but of his own free will," declared Colonel Sam Hughes.[17]

Significantly, the issue of whether the Canadian contingent would be an all-volunteer force was not lost on other Members of Parliament. On the fifth and final day of the special session of the Commons that began on 18 August, A.K. Maclean (Liberal–Halifax) asked the minister directly: "In the event of further Canadian troops going to the front, will the system of volunteering be continued?" Hughes's reply was revealing: "Upwards of 100,000 men have already volunteered, but we are only able to take 22,000 ... So far as my own personal views are concerned, I am absolutely opposed to anything that is not voluntary in every sense, and I do not read in the law that I have any authority to ask Parliament to allow troops other than volunteers to leave the country."[18]

Earlier, on 14 August, the Governor General had forwarded a statement to the Secretary of State for the Colonies summarizing the proposed composition of the Canadian Division – a force of 25,000 men, including just over 10 percent additional troops "to serve as a nucleus for reinforcements."[19] This cable is critically important, first because it verified Canada's official commitment to provide an infantry division, and second because it signalled recognition that "some may not return," and hence the need for reinforcements sufficient to sustain this force in the field.[20] On 1 September, a sobering reply was received from the Secretary of State for the Colonies warning that reinforcements "are calculated to be some sixty per cent of the original strength for the first twelve months of the war." The British, having sustained heavy casualties only the week before in the retreat from Mons, were gently reminding the Canadian government that a 10 percent nucleus of reinforcements was a good start, but that prudent planning demanded at least 15,000 troops be made available over the next year to "replace wastage" – for this one division alone.[21]

So on 23 September, Borden announced that the "approximately 31,200" volunteers who had gathered at Valcartier, Quebec, would all be dispatched to England. Unusually forthright, Borden declared that the additional troops would be "necessary for the purpose of reinforcements," which "for the first year of a great war are estimated at from 60 to 70 per cent."[22] With that the die for future reinforcement schemes was cast, although few Canadians would have understood at this early juncture that such a precedent had been set. By late February 1915, the insatiable demand for reinforcements would become routine, and soon thereafter the original decision to sustain the CEF in the field would be revisited, with near catastrophic results.[23]

In Flanders Fields

The thirty-ship convoy that sailed to England on 3 October 1914, carried with it about 6 percent of all the Canadian soldiers who eventually served overseas in the CEF. Recruitment of the remainder was already well under way, and wisely so. The government of Canada offered a "second over-sea [sic] contingent of twenty thousand men" (2nd Division) only three days after the first had been dispatched. In addition, the government had decided "to maintain continuously under arms in Canada not less than 30,000 men, exclusive of members of the Active Militia called out on active service," with the former being expected to provide "a steady stream of reinforcements [who] would go forward until the end of the war." This was unquestionably a formidable commitment of men and arms, and one that would be significantly extended only a month later, when the number to be kept under training was raised to 50,000.[24] Yet by February 1915 another 45,000 men had come forward to enlist. More remarkable still, as the CEF expanded over the next fourteen months to a corps of two and then three divisions, this tide of volunteers increased fourfold.[25] Thus it appeared, at least until early 1916, that Canada's commitment to the war and to raise the manpower resources needed to sustain it knew no limits. Alas, it was not so – not in Canada, and not even in the mother country.

The first Canadian combat soldiers arrived in France on 21 December 1914. They were the Princess Patricia's Canadian Light Infantry, a privately funded battalion comprised mostly of British immigrants with infantry experience. This unit was promptly deployed into the Ypres salient near St. Eloi on 7 January 1915, as part of the 27th British Division.[26] Within just a few weeks, the commanding officer (CO), Lieutenant-Colonel F.D. Farquhar, along with more than two hundred of his men, had fallen in battle, and on 8 May at the famous Battle of Frezenberg Ridge the Patricias suffered devastating losses – nearly four hundred in this one engagement alone.[27] Elsewhere, and only a bit farther to the north, other significant developments occurred that would ultimately redefine Canada's military contribution to the war. The Canadian Division, having spent the better part of March playing only a minor role in support of IV British Corps near Neuve Chapelle, suffered sixty-seven other ranks killed and two hundred wounded. By mid-April it found itself attached to the Second British Army and to V Corps in a much more turbulent salient, just a few miles directly northeast of Ypres. For Canada, the epic battle that followed, Second Ypres (22 April – 25 May 1915), would be a watershed moment for several crucial reasons. Apart from the fact that some Canadian troops became victims of the earliest use of poison gas by the German army on the Western Front, nearly 6,000 casualties were sustained during four days of non-stop combat – about one-third of the entire division, or more than half the trench strength of its twelve line infantry battalions.[28]

Not surprisingly, the death in battle of nearly two thousand Canadians in just a few days resonated deeply among Canadians. This "European War" was now perceived as a direct threat both to the mother country and to Canada itself. Hence, for all those healthy young men of military age, the pressure to volunteer would increase by the day. Soon they would face an unprecedented and Hobson-like choice – join the CEF and serve one's country honourably, or invite dishonour and a level of public opprobrium that can only be imagined today.

500,000 May Be Beyond the Powers of the Dominion

Even as the casualty figures from Second Ypres were being posted in newspapers and at telegraph offices across the country, recruiters were encountering a steady decline in volunteers – a disturbing trend that bottomed out, albeit temporarily, at 7,094 other ranks (ORs) that April. Nonetheless the War Office, by now well aware of Canada's firm intention to sustain its first two contingents in the field, asked the Borden government to expand its commitment to a whole new level

– that is, to the raising of a third infantry division. Remarkably, Canada agreed to this proposal, and in the wake of the heavy losses at Ypres, enlistment numbers began to rise dramatically, from 7,539 ORs in May to 14,819 in July – the greatest number since the first month of the war.[29] This was a most propitious development, since the Canadian Division had been engaged in hard fighting at Festubert for two weeks in May and again briefly at Givenchy in mid-June; these two engagements together had resulted in nearly three thousand additional casualties.[30]

On 8 July, the Privy Council in Ottawa agreed to raise the limit on men for overseas service, from the prime minister's earlier commitment of 50,000 to 150,000. Moreover, despite earlier suggestions by the British Army Council the previous month that the CEF overseas was already nearing maximum growth, the timing of this decision appeared to be perfect, coming as it did right on the eve of the first of Borden's several wartime visits to England.[31]

Borden's first wartime visit to England and France, in July and August 1915, overlapped with that of his war minister, the newly knighted Sir Sam Hughes, just as the 1st Division was enjoying a relatively quiet period in the Ploegsteert sector of trenches about 5 kilometres north of Armentières. Earlier demands for reinforcements were considerably reduced and would remain so for some time, with the newly formed Canadian Corps of two divisions suffering fewer than 2,700 casualties during the remainder of the year.[32] On his return to Ottawa, though, Borden faced some rather tough decisions, particularly in light of the War Office request for a third infantry division and overwhelming evidence that the conflict would extend far longer and be far more costly in human terms than anyone had previously imagined. Still, with August recruiting totals being the highest since the start of the war, the government appeared to have ample proof that it could adequately sustain troops already in the field in a timely manner and still meet similar requirements for a third division. Not surprisingly then, on 30 October an Order in Council (P.C. 2559) raised the authorized strength of the CEF to 250,000 – a fivefold increase in only one year.[33]

By Christmas 1915, the 3rd Canadian Division was a reality, yet the War Office still hoped for more. British authorities now solicited Canada's support for another twelve-battalion contingent, this one to be sent to Egypt. Canada's reply to these troubling proposals was equally bold. First, and perhaps most significantly, Prime Minister Borden made an unexpected announcement on 31 December: the government intended to double the size of forces then authorized to a total of 500,000 men – ten times the number requested only thirteen months earlier.[34] Stunned, the Governor General expressed "fears that the magnificent total of 500,000 may be beyond the powers of the Dominion of Canada to provide under voluntary enlistment." Nevertheless, less than three weeks later

Canada offered a "fourth division for the Western Front"; at the same time, it signalled a strong desire to keep all Canadian divisions under one command.[35]

Not long after these historic decisions were announced, Canada, like Great Britain, began to feel the heavy burden of sacrifice and the near crippling demands for ever more manpower. Eighteen months of global war and the repeated use of "suicidal infantry assaults" were forcing the British to make a previously unimagined concession to the harsh calculus of the modern battle-field – compulsory service.[36] Soon the British would invest even more heavily in a strategy of attrition, one which suggested that despite the potential for much greater losses, more soldiers might bring an earlier end to the war and perhaps save more lives in the long run.[37]

There Were No "Volunteers" after the Fall of 1914

Meanwhile, as Borden continued throughout 1915 to raise the number of troops promised to the war effort, his ability to meet these challenging goals was sustained by two separate and distinct organizations: the Department of Militia, which took the lead in this vital process, and Citizen Recruiting Leagues, whose formidable efforts would prove invaluable to the Canadian war effort. In particular, after the first casualty lists from Second Ypres were published, there began to develop among the English Canadian public a major cultural shift with regard to what was expected from young men of military age. As James Wood notes, "overseas service came to be viewed as a duty." Buttressed by similar demands in Britain for equalization of sacrifice, many Canadians assumed that most draft-age men would now do their duty as responsible citizens and promptly join the army.[38] Evidence suggests that men who were not so inclined were exposed to an onslaught of public pressure to join, including some very pointed criticism from returning soldiers.

That July, for example, Lieutenant-Colonel James Kirkcaldy, who had been wounded with the 8th Battalion at Ypres and would later command conscripts in combat, declared quite frankly at a public meeting in Winnipeg: "I have nothing but contempt for the man who can go but does not."[39] That "contempt" soon began to manifest itself as a popular public refrain, and before long all men of military age who were not yet in uniform no longer enjoyed the luxury of any real choice in the matter, since not joining carried with it a very real stigma, one that many men found difficult to bear.[40]

In the event, recruiting efforts over the next twelve months achieved re-markable success. But after that, it appears that the wheels began to fall off this impressive manpower machine. The nine months beginning in April 1916 saw a steady drop in total enlistments, which by December had fallen to a record low of just 4,930 men. Then, after a slight increase in January 1917, figures for the rest of that year were even more abysmal, bottoming out at 2,902 in August.[41] According to historians Craig Brown and Donald Loveridge, apart from the impact of lengthy casualty lists, these declines were due not only to the lack of a "central organization and control" for recruiting, and to "ruinous competition" among battalions, but also to a "steadily rising demand for manpower in the agricultural and industrial sectors of the economy."[42] Nonetheless, the volunteer system had reached its limits in Canada.

In the summer of 1915, supported in part by provocative newspaper editorials across the country, the "civilian recruiting leagues" launched much more aggressive recruiting campaigns.[43] These were buttressed by an advertising industry, then being transformed by "new techniques of persuasion," whose efforts encouraged men to join up and implied in subtle ways that they would be betraying their civic duty if they did not.[44] "Appeals were made to every instinct of manhood and patriotism" and were often couched in apocalyptic terms – for example, "the fate of the Empire was at stake."[45] Such lofty rhetoric, cloaked as it was in alarmist hyperbole, may have been easy to dismiss out of hand, but it was also very difficult to escape. Even church pulpits "were thrown open" to recruiters, civilian and military alike, and the clergy itself was no less an advocate – one minister went so far as to declare that "if any young man could go and did not go, he was neither a Christian or [sic] a patriot."[46] Likewise the workplace was no refuge – employers were strongly encouraged to identify potential recruits. In fact, in some cases "recruiting sergeants mingled amongst the workers," recording names and "reasons for not enlisting."[47] When women's organizations actively solicited their members "to give up ungrudgingly our husbands, sons, and brothers," even the home ceased to be a source of shelter. One thoroughly despondent prospect wrote: "I cannot go to a public meeting, I cannot walk down the street, I cannot go to Sunday school, League or Church, I cannot attend any of the district conventions, I cannot even go home and read *Youth and Service* or the *Guardian* without being told that I am a shirker."[48]

By this point the non-volunteer stood derisively accused as a "slacker" and a "shirker." As the following poem suggests, he was also the subject of public ridicule:

> *Mother's Pet*
> See him walking round the streets,
> Mother's darling pet,
> Holding in his fragile hand
> A dainty cigarette.
> He wears the cutest thing in coats;
> If only he could see

The mud stained, blood stained
Coat's that's worn
By boys across the sea.

– MARGARET G. CAMPBELL[49]

The message was loud and clear – join or be shunned, volunteer or be shamed. By mid-1915 even the act of volunteering had been tainted by perceived tardiness. Indeed, these young Canadian men, publicly vilified, "hounded by white-feathering, harangued by recruiting officers, and pressured by family and friends ... knew that there were no [real] 'volunteers' after the fall of 1914."[50]

In a turbulent climate that tolerated such slanderous attacks, one can easily imagine how careless epithets might have had just the opposite of their intended effect. As author and editor J. Castell Hopkins pointed out immediately after the war, "much of ... [this abuse] was unwise and, like most generalizations, in either argument or epithet, untrue."[51] Part of a vast but silent majority, these men had in fact exercised their legitimate and democratic right to reject these often emotional demands. In this respect, they stood on firm ground. First, many were employed in farming or in industry producing essential foodstuffs and other goods for the war effort. Second, regardless of arguments to the contrary, this *was* a "European War," fought principally by Europeans over issues that did not appear to directly concern most Canadians. In this context one is equally drawn to the emerging plight of many Canadian mothers who had already sent more than one son overseas (and perhaps a husband as well) and who were now being shamed into providing more. As one "prairie woman" bitterly recalled, her initial "sense of patriotism and duty" had been challenged by the endless need for sacrifice; for her "the State" had become "an alien and hostile thing."[52] One suspects that few if any of these women would likely have supported the extreme views of one Manitoba judge, a Liberal, who declared in late 1916 that "I would prefer to see my son who is now at the front dead, rather than showing the white feather in the streets of Winnipeg."[53]

Meanwhile in France, the relatively low attrition rates of late 1915 had given way to heavy casualties at Mount Sorrel in June 1916 (eight thousand), and later at the Somme in September 1916 (24,029). Both these battles served as a strong catalyst for Canada's eventual experiment with compulsion.[54] On 23 October, Prime Minister Borden responded to the growing manpower crisis by appealing to all Canadians to provide even greater support to the war effort, first through public participation in a voluntary national registration, and second through "men of military age" promptly placing "themselves at the service of the State for military duty."[55] Enlistments did not increase, however, and as Ian Miller has observed, very soon afterwards "patriotic appeals were largely dispensed

Figure 1.2 Recruiting poster fuels other social pressures to enlist in the CEF. *Source:* Archives of Ontario, C 233–2-4-0-199.

with and citizens openly attempted to shame men into service." Accosted on the street and at work and sometimes humiliated on public transport, these men were now forced to explain why they were not "in khaki."[56]

But it was the cumulative effect of far more compelling events at the strategic and theatre levels in the second half of 1916 and early 1917 that precipitated a full-blown manpower crisis. Apart from heavy Canadian casualties at Vimy Ridge in April 1917, overall losses by the British Expeditionary Force (BEF) "between July 1st, 1915 and January 1st, 1917 totalled seven hundred and eight thousand."[57] In tandem with what author and veteran Vera Brittain described as this "colossal infantry-massacre," the French had suffered devastating losses as well, particularly at Verdun in 1916 and then again in the spring of 1917, prompting a historic revolt among the ranks of the *poilus*; ultimately "about 40,000 troops [in] sixty-eight divisions" would mutiny.[58] With the subsequent French move "to the defensive," even greater demands would be placed on the Canadian Corps, and the call for reinforcements would grow louder still.[59]

There Has Not Been, There Will Not Be, Compulsion or Conscription

While the Canadian Corps was attacking at Vimy that Easter, Sir Robert Borden was overseas inspecting the 5th Division at Camp Witley in Surrey. The organization of this division had been authorized in January 1917 and was, by

Figure 1.3 Recruiting poster highlights the urgent need for more men. *Source:* Archives of Ontario, C 233–2-4-0-203.

early April, well-advanced. Impressed by what he saw, immediately afterwards Borden wrote to Major-General Garnet B. Hughes, the GOC (general officer commanding), expressing his full confidence that this division would go to the front.[60] That the 5th Division would never go to France might have seemed a remote possibility at the time. But Borden was unaware that the tactical triumph at Vimy would come at a very steep price – 10,602 total casualties, including 3,598 dead, making it the costliest battle fought by Canadians up to that point in the war.[61] This costly success helped spell the demise of the 5th Division; it also provided a major impetus for Canada's inevitable march towards compulsory service.

On his return to London and later to Ottawa, Borden would be confronted with two sobering realities: more than twenty-seven thousand casualties in the first five months of 1917, mostly infantry, and ten months of dismal recruiting figures.[62] He could do little about the former; resolving the latter would prove to be his greatest political test. Two-and-a-half years earlier, Borden, speaking in Halifax, had pledged that "there has not been, [and] there will not be, compulsion or conscription."[63] It is clear that when he pronounced again on this subject some two years later, though, he had experienced a conversion on the road to Damascus. Writing to labour leaders, he declared: "I hope that conscription may not be necessary, but if it should prove the only effective method to preserve the existence of the State and of the institutions and liberties which we enjoy, I should consider it necessary and I should not hesitate to act accordingly."[64]

Borden's original pledge had been uttered before Canadians had been blooded on the field. His subsequent reversal reflected harsh battlefield lessons and was made after the mother country had itself approved two Military Service Bills the previous year, followed by New Zealand, the first Dominion to implement compulsory service.[65] And even though the Australian electorate had voted no in the first of two referenda on conscription, soon after the United States declared war on Germany on 6 April, President Woodrow Wilson's administration introduced conscription of all medically fit American men between twenty-one and thirty.[66]

In the wake of heavy losses at Vimy, with recruiting levels at record wartime lows and the promise of creating a force of 500,000 men now in serious danger of being broken, it was clear that the four-division Canadian army could not be sustained in the longer term. Either Canada's contribution in the field would have to be reduced or the mechanism for obtaining adequate numbers of trained reinforcements would have to be radically altered. In early May, as he set sail again for Canada, Borden made a fateful decision: he would honour a solemn covenant made earlier with those brave soldiers still in the field, and equally honour the sacred memory of the nation's ever increasing numbers of war dead.

The Drumbeat for Compulsory Military Service

The great forces that would soon bring Canadian conscripts to the Western Front began to accelerate. If Borden required any further evidence of that, he needed only to review the dismal results from the government's recent and abortive Canadian Defence Force (CDF) recruitment drive. That scheme had attracted "less than 200 recruits" in just over a month. Major-General Sydney Mewburn (then Director General of the CDF) now proposed a new scheme of "Compulsory Selected Service for Home Defence" and – more desperately, it seems – strongly recommended "the enrolment in the Active Militia of all men between the ages of 18 and 45, under compulsion as provided by Section 25 of the Militia Act."[67] The following day, 26 April, R.B. Bennett (Director General of the National Service Board and future prime minister) formally advised the militia minister "that some form of compulsory military service should be imposed in Canada." Shortly thereafter, the Honourable Mr. Justice S. Masten, chairman of the Speakers Patriotic League, asserted that any action to provide "for compulsory military service, if firmly undertaken by the Government will be accepted and loyally supported by the great bulk of our people."[68]

The press echoed this refrain. On 1 May, an editorial in the *Toronto World* chastised the government for its "puttering schemes for recruiting [such] as C.D.F. plans and other voluntary piffle," adding that the Americans' "sensible" plan for a "selective draft" was very similar to the "method of conscription" it had been "recommending for months past." The following day the *Winnipeg Telegram* suggested that compulsory military service, like taxes, was the duty of every citizen, and that "the putting into operation of the dormant clauses of the Militia Act" would simply be tasking citizens to "fulfil the duty they are already, by the law of Canada, under obligation to perform."[69] The *Ottawa Journal-Press* took a much more strident tone: "Volunteering has ceased. Our best men are gone to the front of their own accord. They are falling there for the sake of all of us, including the slackers here who should be with them ... Only one way remains to deal with this situation, namely the way of compulsory service."[70]

Later that month the "moderate" and arguably "pro-Laurier publication" *Saturday Night* suggested that those provinces that had not furnished their fair share of recruits should be forced by the government to do so, and thereby "silence this nest of traitors" in their midst.[71]

Throw Something More to the Wolves

"An air of hushed anticipation gripped the chamber" as the prime minister stood up in Parliament to solemnly address his colleagues, shortly after 3:00 p.m. on Friday afternoon, 18 May 1917. Poised on the edge of a political precipice, Borden began somewhat tentatively before focusing on five major points, the most important being his lack of "hope that the war [would] end this year" and, more crucially, that "four Canadian divisions at the front," could no longer "be maintained without thorough provision for future requirements."[72]

Borden then forthrightly delivered his principal conclusions. First and foremost, he intoned, "the voluntary system will not yield further substantial results." Second, he asserted once more that "all citizens are liable to military service for the defence of their country." And finally, "the time [had] come when the authority of the state should be invoked to provide reinforcements necessary to sustain the gallant men at the front." He concluded that "early proposals will be made ... to provide, by compulsory military enlistment on a selective basis, such reinforcements as may be necessary to maintain the Canadian army to-day in the field ... The number of men required will not be less than 50,000 and will probably be 100,000."[73]

The following day, a *Toronto Globe* headline trumpeted "CONSCRIPTION FOR CANADA," while its editorial ominously enjoined that "those who will not volunteer must be made to serve." Somewhat more cautiously, the *Gazette* in Montreal announced: "Canada To Raise 100,000 By Compulsory Military Enlistment On a Selective Basis."[74] Stunned by this dramatic turn of events, "much of the French Canadian press" paused only briefly before launching major opposition to Borden's proposals.[75] Canada was about to undergo a national catharsis.

The legal instrument that would now be used to compel – by force if necessary – at least 100,000 men to serve in the CEF (and potentially 1,000,000 more if all six classes were called out) was the Military Service Act, 1917. That act seems to have enjoyed widespread support in the press; the public, however, was clearly divided. For example, a rally of some ten thousand people in Toronto on 2 June "endorsed a resolution supporting conscription," but meanwhile, harsh criticism was being levelled against the scheme by farmers, labour leaders, and anti-conscriptionists.[76] In response, Major-General Willoughby Gwatkin, Canada's British-born Chief of the General Staff (CGS), wrote to Sir Edward Kemp suggesting that "in order to placate opponents," the maximum age for men "compelled to serve" should be thirty-four. Furthermore, should it be necessary "to throw something more to the wolves," the government could "limit compulsion to unmarried men and childless widowers" ages twenty to thirty-four, and still obtain up to 195,000 additional soldiers.[77]

Next, Borden campaigned vigorously for the MSA and met privately on four separate occasions with the leader of the opposition, Sir Wilfrid Laurier. The purpose of these meetings was essentially to discuss the legal framework for the MSA and how best to obtain the necessary public and political consensus. In this respect, Borden proposed to form a coalition government; he even offered to withhold implementation of the MSA until a new mandate was given by voters in a general election. Conscription, however, was anathema to the aging Laurier, not least because, in Borden's view, he feared the MSA's "consequences in Quebec," in particular Premier Henri "Bourassa's influence" on anti-conscriptionists. In addition, Laurier was deeply skeptical of the scheme. Writing to Sir Allen Aylesworth, a friend and former colleague, he mused: "How many men will conscription bring in? Just a few slackers, exactly the same as in England." He also noted that only an "infinitesimal number" of conscripts had been "brought to the ranks" in England. The aging statesman proved to be grossly inaccurate on the first count and quite seriously misinformed on the second.[78] Nonetheless, resolute and defiant, Laurier could not bring himself to forsake his fundamental principles or to accept such legislation under any circumstances, and wrote to Borden on 6 June that he could not see his "way clear to join the government on the terms proposed."[79]

Five days later, more resolved than ever to press forward, Borden formally introduced the act to the House. Speaking again at great length, he underscored that "compulsory military service had been embodied in the law of Canada for half a century." He then laid out just "two alternatives": allow the four divisions of the "Canadian Army Corps" to slowly "dwindle from four divisions to three, from three to two, and perhaps from two to one, or perhaps to bring aid by means other than an appeal for voluntary service." Discounting the first option, Borden affirmed "that the need of reinforcements is urgent, insistent and imperative," adding that "the crying need is for physically fit and thoroughly trained troops, chiefly infantry." At the very outset, then, the foundation was firmly laid to conscript primarily for the purpose of reinforcing the ranks of the hardest-hit branch of the combat arms – the infantry. In this respect, Borden noted as well that "a very considerable number of men" who had enlisted in the previous year had "taken [less hazardous] service in Railway Construction and Forestry battalions" and that, while no doubt these units served an "important purpose," the consequent reduction of men "available for combatant service," coupled with high casualties and low enlistments, had created a crisis of reinforcement. The prime minister then repeated the precise number of men needed – 100,000, a number that, based on the Census of 1911, he assured the House "there ought to be no difficulty in providing."[80]

Borden then spelled out a proposal to create ten classes in this "selective draft" (later reduced to six), into which all men called to service would be divided, based primarily on age, marital status, and whether or not the individual had dependent children. Not all draft-age men would be called to arms, however, since a range of exemptions would be judiciously applied (see Appendix 1). To accomplish the latter, though, and in sober recognition that implementation would be complex and challenging from a legal standpoint, Borden declared "that the Act will be under the administration of the Minister of Justice." Finally, he read out Section 4 of the act, noting that upon its proclamation, all men called out "from the date of such proclamation, [shall] be deemed to be soldiers enlisted in the Military Forces of Canada and subject to military law until demobilization."[81]

In short, absent an exemption from service, once an individual and his class were called they were automatically deemed to be "enlisted" for the duration and subject to military discipline, whether or not they even appeared at the recruiting station. Penalties for non-compliance would be harsh, including mandatory prison terms of up to three years. "All citizens are entitled to equal protection of the laws, and upon them is imposed an equal obligation," Borden intoned; and to reject that obligation in this great moment of crisis held, in his view, potentially dire consequences, not the least of which related to that time when Canada's veteran soldiers, having felt "deserted and betrayed," would one day return home "with fierce resentment and even rage in their hearts."[82]

Making the Case for Conscription

Meanwhile, the great conscription debate at home had understandably over-shadowed some major war-related events abroad, principal among which had been the selection on 6 June of the newly knighted Major-General Sir Arthur Currie (GOC, 1st Canadian Division) to take command of the Canadian Corps. Without question, Currie's elevation to corps command was historic: no Canadian had ever commanded such a large military force. Moreover, this appointment, coming at precisely the moment when the Canadian government was attempting to pass legislation to provide the necessary forces to sustain Currie's new command, was seen as a golden opportunity for Borden to gain vital support from the field. The prime minister therefore signalled Sir George Perley, the minister for Canada's overseas military forces (OMFC), that he would send Currie a "message of congratulations," noting that "it would be well if in his reply [Currie] would make clear the need for reinforcements to maintain the Canadian Army Corps at full strength."[83] Drawing the senior military leadership into this fractious debate risked politicizing their views, but clearly the public and especially potential conscripts had every right to know whether or not this latest recruitment enterprise was in fact a *military necessity*. As for the new corps commander, he was most certainly "a forthright advocate of conscription" and, in this matter his voice would unquestionably be heard.[84]

Having first led a brigade and then a division into combat, General Currie was firmly convinced that the volunteer citizen-soldier was a cut above all others, especially those compelled to serve. But now, as commander of the Canadian Corps, he had a much more practical reason to maintain the troop strength of his command, regardless of the manpower source. Fewer rifles meant less fire-power, which inevitably would put the all-important sharp end at a distinct tactical disadvantage and was a recipe for even higher casualties. Therefore, anticipating the great sacrifices that lay ahead and fully cognizant of his new responsibilities, Currie firmly declared that "it is an imperative and urgent necessity that steps be immediately taken to ensure that sufficient drafts of officers and men are sent from Canada to keep the Corps at full strength."[85] For Currie, adequate reinforcements were the *sine qua non* of all military requirements. Yet while he would not wade directly into the national debate over conscription, his personal views on that subject remained quite clear. Writing earlier to a journalist, Currie flatly declared: "The only solution of the problem of Canadian recruiting is conscription."[86]

The Seeds of Discord and Disunion

On 18 June the second reading of the MSA was debated in Parliament. Speaking only briefly this time, the prime minister placed on record crucial estimates from R.H. Coats, the Census Commissioner, regarding the approximate number of men between ages twenty and thirty-four potentially available for service. It was believed that overall there were 636,746 single men in this group, who were in fact part of a much larger group of 1,583,549 draft-age men (married and single, 20–45). Significantly, these impressive figures reflected one other important wartime statistic: although more than 414,000 men had enlisted to date (age 18–45), it appears that nearly 80 percent of Canada's draft-age men had not, and these men were not restricted to any particular region or to one ethnicity. Most of these men were Canadian-born and employed in industry or on farms.[87]

In direct response to Borden, Laurier warned of a "deep cleavage amongst the Canadian people" and called for a national referendum on the issue. He thereby launched a fractious debate in the Commons that lasted for three weeks. In the end, however, nineteen members of his own caucus voted against him and his motion was defeated.[88] The still-evolving MSA Bill then worked its way through committee for two more weeks, after which Borden moved the third and final reading on 24 July. During this period, much time and effort was spent crafting precise language for what would become the act's Achilles heel – exemptions. In the end, though, compulsion remained its core principle, and it was this crucial point of "coercion" that Laurier took up with great vigour and emotion in his final one-hour rebuttal of the act. Having previously argued at length about its questionable constitutional foundation, he now fretfully and accurately warned that the bill "has in it the seeds of discord and disunion."[89] In reply, only one person spoke on behalf of the government. The solicitor general (and future prime minister) Arthur Meighen argued that Laurier himself must be held responsible for any possible "disunion," and suggested that the best way to avoid any further national "cleavage" was for the leader of the opposition to simply give a clear explanation of the measure to the people of Quebec.[90] When the final vote on the bill was taken, not surprisingly it was approved by a majority of 58 members of the House (102 to 44), including "twenty-two liberals ... among them some of Sir Wilfrid's lieutenants."[91] With that the MSA Bill was off to the Senate for a short debate, and thence to the Governor General for Royal Assent, both of which were concluded by 29 August.

Thus, Currie would ultimately get the troops he needed, but Canada would be divided more than ever before. The debates over the MSA had highlighted several unsettling cleavages: English/French, East/West, urban/rural, workers/farmers. Quebec would not be the only centre of "discord and disunion," although it would be perhaps the fiercest.[92] Finally, the intensity of these crucial debates had two other direct and important consequences: first, Borden would proceed with very great caution in implementing the MSA and, in the process, fatefully delay the first call-ups for over five months; and second, the debates had ignited a spirited public discourse, most evident in the press, one effect of which was to cast further negative light on those non-volunteers who, despite still being the great majority of Canadians who had yet to answer the call, would now struggle even harder to avoid being slandered as "slackers" or "shirkers."

The British-Canadian Recruiting Mission

By the time the Military Service Act became law, it was apparent that the imminent prospect of conscription had induced few Canadians to volunteer. Consequently, while the great debate in Parliament ground on, the government busily implemented another important manpower initiative, one that came to be known as the British–Canadian Recruiting Mission (BCRM). Designed to complement recruiting at home, the BCRM sought to take advantage of considerable social pressures being brought to bear in the United States by the Selective Service Act. In this regard, landmark legislation recently approved by the US Congress now permitted "the recruiting of British subjects and others not American citizens within the territory of the United States." Canadian involvement in this initiative was agreed upon in principle by British and Canadian authorities at a meeting in Ottawa in late May, at which both governments decided to "closely cooperate in all Recruiting Matters in the U.S.A."[93] Ultimately, "more than 42,000 were accepted," of whom "30,000 men" met "the required medical standard [and] were enlisted in the different branches of the service." This yielded "upwards of 20,000 recruits ... between January and August 1918."[94]

It is worth examining the direct impact of the BCRM on the CEF, as well as a number of contemporary myths surrounding this important recruiting campaign. BCRM men would not be the reinforcement panacea envisioned by some – at least not at this time of the war – and while they would eventually play a crucial role in the CEF, that role (like that of their MSA comrades) would not be fully realized until the summer and fall of 1918. Second, it is equally noteworthy that one great advantage to volunteering was that it allowed one to select duties other than infantry, and about 58 percent of BCRM men did just that.[95] As will be shown, this option was not made available to conscripts, most of whom were channelled directly into the ranks of the infantry.

Nonetheless, the successes of this program did provide the prime minister with a bit of a political triumph. Specifically, in early July during the debate on the second reading of the MSA, Charles Murphy (a Liberal MP) asked whether "any arrangement had been made to reach the large number of young men who had left Canada for other countries to avoid compulsory service, or to prevent them leaving now. If nothing were done," he added, "it was unfair to those who remained." Borden replied in the affirmative, noting that "an order-in-council [had] been passed to regulate [such] departures" and that relevant discussions were under way with US officials. No public announcement would be made, however, "pending the passage of the [US] bill."[96]

This exchange graphically illustrates how some perceived the circumstances of draft-age Canadians then living in the United States as being quite dissimilar – and unfairly so – from those of their cousins living in Canada. The former would be permitted to *volunteer* for the CEF, while the latter would be conscripted. The apparent injustice of that situation was clear to many, including one correspondent who rather harshly judged these draft-age Canadians working in the United States as simply a group of "young men who had journeyed across the border to escape enlistment."[97]

Winning the Election at Any Cost

Having completed work on the all-important legislative part of the MSA, the prime minister next turned his attention to establishing a Union government, preparatory to the call for a promised election that would provide the necessary mandate to implement compulsory service. The Borden government, first elected on 21 September 1911, had been extended for one year in 1916, but amidst the divisive debate over conscription, it had not received a strong bipartisan mandate in July 1917 for an additional one-year extension.[98] Thus Canadian *realpolitik* had effectively pushed the timeline for implementing the MSA even farther down the road. This seemed quite contrary to the military's expectations if not antithetical to the prime minister's original intent. Nonetheless, in his memoirs Borden maintained that "the supreme issue which overpowered all others was the provision of reinforcements for the Canadian Corps."[99] That position would be tested in the summer of 1917, though, when he received yet another powerful reminder of the war's human costs and of the ever increasing need for reinforcements.

Specifically, the new commander of the Canadian Corps had just conducted his first major offensive against the heavily defended Hill 70 on the northern outskirts of Lens, France. General Currie would later describe the attack as "a great and wonderful victory," albeit one that had come yet again at a steep cost.[100] From 15 to 25 August, another 8,677 Canadians had fallen in battle. Given that these casualties had been suffered in the same month that the CEF attracted fewer than three thousand new recruits, the impact of such heavy losses on the long-term viability of the corps could not have been lost on the prime minister. So it seems even more remarkable that in his subsequent decision to commit

SUPPORT UNION GOVERNMENT

Women of Canada:
"Be True to the Boys At the Front"

Sir Robert Borden in his manifesto says: "The franchise will be extended to women, not chiefly in recognition of devoted and capable service in the war, but as a measure of justice too long delayed. If men die, women suffer; if they are wounded, women heal; if they are maimed, women labor."

The franchise is extended to the women relatives of fighting Canadians, in order that they may help hasten Victory and bring the boys back from the trenches covered with the glory they have won.

A Vote for a Unionist Candidate Is a Vote for Reinforcements

The Union Government is pledged to carry on its work of raising the 100,000 reinforcements so urgently needed to support the Canadians at the front. Laurier and his adherents would stop this work, take a referendum, and experiment with voluntary enlistment, the possibilities of which have been exhausted. The most clear-headed, right-minded Liberals have gladly and without coercion helped to form the Union Government; they have weighed the pros and cons, they have not allowed politics to interfere with their patriotism, or their promise to our brave boys in France to "see them through."

WOMEN WHO CAN VOTE

Every woman may vote who is a British subject, 21 years of age, resident in Canada one year, and in the constituency 30 days, who is the mother, wife, widow, daughter, sister or half-sister of any person, male or female, living or dead, who is serving or has served without Canada in any of the Military forces, or within or without Canada in any of the Naval forces of Canada or of Great Britain in the Present War, or who has been honorably discharged from such services, and the date of whose enlistment was prior to Sept. 20th, 1917.

Such women should vote for the Unionist Candidate to ensure prompt reinforcements at the front.

Every ounce of strength in Canada should be exerted to help right a monstrous wrong the Prussian hierarchy would inflict upon the world. That is why the vote is placed in the hands of those most dear to our soldiers, trusting that the wifely love, and motherly devotion, and sisterly care, will vote as the boys would vote to carry on the work begun, and so far continued in the heroic spirit of self-sacrifice.

Unionist Publicity Committee.

Figure 1.4 The Union Government extended the vote to a select group of women related to veterans of the "Present War." *Source: Toronto Globe,* Toronto, 6 December 1917.

the country to a wartime election, in a single stroke Borden had delayed the timely dispatch of much-needed replacements by several months. Clearly the "supreme issue" was not reinforcements per se, at least not for now.

With respect to the election itself, Parliament passed two highly controversial pieces of legislation – the Military Voters Act[101] and the Wartime Elections Act.[102] Both were designed to help guarantee electoral victory and thereby permit the full implementation of the Military Service Act. As Tim Cook has observed, the outcome of the election was uncertain, and the addition of "400,000 Canadians in uniform" to the voting rolls (who otherwise were "ineligible to vote" but were believed to be government supporters) was seen as one possible margin of victory.[103] With regard to the latter legislation, Robert Craig Brown described it as simply "a bald, reprehensible gerrymander, designed to ensure a conscriptionist vote and to eliminate anti-conscriptionist support in western Canada."[104] It was that and worse, but more importantly for Borden, it was expected to provide wider national sanction for the MSA and, presumably, to offset any opposition to the act in Quebec. In this sense, Borden's fear of losing the election was perhaps surpassed only by an even greater fear of not being able to honour his solemn pledge to the troops in the field. After the government invoked closure on the Wartime Elections Act, this loathsome bill was passed on 20 September and Parliament was "prorogued." Democracy in Canada had suffered yet another two-handed blow.[105]

The next day, nearly five months after the prime minister first electrified the House by proposing compulsory service, a half-million potential conscripts received their first call to register – among them tens of thousands of reluctant warriors whose once-improbable rendezvous with destiny on a far-off battlefield in France would soon become a reality.

"Canada's New Fighting Forces"

CONSCRIPTION
C stands for Conscripts, the youth of the land,
O's for the Order that brings them to hand,
N's for the Nation that issued the call,
S is for Slacker – the cause of it all.
C's for the Camp where the Conscript will stay,
R's for the Rations that he'll get every day.
I's for Instruction in bayonet and gun,
P's for the Pepper to powder the Hun,
T is for Trench he must hold at all costs,
I's for Inoculation 'gainst fevers and frosts,
O is for Overseas, "On to Berlin."
N's for the Name that their valor shall win.

–BILLY M.

First Call for Reinforcements under the Military Service Act

DURING THE MONTHS LEADING up to the fractious federal election of December 1917, Royal Assent to the Military Service Act (MSA) set in train the creation of a vast administrative apparatus that would ultimately bring the entire plan to fruition. On 3 September, a "Military Service Council was constituted by Order in Council 'to advise and assist in the administration and enforcement' of the Act." Chaired by the deputy justice minister (E.L. Newcombe), it included three distinguished lawyers and one military representative.[1] Eight days later, under that council's auspices, the Justice Department posted an "explanatory announcement" in every major newspaper in the country, part of a "publicity campaign" that would continue until the end of the first *reporting* period on 10 November.[2] This unprecedented message underscored the fact that the "first call" for "reinforcements" would be "limited to men between 20 and 34 ... unmarried or widowers without children on July 6, 1917" (i.e., Class 1). In addition, all prospective recruits were advised that a forthcoming "proclamation" would be made that would establish a reporting date for those not otherwise in possession of an exemption. Lastly, anticipating no doubt a public uproar over such "exemptions," and recognizing that an election campaign still needed

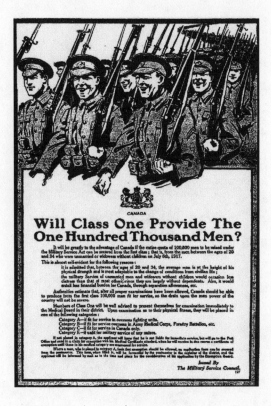

Figure 2.1 "Will Class One Provide The One Hundred Thousand Men?" *Source: Toronto Globe,* Toronto, 15 October 1917.

to be fought in which this sensitive subject would be a key issue, the announcement made it clear that "no advantage [would] be gained by delaying or disadvantage incurred by prompt report for service on the part of those who do not apply for exemption."[3]

This latter bureaucratic attempt to homogenize the new recruitment process was somewhat disingenuous as well as technically incorrect. Ultimately there would be some distinction between draftees who "were classed 'voluntarily reporting' by the military and [those] 'reporting as ordered' by the registrar." In fact, among the very first group of Class 1 men to come forward, even "before the registrar issued [them] an order to report," over 44 percent (8,112) would be classified by the military authorities as "voluntarily reporting."[4] Nonetheless, this *early* act of submission did not win these men any special favours with their new military masters, and certainly not the freedom to select their branch of the service. As for the rest of those draft-age men in Class 1 who had postponed their decision to serve, there remained only a month or so before all would be summarily ordered to report, or to seek the required exemption.

Figure 2.2   Hilaire Dennis, a streetcar conductor, Windsor, Ontario, 1917. *Source:* Author's collection.

"The world ... has no place for the slacker except to die"

One of the many thousands of young men across Canada who did not request an exemption – instead making himself available by "voluntarily reporting" – was a twenty-two-year-old streetcar conductor from Windsor, Ontario, named Hilaire Dennis. Born in New England but raised in Canada, Dennis was a Franco-Ontarian who had long postponed a decision on military service, in part because he perceived this conflict as a distant European war of Britain's own making, and in no small part due to lingering and bitter resentment against the social and political maltreatment of the large French-speaking community in southwestern Ontario of which he was a part.[5] Nevertheless, Dennis and his younger first cousin Leo (a machinist), along with many other kin from Essex County, were soon among the first draftees sent to England for training.

The official call for the rest of Dennis's class to register finally came in the form of a Royal Proclamation, signed by the Governor General the Duke of Devonshire and published in all major Canadian daily newspapers on 13

October 1917, then posted in public places around the country.[6] Citing an urgent need for reinforcements, the decree called upon the Crown's "loving subjects" specified therein to register "on or before the 10th day of November, 1917 ... unless application for exemption shall then have been made."[7] The vast majority of draft-age men did elect to complete a "claim for exemption" based on one or more of the nine grounds defined for this purpose: three "National Grounds of Exemption" (e.g., "the maintenance of the supply of food") and six "Personal Grounds of Exemption" (e.g., financial hardship for the family) (see Appendix 1).[8]

The public's response to the logic of exemptions was less than kind. As historian Jonathan Vance described it, "no amount of rationalization could change the fact that serving in field or factory simply could not carry with it the same honour as serving in the trenches."[9] Yet by 10 November, 310,376 men had made such claims, at which point the formal appeal process began in earnest.[10] Three levels of appeal tribunals were created to render judgment on such claims, the most important being the Local Tribunal, of which 1,387 were created; it was adjudicated by "two members," one "appointed by a County or District Judge" and the other by a "Board of Selection established by a joint resolution of the Senate and the House of Commons." The next level was the single-member Appeal Tribunal (there were 195), consisting of a judge appointed by the Chief Justice of the province. The final level was that of the Central Appeal Judge – the Honourable Mr. Justice Lyman Duff of the Supreme Court of Canada.[11]

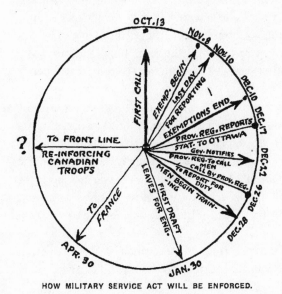

HOW MILITARY SERVICE ACT WILL BE ENFORCED.

Figure 2.3 How Military Service Act Will Be Enforced, *Source: Toronto Daily Star*, Saturday, 13 October 1917.

In a policy memorandum on exemptions, board members were reminded that apart from the need "to provide the essential reinforcements for the Canadian Expeditionary Force," their "function" was "to balance judicially and impartially the necessities of the individual against those of the State, and the civil against the military requirements of the nation."[12] Unsurprisingly, the broad scope for interpreting the guidance, accompanied by liberal interpretations of the complex criteria for exemptions, "tended to slow up the process of selection," except perhaps in places like Toronto, where, according to Ian Miller, "tribunals became stricter over time." There, deliberations apparently found little sympathy for families who already had one or more sons at the front, for men with "infirm parents," or for those claiming an "exceptional business obligation."[13] Conversely, as Amy Shaw notes, in Quebec these tribunals "were perceived as overly willing to exempt applicants."[14] Consequently, two other control mechanisms were introduced. First, the "proceedings of the hearings were published in local newspapers" – a triumph for transparency but a blow to privacy, inasmuch as "for years to come many men bore the stigma acquired from such unwanted publicity."[15] Second, early in the process it was found necessary to insert a military representative at the appeal level whose primary task was to closely scrutinize those cases where, in the words of the prime minister, exemption had "been granted without sufficient grounds or in an indiscriminate manner."[16]

In the event, even though the Department of Militia and Defence achieved a moderate level of success in this endeavour, the "exemptions" provisions in the Military Service Act – a crucial factor in getting this controversial legislation approved – turned out to be a major impediment to obtaining the "essential reinforcements" that the act was meant to generate. Indeed, requests for exemption easily exceeded 90 percent in all provinces except British Columbia, and most of these exemptions were "allowed."[17] In the tumultuous lead-up to the general election, this was another sensitive issue that would require deft handling by the politicians.

And even for that initial group of some twenty-five thousand conscripts who straight away signed reports for service, disturbing attacks on their character continued unabated. In a venomous piece titled "The Slacker" published in *Maclean's* magazine in November 1917, Agnes Laut acidly declared that "the world being gradually and painfully reconstructed by the war has no place for the slacker except to die and fertilize the ground." "Why," she hissed, "should the brave boy go forth and die, that life may be made safe for the coward and the shirker to multiply their kind?"[18]

For some draftees the public opprobrium was too much. Rather than await the results of the upcoming election or further government directives, many men like George Jones simply decided to enlist. Born in Wales, this twenty-seven-year-old steam shovel cranesman from Vancouver was not allowed to volunteer per se, but rather was voluntarily "drafted" on 25 October. Posted overseas much earlier than most draftees, he was eventually assigned to the 72nd Battalion, Seaforth Highlanders of Canada, on 29 March 1918, thus becoming one of the very first conscripts to arrive at the front. Private Jones, neither a coward nor a shirker, would die of wounds suffered at Sancourt exactly six months later.[19]

As for thousands of other conscripts awaiting their orders to report, the unavoidable stigma of simply not being in uniform would continue to hang over their heads, and remain poised there for more than two weeks after the election. In this context, it mattered not a whit that official propaganda had declared that the term *conscript* "under national service has no invidious meaning," or that "failure to volunteer [did] not necessarily mean want of patriotism."[20]

Passchendaele: The All-Volunteer Force and Conscription

After its triumph at Hill 70, the Canadian Corps reverted to static warfare punctuated by the "occasional trench raid or artillery duel" and took a well-deserved rest.[21] On his return in mid-September from two weeks' leave, General Currie oversaw planning for a proposed attack on Sallaumines Hill (east of Lens). But it was farther north, in Flanders, that destiny next took the Canadians – to Passchendaele. There, Currie employed all four divisions of the Canadian Corps (two at a time) during the last week of October and the first week of November 1917. In successive and costly attacks the Canadians eventually secured the great victory that Field Marshal Sir Douglas Haig (commander-in-chief, BEF) had so desperately sought. But it was a pyrrhic victory at best. In seventeen days of bitter fighting the corps had suffered 12,403 battle casualties.[22] Perhaps worse, five months later the Germans would return with a vengeance to this cursed ridge, and all of the corps' hard-fought gains would be entirely lost.

Passchendaele was a watershed for the Canadian Corps, both politically and militarily. Having suffered almost crippling losses, the corps moved back south to the "comparatively quiet" Vimy sector, where it began to rebuild. It would not be called upon again to launch a similar offensive for another nine months.[23] Significantly, too, the Canadian Corps had fought its last major offensive as an all-volunteer force, the extraordinary success of which might be seen in two lights: this highly efficient formation had proven on two successive occasions to be an important key to battlefield success; however, the vital manpower pool that had so consistently sustained the sharp end of Currie's legions had all but dried up. Without massive reinforcement, this once-proud formation would be all but *hors de combat*.[24]

The lingering aftermath of Passchendaele, sustained by lengthy casualty lists soon published in newspapers across Canada, helped generate one more key legacy – a Unionist victory in the election that followed. In fact, only days before this historic ballot, one wartime correspondent wrote: "It is more important to the allied cause that the Canadian people should vote to send reinforcements to the front than it was important that Canadian troops at the front should capture Vimy and Passchendaele ridges."[25] Thus the costly struggle at Passchendaele had brought into sharp relief a fundamental reality for all voting Canadians: without conscription there would not be sufficient reinforcements, and without such reinforcements there would not be a Canadian Corps. Indeed, as historian Dan Dancocks would one day conclude: "Without conscription, Canada could not remain at war."[26]

The Supreme Issue: Conscription

Finding enough infantry troops to quickly rebuild the badly depleted corps was once again Currie's top priority. The long delay in implementing the Military Service Act meant that this once-promising source of manpower was still incapable of satisfying any of his immediate requirements. Although he had pointedly avoided any public hint of political partisanship since first writing to the prime minister the previous June, he had remained a strong advocate of conscription.[27] In private correspondence, however, Currie had become a harsh critic of government delays in implementing the MSA, and he feared for its political success. "Months have already been wasted" in implementing the MSA, he despairingly wrote to Lieutenant-Colonel John Creelman (who had commanded the 2nd Artillery Brigade at Second Ypres before suffering a "breakdown"); "any interference with its provisions, or any delay in its operation, will mean the death of this corps." To Dudley Oliver (a banker friend in London) he ominously declared that he would "do anything ... to see that [the Corps'] strength and fighting efficiency was maintained."[28] Currie's correspondents were able to dissuade him from taking any precipitate action, but only for a time. Shortly afterwards, his tenuous situation altered once again.

Members of Borden's Unionist coalition, worried about their prospects in the upcoming election, thought that Currie's trusted voice might be used once more to remind voters of the overarching military need to implement the act. Hence, Sir George Perley visited Currie's headquarters on 4 December and requested just that – a message from the corps commander reiterating his strong support for conscription. But Currie, who only days before had intimated that he was willing to risk his command if it meant the corps might be saved "as a fighting unit," balked at this flagrant attempt to politicize his role in the debate.[29]

Two days later, Dudley Oliver wrote Currie again informing him that the previous day Sir Wilfrid Laurier had apparently given a speech stating that, in light of the heavy losses at Passchendaele, Currie had "resigned" his command. The following day, 7 December, Stewart Lyon of the *Toronto Globe*, acting on behalf of eighteen other editors of "Canadian Liberal newspapers," cabled "Currie or [the] Acting Commander Canadian Corps in France and General Turner, Commander Canadian Troops in England," expressing his colleagues' full support for "the principle of Union government."[30]

In shock no doubt and in great anger at this curiously worded cable, Currie immediately wrote to Perley, first to protest the doubts being circulated about his command, and second to request that Perley make an official statement confirming Currie's status as corps commander. The damage had already been done, however, and on 8 December the *Toronto Daily Star* mischievously reported that "Gen. Sir Arthur Currie has asked and has been granted a leave of absence from the front," adding that he may have been "superceded [*sic*] in his command."[31] Perhaps worse, it appears that Perley ignored the corps commander's plaintive call for help, and it was not until 14 December that the *Star* finally acknowledged some "suspicion about rumours" surrounding Currie's supposed resignation. Thus Currie's hard-earned reputation appeared safe, at least for the moment, while the fate of his beloved corps hung in the balance. But in just three days' time it would be the voters who would decide the fate of conscription – the "supreme issue" – not the scheming politicians.[32]

"The majority of us are voting for conscription"

While some accounts suggest that the average Canadian soldier in the field knew little about the key issues in this election, the evidence is mixed. For example, in the summer of 1917 the chief recruiting officer for Canada, Lieutenant-Colonel Cecil G. Williams, made a fact-finding trip to the Western Front and "found that the officers and men at the front were extraordinarily well posted in political events in Canada." But clearly "their main interest was in the passing and prompt enforcement of the Conscription Bill," the delay of which "they could not and cannot understand."[33] Moreover, by the time the election took place, any of the surviving troops whom Williams had met would have been blooded twice more – once at Hill 70 and again at Passchendaele – and no doubt their attitudes would have hardened and their cynicism deepened further still. Private Harold Becker of the 75th (Mississauga) Battalion "felt that those who hadn't enough guts to come over and fight should be forced to at least be shown

Figure 2.4   Unionist propaganda – "You Are Here for Life" – gave soldiers in the CEF false hope that they could reduce their time at the front. *Source:* LAC, PA-008158.

what we're up against." Becker, however, was also a thoughtful man and had several issues with the election, not least of which was that a vote for conscription was not only a vote for a government in which he clearly had no confidence, but one that might see his "brother, Fred, being taken into the Infantry and going through what [he] had suffered in the [past] few months."[34]

Ordinary soldiers were not the only ones to convey these types of expectations. Expressing his own private frustration, Lieutenant-Colonel James Layton Ralston, CO of the 85th Battalion (Nova Scotia Highlanders) and future defence minister, would write home in July 1917 stating flatly "that there is not much sympathy here for further temporizing."[35] Captain Leslie Frost, a future premier of Ontario, took a decidedly more hesitant view. While he and his brother Lieutenant Cecil Frost supported conscription, Leslie (like Private Becker) feared that his younger brother Grenville might be drafted and sent into battle. Indeed, according to the legendary field chaplain Canon Frederick Scott, some men "could not bring themselves to do anything which would force others to come and endure the hellish life at the front." After the attack at Hill 70, Leslie wrote to his parents to tell them that he did not intend to "vote under any circumstances for conscription."[36] Conversely, Private Albert Blount, recently wounded and recovering in England, wrote home that "the majority of us are voting for conscription," mainly because without it, fellows like him would automatically be "sent back" to the front due to the lack of "new recruits."[37] Thus for Blount and for most of his comrades, the election offered some hope that all this might change. Wishful thinking to be sure, but it was both logical and a significant battlefield motivator.

Canada Votes Union: Conscripts Ordered to Report

Canada now plunged into a seething election cauldron, one that would divide the nation and transform the political, social, and cultural landscape for generations to come into two solitudes. It saw "Laurier's loyalists and Bourassa's *nationalistes*" pitted against a powerful English-speaking Unionist coalition in a bitter contest that J.L. Granatstein judged as "more viciously racist than any election in Canadian history."[38] Journalist Sandra Gwyn would similarly describe the "Khaki Election" as "more like a civil war than an electoral contest," one in which, for example, readers of the *Manitoba Free Press* were exhorted to "make every ballot a bullet."[39] It was an enormous gamble, but for Borden it would pay off, at least in the short term.

By Election Day, 17 December, the overseas military vote was largely complete. When these votes were officially tallied in Canada on 1 March, it was clear that about 95 percent of the CEF had voted in favour of a Union government, and thus for conscription.[40] In fact, letters, diary entries, and regimental histories from this period are almost universal in stating the soldiers' conviction that this was the right way to go. "I do not believe in conscription but still I have voted for the government," wrote Private George MacKinlay of the 13th Battalion (Royal Highlanders of Canada). But having expressed hope that the vote might "serve to root out a lot of slackers," he also perceptively noted that this act of political submission would take "away the greatest thing we have, in fact what we are fighting for, our Liberty."[41] Meanwhile, back home the Unionists had scored a very impressive victory. Early results gave them a forty-four-seat advantage, one that quickly climbed to a majority of fifty-seven even before the military votes were counted.[42]

Borden, spent "after so long and trying a strain," headed south to Hot Springs, Virginia, for a brief holiday.[43] Just before leaving Ottawa, though, he confirmed the long-awaited order for the first class of conscripts to report. "Instructions were issued to begin the call on 3 January 1918," and on that day draftees began to make their way to seventeen depot battalions across the country. About eighteen thousand men of the first class were available to be recruited on the start date, although their flow at individual depots was limited to "from 25 to

200 per day."[44] In Toronto the quota that first day was for 270 men, but apparently just 200 "answered the call" – the next day only 110 out of 260. Here was evidence of ongoing public resistance to compulsory service, except that now all those who were called and did not report were considered absent without leave – therefore "defaulters" and subject to military law. Lest there be any doubt in that regard, the Military Service Council decided "to publish the names of those men who fail[ed] to report," providing the first hard proof that "conscription had been reduced" to what Desmond Morton described as "a punishment for 'slackers.'"[45]

Still, to the recruiters these new men must have seemed impressive in many ways. The youngest draftee was at least two years older than the youngest volunteer, physically stronger, more mature in most respects, and tougher too in a unique way, since many conscripts arrived at the recruiting centre having been tempered for three years by insults and perhaps even by physical assaults for not having joined the great crusade earlier. "Possessing a spirit as indomitable as the boys of the First and subsequent Canadian contingent," these recruits would soon be worthy and valuable members of "Canada's New Fighting Forces as noted on pages vii, 34, and 248."[46]

The administrative process started with the assignment of a never to be forgotten regimental number. But the most vital document to be completed on that first day of service was unquestionably the "Attestation Paper," and here the military authorities decided to make a fundamental distinction between volunteers and draftees. Whereas the former group had always been required to sign a two-page pro forma indicating their willingness to serve in the "Canadian Over-Seas Expeditionary Force" and to swear allegiance to the Crown, drafted men signed a substantially different document: a one-page attestation titled "Particulars of Recruit Drafted Under Military Service Act, 1917." This did not include either a declaration to serve overseas or an oath of allegiance. Moreover, in what seems an unnecessary and awkwardly redundant act, many conscripts' "Recruit" forms were stamped in large block letters (one to one-and-a-half centimetres tall) with the initials "M.S.A.," thereby reinforcing yet another negative stereotype for anyone in the administrative chain of command who might see these records.[47] These subtle acts of bureaucratic discrimination did not end there. Other documents typically required on enrolment were marked with an "M.S.A." stamp. And for many draftees, the all-important "Casualty Form – Active Service," which tracked the individual's movements overseas to England and on to France and Belgium, was stamped "M.S.A." as well. The ink for that stamp was sometimes red, ensuring once again that a soldier's avenue of recruitment could not be missed by the responsible authorities.[48]

Figure 2.5 Some Military Service Act attestation papers were redundantly stamped "M.S.A.," while the letter "D" for draftee was added as a prefix to the recruit's regimental number. *Source:* See LAC, RG 150, Accession 1992–93, Box 440 – 8.

In fact, from the moment conscripts first received their notification to report, there appears to have developed in the draftee recruitment process an overarching regime designed to treat these new men distinctly differently than their volunteer comrades. That such an approach would generate some hostility on the part of the draftees and their families and friends should not have been a surprise; but that (as will be shown next) it was occasionally reported on in negative terms by the once–highly supportive press would most likely have struck both the government and the military as an entirely unexpected response.

"Unhonored, unsung and even unwept"

One other early indication that many of these recruits would be handled differently was a news blackout regarding the overall number of draftees called up as well as their reporting dates, imposed by Ottawa ostensibly because these facts were deemed sensitive military information. Some newspapers were quick to question the reasoning behind such censorship, especially since it had not been applied during the time of voluntary recruiting. A member of the Military Service Council responded simply that "it is considered unwise to disclose the numbers raised ... Information must not be given to the enemy."[49] One could be forgiven, however, for thinking just the opposite – that telling the Germans that an army of 100,000 reinforcements was beginning to form in Canada, and that this nation's resolve was as strong as ever, would have been a good strategy.

In one revealing case, the authorities did not allow publicity for the departure by train of large numbers of men from Windsor to the 1st Depot Battalion in London, Ontario. These conscripts, unlike their volunteer comrades who had preceded them over the past three years, were ushered off to war in the middle of the night, "unhonored, unsung and even unwept, excepting by a few mothers and dear ones who gathered at the station." Noting by way of contrast that the Americans across the river in Detroit had warmly honoured departing members of their own "draft army" with the "biggest celebration [the city] ever saw," the *Windsor Record* protested that "our draftees deserved and should have received a similar send off," then declared that "one way to bring compulsory military service into disrepute is to eliminate and check public support."[50]

Another disturbing feature of the MSA legislation came forcefully into play – the process for dealing with "defaulters." The director of the Military Service Branch would one day describe those soldiers who had been called up but had failed to register or report as "the very dregs of our young manhood, and every single young slacker to whom the country had given a livelihood."[51] Regulations in effect since the proclamation of 13 October were now implemented across the country with the full force of the law, often by zealous police officers anxious to make their own contribution to the war effort. Jim Smith, for example, the "high constable for Essex County," boasted of "rounding up the slackers," albeit with some difficulty. "The slacker," he declared, "is young and evasive." Still, Smith claimed that he had "pinched seven of the breed to date," six of whom were already "in khaki in the London military camp."[52]

This highly controversial campaign to track down defaulters quickly gained momentum under the glare of national press coverage, including reports that "quite a number of young men fearing conscription" had fled to the United States. In this context, and as noted earlier, negotiations were already in progress to establish a "convention" between the two governments to "conscript Americans in Canada" and "Canadians of military age" in America.[53] Here, however, the MSA codicil exempting non-resident citizens from conscription (i.e., those Canadians who did not live or work in Canada on 4 August 1914) was applicable. Nonetheless, with America at war and approval of this new agreement expected at any time, many young Canadians working in the United States soon exercised a more favourable option – enlisting "voluntarily" through the

BCRM scheme. Consequently, while the "great majority" of the sixteen thousand men who volunteered up until February 1918 would apparently join "units other than the infantry," it was clear that the MSA in combination with the American draft had driven many Canadians (and other British subjects) living in the United States to finally enlist, thus helping secure a robust flow of new men to the front.[54]

"Looks like an early trip overseas"

In many respects the first few weeks in the army for conscripts were no different from those experienced earlier by volunteers. The daily regime the recruits encountered was not a pleasant experience, nor was it intended to be. Yelled at constantly over every detail of their daily lives, they were more than just disconcerted or unbalanced; for some it was pure hell. Survival instincts kicked in, though, and most of them quickly adjusted to the harsh realities of military discipline.[55] Some could not adapt, however, and among these were the first Canadian conscript casualties of the Great War.

Probably the first Canadian draftee to die was Private Harold Earnshaw, a twenty-one-year-old farmer from Loreburn, Saskatchewan. Earnshaw had originally enlisted in Moose Jaw with the 210th Battalion in December 1916. Found to be medically unfit, he was discharged the following May. But after being found fit again in November 1917, he was conscripted on 8 January 1918. Six days later he succumbed to an undisclosed illness. Back east, Private Albert Brooks, a twenty-one-year-old farmer from Sarnia, attested on 9 January in London, Ontario, and "caught cold the first night." He died on 3 February, possibly a victim of London's infamous "ice-box" – a frigid "bunk house underneath the grandstand at the fair grounds."[56] Nearly one thousand more conscripts would perish in Canada before the war ended, and like their volunteer comrades who met the same fate, they too are counted among Canada's war dead.[57]

One of the few surviving first-hand accounts of this life-changing experience was written by Sapper A. Roy Neilson, a conscript originally from Chatham, Ontario, and one of just a small percentage of draftees directed into the engineers instead of the infantry. Neilson attested in London, Ontario, on 4 March 1918. His personal diary is a wonderful compendium of those routine events common to every new soldier's day and covers the full spectrum of basic military training, besides providing a candid look at the social activities available to new recruits. Parade square drill occupied much of his time, followed by lectures, long marches, physical training, and "fatigues" – those additional work details in the kitchen, on the road, and in training trenches, designed to instill discipline and to foster a higher level of toughness, which would constantly be tested. On his third day in camp he watched as an "English [boxing] Instructor" knocked

Figure 2.6   Sapper A.
Roy Neilson, 8th Battalion,
Canadian Engineers.
Source: Courtesy of Dr.
Peter Neilson.

a man down twice," the "second time knocking him senseless." Although he was "quite disgusted" by this affair, the apparent theft of his watch and two towels the following day surprised him even more. And the fact that his bunkmate was put on "open arrest" simply because his "bed wasn't made right" confirmed that his life was no longer his own. If any further proof of that was needed, at the end of that first tumultuous week a medical board again designated him as "A2," prompting Neilson to soberly conclude, "Looks like an early trip overseas."[58]

"No better class of soldiers"

Senior authorities in Canada had generally accepted Lieutenant-General Richard Turner's recommendations regarding the basic training and dispatch of MSA recruits. "Only very elementary training" would be carried out in Canada, and troops would "be sent to [England] in drafts only"– that is, not as formed battalions, but typically in groups of two hundred to five hundred men, who were expected to be "sufficiently drilled to behave in a soldierly manner." Turner requested that the training "be confined to close order drill, manual of arms, physical training and marching" – a program identical to that followed by Sapper Neilson and his mates.[59] In approving these recommendations, Militia Headquarters set forth another key policy: "All men obtained under the Military Service Act will first go into Infantry Depot Battalions. Subsequently those desiring, will be placed in a Machine Gun Corps for a short time before proceeding Overseas so that the best available men can be selected for this branch of the service."[60]

While this decision would remain in force, with minor modifications, for the remainder of the war, the immediate fate of the first large drafts of conscripts remained undecided, principally because of two crucial and unresolved issues. The first had to do with the emerging competition between Canadian and American authorities for troop transport ships: the British Admiralty had made promises to the Americans that threatened to jeopardize the timely flow of Canadian conscripts to their training bases in England.[61] The resolution of the second issue – what to do with the 5th Division – would have serious implications for all draftees heading overseas.

Canadian authorities did succeed in securing sufficient transport ships to move the first intake of conscripts, along with thousands of their volunteer comrades (BCRM men and others), during February 1918. Among the former was the "first draft" from Military District no. 11 in Vancouver, which notably received a "rousing send-off" when their train passed through Mission, BC. One press report noted that "in the view of many military men, probably no better class of soldiers will be found in the ranks of the Canadian army."[62] Meanwhile, the first draft of five hundred new men from Military District no. 1 (London) quietly left for the east coast at 6:00 p.m. on 31 January. Again, departure times were withheld until the last moment, and in contrast to the "large crowd" that had bid farewell to the volunteers of the 99th Battalion some eighteen months earlier, "few relatives were on hand to see the draftees off."[63]

Conscripts and Currie's Plan for an Unparalleled Fighting Force

Overseas, a crucial manpower drama was unfolding. During a visit by Lieutenant-General Turner on 11 January, Currie had been made aware of recent and disturbing plans to restructure the BEF. Those plans, if carried through, would have reduced each infantry brigade from four fighting battalions to three, with those three then being brought up to strength by soldiers transferred from those units being disestablished.[64] Setting aside that advantage, this scheme was seriously flawed in at least one major respect: it would significantly reduce the overall combat power of each brigade. Nevertheless, the War Office had boldly responded to Borden's first dispatch of conscripts overseas by enquiring whether "Canadian Military Authorities [were] prepared to expand the Canadian Expeditionary Force in France ... to six divisions on a 9 battalion basis." If so, the Army Council wanted to "request that the necessary cadres of the 5th Division ... be despatched there as soon as shipping [could] be arranged."[65]

Sir Edward Kemp, who had arrived in England a month before, and General Turner were both favourably disposed to this plan, one which would create a Canadian army in France consisting of two corps, each with three divisions. Currie, on the other hand, was strongly opposed and asked the new overseas minister to visit Canadian Corps HQ, where it was thought that Kemp might receive alternative views on the matter, including details regarding its potential impacts on the "fighting efficiency" of the corps.[66] During his meeting with the new overseas minister on 18 and 19 January, Currie expressed serious doubts that any tangible benefits would arise from the army expansion scheme, but apparently to no avail. "The Dominion has quite enough men to keep its glorious divisions up to strength," Kemp declared, and a week later, in a cable to Ottawa, he expressed support for the British proposal.[67] Four days later, "Cabinet approved [Kemp's] proposal," albeit with significant caveats, not least of which was Borden's warning that the plan "involves a supply of reinforcements during the next twelve months which it will be extremely difficult, if not impossible, to provide."[68]

Shortly thereafter, Kemp wavered in his resolve. Notwithstanding what appeared to be an encouraging number of reinforcements in the manpower pipeline, the prospect of a new German offensive and the strong possibility of even higher Canadian casualties combined to suggest a more sobering calculus. So he decided to place in temporary abeyance any further decisions on the matter, and the next day he instructed Currie to report to London for further consultations.[69]

Currie met with Kemp on 6 February and again advanced substantive arguments against the formation of what he firmly believed would be a larger but significantly weaker army. Still unconvinced, Kemp asked the corps commander to put his objections in writing, whereupon Currie promptly produced a cogent and compelling argument, one that countered the War Office plan and offered a practical strategy for rapidly enhancing the overall combat power of the Canadian Corps. The essence of Currie's counter-proposal was that the sustained striking power of his infantry brigades was a direct function of the four-battalion (two up, two back) attack formation. Hence, he strongly suggested that making these four battalions even more robust, not less, in terms of both manpower and weapons, would not only strengthen the impact of any assault but also go a long way towards preserving the crucial integrity of the formation itself, especially at the platoon level. That would increase the likelihood of battlefield success while offering offer the best chance for minimizing overall casualties.[70]

In the end, Kemp accepted Currie's logic and his ambitious plans to create a corps unrivalled in both its striking power and its ability to effectively sustain itself in the face of significant losses. In an abrupt volte-face, the minister wrote to Borden on 8 February and acknowledged that having conferred again at length with Currie, "we are justified in declining to accede to the War Office request." One key factor affecting the minister's decision was the ongoing challenge of "getting a sufficient number of recruits to cover wastage," particularly in light of a recent cable from Mewburn, who had replaced Kemp as militia and defence minister, noting that the "numbers drafted under the Military Service Act have so far fallen short of anticipation." Apart from the unresolved "difficulty with respect to transportation of troops from Canada," Kemp's most salient point, though, was this simple assertion: Currie's "scheme will give us a better fighting force than the War Office proposal."[71]

On that same day, 9 February, the 5th Division was "ordered to furnish drafts of 100 men each to the units in the field." Shortly afterwards, this division was completely disbanded, after which, as historian A.M. Jack Hyatt argues, Currie "lost interest in the Military Service Act."[72] Even so, while the breaking up of the 5th Division would solve most of Currie's immediate reinforcement challenges, it was not a long-term panacea. The relentless costs of daily battlefield wastage alone meant that Currie had at most six more months until the next crisis hit.[73] At that point, in a remarkable case of just-in-time manpower delivery, thousands of long-promised conscripts would swell the ranks of the infantry and play a vital role in the epic battles of the Hundred Days.

3
The First Canadian Conscripts in Combat

A Rough Passage

THE FIRST WAVE OF conscripts landed in Liverpool in February 1918. Remarkably, despite the increased threat from deadly U-boats, their Atlantic crossing had been largely without incident. In time, sixty-seven conscripts would perish at sea, not because of U-boats but from two other deadly killers – pneumonia and influenza.[1]

Heading south almost immediately by train, this draft arrived at a "segregation camp" adjacent to the main training base at Bramshott in Surrey, where all were medically quarantined for about two weeks.[2] For each conscript, military life now presented three great unknowns: the daunting challenge of basic infantry training; the potential for physical and mental abuse by their instructors and perhaps by others not sympathetic to the mode of their recruitment; and, finally, the ever approaching spectre of combat. Political events at home and abroad would shape all three, but action on the battlefield would determine most of their destinies.

Fortunately for these reluctant warriors, they had a strong ally in Lieutenant-General Sir Richard Turner, GOC Canadian Forces in the British Isles. To help neutralize the threat of any possible maltreatment, Turner had issued stern instructions directing all commanding officers to ensure that these new men were afforded "the same treatment and goodwill as has been extended to those who, in the past, enlisted under voluntary conditions. Any inclination to treat [these] reinforcements ... in a manner that would harbour ill feeling [was] to be dealt with promptly and severely."[3]

Similar orders were later issued abjuring the use of the term "conscript." Soldiers ignoring that directive were threatened with harsh discipline, including the possible loss of pay and up to twenty-eight days of Field Punishment no. 1, which involved being "secured ... to a fixed object" (typically a wheel or a fence) for up to two hours a day.[4] These were draconian measures by today's standards of discipline, but evidence suggests that such a firm policy was entirely necessary. "Conscripts will have kind of a rough passage over here," wrote driver Bill Calder that January, "not from Fritz but from the boys that are hear [sic] now." However, Private Jack Row mused: "It won't be long before some of them are back wounded and made as much fuss of as we were." At the front, though, this tone would take a darker turn. Writing to his brother in June 1918 on the subject of conscription and of those men then being "called up," gunner Bertie Cox harshly declared: "I am as bitter against conscripts as you are against Germans. I'd soon kill with my own hand, a man who is made to fight for his country, after 3 1/2 years of war, than any German, including the Kaiser."[5]

In the face of such raw and pent-up emotions, Turner's decision was prudent and reflected a strong grasp of the widespread antipathy throughout the ranks towards men who had to be fetched. Nonetheless, decades later Private Ben Wagner would recall that while "the army clamped down on an attempt to bully them both in France and in England," once the draftees "got to France, they were just absorbed into the group without much fuss about it."[6] Indeed, the battlefield would test the depth of any latent hostility towards conscripts; that is where they would have the opportunity to prove themselves worthy successors to the men who had come before them.

"Surrounded by barb wire and fenced"

On Sunday morning 17 February, a draft of reinforcements, typical of what all the rest would soon look like, arrived at the Bramshott "Segregation Camp." This was a large contingent of conscripts plus a strong element of BCRM men, along with a smaller group of traditional recruits – all told more than five hundred young men and ten officers from the Western Ontario Regiment. "Surrounded by barb wire and fenced," the new arrivals began their first full day in England with yet another medical inspection – and for good reason. Seven men had been left behind in Liverpool with the mumps, one with scarlet fever, and another with the measles; two others had pneumonia. But apart from about twenty cases of "vermin," the medical authorities did not detect any further outbreaks of infectious diseases. The men appeared to be in good shape to commence full-time training, which got under way on their fourth day in camp.[7]

Prior to 1917, basic infantry training in the CEF had been the responsibility of individual units deploying overseas. Later that responsibility was assigned to a labyrinth-like system of reserve brigades and battalions, and eventually to two separate Canadian training divisions, over top of which British authorities had imposed further direction. This bureaucratic formation proved to be inefficient and ineffective; it did not produce trained soldiers at anywhere near its capacity, or worse, it produced what Desmond Morton described as "inadequately trained" soldiers. Thus, in December 1916 the old approach was summarily scrapped and "Canadian authorities in England assumed the entire responsibility for training their own reinforcements."[8] Shortly thereafter a new standardized fourteen-week course in basic infantry training was introduced.[9]

It was felt that by consolidating lessons learned from two-and-a-half years of previous instruction and battlefield experience, significant improvements could be made both in the quality of training and in the flow of reinforcements to the front. Indeed, the authorities would be proven correct on both counts. A year later, though, with the imminent threat of a new German offensive and with the arrival of thousands of fresh recruits, it was decided to revisit the requirement for a fourteen-week basic training syllabus, which, depending of course on the ever-increasing manpower demands from the front, was at best a very soft requirement. As will be shown, the subsequent decision to temporarily reduce the length of the basic infantry course has been widely misinterpreted ever since, particularly with respect to its impact on conscripts and on their performance in battle.

"The fate of the British Empire hangs in the balance"

By early March 1918 the long-expected build-up of German forces on the Western Front was mostly complete.[10] But not until Thursday, 21 March, did General Erich Ludendorff launch what became the last great German offensive of the war. Code-named Operation Michael, the main German assault began with a massive four-hour artillery barrage along a 70 kilometre front between Arras and La Fère. No fewer than sixty-four German divisions were opposed by just twenty-nine under-strength British divisions. Within a few hours, the Third and Fifth British Armies had reeled back, and the latter had faltered fatally, almost disintegrating in a rout.[11]

The Canadian Corps was then holding a quieter section of the front farther north at Lens. General Currie had just left for London to consult further with Kemp on the latest proposals to reorganize the CEF. That evening, Currie was recalled to France. In time, all four divisions would be temporarily removed from his command, but surprisingly, the corps itself would not be "directly involved."[12] At the same time the ordinary Canadian soldier in the field was shocked by all these turbulent events, since it was generally believed that "the English soldier was as good as the best in the world." To gunner William Kerr, the British "reverses" seemed inexplicable, although in his postwar memoir he expressed serious doubt as to the "qualities of many English Divisions, reinforced as they now were by conscripts."[13] This was faulty logic at best. British conscripts had been flowing to the front for nearly two years, and compared to Canadian volunteers, many of them had as much or even more battle experience. Nonetheless, if Kerr and his comrades assumed that "conscripts" were partly responsible for this setback, then Canadian conscripts just arriving in the theatre would clearly have yet another burden to bear.

This tortuous week had at least one other disturbing result – there appears to have been "panic" at all levels of the military hierarchy, especially among those responsible for providing the BEF with trained reinforcements. In England, the news of a possible collapse prompted the British to scour the country for potential reinforcements; eventually, 170,000 personnel "were instantly made available for France."[14] This precipitous and alarming action then triggered a number of precautionary and somewhat questionable decisions on the part of Canadian authorities. First, on Sunday, 24 March, HQ OMFC directed the staff at Camp Witley to "prepare for immediate despatch every available fully trained infantry man" – a seemingly desperate move that resulted in the wholesale cancellation of advanced training.[15] In short, the suspension of vital training programs – a rarely invoked military option that typically comes at a steep cost – was considered an operational necessity. But it was the decision the OMFC took next that would shake the foundation of the Canadian training system.

On the fifth day of the crisis, citing the gravity of the situation, the Brigadier-General, General Staff (BGGS) at HQ OMFC in London directed that the training syllabus at all of Canada's main training bases (Bramshott, Witley, Seaford, and Shorncliffe) "be revised to ensure that the training of all 'A-2' men in essential subjects ... be completed at the end of the ninth week." Emphasizing the "severe fighting" then under way, this directive noted the strong likelihood that this latest German offensive would generate "heavy demands" for reinforcements: thus the need for more "strenuous efforts" on the part of the instructing staff. Then, in what might be seen today as a bit of micromanaging, this extraordinary missive suggested a specific "distribution of hours" for weeks five through nine of the new training syllabus, and even identified those core subjects on which the instructors needed to concentrate more heavily.[16]

These were tumultuous times. Only one week into the German offensive, General Currie issued a historic "special order" to the troops in which he dramatically declared that "the fate of the British Empire hangs in the balance." He then solemnly exhorted his troops to "advance or fall where you stand ... to fight as you have never fought."[17] Fortunately for Currie and for the Canadian Corps, fate and circumstance would prove to be on their side.

As for General Turner, his decision to accelerate the production of trained reinforcements had likely been endorsed by his deeply concerned minister. Abandoning his typically phlegmatic style, Kemp had worriedly written to Mewburn describing this "awful push of the Germans" as "the most anxious time since the war began."[18] While not yet in a "panic" per se, the next day Kemp expressed great alarm when he urgently requested that Canada dispatch

"15,000 infantry ... by the end of April."[19] Clearly, the recent break-up of the 5th Division had not met expectations in this regard; in the words of historian Robert Craig Brown, it was "a temporary expedient."[20] Meanwhile, General Currie continued to press hard for more men, writing urgently to Kemp the same day he issued his "special order" to express his fervent "hope that the calling up of men in Canada will be pushed with greater vigour."[21]

What of the changed training program? Was it ever fully implemented? It would appear that, notwithstanding the initial knee-jerk reaction, it was not, although high casualty figures in August would trigger a similar contraction in training. In fact, shortly after the abbreviated syllabus was introduced, it became increasingly evident that the minimum training period established for new recruits had quickly evolved, and would soon extend well beyond the mandated nine-week course approved during the dark days of March 1918. Nevertheless, collective anxieties about German advances had combined with a perceived lack of manpower to propel a tectonic albeit temporary shift in training policy for newly arrived recruits. And, as noted in the Introduction, these historic events would create the foundation for another enduring myth – that of the partially trained conscript.

Insurrection: Conscripts Deployed to Quebec

Back in Canada, the alarming news from the front was completely subsumed by another quickly developing crisis: a sudden insurrection in Quebec instigated by opponents of conscription. What became known as the "Easter Riots" began on Thursday evening, 28 March, when federal constables attempting to enforce the MSA in Quebec City arrested a suspected defaulter, who was not carrying a "certificate of exemption."[22] Although he was promptly released, angry crowds rioted over the next three days, prompting Borden to dispatch seven hundred soldiers to Quebec.[23] Subsequently, the city witnessed "one long continuous riot" on Easter Sunday; "four civilians were killed, many wounded and about seventy arrested." "Public order" was soon restored; but even so, Borden dispatched one thousand additional English-speaking soldiers to Quebec City, along with another twelve hundred to Montreal.[24]

In a remarkable twist of fate, and one that certainly stands out as one of the war's great ironies, a great many of the reinforcements shipped out to Quebec to subdue this anti-conscriptionist revolt were themselves conscripts. One of them was Sapper A. Roy Neilson, who found himself that Easter Monday at the Engineer Training Depot in "St Johns" (Saint-Jean-sur-Richelieu, Quebec). "Getting us ready for action in Quebec or Montreal," Neilson scribbled in his diary.[25] Fortunately, it was not to be. Nevertheless, for some conscripts deployed to Quebec City, their first taste of action would come in Canada, not in France. Moreover, many of these draftees would remain in Quebec for the duration.[26]

With the crisis in Quebec contained for the moment, Borden turned to the other great dilemma he still faced: where to find the necessary reinforcements urgently needed overseas, absent a strong response to the first call-up by the MSA. On 12 April, Kemp had advised that there would be "practically no trained infantry reinforcements available after July 1st." Worse, given the heavy casualties expected in the "immediate future," it would not be possible, he warned, to sustain the necessary Canadian Corps infantry "beyond June 1st."[27] Pressured by colleagues and confronted with alarming reports on the war, Borden was compelled to act. Accordingly, a draft Order in Council was prepared that essentially cancelled all MSA exemptions granted so far, prohibited "future exemptions for men in Class 1," and called up without exception "all men between 20 and 24 years of age."[28]

The Commons met *in camera* for two hours on 17 April (a historic first). There, Borden made a strong case for Canada to "supply the men necessary to keep our divisions up to full strength, no matter what casualties were suffered."[29] Then, two days later, eschewing normal parliamentary procedure, which would have seen a revised Military Service Act submitted for an expected time-consuming debate, Borden chose instead to summarily expedite the entire legislative process. He did so by submitting to Parliament not a government bill, but rather a revised Order in Council amending the MSA, in what Borden himself described as "a rather novel method" for the requisite consultations.[30] Tabling the "Order" to a full house and a packed gallery, Borden declared that "the exemptions of 1917 are being abolished"; hence, all unmarried men and widowers without children aged twenty to twenty-two would immediately be called up. In addition, Class 1 registration would be expanded to include all nineteen-year-old men, although any decision to order this group to report for service would be temporarily held in abeyance pending a further review of requirements. Shortly thereafter, the necessary measures were passed by a majority of forty-nine (114–65). The selective draft in Canada was no more.[31]

In a single stroke, Borden had overcome two great obstacles to harnessing Canada's untapped supply of draft-age men: first, the extremely troublesome issue of exemptions, a debilitating chokepoint for the MSA; and second, the need to establish a continuous and reliable flow of reinforcements to the front. Yet the toxic effects of these decisions would further alienate large groups of Canadians, including farmers, fishermen, and labour leaders, not to mention most of Quebec.[32] Borden's party would one day pay a steep political price for such measures, but for Currie and the Canadian Corps, this was all most welcome news.

A Very Credible Appearance

In this the forty-fifth month of the Great War there were some very desperate moments. On 11 April, with the fate of his armies seemingly hanging in the balance, Field Marshal Haig's "backs to the wall" message, with its shocking declaration that "every position must be held to the last man," indirectly high-lighted what appeared to be the British Army's own principal weakness – the lack of trained reinforcements at the front.[33] In what the *Times* described as "the most drastic and comprehensive measure for national defence ever passed by the Imperial Parliament," the British government approved a fifth Military Service Bill.[34]

In the meantime, to its great credit, the Canadian training system in Britain responded positively to the grave crisis in France and produced in short order the syllabus necessary to ensure that training in all "essential subjects" would be completed by the end of the "9th week."[35] This difficult task was accomplished first by an overall effort "to intensify the training" and second by the earliest move yet to "summer time" in the United Kingdom (24 March instead of 8 April), which provided more daylight hours and lengthened the training day itself. In short, "every effort [was] made to utilize as many hours of daylight as possible" and to do so in the most effective manner.[36] In addition, excessive drill time was eliminated, as was extra physical training and several forced marches – the latter a useful exercise for toughening up the trainees, but one that most recruits saw as practice bleeding. As a result, while the goal of producing a "fourteen week" soldier was temporarily abandoned, the revised syllabus helped mitigate the overall impacts of a shortened course, and ultimately produced graduates with the nominal equivalent of nearly eleven weeks of essential training under the old program.

The other requirement necessary to make an abbreviated syllabus work was of course a well-motivated recruit. In this respect, the authorities at Bramshott reported in early May that "the recently arrived drafts from Canada under the Military Service Act present a very creditable appearance and show a keen interest in their work."[37] Not only were these new men highly motivated, but some of them were quite adept at mastering basic military skills, especially in musketry. For example, Private Austin Kempffer of the 3rd Reserve Battalion, a stationary engineer and draftee originally from New Carlisle, Quebec, scored an astonishing "161 points out of a possible 170 ... said to be [the] Canadian Record in England."[38] As for the nine-week training experiment, clearly the plan to produce an equivalent ten-week or eleven-week soldier was not ideal. However, the crisis that precipitated these changes would pass in less than a month. In addition, a survey of hundreds of relevant files reveals that most new men then in the pipeline benefited from formal training that routinely extended well beyond the temporary nine-week minimum and, for many, exceeded even the original goal of "fourteen weeks."[39] Moreover, within just two months Camp Witley reported that "additional arrangements are being made for the training in Platoon tactics of the men who have completed their 11th week of training," after which another status report confirmed a return to the *status quo ante*: "Tactical Schemes are being carried out by men who have completed their individual training. [Thus] it is hoped that all men who complete their 14th week of training will have a good knowledge of elementary tactics in Open Warfare in addition to Trench and Semi-open Warfare."[40]

Bramshott's summary for the month of July echoed this same trend, noting that its own training program featured "a number of units in the area" comprising "a considerable number of men in the 12th, 13th and 14th weeks of training, and over, [whilst] great attention is being paid to field work consisting of Platoon and Company in attack, both on main and isolated positions, withdrawals under pressure, and general outpost work."[41] Thus, while the notion of the half or partially trained conscript would soon become an enduring myth, it does not appear that most new men who joined the Canadian Corps that summer were generally lacking in requisite field skills.[42]

Conscripts: Fuel for Currie's Reorganization

Meanwhile Currie worked assiduously throughout April to regroup the Canadian divisions under his control, pressing forward with several key organizational changes. Having obtained OMFC approval to augment his infantry battalions with one hundred more men each, he decided to dramatically increase the firepower of the corps. To that end, he provided each of these units with enough light machine-guns that every rifle platoon was now equipped with the formidable punch of "two Lewis gun teams."[43] Currie also reorganized the corps' existing machine-gun companies into "2-company battalions, one with each infantry division," and added a third heavy machine-gun company to each machine-gun battalion. The net result was the creation for the first time of a "machine gun service ... a distinctive arm, intermediate between the infantry and the artillery, and with tactics of its own." This landmark decision would later pay handsome dividends on the battlefield, but like all such initiatives it would be manpower intensive. The soldiers required to establish these elite units had to come from the ranks of existing formations. So in a somewhat controversial move, Currie directed each infantry battalion to provide fifty of its "best and brainiest men" for this purpose.[44] Thus the infantry, ostensibly left with only half the manpower gain originally anticipated, had to await the arrival of

Figure 3.1   Private Russell Crarey (third from left, killed in action 11 October 1918) and comrades, 6th Canadian Reserve Battalion, Seaford Camp, summer 1918. *Source:* Courtesy of Doreen Williamson.

Figure 3.2   Private Jim Young (back row, second from right) and comrades at Seaford Camp, summer 1918. *Source:* Courtesy of Jim Vallance.

at least twenty-four hundred new men – mostly conscripts – in order to backfill behind their departing "best."

Lastly, Currie made the long-sighted decision to expand his pioneer companies into full-fledged engineer battalions (one per brigade), with each of these units reporting directly to newly established engineer brigade headquarters (one per division).[45] Once again, though, the corps commander had not yet figured out just how to sustain so many trained engineers in the field. Nevertheless, the authorities in Canada reacted quickly to Currie's ambitious plans and diverted a modest number of new recruits away from the infantry. Consequently, a few lucky drafts of conscripts, among them Sapper A. Roy Neilson, soon found themselves in England, not at infantry training camps like Bramshott, but at the engineer training school in Seaford.[46]

"All new men, who have the appearance of making good soldiers"

By early May, General Currie had regained control of three of his divisions, but the 2nd Division (Major-General Harry Burstall, GOC) remained in the line with VI Corps (Third British Army) in the ever-volatile sector of Neuville-Vitasse. Burstall's men held "this front for an uninterrupted period of 92 days, during which time [they] repulsed a series of local attacks and carried out no less than 27 raids."[47] In fact, "the month of May ... brought to the 31st Battalion more actual action than had the momentous five weeks which had preceded it." So it is somewhat surprising that Currie did not mention in his postwar "Interim Report on the Operations of the Canadian Corps during the Year 1918" any details regarding casualties during this phase of the war, nor anything about how the 2nd Division was reinforced. Given that the 2nd Division sustained more than twenty-eight hundred combat casualties during this time, along with the normal wastage associated with front-line service, it does raise the question: Where did the replacement personnel come from, particularly in light of Currie's ongoing reorganization of the corps?[48]

The answer of course is that some of the replacements were returning from hospital, some were genuine volunteers (mostly the last remnants of the 5th Division infantry), and some were BCRM men who had enlisted the previous summer but who only now were being posted to the front. And, lastly, infantry battalions were now beginning to be reinforced by a small but growing cadre of conscripts, including Private George Jones, who had joined the 72nd Battalion in late March. Mixed for example among a batch of nineteen reinforcements arriving at the 7th Battalion (1st British Columbia Regiment) transport lines on 12 April were two other conscripts – Private Alexander Bey, a labourer from Fernie, BC; and Private Werner Olson, a Swedish merchant from Vancouver, both of whom had been recruited in early November. They were followed into the trenches on 18 April by another draft of seventy reinforcements, among whom were at least eleven more conscripts, all of whom had been attested well before Borden had officially called them to the colours. Significantly, these men did not have to wait long for their first taste of action: the 7th conducted trench raids on 19 and 21 April. By that time many conscripts were truly at war, and luckily most would survive unscathed – at least for now. Among them was Private Niels Pedersen, a Danish-born fisherman from Prince Rupert. His luck eventually ran out on 17 August near Damery, east of Amiens. By that time though, he and his fellow draftees had become veteran soldiers in every respect.[49]

Apart from normal attrition, Currie's reorganization – a shell game of sorts – was claiming thousands of infantry from the ranks of his newly reconstituted divisions. The 7th Battalion, for example, surrendered fifty of its "best men" to the 1st Canadian Machine Gun (MG) Battalion on 13 April. The 85th Battalion made a similar contribution two days later. Among the twenty reinforcements sent initially to backfill the depleted ranks of the 85th were four conscripts who, the very next day, were plunged into the cauldron of battle opposite Arleux, 10 kilometres southeast of Vimy Ridge. There, besides conducting two trench raids over the next two weeks, the 85th was subjected to "numerous and concentrated enemy shoots on the whole area." During one such attack, two conscripts suffered wounds, one of them being Private Archibald Forbes, a teamster from Stellarton, Nova Scotia. Wounded by shrapnel on 2 May, Forbes thus became the first Canadian conscript to become a battle casualty in the Great War.[50]

Over the next two months other units in the 2nd Division conducted similar patrols, punctuated by periodic trench raids and the occasional "daylight reconnaissance." During one of these latter operations, at about 4:30 p.m. on 10 June, the 18th Battalion (Western Ontario) sent out an officer and four scouts to reconnoitre the enemy wire on the banks of the Cojeul River, 2 kilometres east of Boisleux-au-Mont. The unit war diary provides scant details of what happened next, but does note that two ORs became casualties that day. One of these men was Private George Allsop, a twenty-one-year-old machine operator from Woodslee, Ontario. In fact, Allsop was killed in action – the very first in a long line of reluctant warriors to die in battle for King and Country.[51]

These types of raids and counter-raids were the principal feature of combat during this unusual chapter in the history of the 2nd Division.[52] Arthur Lapointe, a signaller then with the 22nd (French Canadian) Battalion, recorded the sudden fury of one such raid on 8 June, which had been preceded only hours earlier by the arrival of more than one hundred reinforcements, most of whom were conscripts. At 9:45 p.m. the Germans provided these fresh troops with a shocking introduction to the trenches – a brief but "intense" artillery barrage. Five minutes later, "3 hun parties each numbering approximately 50 rushed forward" across the battalion front, and in the fierce battle that followed many new men along with numerous veterans became casualties. Lapointe later wrote that a dozen conscripts had been killed, although in fact not one had died. Several draftees had been wounded, though, and all had been blooded.[53] By the time the "Van Doos" went over the top two months later at Amiens, all would be experienced veterans.

Elsewhere in the VI Corps sector that month, other 2nd Division conscripts encountered a similar fate. On the night of 24–25 June, two companies, one each from the 31st Battalion (Alberta Regiment) and the 27th (City of Winnipeg) Battalion, conducted a "minor operation" against strong enemy defences at the village of Neuville-Vitasse. In fact, this was a large-scale, well-rehearsed, and complex raid, preceded by a heavy artillery and shrapnel barrage and marshalling the firepower of nearly five hundred men attacking in two spirited waves. German resistance was equally fierce, and in the wake of "heavy machine gun and Trench Mortar fire," the 31st Battalion alone lost 68 men, including 13 ORs killed and 6 missing.[54] Among them were two conscripts – Privates William Laidlaw, a labourer recruited from Merlin, Ontario, and Ernest Laforet, a sailor from Tecumseh, Ontario; both had joined the battalion with great promise only a few weeks earlier. Indeed, in describing the draft of "32 O.R. reinforcements" who arrived at the horse lines on 28 May, the war diary confidently reported that these were "all new men, who have the appearance of making good soldiers." Similarly, a draft of "34 O.R's" arriving two days later was described as follows: "about 12 of these men are returned casualties, the remainder are new men and of much better physique than recent drafts." They were that and much more, by most accounts. Laforet was "severely wounded" at Neuville-Vitasse and, "while proceeding to the Dressing Station, was instantly killed by enemy shell fire." Laidlaw's fate, on the other hand, remains somewhat of a mystery. Records indicate that he too was "killed by machine gun bullets during [the] raid," but apparently his body was not recovered. Today he, along with eleven thousand comrades who also fell in France and have no known grave, is honoured at the Vimy Memorial.[55]

Among the six missing soldiers was Private Ernest Hanson, born in England and recruited in Windsor, Ontario. Originally assigned to the 18th Battalion, Hanson was transferred to the 31st Battalion on 7 June. There he experienced only one – albeit event-filled – four-day tour in the line, before participating in an epic raid at Neuville-Vitasse. Slightly wounded in the left arm and captured during the attack, Hanson was quickly dispatched 900 kilometres to the east to the German prisoner-of-war camp at Gustrow, in Mecklenburg. There the first Canadian conscript to be taken prisoner was held until his release in January 1919.[56]

In many ways, this multi-battalion raid at Neuville-Vitasse signalled a new level of boldness in the Canadian Corps, one which seemed to be rooted in a strategy of vengeance and attrition. Nonetheless, and despite many high-level messages offering both units "heartiest congratulations on the success of [this] operation," brigade headquarters was more reserved in its praise, acknowledging that the "difficulties are fully realized and your casualties greatly regretted being so high."[57] The implications of this latter point were quite clear. While difficult and hard-won successes were laudable, the ability of each brigade to sustain itself during extended periods of operations such as these would, in the face of such attrition, depend most heavily on one vital resource – trained reinforcements. Quite fortuitously, though, at that very moment thousands of such men were then arriving in France, including, as Tim Cook notes, "the first conscripts."[58]

"You know my life is not worth ten cents in the army"

Among the thousands of new men still in England was Private Hilaire Dennis. By early May, he had completed twelve weeks of basic infantry training with the 4th Reserve Battalion, when suddenly many of his comrades were selected for an overseas draft, one that Dennis was "much disappointed" to learn did not include him. "It broke my heart to see them go," he wrote, and to learn that he would have to stay behind until the "next draft." In fact, it would be another three weeks before Private Dennis got the call, and his letters home (those that have survived) offer an intriguing look at the type of soldier that the Canadian training system was then churning out. Strong, healthy, well-trained, and apparently well-motivated, Dennis was also somewhat fatalistic. His attitude, overall, contrasts sharply with the perceived lack of dedication typically ascribed then and afterwards to conscripts. Evidence of his remarkable conversion from a skeptical citizen who objected to fighting in this "European War," to a trained soldier keen on doing his duty, was even more apparent when he wrote: "I am qualified for a machine gunner and Bomber, and believe me Uncle if they ever give me a chance at those wild Germans I will cut them down like hay. I am a good bayonet fighter – also I don't think that I will be afraid to use the cold steel because I can use it."[59]

Clearly the veteran instructors at Camp Witley had instilled in this young man the requisite killer instinct necessary to perform the brutal tasks that lay ahead. Dennis and his fellow draftees would not disappoint in this regard.

However, they would not go to their fates mindlessly either. Addressing this latter thought in sober terms, Dennis added:

> I may drop off over here ... You know my life is not worth ten cents in the Army and I know it. If I die in this war I will die game because I don't care if I die now. It used to worry me quite a bit you know. I used to worry about all those things at home and war over here but now I have to cut all this out and I don't care what becomes of me ... as I said before, I am ready as many other Canadian lads did to make the supreme sacrifice for my people and country.[60]

Meanwhile back in Canada another draftee, Sapper A. Roy Neilson, had embarked from Halifax on 11 May aboard the Australian troopship HMAT *Runic*. His was an eventful journey worthy of a closer look, especially since he followed in the wake of those Canadians whose first glimpse of war came not at Ypres or on the Somme but on the fierce and often unforgiving North Atlantic. The *Runic*, loaded with flour and "about 540 Australian troops," was briefly home for Neilson and "about 225" Canadian troops as well, who were accommodated in a fifty- by eighty-foot section in the front hold. Typically, a transatlantic crossing afforded few creature comforts for enlisted men and was especially traumatic for those who could not swim and for those who deeply feared the sea. In addition, as the convoy pressed slowly eastward at a fixed speed of about eight knots, the threat of U-boat attack continued to mount and personal anxieties increased by the day. On Thursday, 16 May, the other great menace of the sea had returned with a fury. Waves "like mountains" repeatedly flooded the deck with at least two feet of water, and soldiers scrambled into the ship's heaving cargo hold for shelter.[61]

On the seventh night of the crossing, the *Runic* began to lurch about, its steering gear having temporarily failed, causing the soldiers to be thrown around quite violently. Next, Neilson recalled, having entered the primary operating area for German submarines, on the tenth day of the voyage the men were ordered for the first time to sleep in their clothes. For some this was pure misery, as many men quickly discovered that their uniforms were infested with "big woolly" lice. But the caution was justified, for Neilson's convoy soon came under attack. At about 2:30 a.m. on Thursday, 23 May (day thirteen), Neilson was awakened when he "heard a shot fired," followed by a "real loud report." Thinking the ship could be torpedoed at any moment, "250" men flung themselves up the sixteen steps to the deck just in time to see the *Persia* swing away from the stern of the *Runic*, with which it had just collided after successfully manoeuvring to avoid an enemy torpedo.[62]

Figure 3.3   Sapper A. Roy Neilson (centre), 2nd Engineer Reserve Battalion, and eight comrades in quarantine at Camp Seaford, May 1918. *Source:* Courtesy of Dr. Peter Neilson.

Not so fortunate was the escort RMS *Moldavia*, which had been "converted into an armed merchant cruiser" in 1915. On this fateful night, she was transporting the US "58th Infantry Regiment" and leading five other troopships through the English Channel, including Neilson's *Runic*, when at about 2:40 a.m. she "was torpedoed and sunk by a German submarine with the loss of 56 men."[63] Notably, some of these men were American draftees. Ironically, it was their sacrifice that apparently allowed *Runic* and the other ships in the convoy to escape, thus permitting at least one more contingent of conscripts (the Canadians) to live and fight another day.

As for Sapper Neilson, in the immediate aftermath of his lucky escape from the worst of a U-boat attack, he summed up this traumatic experience by echoing a theme curiously common to all veterans. "We now feel life," he wrote, "none of us being sorry." The next day, Friday, 24 May, he and his mates disembarked in London, were "packed into a troop train," and swiftly whisked off to their next assignment – the 2nd Canadian Engineer Reserve Battalion (CERB) at Seaford Camp in Sussex.[64] For these draftees, the front was now one giant step closer.

Keeping the Corps Intact as a Fighting Organization

By late June, Currie had finally secured relief for the 2nd Division, but only in exchange for the 3rd Division as its replacement. In the meantime, the reorganization of the Canadian Corps and the arrival in England of thousands of fresh troops from Canada (and the promise of many thousands more) had not been lost on the British senior staff. These facts, coupled with the latest casualty reports, compelled the new Chief of the Imperial General Staff, General Sir Henry Wilson, to privately solicit support from Sir Edward Kemp "to raise another Division, if only as a temporary measure." The Canadian authorities were stunned by this suggestion, inasmuch as this latest proposal to reduce "the four Divisions of the Canadian Corps to 9 battalions each instead of 12" was one that had been safely put to bed, or so it was thought, the previous February. Moreover, Wilson boldly proposed that this new formation "might be made by combing out 'A' men from forestry and other non-combatant units, supplementing them with some of the excess numbers and reinforcements at present in the depots both in France and England."[65]

Kemp's detailed reply to Wilson nine days letter was a masterpiece of diplomacy. In a carefully worded rebuttal of Wilson's faulty battlefield logic regarding reduced-size divisions, it challenged any implied misconceptions regarding so called "excess numbers." Ultimately Kemp rejected the British proposal outright, underscoring once again the importance of keeping the corps "intact as a fighting organization" and declaring as well that "its value as a striking force would be impaired" were it to be "reduced in strength or diluted with other troops."[66]

In fact, Wilson and the War Office had seriously misjudged the matter and had delivered their calcified proposal at the most inopportune time. Sir Robert Borden, in London since 8 June for the latest meetings of the Imperial War Cabinet, had just summoned General Currie for a war update, during which he demanded the "unvarnished truth." Currie complied and provided Borden with "a lurid picture" of the situation, one that was highly critical of British leadership during the recent German offensive, and one that likely strengthened Borden's resolve to avoid at all costs a potentially dangerous reduction in brigade strength. One week later, Kemp's stern reply to Wilson strongly suggested that Canada was fully prepared to "fight it out to the end," but that it would do so only on its own terms and with an army corps fully manned and equipped to do the job. Otherwise it would be increasingly difficult for Borden and his Union Government to continue to justify to the nation its ongoing sacrifice of Canada's youth, including that of men who were now being compelled to fight.[67]

"They were a fine-looking lot of men"

As the Imperial War Cabinet debated the conduct of the British war effort, the appearance of large numbers of conscripts was increasingly evident at training bases throughout England, both to the instructing staff and to most volunteers who began to follow with greater interest this band of reluctant warriors. In a

Figure 3.4   Prime Minister Borden and Lieutenant-General Sir Arthur Currie review CEF troops during march past in France, July 1918. *Source:* LAC, PA-002746.

letter home on 2 June, Percy Wilmot, then newly commissioned from the ranks and serving with the 17th Reserve Battalion at Bramshott, noted that "Mr Conscripto – (which name is not used here. They are called 'Drafters' [*sic*]) are now fast arriving and are being put into training. They are quite a good lot of men and are taking to the work quite eagerly."[68]

The venerable padre Canon Frederick G. Scott would likewise recall in his postwar memoir that during a visit to the Canadian Corps Reinforcement Camp (CCRC) at Aubin-Saint-Vaast in July 1918, he had "addressed a battalion of draftees who were about to be sent up to the front. They were a fine-looking lot of men," he declared, "and knew their drill." This was high praise indeed coming from a man of the cloth who had lost a son in battle and had actively campaigned for conscription.[69]

Canon Scott's brief albeit positive description of these draftees seems to have reflected a slowly developing attitude – fuelled in part perhaps by direction from the corps and division commanders – that veteran soldiers ought to avoid "criticism or recrimination" in their treatment of the new men. This made very good operational sense, since it was presumed that soldiers who were treated with a modicum of respect were much more likely to perform their duties more effectively than those who were held in contempt. As historian

Larry Worthington has acknowledged, "the integrated draftees seemed to conform to the spirit of the Corps," and these same men were seen "fighting later with skill and courage."[70] Regimental historian Kim Beattie agreed: once blooded, "they [the conscripts] made good soldiers." As it turned out, the method of an individual soldier's recruitment would matter far less than whether he was a reliable soldier in battle and, more importantly, whether he could be depended on not to fall asleep while on sentry duty. In the meantime, though, the conscript continued to be an easy target, as in this example of soldiers' humour:

> *Onward Conscript Soldiers,*
> Marching as to war,
> You would not be conscripts
> *Had you come before.*[71]

Pandemic Flu and the Summer Offensives

For many of these new men, bullying would be the least of their worries. Before many of them could even join their units in the field, they would first have to survive the next great peril – the Spanish influenza. This "new type of Influenza" began to sweep through the corps and its training establishments around the end of May, and by mid-June the scourge had become a full-scale epidemic with "devastating effects" on some units. For example, the 14th Battalion (Royal Montreal Regiment), then in "Special Army Reserve," was forced to cancel a move to Écoivres because "several hundred men were sick."[72]

For most of those severely affected, the sickness lasted only three to four days. But it was characterized by "very high temperature, splitting headache, some conjunctivitis and racking pains." Collectively, these symptoms ensured that the individual was *hors de combat* for at least a week. Moreover, since the disease was so prevalent, medical facilities were quickly taxed to the limit. So except in extreme cases, hospitalization was out of the question, and most patients had to be treated *in situ*. Worse, over the next few weeks all units were affected by this persistent and seemingly interminable plague. As late as 4 July, Major Arthur Bick, a divisional artillery officer, reported in his diary that the "epidemic of what is called Influenza, Spanish Fever or Bolshevism seems to be dying out very slowly."[73]

Yet the news was not all bad. This paralyzing epidemic had struck when most of the Canadian Corps was in reserve; this meant that Currie did not have to fight two enemies at once. Second, although the Canadian forces recorded about forty-six thousand total cases of influenza and nearly eight hundred fatalities, the vast majority of deaths occurred in Canada, at sea, or in England, which, it must be said, was much less debilitating to the corps in the field. Thus, as historian Bill Rawling has noted in his seminal paper "A Resource Not to Be Squandered," in a propitious turn of events the "first wave [of the flu] subsided, coincidentally in time for the summer offensives to begin."[74] Reorganized, revitalized, and reinforced, Currie's beloved corps would now take its place in the line once again with Haig's other legions – this time at Amiens.

4
Conspicuous Gallantry at Amiens

*It became necessary to resort to conscription in those dark months which
preceded the triumphant Hundred Days ... It was regrettable but imperative ...
and it stands to the everlasting credit of the volunteers that the conscripts
were absorbed so unostentatiously as reinforcements to tried units, that their
arrival hardly called for comment, and it became the worst of "form" to cast
compulsion in a man's teeth.*

– RALF FREDERIC LARDY SHELDON-WILLIAMS

BY THE EARLY SUMMER of 1918, Canadian conscripts had begun to flow to France
in large numbers, just in time it would seem for Currie to support General
Ferdinand Foch's strategy of continuous attack – "Tout le monde à la bataille!"
– everybody into battle![1] In this respect, Currie was offensive-minded as well,
and did not relish the thought of the Canadian Corps wasting away in a static
defence. This much-tempered battle philosophy would soon intersect with that
of Foch's; when combined with a new capacity to rapidly replenish the ranks of
the Canadian infantry corps, it would shape all of Currie's key battlefield decisions for the remainder of the war.

Meanwhile, Ludendorff's spring offensives had, for him, proven a disappoint-
ing failure. His four-army assault east and south of Reims on 15 July (the Second
Battle of the Marne) had been soundly defeated by French and American forces.
For all intents and purposes, the German army had ceased to be an instrument
of attack. Still formidable but now exhausted, poorly supplied and not well reinforced, his battered legions were experiencing a precipitous drop in morale
and the debilitating effects of the Spanish flu.[2] All of this set the stage for a
spectacular Allied counterstroke. Meeting in late July for what would be the
first and last such conference with his principal commanders – Haig, Pétain,
and Pershing – Foch laid out his strategy for the next six months. Afterwards
he formally requested that the Allied armies provide him "as soon as possible
with the total forces they could put in the line on January 1 and April 1, 1919,
respectively."[3] That done, Foch now turned his attention to the next major
summer offensive – Amiens.

"Foch's Pets"

Shortly after Foch's command summit, Lieutenant-General Currie was informed by Major-General John Davidson (Haig's Chief of Operations) of pending plans for the new offensive. It would include the Canadian and the Australian Corps, but was expected to be "of limited scope."[4] In fact, General Sir Henry Rawlinson, GOC Fourth British Army, initially intended merely to "assure the safety of Amiens" by freeing "the Amiens-Paris railway line." On 5 August, however, Haig decided instead on a much more ambitious and general offensive "to capture the line Chaulnes-Roye" 25 kilometres farther to the east.[5]

As for the Canadian Corps, fully reinvigorated after a long rest, many wondered when this splendid formation, sometimes known as "Foch's Pets," would again be put to the test, given that it had not participated in a major offensive since Passchendaele some eight months earlier.[6] No doubt Currie would have been sensitive to such criticism, so he enthusiastically embraced this opportunity to re-engage the enemy, although his motivation appears to have been influenced somewhat by a number of other concerns.

First, apart from the extraordinary developments taking place farther south, Currie was likely aware of strategic discussions to postpone the next major Allied offensive until the summer of 1919, by which time overwhelming numbers of American troops would be in place. In this context, the prospect that the Americans might quickly turn the tide was not unpleasant, although it would likely mean a diminished role for the Canadians. But Currie had a far more practical objection to any further delay in the operational employment of the Canadian Corps. Foremost on his mind was the high number of battle *and* non-battle casualties that the corps experienced on a daily basis, "even on a quiet front" – about "two hundred a day."[7] Far better, he thought, to be on the offensive, where losses were typically measured against the success of an attack – yardage gained, prisoners taken, and, most important, enemy dead. Notably these views were remarkably similar to those of General Ludendorff, who later wrote that "of the two [offence and defence], an offensive makes less demand on the men and involves no higher losses.[8]

And as a *national* commander, Currie had even broader, more complex issues to confront. How, for example, could one reasonably justify mounting losses (over ten thousand casualties since January 1918) absent any clear evidence that these sacrifices had not been in vain? Worse, for the corps to continue to hemorrhage indefinitely, even at this lower rate, would be even more disturbing. Why, one might reasonably ask, had it been necessary for Canada to implement conscription in the first place if the men produced in that most divisive of recruiting efforts were only to become victims of routine battlefield wastage, rather than essential participants in a great Allied campaign to help end the war? Amiens it would be then and, in Currie's words, "God help the Boche."[9]

The Hundred Days Begin

By August 1918 the Canadian Corps was the largest and perhaps the most effective formation of its kind on the Western Front; but it was not, as generally thought, at full strength. Indeed, despite the corps receiving thousands of reinforcements over the previous six months, it "was considerably under strength on the date when [the Amiens] operations began."[10] Further evidence of this peculiar manpower shortage was apparent in Currie's decision on 4 August to release "all men in arrest awaiting trial [with notable exceptions] ... without prejudice to re-arrest."[11] Thus Amiens would be a maximum effort in every sense, but the corps would never be at full strength until the very end of the war.

On this same date, the fourth anniversary of Britain's declaration of war on Germany, Sir Robert Borden issued a press statement in London reaffirming Canada's continuing resolve and declaring that "in the end, no army in such a war as this is stronger than the spirit of the people behind it."[12] But it would be the strength of the men up front that would carry that "spirit" into battle, and very soon their ranks would be fully reinforced by a new kind of citizen-soldier – the Canadian conscript. Thousands of these new men were now making their way to the front, and their journey was about to accelerate, for on this day the Battle of Amiens had already begun. Earlier that morning, leading elements of the Canadian Corps had come under fire at the Domart Bridge, about 10 kilometres southeast of Amiens, where Canadian sappers had courageously removed several enemy demolition charges to make the bridge safe. In fact, this obscure action marked the actual beginning of what would become known as the Hundred Days.[13]

The following day, about 5 kilometres north (outside Villers-Bretonneux), the 21st Battalion (Eastern Ontario) arrived in the main battle area to relieve the 16th Australian Battalion. Like most other Canadian units, this weary battalion had travelled a circuitous route of nearly 150 kilometres, all on the march except for a 60 kilometre run by train.[14] Then, having rested most of the day, the battalion moved forward from Fluy into new positions, where at about midnight and in the pouring rain, the 21st suffered its first serious blow of the operation. A German 5.9-inch heavy artillery shell landed with a crashing roar directly on a small ammunition dump just as two platoons of "A" Company were passing by. The ensuing blast caused wholesale carnage, instantly killing seventeen men and wounding ten more. Among the dead and wounded were four conscripts, including Privates Patrick Belanger, a barber from Ottawa, and

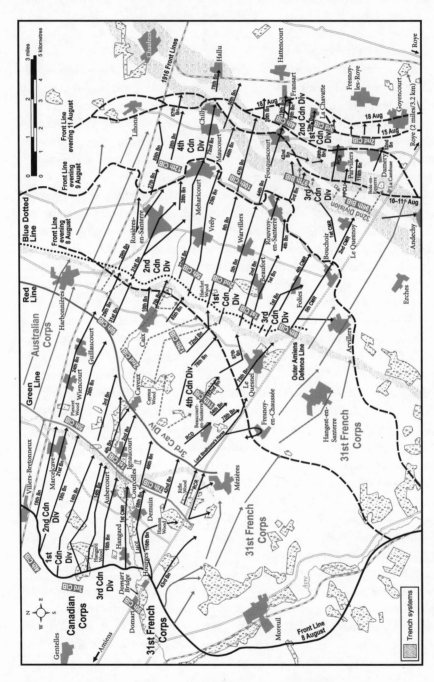

Map 2 Amiens, 4–24 August, 1918. Map by Mike Bechthold.

Arthur Brabant, a farmer from L'Original, Ontario – the first of Canada's reluctant warriors to die in Picardy.[15]

"I never saw such a concentration of men and guns"

By the evening of 7 August, Haig had deployed four separate corps at Amiens under Rawlinson, consisting (north to south) of III British Corps, the Australian Corps, the Canadian Corps, and the 31st Corps of General Marie-Eugène Debeney's First French Army. As historian Brereton Greenhous has pointed out, "twenty-one divisions" were thus opposing General Georg von der Marwitz's fourteen.[16] Indeed, in his diary, Major-General Sir David Watson would record that he "never saw such a concentration of men and guns."[17] The Foch/Haig plan to penetrate as far east as the Roye-Chaulnes Line was without precedent for the Allies. Moreover, the date of the attack had been moved up two days, from 10 to 8 August, thus placing enormous stress on the attacking forces and leaving precious little time to prepare the necessary plans to fully support such a complex scheme.[18] In the end, this latter decision seriously compromised the ability to exploit success, particularly on the second day of the battle.[19]

The Battle of Amiens, informally code-named "Llandovery Castle" ("L.C. Operation" for short), featured a fairly simple plan of execution.[20] The Canadian Corps, then fully deployed with three infantry divisions up and one in reserve (the 4th), each supported by a battalion of tanks, would strike "the main blow on the Fourth Army's right." There were three major objectives: first, penetrate some 3 to 5 kilometres to the "intermediate objective" – the "Green Line" – site of the enemy's line of forward outposts; then, after a brief pause, advance a similar distance to the next key objective – the "Red Line" – site of the Germans' "static reserve defense [*sic*]" and its "gun lines." Finally, the 3rd Cavalry Division, led by the Canadian Cavalry Brigade and followed closely by the 4th Canadian Division, was expected to drive another 7 kilometres farther to the east, this time to the "Blue Line," otherwise known as the "Outer Amiens Defence Line."[21]

Besides a determined enemy, the "highly varied terrain of a very large battlefield" also had to be overcome. The river Luce, flanked by "very marshy" areas, was an "unfordable obstacle" at the time; in addition, it protected a plateau that was covered with enemy defences and "intersected by some deep ravines." Consequently, the 3rd Canadian Division would be especially hindered in its advance. But, aided by Currie's bold investment in engineer brigades, not one of these obstacles would prove insurmountable.[22]

Thursday, 8 August 1918: Like Hell Let Loose

Major-General Watson's chilling description of the opening barrage was echoed by another eyewitness, who reported that at 4:20 a.m. "the shells screamed

Figure 4.1   Private Dewart Keir, 19th Battalion, killed in action, 8 August 1918. Crucifix Corner Cemetery, Villers-Bretonneux, France. *Source:* Author's collection.

overhead like countless legions of destroying angels," after which seven thousand men in three Canadian lead-off brigades were up and over the top.[23] Remarkably, just forty-five minutes later the corps had taken all its first objectives, albeit at some notable cost. In particular, the 4th Brigade (four Ontario battalions) had sustained serious losses.[24] Checked by dense morning fog and heavy machine-gun fire, the 20th Battalion (Central Ontario) suffered twenty fatalities, including several conscripts. One, a twenty-two-year-old Italian-born shoe repairman from Toronto, Private Gus Izzo, whose exemption claim had been "disallowed," was "killed by a machine gun bullet" in his unit's successful attack on Marcelcave. As for the 18th Battalion, its thirty dead included Private William Hudson, a cashier from London, Ontario, who had been "hit in the head by shrapnel." Among those lost in the 19th Battalion (Central Ontario) was Private Dewart Keir, a stove mounter from Toronto. A month later, Keir's mother would receive a moving letter from Lieutenant R.O. Spreckley, reassuring her that her cheerful and dependable son had died "whilst so nobly and courageously doing his duty for his King and Country." Finally, the 21st Battalion lost its commanding officer, Lieutenant-Colonel Elmer Watson Jones, and nineteen ORs killed, including Private David Barr, a farmer from Clayton, Ontario, who had first joined this unit on 23 June. For his parents, David and Grace Barr, the nightmare was only beginning. Three weeks later they would receive word that their younger son Wilford had been killed in action as well. He too was a conscript.[25]

At 8:20 a.m. the attacking battalions of the 7th Brigade "jumped off from the Green Line." Less than two and a half hours later, they seized their objective (the Red Line) "without serious casualties." Still, among the ten fatalities of the 49th Battalion (Edmonton Regiment) were four conscripts, including an English-born blacksmith – Private William Powell – "hit in the throat and killed by an enemy machine gun bullet" only four days before his twenty-second birthday.[26] Farther to the north, the Canadian Corps was getting an even warmer reception. The 1st and 5th Infantry Brigades had launched their assaults on the Red Line without benefit of field artillery. Each had run into "stubborn" defences, starting with enemy artillery fire, which claimed the life of Private Guy Blanchette right at the start line. This would be the first of two war tragedies for the Blanchette family from Huntingdon, Quebec. Exactly two months later, Guy's younger brother George (also a conscript but serving in the 22nd Battalion), would be slain in battle as well.[27]

In the event, "hard fighting" continued on the Corps' left flank, particularly at Pierret Wood, where "heavy fire" from "enemy machine guns" stymied both the 24th Battalion (Victoria Rifles of Canada), a Montreal regiment, and the 26th Battalion (New Brunswick Regiment).[28] Subsequently the 24th engaged in "house-to-house" combat, both in Wiencourt and Guillaucourt, some of it "hand-to-hand," and "the Battalion lost heavily." No fewer than 191 casualties were sustained on this first day at Amiens (nearly one-third of the 24th's trench strength), including 27 dead ORs, 4 of whom were conscripts. Among the dead was Private Joseph Biron, a twenty-two-year-old shoe cutter from Lachine, Quebec; wounded by machine-gun fire "in the leg and groin," he died shortly afterwards.[29]

By 11:00 a.m., though, the third and final assault of the day was well under way. Despite stiff resistance, by 3:00 p.m. the 2nd Brigade had reached the old Amiens Defence Line, three hours ahead of plan. Among its relatively light casualties was Private Herbert Fahrenkopf. Drafted at Springwater, Saskatchewan, but originally from the close-knit German farming community of St Clements, not far from the city of Kitchener (formerly Berlin, Ontario), Fahrenkopf had arrived in France on 3 June. Joining the 5th Battalion (Saskatchewan Regiment) in the field on 19 July, he likely experienced his first combat during a raid on German lines one week later. This day, however, Fahrenkopf was "instantly killed by an enemy shell" in the village of Caix.[30]

Caix itself had been overrun earlier by the 7th and 10th Battalions, thus capping what at the time was the deepest one-day penetration of enemy lines in the history of the Canadian Corps. By then, however, "hostile aircraft [had begun] to make their presence felt," sufficient for the Germans "to hold a local superiority in the air." For one Canadian conscript, Private Vincent Rawlins – a rancher from Pincher Creek, Alberta – this was a fateful development. Around 3:30 p.m., as the 10th Battalion was establishing "outposts" a few hundred yards east of Caix, Rawlins "was wounded in the kidneys by shrapnel from a bomb dropped from an enemy aeroplane." He succumbed the same day – one of 1,036 Canadians to die on 8 August.[31] Thus, while the great victory at Amiens would one day be described as "the black day of the German Army," for Canada it had been a costly triumph.[32] Moreover, with more than twenty-eight hundred other Canadian soldiers wounded in the initial action, the call for reinforcements, a great many of whom were conscripts, was immediate and urgent. Of these soldiers and their comrades who had already fallen in battle, one veteran later observed: they "did their duty as gamely as any, and I know of no instance where discredit was brought on the Army by one of them."[33]

Amiens, 9 August: For Conspicuous Gallantry and Devotion to Duty

The startling victories of 8 August, having "gone far beyond expectation," surprised both Haig and Rawlinson almost as much as the Germans. Indeed, there were only vague provisions in the chief's battle plan to exploit such success. When asked what should be done next, General Currie, recognizing that "GHQ had no definite ideas what to do," simply decided that since "the going seems good: let's go on!"[34] But by this time the Germans had moved six divisions into the line in order to stem the Allied tide. Further progress therefore proved to be very costly, in no small part because of confusion and delays as senior headquarters endeavoured to grasp entirely unexpected opportunities. First, not until very late on 8 August did the Canadian Corps receive orders to continue the advance the next day. Second, hampered by last-minute changes from Army Headquarters, Currie was forced to modify his own plans numerous times, moving zero hour first from 5:00 a.m. to a much more disadvantageous 10:00 a.m., then later still.[35] Worse, the deadly domino effect on subsequent attacks would affect all Allied armies engaged at Amiens on 9 and 10 August.[36]

First into the fight on the Canadian Corps' far left flank was Burstall's 2nd Division. His 5th and 6th Brigades were caught up in the great confusion of the conflicting zero hours that morning. In particular, the 29th (Vancouver) and 31st Battalions jumped off at 11:00 a.m., one hour later than the revised plan.[37] Straight away they encountered devastating machine-gun and artillery fire coming at them "point blank from the neighborhood of Rosières," which resulted in numerous casualties, including the 29th's commanding officer, Lieutenant-Colonel W.S. Latta. Nonetheless, by 1:00 p.m. his battalion had pressed on past the village and had advanced another "800 yards" to the east, at which point a thirty-year-old BC logger and conscript by the name of Private Frederick Bennett was "shot through the head ... and killed" – one of the last of almost 230 casualties suffered by the 29th this day.[38]

The situation to the south was even more perilous. The 31st Battalion was forced to attack across "a thousand yards ... [of] ground that was devoid of cover." "Thus, to proceed in the face of such murderous cross-fire meant suicide." Yet still the 31st pressed on to Rosières, where it quickly found itself in a duel of "bayonet versus machine gun."[39] Ultimately the battalion would award thirty-two Military Medals (MMs) for conspicuous gallantry this day, including the first ever to a Canadian conscript – Private William Thomas Mott, a twenty-two-year-old farmer from Merlin, Ontario. As his citation reads:

> This man showed exceptional bravery under intense machine gun and shell fire. Noticing his platoon being held up by a party of the enemy armed with automatic rifles, with utter disregard to danger rushed ahead, killing two of the enemy and capturing the rest. This man has at all times shown great courage under fire, and his conduct has been a fine example to the other men of his platoon.[40]

But the stark casualty numbers told a more poignant tale: 238 other ranks had been killed or wounded by an "enemy determined to hold his ground, or, at the worst, to sell it very dearly." Among them were at least two dozen reluctant warriors, including Private Arthur Barley, a twenty-two-year-old American-born farmhand from Claresholm, Alberta, who died after his "leg was shattered by enemy machine gun fire."[41]

Across the Canadian sector, it was clear that the corps was once again facing a resolute enemy, one whose ranks would soon include at least five fresh divisions.[42] For this reason Currie deployed two other divisions on 9 August – the 1st and the 3rd. In the 1st Division's 2nd Brigade, the 8th Battalion (90th Rifles) was hit especially hard, losing its CO, Major T.H. (Tom) Raddall, early in the attack. By late afternoon the next day, of its 435 casualties, 8 officers and 59 ORs had been killed in action, leaving the unit with about "one quarter of the strength it had when it first took the field in 1915." One of the wounded was Private John Gibson, a Scottish-born streetcar conductor and conscript from Winnipeg, who was shot in the head and died of his wounds eight days later. Among the dead were five other draftees, including Private George Christy, a twenty-two-year-old clerk with the Eaton's department store in Winnipeg. Christy had been with the battalion in the field since mid-May.[43]

Farther south still, Brigadier-General W.A. Griesbach's 1st Brigade did not begin its attack until 1:15 p.m. But it too was met by "intense" machine-gun and artillery fire.[44] Leapfrogging ahead at the village of Rouvroy-en-Santerre, the

Figure 4.2   Private William
T. Mott, 31st Battalion, was
awarded the Military Medal
for "exceptional bravery" at
Rosières, 9 August 1918.
Source: Chatham-Kent
Museum.

4th Battalion (Central Ontario) quickly found itself "enfiladed" and facing "Field
Guns ... firing Point Blank." Private Thomas McMinn, a barber from Toronto
who had joined this unit the previous May, was one of the first to fall. Fatally
"struck on the head by a splinter from an enemy shell," he was one of 139 OR
casualties this day.[45] Clearly the German army had regrouped at Amiens. Once
again progress would be measured in hundreds of yards or metres, while the
demand for reinforcements would dramatically increase.

"We left numerically stronger than when we came in"

The quandary now faced by Currie for this third consecutive day of the offensive
was both daunting and multidimensional; his troops were nearly exhausted,
the enemy was rapidly being reinforced, the number of tanks available had been
drastically reduced, and the terrain to be confronted next presented a much
greater tactical challenge. In addition, the Germans had deployed a "machine
gun defence in exceptional depth."[46] For Currie, perhaps the only reassuring
news was an adequate and timely flow of reinforcements. Even so, the sixty-five

hundred casualties sustained over the previous two days included a galaxy of all-important NCOs and junior officers, whose leadership skills were, at least in the short term, simply irreplaceable.

Undeterred, Currie dutifully launched a much less ambitious two-division-plus offensive starting at 4:20 a.m. on 10 August. It began in the south with a one-brigade assault by the 3rd Division on the village of Le Quesnoy. There the 8th Brigade attacked with two battalions: the 2nd CMR (British Columbia Horse) in the lead, with the 1st CMR (Saskatchewan) in support. Again, there were heavy casualties.[47] Forty-five men from the 2nd CMRs were killed in this one attack, among them Private Frederick Wood, a British-born draftee and "assistant buyer" with the Swift Canadian Company. By the time they were relieved the next day, the 2nd CMRs' total losses numbered 213 ORs alone.[48] Withdrawn from the line, it did not fight again at Amiens. Nevertheless, the CO, Lieutenant-Colonel G.C. Johnston, later observed that thanks to a very robust reinforcement pool, "we left numerically stronger than when we came in." Unrecorded here, though, was one other significant fact: about 30 percent of his new men were conscripts.[49]

The 3rd Division subsequently handed over its responsibilities to the 32nd British Division, while on the northern half of the Canadian front, Watson's 4th Division replaced the 1st and 2nd Canadian Divisions. Thus, around mid-morning of 10 August, Currie had just one Canadian and one British division available to recommence the offensive. Leading with two brigades (the 10th and 12th), Watson's troops jumped off at 10:15 a.m. In the centre of the attack, the 72nd Battalion quickly overcame "strong opposition" at Maucourt before pushing on to the village of Chilly, where the Kilties "encountered what was then an entirely novel means of resistance – the point-blank fire of field guns" from "a range of only 500 yards." Still they routed the defenders in exchange for only light casualties, then dug in for the inevitable counterattack. Among the many Seaforths who fell that morning was Private John McPhail, a thirty-year-old smelterman and conscript from Trail, BC. Struck "in the face by an enemy machine gun bullet," he quickly succumbed to his wounds.[50]

The rest of the attacking battalions would be less fortunate. Severe enfilade fire forced the 50th (Calgary) to wait nearly all day to leapfrog its sister battalion the 46th (Saskatchewan Regiment), thereby delaying the start of its main assault until 7:40 p.m. Nonetheless, plunging forward across 1,500 metres of well-defended terrain to the railway line in front of the village of Hallu, it managed to reach its final objective in just one hour. It was a historic moment: the 50th, together with the 78th Battalion (Winnipeg Grenadiers) and supported by two companies of the 38th Battalion (Eastern Ontario), had made the deepest penetration of German lines for the entire Canadian offensive at Amiens. But, short of water and ammunition, the Albertans were forced to dig in and defend against a second enemy counterattack. One of this unit's many casualties later that evening was Private David Paterson, a farmer and draftee from Nanton, Alberta, who was "wounded in the abdomen by an enemy bullet." Evacuated to No. 48 Casualty Clearing Station (CCS) over 50 kilometres to the rear, Paterson succumbed to his wounds some four days later, no doubt having endured what must have been a very painful death.[51]

The next morning, 11 August, the Germans launched another major counterattack, starting with a heavy bombardment at 10:00 a.m. Struck down in this barrage and subsequent assault was Private Gordon Beall, a draftee and electrician, formerly with the Renfrew Power Company (on the Ottawa River). Beall, who "was last seen at his machine gun post in the village of Hallu," had one brother serving with the PPCLI and another (a conscript) en route overseas with the Canadian Engineers.[52] At about the same time, at an isolated outpost in the besieged village itself, Private Howard Slater (78th Battalion), a farmer and draftee from Neepawa, Manitoba, was manning a Lewis gun along with four comrades. Surprised by a party of ten Germans, he and two others were captured but then quickly abandoned in a shell-hole just 20 metres farther back in the village. Luckily for Slater and his mates, the Germans had no time to deal with prisoners, nor were they apparently inclined to ill-treat them. In fact, within a few hours, Slater and his group were able to safely make their way back to friendly lines. By then the Canadians had surrendered all ground gained the previous day and the 78th had suffered the loss of 174 ORs, while the 50th had 240 casualties among its other ranks.[53]

12–15 August: Facing the Uncut Wire at Amiens
By the end of the fourth day of sustained combat at Amiens, nearly ninety-one hundred Canadian soldiers had been killed or wounded, or were missing. What must have been particularly worrisome for Currie, though, was that significant casualties had occurred on 11 August (the last day of the "general offensive") in exchange for negligible tactical gain and despite his cancellation of a 4th Division attack. More ominous still was Foch's insistence that the offensive be renewed – a plan that Haig reluctantly endorsed, albeit in exchange for a crucial operational respite of four days.[54]

In the interim, the 2nd and 3rd Divisions re-entered the line to replace the 4th and the 32nd British Divisions before being committed to several local actions, each of which proved to be costly in its own right. At the same time, Currie began to develop a detailed argument for suspending the army's planned offensive altogether, one that included other challenging options for his own formation. But before the Canadian Corps could fight effectively again, it needed to reconstitute. Fortunately for Currie there were still sufficient trained personnel in the manpower pipeline to help make that happen. In fact, during the first week of Amiens (up to 15 August), the CCRC had sent forward no fewer than 9,045 reinforcements – mostly new men – plus about 2,000 "casuals" (soldiers returning from leave, course, or hospital stay), signalling once again a robust regenerative capacity that was then unknown either to the British or to the Australians, and one that was clearly sourced primarily by conscripts.[55] For example, the 7th Battalion received forty reinforcements on 8 August, twenty-seven of whom were conscripts; within a week it received 120 more, including fifty-three additional conscripts. Just eight days later, the 72nd recorded 93 ORs taken on strength, of whom 63 were conscripts; significantly, of this latter number, 52 would become casualties by the end of the war, including 14 who were killed in action or died of their wounds.[56]

As his corps reconstituted, Currie forwarded a concise appreciation to General Rawlinson on 13 August, one that spelled out six reasons why the attack scheduled for the 15th should not go forward, or at least should be delayed sufficiently to deceive the Germans as to the Allies' true intentions. One of Currie's key arguments, however, would come back to haunt him. "Four years of experience has taught us," he declared, "that troops attempting to cross uncut wire suffer casualties out of all proportion to any gains they make."[57] With the deadly wire at Amiens still intact, Currie was loathe to attack again, and for good reason – at least for now.

A Deadly Lull in the Fighting

The Oxford Dictionary defines "lull" as a "temporary quiet period in a storm or in any activity." Comparatively speaking, there *was* a lull of sorts at Amiens, but it would be misleading to suggest that the period that followed the first four days of that battle was at all quiet, or that hostilities had ground to a halt.[58] For some battalions, like the 42nd (Black Watch) and the PPCLI, this would be among their most intense periods of combat in the entire war. Indeed, while the British official history assessed that "during the eight days which followed 11 August, no important action took place on the front of the British Army," it is not likely that the ordinary foot soldiers in the 2nd and 3rd Canadian Divisions would have agreed.[59] In this context a closer look at this later action is revealing in a number of key respects.

First, as historian Shane Schreiber notes, the Allied offensive at Amiens had come hard up against the "deadly law of diminishing returns," when "by the end of the third day of almost any operation, the attackers' increasing entropy has reached the same level as the defenders' incoming energy," thereby creating "a state of equilibrium [on] the battlefield."[60] In fact, that lethal level of tactical "stasis" had been reached at Amiens by the end of the second day, a harsh reality that would confront Currie again later and with even deadlier consequences both at Arras and at Cambrai. Still, the Canadian Corps had been tasked "to maintain a steady pressure on the enemy." Its subsequent operations included a costly 7th Brigade assault against the village of Parvillers on 12 August. In a pitched battle that ebbed back and forth over the course of three days and three nights, the 42nd Battalion sustained 143 OR casualties, including 30 dead and 10 more who later died of wounds.[61] In this same action, the 49th had to send all four companies forward as reinforcements, while a third battalion, the PPCLI, launched an assault from the south of Parvillers. On the evening of 13 August, the 49th engaged in "very severe fighting" that saw Private Cecil Kirkpatrick, a teamster and draftee from Livingstone, Alberta, "instantly killed by a shell that exploded near him" – one of thirty-two men from the Edmonton Regiment to make the ultimate sacrifice at Amiens.[62]

Elsewhere the going was equally tough. South of Parvillers at the village of Damery, the 52nd Battalion (New Ontario) had tried its own hand at a raid, a costly and "unsuccessful" two-company effort on 14 August that resulted in heavy casualties – "9 Other Ranks killed, 21 wounded [and] 22 [ORs] gassed," including Private Horace Mallinson, a milk sampler and draftee from Winnipeg, who fell to German machine-gun fire in this assault. Undeterred, the 52nd renewed its attack the next day, this time led by its commanding officer, the redoubtable Lieutenant-Colonel W.W. Foster. In just a few hours Foster's men cleared the entire village and pushed well beyond Damery before finding their left flank fully exposed and themselves the object of a German counter-attack. In this latter action, twenty-one-year-old Private William Sibbald from Stonewall, Manitoba, was killed by rifle shot as he manned a trench east of Damery. Sibbald had been drafted on 5 January, the same day as his friend and fellow farmer Private Roy Hand. Sadly, Private Hand had been wounded by shelling at the very start of operations in Damery and succumbed to his own injuries four days later. Thus, for one small, hard-hit, farming community 35 kilometres north of Winnipeg, two more reluctant warriors had paid the ultimate price.[63]

"A soldier of the King now"

Still more dramatic events began at 11:00 a.m. on 16 August, when the "B.G.G.S. Canadian Corps advised [1st and 2nd Division] that the French think [that the] enemy has gone" and were planning a noon attack "to push beyond Roye" another 3 kilometres to the east. Currie was compelled to cooperate in this attack, and directed his lead divisions to advance in support of the French. Apparently he did so with some reluctance, as he still firmly wished to extricate the corps from this sector of the front.[64]

First into the fight was the 9th Brigade (temporarily "under instructions from the 1st Division"), which immediately tasked the 43rd Battalion (Cameron Highlanders) along with the 58th (Central Ontario) "to push forward and keep up with the French advance" on Goyencourt, just north of Roye. Their noon attack was met by a deadly German counter-barrage coupled with heavy machine-gun fire, and the 43rd sustained "a large number of casualties," including their CO, Lieutenant-Colonel Hugh Urquhart. For its part the 58th had found it "impossible for any troops to move in the open," and thus the 43rd had essentially been left on its own. "Too weak" to advance any farther, by the time their welcome relief began at 4:30 a.m. the following morning, the Camerons counted 14 confirmed dead, 109 wounded, and 36 missing among their 159 total OR casualties.[65]

The 43rd Battalion's losses included seven conscripts, two of whom were evacuated from the battlefield only to die of their wounds shortly thereafter; they were Privates Homer Cronk and William Bawdon, both aged twenty-one. In addition, Private James Reid, a farmer from Reston, Manitoba, fell in this action. Reid, whose sacrifice is honoured today at the Vimy Memorial, left Canadians one other poignant reminder of his fateful journey as a citizen-soldier. On 14 January, still at the depot in Brandon and a mere nine days after being drafted, he had scribbled on a postcard to a friend, Olive Nairn, perhaps with some measure of solemnity and trepidation, "I am a soldier of the King now."[66]

As for the 2nd Division, it had responded to news of the French advance by tasking its 4th Brigade to push "forward strong patrols" starting at 2:00 p.m., the principle objective being to secure the village of Fransart. It seems, though, that the 4th Brigade made a somewhat liberal interpretation of its guidance regarding "strong patrols," and chose instead to launch a much more ambitious and vigorous assault, using all of the 19th Battalion supported by two companies each from the 18th and 20th. Subsequently, in an attack marred by a dangerous misunderstanding about zero hour, the attackers immediately ran into "considerable opposition," yet still managed to invest the whole of the village, albeit at a dear price. Among the 4th Brigade's casualties were eight men dead and sixty-one wounded or missing. The 19th Battalion's Private William Taylor, a miner and draftee from Timmins, Ontario, was one of those whose body was not recovered. And Private Carmelo Grech, a carpenter from Toronto but originally from Malta, was "hit through the head by a bullet from an enemy's sniper rifle ... the bullet passing through his eye and out at the back of his head." Immediately evacuated to No. 48 CCS, Private Grech succumbed to his horrible wounds eleven days later.[67]

"He died for justice and freedom"

At 5:00 a.m. on 17 August the French (47th Infantry Division) renewed their advance at Goyencourt, supported in part by the 1st and 2nd Brigades (CFA) and the 7th Battalion. The BCR's cooperative attack failed to make any material progress, however, and earlier orders "to keep in touch" with the French were later cancelled. In short, the Canadians were done. "Under orders from Corps," even a personal request from the French division commander, for the Canadians to once again attempt to "take Fresnoy-les-Roye," was refused. As for the 7th Battalion, by late that evening it had suffered another nine ORs killed and twenty-nine wounded.[68] Among them were several draftees, including Private William Knowles. Knowles, who had joined this unit just three days earlier, was severely wounded by enemy shelling and died "on the way to the dressing station."[69]

Over the next few days, many of the last Canadian soldiers to fall at Amiens would be struck down by shelling, sniper fire, or enemy air attacks. Not all were infantry: two gunners from the 2nd Trench Mortar Battery – John Mills and Alexander Noble – along with five comrades, were killed in a brief but deadly barrage that suddenly rained down on their position southeast of Le Quesnel. Mills, from Saint John, New Brunswick, was an early conscript, having attested in late November 1917. Noble, a twenty-one-year-old cannery man from Port Essington, BC, had also enlisted more than two weeks before the first MSA troops were officially called.[70] Clearly, the so-called rear echelons were not immune from attack. Two days later another deadly blast southeast of Caix killed an astonishing twelve men "outright" and wounded twenty-two others. Among the dead was Sapper John Knox, a twenty-two-year-old construction engineer with the 1st Tramways Company. A bridge builder from Portage la Prairie, Manitoba, Knox too had fatefully signed up the previous November.[71]

Closer to the front, enemy shelling continued to take its toll. On 18 August, a relatively quiet Sunday morning, Private James Fox (7th Battalion) died of shrapnel wounds to the abdomen during a German counterattack east of Damery, while his fellow conscript Private James Hooppell (14th Battalion) fell victim to shelling on the outskirts of La Chavette. The next day, while marking time "in the vicinity of Hattencourt," Private Jesse Barmby (50th Battalion), a British-born labourer and draftee from Calgary, was killed by shellfire. Then on

22 August, just one day prior to its relief, the 85th suffered its last two casualties of the Amiens campaign. One of them was Private Evan Pugh, a baker and conscript from Sydney, Nova Scotia. "Hit in the back and legs by shrapnel" near Chilly that morning, he died "before he could be evacuated."[72]

Two days later the Canadian Corps received yet another forceful reminder of how deadly this sector remained. On the evening of 24 August, the 78th Battalion found itself marching west under a full moon towards a troop train in Longueau, a risky journey given the large increase in enemy air activity over the previous week.[73] No one was more aware of the peril than the soldiers themselves: "Not one of the marching troops appreciated the moonlight ... its brilliance silhouetted them fatally against the white ribbon of dust over which they passed ... Straight over the road came the planes. Up and down at irregular intervals came the swishing whistle of the heavy bombs, culminating in fountains of flame-crowned smoke and noise."[74]

In the grim aftermath, the 78th counted more dead that night than any other single day's fatalities at Amiens – twenty-three ORs, plus forty-five men wounded. Among the former was Private Stuart Grigg, a twenty-one-year-old draftee and express messenger with the Canadian Pacific Railway (CPR) in Winnipeg, who was interred at Hillside Cemetery near Caix and Le Quesnel. Years later, Grigg's permanent memorial headstone would be inscribed with this simple and enduring message: "He died for Justice and freedom."[75]

Amiens – L'envoi

In his "Interim Report" on Canadian operations in 1918, General Currie observed that "the [10,783 OR] casualties suffered by the Canadian Corps in the 14 days' heavy fighting [at Amiens] ... were very light," considering "the number of German Divisions engaged, and the results achieved."[76] Such a sanguine assessment was not likely shared by his soldiers. Moreover, it is tempting to ask how Currie could possibly have pressed on, or engaged in large-scale raids after the so-called "lull" in the battle began, were it not for an immediate and continuous flow of reinforcements. Nevertheless, the Canadian Corps did press on, in the process sustaining no fewer than 2,748 additional casualties – more men than it had lost on 9 August, and all for what one correspondent later described as "tactical adventures."[77] In fact, measured against the total number of Canadian soldiers actually engaged (elements of five brigades and ten battalions at various times), this was one of the costliest weeks of the war. And ironically, those casualties were a consequence of costly attritional warfare of the type that Currie was attempting to avoid as he struggled to pull the corps back from Amiens.[78] Amiens had also claimed thousands of highly experienced junior NCOs and nearly six hundred officers – mostly platoon leaders and company commanders – men whose tactical acumen and battlefield savvy would be sorely missed in the crucial days to come. Now, blessed by a massive and continuous infusion of manpower – mainly infantry – Currie redeployed the Canadian Corps for an entirely new major offensive some 50 kilometres to the north, for what many later described as the corps' most brutal fighting yet.

"Draft Men" and the Battle of the Scarpe, 1918

"Act with the utmost boldness and resolution"

IN THE WAKE OF the Allied triumph at Amiens, General Currie left that sector of the front on 22 August, departing almost in haste and likely relieved to escape what he feared would be a military disaster. Any further "attempt to force ... this uncut wire would be altogether too costly an operation," he had mused a week earlier; he would not "have a good operation spoiled by overzealousness."[1] In the event, upon arriving at his headquarters in Hautecloque that evening, Currie received orders from General Henry Horne (First Army) directing him to prepare for offensive operations east of Arras "on or after the 25th instant."[2] Included with these instructions was a letter from Haig urging his army commanders to impress on "all subordinate commanders" the need "to act with the utmost boldness and resolution," and adding that "risks which a month ago would have been criminal to incur, ought now to be incurred as a duty."[3] Currie was inclined to take such risks. As will be shown, however, in doing so the Canadian Corps would suffer its first major setbacks – a historical fact often overlooked in standard accounts.[4]

Setting aside the daunting nature of the task at hand, Currie was well aware that "all Units were not up to strength" – particularly his infantry battalions, some of which had replaced more than half their trench strength since the start of Amiens. Furthermore, the initial assault at Arras would be a night attack, a bold and difficult manoeuvre for his veteran soldiers, and an even riskier one for thousands of less experienced troops. Finally, Currie would have just two Canadian divisions and one British (the 51st Highland) to deploy in what would be "the hardest battle in [the corps'] history."[5]

Despite some continuing manpower shortages, the foremost change to Currie's new battlefield calculus was that the strength of the corps had in fact been largely restored at Amiens, even while operations were still under way. But numbers alone did not make an army. As Bill Rawling suggests, apart from a good rest, what Currie's exhausted troops really needed was adequate time to absorb basic "lessons learned" from the corps' first experience in open warfare. But there would be no such interregnum: in the words of the official historian, "unprecedented demands [would] be made on the stamina of the forces employed."[6]

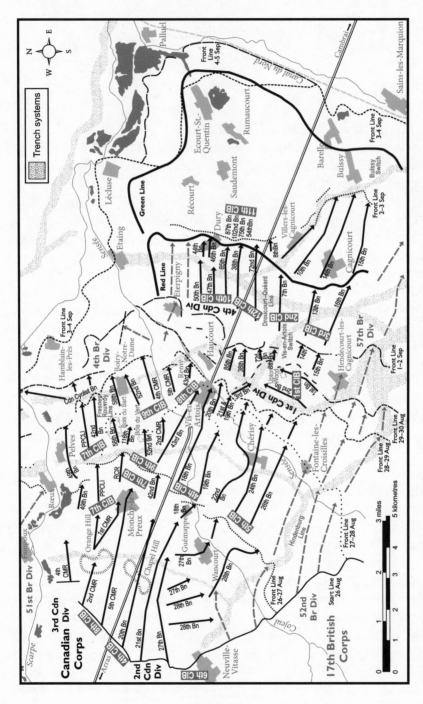

Map 3 Arras and the D-Q Line, 26 August–5 September, 1918. Map by Mike Bechthold.

"Not a word of criticism was uttered regarding the draft men"

Back at Amiens, the corps staff scrambled to move the 2nd and 3rd Divisions north in time to take the handover from British XVII Corps on 23 August. It was a rushed and fatiguing affair for all concerned. Typical of many units, the men of the 20th Battalion enjoyed just one full day's respite prior to re-entering the line at Arras.[7] Nevertheless, as war correspondent Roland Hill later recalled, all the "men and officers alike were proud, keen and on their mettle," while,

> the reinforcements were of the finest ... [and] had been through the severe train-
> ing necessary to open fighting ... Not a word of criticism was uttered regarding
> the draft men, who were in large numbers; they, too, had proved their breed and
> skill in active training. Most of them had seen service in the line at Arras before
> the trek south in August.[8]

Hill was perhaps idealizing what he had seen; there are conflicting reports about how conscripts were treated. For example, one young volunteer in the 46th Battalion remarked that the draftees "were good men, but the poor devils ... didn't have a chance." Veterans "picked on them and ... thought that they should have been in there earlier," adding that it was "too bad we took that attitude to the conscripts."[9] No doubt Lieutenant Don Goudy (OC "C" Company, 21st Battalion) would have emphatically agreed. Twenty years after the war, he wrote that he too experienced the same "unreasonable prejudice" that all new men were confronted with on arrival at the front. But while conscripts "were not given full credit due them by the volunteers," he observed, they did everything that volunteers did. "Once in it they began to get the spirit of the thing. If they didn't enjoy it they at least didn't shirk their duties ... I never had occasion to consider a draftee a 'coward.' After all, there were very few cowards among the Canadians, draftees or volunteers."[10]

One young draftee then preparing for his second major battle was Private Hilaire Dennis of the 18th Battalion. After four months' training in England and France, Hilaire had arrived at the CCRC in Aubin-Saint-Vaast on 17 June, along with 1,000 other fresh troops. Eight weeks later he joined his unit in the field at Amiens in time to experience the full panoply of combat, including a savage two-battalion assault on the village of Fransart. Less than two weeks later, having endured a whirlwind journey north, Dennis and his fellow draftees found themselves in Pierremont, 35 kilometres west of Arras. There, on 23 August, he scribbled the following poignant words to close family in Canada:

> I am on rest for a few days and certainly need a little rest ... I have been through
> something most awful in the last few days ... the experience tells on my face quite

a lot, and I know that it is through the good prayers of everyone at home that I have been so well protected from the awful claws of this machine of destruction.[11]

Writing hastily on sheets of paper ripped from a pocket diary, Dennis fretted over his inability to get some legal papers notarized in the field, before finally declaring to his uncle: "If anything should happen to me, well everything I own is yours." Clearly he was preparing for the worst, but lest he leave folks back home on a sour note, he offered his simple gratitude for a welcome care package, along with a short but striking declaration: "I was very glad of all the things you sent because tobacco like we get in Canada we can not get it here, and uncle when we go up to the front Line with a good shot of rum and a mouthful of good Canadian tobacco, I figure myself to be a real soldier and feel no fear."[12]

"Do you think it can be done?"

The original plan for the Canadian attack south of the Scarpe River was an integral part of Haig's grander scheme to employ two of his armies (the First and the Third) in a massive assault against the vaunted Hindenburg Line (known by the Germans as the *Siegfriedstellung*). His plan was a fluid one, though, and from the moment that Currie briefed it to his division commanders, it began to change, literally by the hour. Moreover, Currie was still wrestling with other significant challenges that threatened to jeopardize his entire operation. Similar to the action at Amiens, for the most part fit but poorly rested Canadian troops would be required to attack almost immediately after their arrival in front of Arras. More remarkable still, Currie intended to accomplish this perilous frontal assault at night, largely without the benefit of surprise, and with just half his infantry corps (supported by insufficient artillery). Given these great risks, Field Marshal Haig visited corps headquarters on the afternoon of 24 August in the company of General Horne and posed a simple, straightforward question to Currie: "Do you think it can be done?" In fact, Haig called again on the next three successive days, each time seeking (and receiving) unequivocal confirmation that the Canadians would achieve the near impossible.[13]

Haig *was* pressing for the impossible. The replenished albeit much fatigued Canadian Corps was being called upon to advance nearly 10 deadly kilometres against what were perhaps the German army's most formidable defences. But the fundamental flaw in the planning for this attack was the simple fact that the entire offensive was far too rushed.[14] Late on 25 August, Currie attempted to inject some element of surprise into the tactical equation by rolling zero hour forward from 4:50 to 3:00 a.m. He was counting (a lost hope, as it turned out) on bright moonlight (which there had been on the previous two nights) to help the soldiers navigate their way forward.[15] But the corps commander's last-minute decision deprived the troops of two hours of much needed rest; it also appears to have ramped up everyone's stress levels. The 8th Brigade recorded that Currie's decision "created a dangerous situation owing to the difficulties of communication after dark in strange country" and expressed considerable doubt as to whether the revised zero hour could be relayed down the line in time.[16]

On the eve of the great battle, Currie issued another "Special Order," essentially a two-page summary of all the congratulatory messages received at corps headquarters to date since the stunning triumph by the Canadians on the first day of Amiens. Notably, buried in the text of one congratulatory message was an important signal for Currie from the militia minister, Major-General Mewburn, reaffirming that "a steady flow of reinforcements from Canada will support you in your efforts."[17] Thereafter Currie would indeed command the Canadian Corps with "boldness and resolution"; and, on occasion, he would take those very "risks which a month ago," in the words of Field Marshal Haig, "would have been criminal to incur."

"Cheer up boys, *nous prenons notre objectif ou nous mourrons*"

Just moments before the battle, a shot of rum and these sobering words from his company commander were enough to steel Private Armand Thérien, a conscript from Montreal, for his first fight.[18] Then, at precisely 3:00 a.m. on Monday, 26 August, a great artillery barrage exploded across the Artois hills. Awed by the spectacle, Private Dennis was moved to write,

> the heavy guns were roaring something awful and the sky was red with fire ...
> There was fire splashing through the sky and fire rolling on the mountain in
> front of us [Orange Hill] ... When we reached the other mountain [Chapel Hill]
> I certainly did see some sight in the dark. We had to walk through dead bodys
> [*sic*] all over. And then I was wild. I was right after blood.[19]

The German defenders were definitely surprised by the very early hour of this assault – so much so that Canadian troops managed to make it into Monchy-le-Preux "before breakfast."[20] Thereafter, progress was much more difficult. Moreover, it appears that Currie was slow to recognize that the Germans' tactical withdrawal was not a headlong retreat and, more importantly, that his two lead divisions were operating at very nearly the limits of their endurance.

Even so, the corps' early morning triumphs were significant. In particular, the 2nd CMRs crested the fortified heights of Orange Hill shortly after 5 a.m., suffering just seven dead in their successful attack, including a twenty-one-year-old law student and draftee from Bracebridge, Ontario. Having arrived in France only two weeks earlier, Private William Johnson was struck down by a bullet in the head. Years later his grieving father, Crown attorney Thomas Johnson, would add the following poignant words to this young conscript's memorial headstone: "Faithful Unto Death."[21]

In similar action to the south, the 21st Battalion had begun its attack with a trench strength of 593 men. Rolling nearly unbroken in its advance, this unit quickly captured its "second and final objective" within an hour after zero. Among its twelve OR fatalities were four draftees, including Private Archie McDonald, a bridge builder from Killaloe Station, Ontario – killed a mere five days after marking his twenty-second birthday.[22] The corps had advanced nearly 6 kilometres, captured large numbers of enemy prisoners, and taken the great prize of Monchy itself. Yet, as historian Shane Schreiber has perceptively noted, the harsh realities of the Germans' elastic defence had come sharply into play. By "10:00 a.m., confusion caused by the quick success" had begun "to slow the Canadian advance, and strong German counterattacks later in the day" decisively "checked the Canadians' progress."[23] By late afternoon the 4th Brigade had been stopped cold at Guémappe, and the 6th Brigade at Wancourt Ridge, and to the north of the Arras-Cambrai road, the 7th Brigade had been forced "onto the defensive." Indeed, in Ludendorff's view, his troops had fallen "back according to plan," and "the early stages of the fighting" had developed "favourably" for the German army.[24]

Despite heavy losses, Burstall initially agreed with Major-General Louis Lipsett (GOC, 3rd Division) to set zero hour for 4:55 a.m. the next day. Such an early start posed major challenges, not only for his beleaguered 4th and 6th Brigades but for his fresh 5th Brigade as well.[25] Thus he compromised and moved the 2nd Division attack back until 10 a.m., even though it seems clear that he ought to have demanded a much longer delay. In this context, the question remains: Why, in the face of so many uncertainties, coupled with high casualties and seriously fatigued troops, did Burstall not insist on holding Currie to his original plan for a twenty-four-hour operational pause?[26] As for Currie, he would end the day by issuing another "Special Order," this time demonstrating an almost theatrical flourish in a decidedly hollow attempt to further inspire the troops: "I desire to congratulate all concerned on the magnificent success achieved this day. It has paved the way for greater success tomorrow. Keep constantly in mind Stonewall Jackson's motto 'Press Forward.'"[27]

"He died for freedom and honour"

As preparations to renew the Arras offensive continued, the weary Canadians found themselves "beyond the range of [most] counter-battery groups" and suffered accordingly at the hands of German artillery. Planning for day two called for a very ambitious attack, the first objective being the enemy defences along the Sensée River (nearly 4 kilometres to the east), followed by the "high ground" another kilometre beyond the river – the Fresnes-Rouvroy Line. The improbable "final objective" would be the distant villages of Étaing, Dury, and Cagnicourt, just past the more formidable Drocourt-Quéant (*Wotan-Stellung*) line, 4 kilometres farther to the east.[28] Thus the depth of this planned penetration was Amiens-like in scope, without the same impressive array of supporting artillery and machine-gun fire, or the powerful punching weight of what had been five fresh divisions. Given the magnitude of the physical defences to be overcome, and the growing strength of the opposing forces, the once-planned twenty-four-hour delay seems to have been fully justified, yet Currie chose to "Press Forward." His only concession to the troops was to alert the 2nd and 3rd Divisions that they would be relieved a day earlier than planned, on the night of 27–28 August.[29] Even this was not to be.

The second day of this Battle of the Scarpe began like the first, with a "heavy rain" that hampered assembly, movement, and navigation alike. Striking at 4:55 a.m., the 52nd Battalion (9th Brigade) successfully invested the Bois du Vert by 7:00 a.m. despite significant casualties. Among the first of Lieutenant-Colonel Don Sutherland's weary troops to fall was Private Reginald Edwards, a twenty-five-year-old Winnipeg barber and draftee from Boston, Massachusetts, who was fatally wounded even before exiting the "jumping off trench."[30] Likewise, just to the north, the 58th (Central Ontario) Battalion attacked the Bois du Sart, claiming the wood as their own by 7:30 a.m.[31] But with one exception, all other advances were sharply checked as enemy reinforcements poured into the area and German defences stiffened further still.

That exception was a cooperative attack along the Arras-Cambrai road against the fortified village of Vis-en-Artois. This was made by fresh troops of the 43rd Battalion (9th Brigade) on the north side of the highway, and by the 18th Battalion (4th Brigade) on the south. There, just as the Cameron Highlanders began their attack at 10 a.m., Private Archie Blanchard, a twenty-one-year-old farmer from Nipigon, Ontario, fell victim to heavy enemy shelling with a serious head wound. Even though his injuries were "immediately dressed," Blanchard's comrades were forced to leave him behind. Shock and blood loss took its toll, and he died the following day at No. 7 [British] CCS at Ligny-St.-Flochel. "Men were falling fast" recalled one eyewitness. But curiously, while "considerable fighting was encountered," the battalion diarist later recorded that enemy resistance was not as stubborn as had been expected.[32]

South of the Arras-Cambrai road, the attacking battalions also met with early success. By noon, the 18th and 19th Battalions had fought their way to the irregular near bank of the Sensée River (a narrow but forbidding stream), "taking many prisoners and causing the enemy severe casualties."[33] Of this infernal scene, Private Dennis recalled: "We took a big bunch of prisoners one morning ... They were coming to us with their hands up by the hundreds and some of them were crying like babys [*sic*], and I'll tell you they should rather see old man Satan himself than see a bunch of Canadians facing them with cold steel."[34]

These young soldiers could be forgiven their optimism; it would be very short-lived. Unbeknownst to Burstall, let alone the 4th and 5th Brigades, the Canadian Corps had just collided with the heart of the German defence – the killing grounds of the Sensée River valley. The 4th Brigade war diary describes best what happened next: "Here strong resistance was met with, the enemy Machine Gun fire being intense. The artillery barrage failed and eventually subsided altogether. Any attempt to advance against the enemy's strongly organized system of trenches – Olive Trench [and] Ocean Works ... caused severe casualties."[35]

No doubt Brigadier-General Robert Rennie (GOC, 4th Brigade) would have preferred to establish his battalion outpost lines on the far side of the river. But this proved impossible. Thus, the more exposed west bank of the river became the temporary home of the 18th Battalion. Soon enemy shellfire claimed many lives, including that of Private Fred Readhead, a twenty-two-year-old bank messenger and conscript from Woodstock, Ontario, who was slightly wounded near Vis-en-Artois, then killed instantly by an enemy shell as he tried to make his way to the rear. By the end of the day, with 19 dead and 150 others wounded, the effective trench strength of the 18th had been reduced to a critical level.[36]

To the immediate right, casualties were very heavy for the 19th Battalion as well. Around 2:00 p.m., Private Lorne Cox, a tall (6'1½" – 187 cm) twenty-one-year-old salesman and draftee from Colborne, Ontario, was "killed by a machine gun bullet through the heart" near the village of Chérisy. Originally reported missing, Cox was later mourned as a "gallant soldier who has given his life for the cause of liberty."[37] As for the 21st Battalion, which had started the day in "reserve," it too suffered very heavy losses – 119 all told, including 14 ORs killed, mainly by artillery and machine-gun fire. Among these fatalities were nine conscripts, a very diverse mix of young Canadian men including a rubber worker, a cheesemaker, a sawmill hand, a blacksmith, and four farmers. All but one had been taken on strength in France at the Canadian Infantry Base Depot (CIBD) on 9 August, including Private Wilford Barr, a young farmer from Clayton, Ontario, who was still mourning the loss a week earlier of his older brother David (also a conscript).[38]

Farther south still, the 5th Brigade, led for the past two weeks by the redoubtable Brigadier-General T.L. Tremblay, had launched its own attack at 10:00 a.m.

By noon these troops had met with early success, having crossed the river bed (largely dry at these points), and having captured an "enormous number of prisoners" in exchange for only "light" casualties. At 2:00 p.m., however, Lieutenant-Colonel Clark-Kennedy, CO of the 24th Battalion, arrived at brigade HQ to personally report that both the 22nd and 24th were "held up 500 yards East of [the] Sensée River," in part because the Canadian attackers had moved beyond the protection of friendly artillery. Casualties had quickly mounted, and successive attempts to advance farther had been quickly checked.[39]

The 22nd (Van Doos) would survive this day, although just barely. Its acting CO, Major A.E. Dubuc, had been severely wounded, two other officers were dead, and another dozen were wounded. Worse, the battalion had suffered the devastating loss of at least 21 ORs killed, 193 wounded, and 11 missing. Seven of the dead were conscripts, all of whom had been killed by machine-gun fire in the advance from Wancourt to Chérisy. They included one of Canada's older conscripts, Private Jean-Baptiste Degagné, a labourer aged thirty-five from Mistissine, Quebec.[40] Meanwhile, the 24th had been equally savaged, having lost one officer killed and 9 more wounded; 19 ORs were fatalities, another 190 were wounded, and 33 more were missing. Among the dead were 7 draftees, including Private Joseph Brochu, a carter from the tiny South Shore village of Saint-Gervais. Back in Quebec, Brochu's grieving parents Alexandre and Marie would one day receive a small memorial plaque (sometimes referred to as the "dead man's penny") with the name of their son inscribed thereon, along with the immortal words "He died for freedom and honour." [41]

Doubtless by this point in the battle, Currie was impressed by the tenacity of the German defenders, and likely alarmed as well by reports of heavy casualties in exchange for little progress. At 5:45 p.m. he called General Burstall to advise him that contrary to earlier direction, further advance "was to be limited." Having failed to capture the Fresnes-Rouvroy Line, the corps commander was compelled to scale back his objectives; now he would seek only to make "good the crossings over the Sensée River." Here it appears that Currie made another fundamental change in his battle strategy. At 8:35 p.m. the 2nd and 3rd Divisions received orders for "the attack to be continued" the next day – a decision that likely astonished Burstall if not Lipsett as well.[42] Apart from the fact that both commanders had fully expected to be relieved that night, they had nearly exhausted their forces in attempting to seize the corps' first objective. Now they were expected to renew the advance after a pause of just twelve hours. In the event, elements of five German divisions would deliver a crippling blow to the 2nd Division and the first major setback to the Canadian Corps in the Hundred Days. It would not be its last.

Fateful Decision: A Rare Mistake by Currie

In the corps' "Interim Report," Currie states that while his intention was "to continue the battle on the 28th with the 1st Canadian Division on the right and the 4th (British) Division ... on the left," the fact that the latter "was unable to reach the battle position in time" forced him to change his plans. He cancelled his original orders "and the battle was continued by the Divisions then in the line."[43] The implications would be enormous.

At least two less costly options had been available to Currie. First, he could have simply suspended the offensive altogether for twenty-four hours, just as he had wisely envisioned two days earlier. This would have allowed adequate time to replace both tired divisions and then continue the offensive on 29 August. This is probably what he should have done, instead of pressing tired and much reduced formations into a frontal attack against well-fortified defences, which violated his own battlefield doctrine. Second, he could have chosen to replace just the 2nd Division and attacked on 28 August with a much higher probability of success. Evidently the 3rd Division had not been as severely battered as the 2nd, and as subsequent events would prove, it was effectively a stronger formation.[44] To thrust the exhausted 2nd Division once more into the breach, though, risked a catastrophe – killing off even greater numbers of experienced leaders and thereby reducing the 2nd to a hollow shell, incapable perhaps of further attacks for weeks to come. Yet in what one Canadian historian described as a "rare mistake by Currie," he decided not to replace either division, and compounded the risk by not opting for a twenty-four-hour suspension.[45]

Why *did* Currie gamble in the face of such obviously unfavourable odds? Apart from top-down pressure from Haig, what most likely prompted him to act so boldly just two weeks after the corps had sustained nearly twelve thousand casualties at Amiens was a near-continuous flow of reinforcements. Currie had once been much more cautious in husbanding his precious manpower resources, but the high casualties at both Amiens and Arras suggest that personnel shortages were no longer an overriding factor in his command decision making. Indeed, the fateful decision taken on the night of 27 August to push forward thoroughly spent divisions against well-entrenched superior forces would be repeated by Currie some five weeks later at the Canal du Nord, this time with even more deadly results.

"The men were in extremely exhausted condition"

Lipsett chose to attack on 28 August with all three of his infantry brigades; Burstall elected to recommit just his 4th and 5th Brigades. The 7th and 9th Brigades stepped off at 11 a.m., ninety minutes before the troops of the 2nd Division, and "carried everything before them."[46] But one battalion in the 9th

Brigade, the 52nd, its "losses of the previous day [having] been heavier than at first anticipated," had been able to muster only "about 220 men" for this attack," about one-third of its earlier trench strength. Worse, the following report suggests that these soldiers were hardly in any condition to fight: "The men were in extremely exhausted condition ... they had been shelled very heavily all day, and secured very little or no rest, so that physically they were in very poor shape besides being very weak in numbers."[47]

By the time the 52nd was relieved at 3:00 a.m. the following morning, its four companies had been reduced to a mere one hundred souls. It had advanced nearly 3.5 kilometres, and had claimed its share of the Fresnes-Rouvroy Line, but the human cost for two days had again been very high – twenty-three ORs killed, ten of whom were conscripts. Among these was Private Thomas Fraser, a carpenter originally from Whycocomagh, Nova Scotia, but conscripted in Port Arthur, Ontario – killed by shellfire near Boiry. Then there was twenty-two-year-old Chicago-born Private William Frank from Oak Bluff, Manitoba; drafted on 27 November 1917, he had taken a machine-gun round "through the stomach."[48]

Farther south, the 8th Brigade (the 5th CMR along with the 43rd Battalion) was subjected to "intense [gas] shelling" in its initial advance and the "attacking companies ... suffered very heavy casualties" – about 125 wounded. Among the dead in the 5th CMR was Private Rosario Larivière, a twenty-three-year-old draftee and stone cutter from Philipsburg, Quebec, who was "instantly killed by enemy shell fire" and whose remains were never fully identified.[49] Meanwhile the 43rd Battalion operating north of Vis-en-Artois, its trench strength having been reduced to "40 and 50 per company" (as opposed to the normal 150), had fared even worse. It had seized all its primary objectives within an hour of zero, but its "losses had been over 50%," and this despite having taken on 316 reinforcements a mere two days earlier. Among the fallen was Private William Hamilton, originally from London, Ontario, but drafted the previous January in Brandon, Manitoba. He was killed by shellfire as he sheltered in the sunken road north of Vis-en-Artois.[50]

Still, by late afternoon all 3rd Division brigades could claim a certain measure of victory, even though the German army had effectively stopped their advance cold just a few hundred metres beyond the Fresnes-Rouvroy Line. Most of the fighting battalions then rode out occasional shelling for the rest of this day while anxiously awaiting their relief. But Currie's original plan for this controversial relief never fully materialized, since the 4th Canadian Division was still en route. Consequently, the 7th Brigade was relieved by a newly created "Canadian Composite Corps, consisting of Motor Machine Gun Batteries, Cyclists and Trench Mortars," whose harried troops, in the case of the 2nd Canadian Motor

Machine Gun Brigade (CMMG), had to carry their heavy kit on their backs for about "2½ miles" across unfamiliar terrain, under fire and at night.[51] In short, Currie was forced to replace exhausted infantry with equally fatigued and battle-weary machine-gun troops, who soon found themselves in their own desperate fight, one that would last nearly another twenty-four hours.

"It was just like a hail storm forced by a hundred mile an hour wind"

South of the Arras-Cambrai road, the ever confident General Burstall and his beleaguered 2nd Division had likewise made another attempt to pierce the Fresnes-Rouvroy Line. The results were decidedly different from those achieved by General Lipsett. Nearly a decade later, Lieutenant-General Sir Archibald "Batty Mac" Macdonell, GOC 1st Division, would recall having tea with Currie and Burstall that day, and that Burstall "was in a jubilant mood." In this context, it is evident that Burstall must share equal responsibility with Currie for the coming defeat. Just three days earlier, Field Marshal Haig had visited the 2nd Division headquarters, where Burstall apparently impressed the commander-in-chief with his resolve to succeed in the forthcoming operation. Now, despite having suffered grievous losses over the previous two days, Burstall appears to have been more determined than ever to make good his promise to Haig. It was not to be. Late that evening Macdonell's troops would be forced to relieve a much-troubled sector, one that was in complete disarray.[52]

Brigadier-General Rennie's badly depleted 4th Brigade, which had started off the previous day with a frontage of 4,200 yards, would now attack at 12:30 p.m. across a narrow front of just 700 yards. Burstall would later acknowledge that the 4th Brigade had been "very short of troops" at that moment – "practically a composite battalion ... their reserve consisting of Headquarters details, batmen, cooks, etc." The 5th Brigade was not much better off. Nonetheless, despite having employed a much larger and fresher force without success in a similar effort just a day earlier, Burstall still followed Currie's instruction to press forward and seize the Fresnes-Rouvroy Line, 1,000 metres distant. Knowing that his "troops were both mentally and physically exhausted," that "the wire opposing them was practically uncut," and that "the enemy's trenches were extremely strongly held," and given that his left flank remained exposed, Burstall should have demanded a one-day pause in operations. Inexplicably, he did not. At zero hour, Rennie ominously reported that his troops "were nearly all in."[53]

Leading off this assault on the far-left flank was the 20th Battalion, which by early evening had advanced "about a thousand yards," even though "nearly all the officers and section commanders were killed or wounded" in the process. When relieved the next morning, the 20th was down to 120 ORs, having lost nearly 80 percent of its trench strength over the previous three days. Among its hundreds of casualties was Private John Bratti, a diminutive (5'2¾" – 159.4 cm) Italian-born plumber and conscript from Toronto, who suffered a gunshot wound to the chest. Despite four broken ribs and a collapsed lung that demanded a week of surgical treatment, Bratti miraculously survived the war and lived to a very old age. Not so his comrade Private Walker Patterson, a barber who had been working in Toronto when he too was drafted. Just twenty-two years old, Patterson was "severely wounded" in a hail of machine-gun and artillery fire. His body was never fully recovered. He too is commemorated at Vimy.[54]

In its so-called reserve role, the 18th Battalion again suffered heavy casualties – 21 dead and nearly 70 wounded to add to the 169 casualties from the day before.[55] One of the wounded was a twenty-one-year-old druggist from St. Thomas, Ontario, by the name of Private Harold Penwarden, who was shot straight through the "left forearm." Only a day earlier, Harold had carried his severely wounded platoon commander (Lieutenant Henry Gerrard) off the battlefield. Now wounded himself and enfiladed by heavy machine-gun fire, he "had to wait in [a] shell hole from 2.30 p.m. ... til dark, about 8 o'clock" before being able to evacuate from the front line.[56] Similarly, Private Dennis described his own brush with death as follows:

> Fritz open up [*sic*] with his machine gun and it was just like a hail storm forced by a hundred mile an hour wind ... I was lucky that there was only one bullet that went through me because I was hit in different places through my clothes ... It was about one p.m. o'clock when I got hit and I drop[ped] in a big shell hole, and there I had to stay until nine p.m. before I could get out for help. I was certainly an awful sight after rolling myself in my own blood for all that time.[57]

Four other 18th Battalion draftees were not so fortunate. Private Lloyd Claus, a clerk from Chatham, Ontario, was "killed by an enemy shell," while Private Leslie Allison, a shoe salesman from St. Thomas, was felled "by enemy machine gun fire." Neither soldier had made it even close to his unit's first objective.[58]

At about the same time on the immediate right, the 21st Battalion was attempting to fight its way down past "the dry bed of the Sensée ... [where soon] the men began to drop in large numbers." Failure to make any substantial progress would not be the result of any lack of courage or effort on anyone's part. In particular, Lieutenant Don Goudy would recall that the battalion, "largely seeded by new drafts," performed remarkably well, despite serious fatigue and a significant shortage of riflemen. His one critical comment about the "draftees," soldiers he generally deemed to be "of a high standard," was that as the men were enfiladed by machine-gun and "field gun" fire, they tended to "cluster in one spot."[59] Even so, British-born Sergeant Walter Lloyd, who commanded a platoon at Vis-en-Artois and also "thought highly" of these new men, later recalled "how well the draftees maintained their distance and interval that day on the way down the first slope" – a noteworthy compliment from a veteran NCO about the training and discipline exhibited by these conscripts under very desperate circumstances.[60]

In the end, the Scarpe claimed the lives of 42 ORs in the 21st Battalion alone. Apart from the 289 men wounded or missing, fully one-third of its dead were conscripts. Among them were Privates Jack Bevis, an English driller from Kingston who had been with the battalion for barely two weeks, and John Lober, a labourer from Bainsville, Ontario. Lober was just twenty years old and could not even sign his own name. He had been conscripted the same day as his older brother Joseph, who would be wounded in October but would survive the war.[61]

The 19th Battalion, following in the immediate wake of the 21st Battalion's human debris field, also came swiftly under heavy fire, and their forward progress was immediately checked. Still suffering from the severe losses of the day before, and especially from a critical shortage of junior leaders, the lead companies quickly "became fused into one mass."[62] Casualties mounted rapidly. Corporal Deward Barnes, who had been promoted only a week or so earlier, suddenly found himself "in charge of half a company." Later, as these men sheltered in a deep trench, Barnes ordered the men "to make [fire] steps" in order to see and shoot over the parapet. Paralyzed by fear no doubt, "one or two of the draftees ... refused," he recalled, and "although the majority were good men," he "threatened to shoot them if they didn't dig." By this time, though, the 19th had become "badly disorganized."[63] Despite valiant efforts to outflank the enemy, it could advance no further and was forced to withdraw all the way back to its original start line.

The next day, Lieutenant-Colonel L.H. Millen calculated that his unit had suffered at least 30 dead and 255 wounded or missing over the previous seventy-two hours. On 28 August alone, six of those killed had been conscripts, including Privates Robert Pickens and Harry Walker, both fishmongers from Toronto. Pickens had suffered a bullet wound to the groin "and died almost immediately." Walker, who was British-born and had previously served two and a half years in the militia with the Army Service Corps, had fallen in action precisely on his twenty-seventh birthday.[64]

The 22nd Battalion No Longer Existed

Tremblay's 5th Brigade fared no better than Rennie's. Having relieved the 156th British Brigade the previous evening, the 5th had expanded its front accordingly. In response, Brigadier-General Tremblay deployed a third, somewhat fresher battalion, the 26th, on his right flank to help better cover the extra ground and, no doubt, to help stiffen the overall advance. This it would do, but not nearly enough to save the day.

Pressing forward to the first enemy trench line, the 24th Battalion was immediately stopped, both by heavy machine-gun fire and by barbed wire, "great belts [of which] had remained uncut by the artillery barrage." One of the first to be wounded was Lieutenant-Colonel Clark-Kennedy, who despite a "shattered leg" continued to command the remnants of his force (about 150 men) from a shell-hole until evacuated late that afternoon. Many of his young soldiers were new men "fighting in their first engagement."[65] Others, like Private Joseph Field, a baker from Montreal and a mere five feet (152.4 cm) tall, had joined the 24th the previous June and had fought throughout the Battle of Amiens. Tragically, Field survived a machine-gun round to the arm in this action only to perish en route to an aid post. Also killed this day along with a half-dozen other conscripts was Private Arthur Daigle of Culbert, Quebec. Daigle had been helping evacuate a wounded comrade "when an enemy shell landed beneath the stretcher" he was carrying. Daigle and the wounded man were both killed.[66]

By the time Clark-Kennedy was finally evacuated from the battlefield late that afternoon, the 24th Battalion had been crippled by 152 casualties, to go with the dreadful losses of a day earlier (242). If not for the "valorous leadership" of the 24th's commanding officer, it might have been much, much worse. Taking temporary command, Major P.L. Hall, M.C., immediately tried to make contact with the 22nd on his left flank, a "difficult" effort at best, since "the 22nd Battalion, as a battalion, no longer existed, all officers having fallen, killed or wounded, together with the great majority of their N.C.O.'s and men."[67]

The Van Doos did not produce a narrative of operations for this day, mainly because all of their officers had become casualties. Major Georges Vanier (acting CO and future Governor General of Canada) suffered a bullet wound to the chest and was very nearly blown up by an enemy shell, as a result of which he lost a leg. Along with 6 other wounded officers, the battalion counted 186 OR casualties, including 22 killed in action. Among its half-dozen conscript fatalities were Privates Alfred Maher, a twenty-year-old labourer from Saint-Jérôme, Quebec, and Arthur Lamarche, a moulder from Cowansville, Quebec. Like hundreds of their comrades who had assaulted the Ulster and Union trenches this day, both men had been mortally wounded by "enemy machine gun bullets." There would be little time to mourn, however. Over the next two weeks, the 22nd alone would bring on board more than 350 replacements.[68]

"We are almost speechless when we see the lists of casualties"

As Currie would later record in his diary, by late in the afternoon of 28 August, Burstall "was somewhat disappointed at [the] progress" of his troops.[69] All three of Burstall's lead battalion commanders had fallen in battle, among them Lieutenant-Colonel Archibald Mackenzie, CO of the 26th Battalion, "killed by machine-gun fire."[70] Troops who one day earlier had confidently been expected to first overpower stubborn German defences at the Sensée, and then carry out similar feats at the Fresnes-Rouvroy and Drocourt-Quéant Lines, had found themselves hunkered down in shell-holes not far from their jumping-off points. By nightfall the Canadians essentially owned only one part of the Fresnes-Rouvroy Line to the north of the Arras-Cambrai road and none of it to the south. In short, both Currie and Burstall appear to have ignored the ominous warnings of the previous day – that is, that under-strength units and exhausted troops would be no match for a determined opponent protected by vast fields of well-organized trench defences and uncut wire – ironically, just the scenario that Currie had set out to avoid when he extricated the corps from the Amiens sector.

As historian Tim Travers has observed, both Rawlinson and Currie appear to have "pressed their frontal attacks in late August longer and further than was prudent" – an understatement if anything, in light of the near disastrous battle that followed. Dancocks was even blunter in his assessment: "The Second Division's attack was a failure." This brought a stunning and predictable halt to a remarkable string of Canadian victories.[71]

The German army, in a resolute and well-executed defence of the Hindenburg Line, had sent General Currie a clear and powerful signal that any further Allied gains would be made at an increasingly steep price. Nonetheless, Currie was clearly blessed with one crucial commodity that the Germans did not possess – a reliable and steady flow of reinforcements.[72] Thus, in the great war of attrition, Currie was ahead, at least in the Canadian sector. Moreover, because his divisions had been able to continue moving forward, at best the Germans had won a passing tactical victory at the Fresnes-Rouvroy Line, not an operational reprieve.

Meanwhile, Currie had finally been forced to take an operational pause, albeit for part of just one day. But owing to the ever-increasing tempo of the offensive, the harsh lessons of this vicious battle would not be learned. Moreover, as the shattered remnants of the 4th and 5th Brigades limped to the rear, not to fight a major offensive for another five weeks, there remained another troubling reality for Currie. Casualties over the previous three days totalled "254 officers and 5,547 other ranks," significant losses that historian J.P. Harris has described as "appalling by any standard."[73] But perhaps a more accurate impression of these grim numbers is best conveyed by the voice of one concerned mother. Writing on 29 August to her son Private Will Antliff at No. 9 Field Ambulance, located at the time near Arras, Mrs. Antliff plaintively declared: "While we read daily accounts of the victories and the advance of the allies, we are almost speechless when we see the lists of casualties that follow."[74] Little did Will's widowed mother know that those lists were about to exceed anything seen at home since April and November 1917.

The Hardest Single Battle: The Drocourt-Quéant Line

"The battalions engaged suffered severely"

THE DROCOURT-QUÉANT (D-Q) Line, a "northward extension of the main Hindenburg Line" between Drocourt and Quéant, anchored "one of the most powerful and well-organized German defence systems," a complex network of "concrete shelters and machine gun posts ... protected by dense masses of barbed wire." A German defeat here would likely accelerate the retreat of their forces farther south, while a successful defence would extend the war, perhaps well into 1919.[1] Rising to this challenge, Currie would direct several days of preliminary attacks before then using what Tim Cook described as "brute force rather than careful planning" to execute one of the most successful assaults in Canadian military history – itself "a plan fantastic in conception and, from the start, improbable of success."[2] Nearly exhausted by three days of intense fighting and opposed by "eight fresh divisions," Currie's weary troops were left with almost no time to prepare for an attack that might have taken "months" to organize earlier in the war. Nevertheless, in the words of Dan Dancocks, the D-Q Line would be "smashed with surprising[,] almost ridiculous, ease," thanks in no small part to Currie's new men, who formed a substantial part of every front-line unit and who yet again would perform remarkably well.[3]

The failure of Burstall's 2nd Division to capture its share of the Fresnes-Rouvroy Line had placed a heavy burden on Batty Mac's "Old Red Patch" (as the 1st Division was known), which had to complete this task before the next offensive could be launched. From 30 August to 1 September, the 1st Division engaged in a number of so-called minor operations that succeeded, although at great cost. Starting at 4:40 a.m. on 30 August, Macdonell sent the 1st Brigade forward to establish a secure jumping-off point for the main assault. Brigadier-General Griesbach's 1st and 2nd Battalions conducted a brilliant right flanking manoeuvre that stunned the German defenders. At the same time, the 3rd Battalion on the left executed a frontal attack, culminating two hours later in the capture of a half-dozen enemy trenches, although not the fortified redoubt called "Ocean Work," the same impenetrable obstacle that had earlier stymied the 4th Brigade on two successive days.[4] All "the Battalions engaged suffered severely," and by the end of the operation, Griesbach's modest success had come at a steep price – 620 killed, wounded, and missing ORs – about 25 percent of the brigade's trench strength.[5]

For Lieutenant-Colonel L.T. McLaughlin's 2nd Battalion (Eastern Ontario), this protracted action was a mix of success and misfortune. One of his first casualties was Private George McLaren, a young clerk from Renfrew, Ontario, who had joined the unit at Amiens on 8 August. Struck down "by shrapnel from an enemy shell" just as his company was assembling for the dawn attack, McLaren was the first of eleven 2nd Battalion conscripts to die in front of Upton Wood.[6] The early success of the 3rd Battalion (Toronto Regiment), then being led by Major D.H.C. Mason, was followed by "three and a half hours of severe fighting" that culminated in 34 dead ORs and a dreadful 202 casualties overall.[7] Among the killed and wounded were ten draftees, including Private Kilby Hickling, fatally wounded in front of Upton Wood (perhaps by a sniper) as he attempted to carry water and rations up to the front line. Nonetheless, that afternoon and evening the 4th Battalion (then operating in direct support of the 1st) did carry the wood along with its adjacent network of troublesome trenches. This was a small triumph, but one that came at a steep cost – 75 OR casualties and 12 dead, 5 of them conscripts.[8]

Currie postponed the main assault on the D-Q Line for one more day (until 2 September), which forced Macdonell to fight elements of two brigades for a further two days in order to properly position his forces. This follow-up action began at 5:00 a.m. on 31 August with two companies of Major A.L. "Bug" Saunders's 8th Battalion attacking "Ocean Work," which they surprisingly captured in less than one hour. By that time the battle had claimed a dozen more ORs and the lives of several conscripts.[9] Next, in a final effort to ensure a secure jump-off for the big offensive to come, Macdonell launched a three-brigade assault north of Hendecourt. Beginning with an "exceptionally good" barrage at 4:50 a.m. on Sunday, 1 September, Lieutenant-Colonel Dick Worrall's 14th Battalion, whose leading company was reinforced by "a large proportion of new draft [*sic*] who had joined the Battalion but a few hours before," gained "with ease its objective with practically no casualties."[10] However, despite being cautioned at the outset of the battle not to rush too quickly forward and get caught underneath the friendly barrage, about a half-dozen of the new lads did just that. At least two were killed, including Private Alexander Niven, a Scottish conscript and former blacksmith from Montreal.[11]

Lieutenant-Colonel Paul Tudor's 5th Battalion also enjoyed early success, seizing its main objectives within thirty minutes despite having suffered "considerable casualties in the attacking wave" – 5 junior officers and 100 ORs. Later that afternoon and evening another 150 men were lost during fierce enemy counterattacks, actions that did not conclude until just before zero the next morning, at which point the 5th had suffered 40 dead ORs alone. Nine of these men were draftees.[12]

"The hardest single battle of the war for the Canadian Corps"

The final convulsive attack on the D-Q Line began on Monday morning, 2 September, at precisely 5:00 a.m., with a spectacular barrage delivered by "Twenty brigades of field artillery and eleven of heavy artillery" – more firepower than the Canadian Corps had employed on the first day at Amiens.[13] Behind this curtain of steel, Currie launched three infantry divisions (the 1st on the right, the 4th British on the left, and the 4th Canadian in the centre) across a front spanning more than 7.5 kilometres. But what began almost in a near rout of the enemy soon turned into "the hardest single battle of the war for the Canadian Corps."[14]

Leading the way for Macdonell on the right was Brigadier-General George Tuxford's 3rd Brigade (13th and 16th Battalions), which moved smartly forward despite absorbing several casualties from at least "one battery firing short." Lieutenant-Colonel Cy Peck's 16th Battalion (Canadian Scottish) encountered more serious difficulties: his men were almost immediately held up by heavy enfilade fire on their right flank, predictably so given that Brigadier-General George Paynter's 172nd British Brigade was not scheduled to step off until ninety minutes after zero. Ultimately Peck's troops seized control of the unit's first objective, the "Red Line" (D-Q support line), but they paid a steep price – 203 casualties. Among its 33 ORs killed were several British-born draftees from Manitoba. They included two farmers – Henry Simpson, a Scot from Elva, and Norman Kirk, English-born, from Ochre. Kirk suffered multiple wounds to his left arm and stomach but miraculously survived, only to perish the next day at No. 33 CCS.[15]

Jumping off on the left at 8 a.m., hard on the heels of the 13th, was Dick Worrall's 14th Battalion. It stormed the village of Cagnicourt (the 5th Brigade's second objective the previous week), surprised many defenders, and captured "practically a Battalion" before running into major opposition around 9:00 a.m. There the Royal Montreal Regiment found itself enfiladed from both flanks and from air attack by "30 hostile aeroplanes," resulting in heavy losses. By the time that the RMR was relieved the next morning it had suffered over 280 total casualties – nearly half its trench strength and "practically the whole of [its] Senior N.C.O.'s."[16] Perhaps this should not have been a surprise, though, given Tuxford's later assessment that the "men actually were so worn out with the continuous operations that they [fell] asleep in shell holes practically during the fighting." Nevertheless, the GOC offered high praise for the 363 reinforcements he had received just prior to this battle, stating in no uncertain terms that "so far as fighting goes," these drafts "seem to have been all that was desired from new men to battle [*sic*]."[17]

Thrust directly into combat without any time to assimilate into their new sections, these new men had quickly proven their mettle. Indeed, Private François Cardinal, a farmhand originally from Lebret, Saskatchewan, would be awarded the Military Medal for conspicuous gallantry this day, and many other conscripts who fought just as valiantly would be counted among the unit's thirty-three dead ORs. They included Privates Aquilas Côté, a carpenter originally from St-Hilaire, Quebec, and Haviland Hunking, a woodworker from Oshawa, Ontario – both killed in the attack on the Buissy Switch.[18]

Farther north, between Cagnicourt and the heavily fortified village of Villers-lès-Cagnicourt, other efforts by the 1st Brigade to advance to the Buissy Switch had been less successful. In particular, the 4th Battalion found itself "checked" almost immediately and completely pinned down by heavy machine-gun fire. Over the next twenty-four hours it would sustain 130 casualties and count 4 conscripts among its 14 dead ORs.[19] Killed by shrapnel wounds to the head and body in the initial advance was Private Clifford Lockley, an English-born, twenty-one-year-old shoe cutter with the Hamilton Shoe Company in Toronto. Lockley, a well-known "local concert entertainer and humorist," had served for two years with the 48th Highlander of Canada prior to being conscripted.[20]

Among this battalion's ninety-two wounded this day was one very lucky conscript, whose story illustrates two other crucial points regarding the fate of draftees. Private John Edwards had worked as a fireman with Croesus Gold Mines near Matheson in Northern Ontario until conscripted on 18 January 1918. Arriving in Camp Witley on 4 March, he underwent an abbreviated course in basic infantry training before being transferred to France on 22 May along with forty-seven other new men. There he spent another eleven weeks training at the Canadian Infantry Base Depot (CIBD) and at the CCRC. Out of his group of 48 reinforcements, 11 were eventually killed in action and 23 wounded – a 70 percent casualty rate. As for Edwards, his war began on 8 August, when he joined the 4th Battalion in the field at Amiens. Less than four weeks later, Private Edwards and his mates were caught in the terrible enfilade fire in front of Villers-lès-Cagnicourt, where a bullet wound to the left arm quickly brought an end to his combat service. Thanks to a quick evacuation by the 2nd Field Ambulance, Edwards received excellent medical care the next day at 26 General Hospital in Étaples; just one day later he found himself recuperating in England at the Military Hospital in Chatham.[21] For Currie and his division commanders, this highly efficient medical system was one of their greatest allies; not only did it save soldiers' lives, but it also enhanced the possibility that many of these men could be rapidly returned to combat.

"Only three weeks in the trenches"

Farther north, Brigadier-General Fred Loomis's 2nd Brigade did not have an easy time of it either. Lieutenant-Colonel W.F. Gilson's 7th Battalion had attained its objective (the Red Line) by 7:30 a.m. However, in addition to taking between "six and seven hundred prisoners," the BCR recorded twenty-three of its own killed and eighty-nine wounded. Among them were a dozen draftees, including Private John Michell, a thirty-one-year-old clerk from Kamloops, who had survived a wound in the attack near Villers-lès-Cagnicourt, only to be killed by shellfire shortly thereafter while en route to the nearest dressing station.[22]

The 10th Battalion had launched its own ambitious assault from the Red Line at precisely 8 a.m., but it too soon came to a halt under heavy enfilade fire from "German Field Artillery and Mobile Trench Mortars." Lieutenant-Colonel E.W. McDonald wisely abandoned his frontal assault at Villers-lès-Cagnicourt and instead commenced a slow, methodical manoeuvre to outflank the "fortress" there. Nine hours later, the 10th would capture the much-prized enemy redoubt on the Cambrai road – the "Factory" – just in time to execute its main attack against the heavily fortified trenches of the Buissy Switch. Then, after another five-hour struggle in which they defeated an enemy who "fought bitterly until the end in almost every instance," MacDonald's spirited troops were finally able to claim their share of the switch – albeit at a severe cost. By the time they were relieved the next day, the Calgary Regiment had sustained more than 230 OR casualties alone and 26 dead – well over one-third of the unit's trench strength.[23] Among them were several draftees, including Privates Harvey Driscoll, a young American-born (Arkansas) farmer from Mountain Park, Alberta, and Fred Steele, originally from Alliston, Ontario, but more recently a clerk at the Peacock General Store in Carmangay, Alberta. Driscoll's left leg had been "blown off" and his "right leg badly cut up" by an enemy shell. Although "evacuated to No. 11 Field Ambulance ... he succumbed to his wounds the same day." Likewise, with "only three weeks in the trenches," Fred Steele also fell in action. Once a well-known lacrosse player and "all round athlete," Steele would be honoured by the *Calgary Daily Herald*, which soon posted a lengthy lament to mourn the passing of this once-"brilliant hockey star."[24]

"I doubt if it can be carried through"

While Macdonell's troops were pushing steadily eastward, Currie sent his one fresh formation into the fray – Watson's 4th Division. General Watson first

Figure 6.1 Private Fred Steele, 10th Battalion, CEF, a once-"brilliant hockey star," killed in action 2 September at the D-Q Line. *Source: Calgary Daily Herald,* 24 September 1918.

learned the "policy for the employment of [his] Division in future operations" on Thursday, 29 August, and immediately confessed to his diary: "It is a very ambitious programme and I doubt if it can be carried through to the extent that they have laid down."[25] Given that two other Canadian divisions had just been savaged during their extraordinary efforts to take just one part of the Fresnes-Rouvroy Line, perhaps Watson could be forgiven for his momentary lack of confidence.

Leading the way south of the Arras-Cambrai road on 1 September was Brigadier-General James MacBrien's 12th Brigade, whose primary task was to help secure the jumping-off line (JOL) for the next day's assault. After the battle, the brigade's overall casualties would be considered light, but this assignment proved to be much more difficult than expected. For example, Lieutenant-Colonel J.A. Clark's 72nd Battalion encountered stiff resistance at the outset, particularly from machine-gun posts that had barely been touched by the opening barrage. Private William Moul, a British-born clerk and conscript from Silverton, BC, was one early casualty – fatally "hit in the body by shrapnel"

– while two of his wounded comrades were "taken prisoner by the Bosche." One of these was Private Arthur Sellwood, a barber and draftee recruited in Vancouver, who was fortunate to be "recaptured by [his] own company the following morning." Thus by nightfall, when MacBrien was ready to attack the D-Q Line, his battalions were operating at somewhat lower trench strengths than is commonly thought, in fact averaging about 560 men each.[26]

To complete the lineup for Watson's set piece attack, Brigadier-General Victor Odlum's 11th Brigade (including one company of the 4th Battalion, Canadian Machine Gun Corps) was tasked with leapfrogging the 12th Brigade. It too completed its assembly by 1:00 a.m. that night; not long after, its machine-gun company suffered its first casualties of the battle, one of whom was Private Myles Russell, a young American-born barber who had been drafted in Fort Qu'Appelle, Saskatchewan. Sheltering just prior to zero in a dugout outside Vis-en-Artois, Russell was killed by an enemy shell that burst nearby. As for the rest of Odlum's brigade, tasked to seize the Dury heights, it was also expected to "press on to the Canal du Nord" and, "if possible, cross the Canal and seize the high ground beyond." Again it was not to be.[27]

A Bitter Legacy: One Family, Two Telegrams

Stepping off at 5 a.m., Watson's 4th Division encountered difficulties straight away. First, on the 12th Brigade's left flank, the 85th Battalion had to deal with unfinished business from the previous evening – a nasty enemy redoubt of at least 18 heavy machine guns located a mere fifty yards in front of its JOL. In the costly frontal assault that followed, (acting CO) Major J. MacIntosh Millar's Nova Scotians sustained 50 percent of their losses for the day in a Somme-like advance over "the first 300 yards." Ultimately, they would gain all of their objectives, but in doing so the 85th suffered a stunning total of 273 casualties (13 officers and 260 ORs) – about 43 percent of its trench strength – including 62 ORs killed in action. Among the dead was Private Howard MacPherson, a twenty-one-year-old mechanic from McLellans Brook, Nova Scotia, who had served with the unit since the previous May. Many of his fellow draftees were much luckier, seventeen having received survivable wounds during this assault. Replacements came forward quickly, though. In fact, over the next three weeks this unit would receive 197 reinforcements, including 110 conscripts, once again bringing the 85th nearly up to strength.[28] Memories of this timely replenishment most likely informed key judgments by its CO, Lieutenant-Colonel Layton Ralston, when a quarter-century later, as Canada's defence minister in another war, he openly advocated the deployment of conscripts overseas, primarily to reinforce depleted infantry battalions.[29]

Meanwhile, farther south on the 12th Brigade's right flank, the 38th Battalion had fought an equally fierce battle. Initially it encountered "no serious opposition." But after crossing the Arras-Cambrai road and cresting the ridge beyond, the 38th came under much more intense machine-gun fire and shelling from both flanks, resulting in what Lieutenant-Colonel Edwards later described as "very heavy casualties." Stripped of any protective artillery barrage and almost devoid of field cover, his men were doomed. Later, Edwards would rightfully assert that had the final objective been on the third D-Q Line and not, as it fatefully was, on the forward exposed slope of the Dury ridge, his "casualties would have been very light in comparison." Instead, the 38th suffered a total of 269 casualties – nearly 50 percent of its trench strength – and 57 dead ORs.[30] Nine conscripts were among the latter, including Private Orville Publow, a painter from Perth, Ontario. Just twenty-two, Publow was "instantly killed by machine gun fire" near Dury. Newspaper accounts later revealed that Orville, one of David Publow's four sons, was the younger brother of Robert, also a draftee, who himself would fall in action some two months later.[31]

On the 12th Brigade's far-right flank, the 72nd Battalion likewise encountered early success. Within the hour the Seaforths quickly captured their share of the D-Q Line, but in their headlong advance to the enemy support line they lost many men, including the Scottish-born Price brothers of Vancouver – John and Alexander – both conscripts who had been in France since early June. The first to fall was likely the older brother John, a steward in civilian life, who died from wounds to the head in this unit's second attack south of Dury. Twenty-one-year-old Alexander then perished when "an enemy shell exploded close to him." For Alex Sr., the two telegrams he received shortly thereafter would be another parent's tragic and bitter legacy from the Canadian conscription crisis in the First World War.[32]

The 72nd Battalion made quick work of all four enemy defence lines before it too ran into much stronger opposition in its advance to the Red Line. There the kilted Seaforths would make periodic but futile attempts to advance beyond a "sunken road," only to suffer further from what MacBrien later described as "the most severe Machine Gun opposition which this Brigade has ever encountered." Among the 72nd's many afternoon casualties was the American-born Private Henry Heslop, who had previously worked as a fisherman in Ladner, BC. Heslop, who had enlisted on 27 November, a full five weeks before his class was called to the colours, was acting as a stretcher-bearer when he was "killed ... by a bullet which passed through [his] left breast." He was just one of the battalion's fifty-seven ORs to die this day, a grim total that included at least eighteen draftees.[33]

Despite the capture of nearly 450 prisoners, this was a pyrrhic victory of sorts. Having lost 268 men or about 48 percent of its trench strength, including 14 officers and dozens of experienced and irreplaceable junior leaders, the 72nd was now a seriously broken fighting unit. Curiously, in a pointed but carefully worded battle narrative, Lieutenant-Colonel J.A. Clark suggested that "the present drafts require more training," since they appeared to "bunch together and stick" when "under fire" (typical for most soldiers in combat for the first time), adding that in his view "the meaning of 'pressing on' must be drilled into them."[34] In this respect Clark may have been a bit harsh, since the overall success of his men in this engagement belied to a great extent this latter criticism. Moreover, sixty-six of his OR casualties this day had been conscripts – 26 percent of his total losses – further testament to their apparent courage and sacrifice under fire. One of their number, Private Edward Rich, a farmer from Salmon Arm, BC, would be awarded the Military Medal for conspicuous gallantry in this action.[35]

"Many new recruits were eager for their first show"

Farther to the north, Brigadier-General Ross Hayter's 10th Brigade initially enjoyed similar success to MacBrien's, but became completely bogged down when his troops attempted to push beyond the village of Dury. There the belts of enemy wire were "dense and almost entirely uncut," and though Lieutenant-Colonel Herbert Keegan's 47th Battalion quickly penetrated this obstacle, success came at a high cost. By the end of the day, Keegan had lost seven junior officers and counted another 155 OR casualties – 12 of whom were killed in action.[36] Half of those in this latter group were draftees, including Private Denny Caza, a painter from Walkerville who had been in France since early June but had only joined his unit three weeks earlier at Amiens. Caza was killed by shellfire that morning during the initial assault on the D-Q Line; tragically, his older brother Theodore (also a conscript) would meet a similar fate less than one month later. Among the battalion's 116 wounded were Privates Ernest Charbonneau, a salesman from Sandwich, and Albert Eberly, a traction engineer from Sarnia, Ontario. Charbonneau received the perfect *blighty* – a gunshot wound to the right leg and foot that saw him back in England within a week, never to return. But Eberly, who on recruitment had claimed two years' prior service with a militia regiment, was not so fortunate. "Severely wounded in the back and left thigh by an enemy shell," he died from his wounds at No. 42 CCS the next day.[37]

Lieutenant-Colonel Lionel Page's 50th Battalion, whose "many new recruits were eager for their first show," also experienced "extremely light" casualties until about 7:30 a.m., when a violent German barrage exploded on its "newly

Figure 6.2 Private Denny Caza, 47th Battalion, killed in action at the D-Q Line, 2 September 1918. *Source:* Courtesy of Danielle E. Reaume.

captured positions" in front of Dury. Ultimately this unit would document 241 total casualties, although the CO later reasoned that "in light of the results obtained," these losses were "not heavy." Moreover, Page was quite fulsome in his praise for all ranks, noting in particular that "the new drafts were splendid and their only fault overkeenness [*sic*]."[38] Indeed, ten of the thirty-one dead ORs were new men, many of whom no doubt were among the "human cannon fodder – 150 fresh reinforcements" that the battalion had taken on strength just days earlier at Beaurains. "They looked good to us," recalled veteran Victor Wheeler, knowing full well that many would soon "be sucked into the fatal whirlpool."[39] Among the draftees to fall into that whirlpool were Privates Hubert Fournier, an Acadian watchmaker from Edmundston, New Brunswick, who had settled in Calgary, and the French-born Alphonse Garnier, most recently a farmer in Clover Bar, Alberta. Shellfire in front of Dury had claimed the life of Garnier; Fournier had perished from a bullet wound to the head.[40]

Meanwhile the 46th Battalion, led by Major Jock Rankin, passed through the 50th, and by 7:50 a.m. had successfully overrun the village of Dury. Early success led once more, as it did all across the D-Q Line, to a fierce struggle resulting in fairly severe losses. Over the next three days the "Suicide Battalion" once again lived up to its reputation, absorbing an astonishing 310 casualties, including 48 killed in action, a grim accounting that "equalled anything in its brief history."

Among the dead were two young immigrants: Private Ole Botten, a Norwegian-born farmer from Star City, Saskatchewan, and Private William Walberg, a twenty-one-year-old American-born farm worker from Roche Percée on the North Dakota border – both conscripts.[41]

Remarkably, the fight was still far from over. Phase Two of the 4th Division battle plan involved a continuation of this advance, first by the 44th Battalion on the left and then by the 78th on the right. But while the Germans appeared to have yielded the D-Q Line and surrendered in near record numbers, they had also reorganized and, as mounting Canadian casualties would prove, they were now about to mount a fierce and deadly defence of all ground east of the Red Line. In particular, the 44th, led by Major D.B. Martyn (acting CO), found itself pinned down at its jumping-off point (the D-Q support line), where enemy shells "rain[ed] on the 44th positions throughout the day." The results were predictable: 278 total casualties and 41 ORs killed, or about "two-thirds of the Battalion's trench strength." As the unit historian E.S. Russenholt would one day grimly note, by the time the "Manitobans" were relieved two days later, "the survivors in No.2 Company number[ed] less than a dozen."[42]

Among the 44th's dead were eleven draftees, including Private John McAuliffe, a plumber from Winnipeg, by way of Alberton, PEI. Just twenty-one, having reached that milestone only four days earlier, McAuliffe was killed by shellfire on this terrifying day, one that was "so clear that enemy howitzer shells [were] seen as they descend[ed] on the trenches." Available records indicate that, with one exception, all of the 44th's conscript casualties this day were due to this murderous enemy shelling and not, as perhaps one might expect, from intense machine-gun fire. Finally, one other noteworthy fatality was Private Arthur McKeeve, a British-born stone mounter and fitter from Wynyard, Saskatchewan. Like many of his comrades, McKeeve's remains were not identified, so it is somewhat ironic that the sacrifice of this "stone mounter" is honoured today, in carved stone, at Canada's Vimy Memorial.[43]

Two weeks later Hayter signed his official report and declared that "the operations of the 10th Infantry Brigade were an unqualified success." To this optimistic analysis, he dutifully added about a dozen "conclusions and deductions," the most crucial of which seems to have been his unequivocal assertion that an operational "pause of quite six hours" was "essential" in this type of operation, first to help avoid thrusting battalions into a completely obscure and disorganized tactical situation, and second, to allow sufficient time for field artillery brigades to move forward to cover the next advance. In this context, it appears that Hayter's veiled criticism of pushing too hard too fast may simply have been one attempt to highlight the bitter cost of Watson's and Currie's flawed but ultimately successful strategy.[44]

"The helplessness of infantry on exposed ground"

Elsewhere, Odlum's 11th Brigade had advanced at 8:00 a.m. Within the hour his three leading battalions (Carey's 54th, Harbottle's 75th, and Perry's 87th) had encountered intense enfilade fire from Dury on the left, and on the right from the same "Factory" redoubt north of Villers-lès-Cagnicourt (the "old Mill") that had proven so troublesome for the 10th Battalion.[45] After only a very brief advance the 54th could progress no further, having suffered the loss of over half its officers, plus 28 ORs killed and 169 total casualties. Among these were two men who had been drafted the same day in Hamilton: Privates Charles Clarkson, a driver from Ancaster, and William Lane, a British-born cotton mill worker. Clarkson died after being "hit in the stomach by an enemy machine gun bullet." Lane, "the second son of [Edward] Lane to make the supreme sacrifice," had perished from the nearby "explosion of an enemy shell."[46]

As for the 75th, Harbottle's men suffered even more grievous losses. Between 8:00 a.m. and 10:00 a.m. the 75th "literally fought foot by foot" to finally establish a line about 200 metres in front of the "sunken road" west of Mont Dury. But then, having already sustained "heavy casualties" from "machine gun fire ... of almost unparallel [*sic*] fury," it was forced to ride out the storm hunkered down in unsheltered slit trenches. In the end it was nothing less than a slaughter. The 75th experienced its worst day yet of the war – 6 officers killed and 16 wounded (including the CO), plus 53 ORs killed and another 230 wounded – a grim total of 305 casualties. Reflecting the curious logic typical of the day, Odlum later declared in his after-action report that "the officers led splendidly, as the casualties, particularly those of the 75th prove."[47]

Among the 75th's lucky wounded was Private Joseph Allaire, a blacksmith from Timmins, Ontario, by way of Buckingham, Quebec, who had joined the battalion in late July, just in time for Amiens. Allaire, having suffered a slight gunshot wound to the left leg, was evacuated to England never to return. Not so lucky were two chums from South Porcupine, Ontario: Privates Herbert Devine, a diamond driller, and Thomas Dinning, a stationary engineer. Both men, like Allaire, had been born in Quebec, both had been drafted the same day in Toronto (21 January), and both were killed during the abortive attack at Dury.[48]

On the left flank and south of Dury, the 87th Battalion was experiencing its own worst day. Initially, Lieutenant-Colonel Ken Perry hesitated to push his troops forward as scheduled at 8:00 a.m., since the tactical situation was simply too "obscure." Upon learning that the 75th was entirely pinned down, however, he began a tentative advance about 8:30 a.m. Unfortunately, as his two leading companies crested the ridge east of the "sunken road," his men, like all other assaulting troops in this sector, immediately came "under heavy Machine Gun and shell fire."[49] Desperate at his own mounting losses, Perry advised Odlum that no further advance was possible, only to be ordered "to hold on to what [he] had and await further orders." Again, the resulting casualties were extraordinarily grim – 320 officers and men including 60 ORs killed in action, 14 of whom were draftees, and many of whom were likely among the 48 reinforcements who had arrived just a day earlier. Private Joseph Dubé, a twenty-one-year-old filler from North Coaticook, Quebec, was probably one of the first of these Canadian Grenadiers to die when he was felled by enemy shellfire, just as his unit was moving up to its assembly position. Most of his comrades, though, were cut down in the actual attack on or near the infamous Dury hill. Among them were many men from Montreal, including Privates Louis Bourgeois, a waiter, and Charles Alarie, a labourer, the latter having suffered one gunshot wound to the chest and another that fractured his right thigh. Evacuated to No. 8 Stationary Hospital in Wimereux, Alarie died of his wounds some three weeks later.[50]

The story of the 11th Brigade's epic battle at Dury hill would not be complete without noting the part of Odlum's fourth battalion – the 102nd (Central Ontario). Tasked with following closely behind the 87th, Major E.J. Ryan's troops likewise suffered heavy casualties on the slopes of Dury ridge. Among the first to fall was Private James Dick, a Scottish-born farmer and draftee from Midland, Ontario, who died from the concussion of a shell exploding nearby. Unsettling, though not uncommon, his body "did not bear any visible wounds after death." Later, in response to reports (quickly confirmed) that the enemy was withdrawing, the 102nd renewed the assault and, in the historic advance that followed, pressed forward largely unopposed all the way to the "Green Line" (not far from the Canal du Nord). But it was a bittersweet triumph: 33 more infantry lay dead and 153 wounded. Nonetheless, Ryan later declared: "All ranks [had] performed in a magnificent manner."[51]

Judging from his after-action report, the brigade commander did not fully share this assessment. Partly in response to very heavy losses – 950 men – in executing what he clearly perceived to be a faulty plan, Odlum (like Hayter) sharply delineated several "lessons which struck [him] most forcibly" in the battle's aftermath. Foremost among these was a lament of sorts for "the helplessness of infantry on exposed ground." Odlum felt very strongly that the decision for his brigade to "leap-frog" the 12th ought to have been delegated to a "competent [i.e., informed] commander who should not have his hands tied from behind." With an additional hint of rancour, Odlum railed against the "repeated failure" of adjacent formations to assist in protecting the flanks of their "hard pressed neighbor." Finally, in what appears to have been a direct challenge to Watson, if not to Currie himself, Odlum acidly noted that the attack plan had been based on a false assumption – that is, that once they were through the D-Q Line, enemy resistance would substantially diminish, thus negating the requirement for an operational pause to allow the guns to be brought up in support of a follow-on artillery barrage. In fact, just the opposite occurred. The attacking battalions were left pinned down, utterly exposed, without benefit of effective artillery support and with near catastrophic results.[52]

"The unparalleled striking power of our battalions"

Odlum's acerbic findings again raise the question of whether Currie would have taken such grave risks had his divisions not been fed a reliable stream of reinforcements. The answer is to be found partly in Watson's and Currie's actual responses to the events of 2 September. That evening, having been provided a more complete picture of the enemy's defences, the "severe losses" sustained by his troops that day, and the attendant risks of continuing the "advance without adequate preparation," Watson "in turn informed the Corps Commander, placing the entire situation clearly before him." Emboldened by the capture of the D-Q Line, General Currie chose to gamble yet again and abjured, at least initially, any operational pause. Yet only a few hours later, in what must be considered another example of his battlefield acumen, he carefully reconsidered Watson's ominous report and wisely decided to postpone the next attack – for twenty-four hours.[53]

In his diary entry for 3 September, Currie reflected on the significance of the Canadian victory at the D-Q Line and compared its success with that achieved at Amiens on 8 August; of the two, he declared the D-Q Line to be the "greatest." After the war he rightfully attributed this great triumph to "the unparalleled striking power of our Battalions and [to] the individual bravery of our men [who] had smashed all resistance."[54] Left unstated was the fact that despite thousands of casualties, the "striking power" of Currie's victorious battalions had been continuously reinforced, mainly by conscripts, who by most accounts had fought courageously, and without whom it is likely that this latest offensive could not have been mounted.[55]

The Canal du Nord and the Brotherhood of Arms

*A feature of the battle was the excellent account given of themselves by the new
reinforcements ... Many of these were one year men, and if they suffered, perhaps during their training under the stigma of being conscripts, they learned
when they reached the battle line that they were regarded as comrades in arms.
Imbued with that spirit they gave a magnificent account of themselves.*

– J.F.B. Livesay, *Toronto Daily Star*, 28 September 1918

"The door was shut"

The Canadian Corps had rapidly broken through one door at the Hindenburg
Line – Drocourt-Quéant – but according to Major-General W.H. Anderson
(Horne's chief of staff), "the door was shut" to the bigger prize – the Canal du
Nord. Canadian and British forces were simply too weak to continue an all-
out offensive. There would be "no major operations on the First Army front"
for nearly four weeks, which would still prove to be a costly interregnum for
Currie's 2nd and 3rd Divisions.[1] Meanwhile, his two other divisions (the 1st
and the 4th) would rest and replenish in preparation for what would become a
stunning and decisive breakthrough at the Canal du Nord, arguably Currie's
greatest tactical triumph of the war.

The corps' 8 kilometre advance to the Canal du Nord on 3 September had not
been without cost. More than one hundred men were lost in the 2nd Battalion
alone, including Private Arthur Bailey, a schoolteacher and draftee from Dart-
ford, Ontario – "hit in the arm by shrapnel" and later killed en route to the
dressing station. Farther north, across the Arras-Cambrai road, the 47th had
suffered nearly 100 casualties as well and 29 ORs killed, among them 5 draftees. That was more than twice the fatalities incurred the day before at the D-Q
Line.[2] Thus, while it was clear that the enemy was in the midst of a tactical
withdrawal, it was also evident that the still formidable German army was not
about to surrender the canal.

Currie had at last been forced to take a lengthy pause, while a "steady stream
of reinforcements, most of them conscripts, filled the depleted ranks of the
Canadian infantry."[3] For example, Lieutenant-Colonel Cy Peck's 16th Battalion
had received 322 reinforcements in August, and another 210 would arrive in
September, most of them just in time for this unit's greatest test yet. But, in the

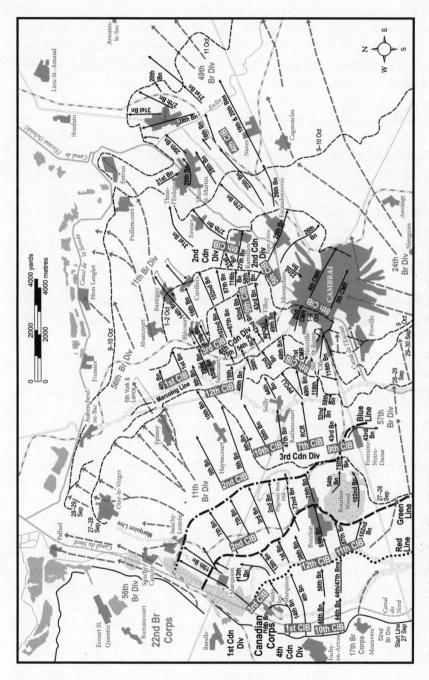

Map 4   Canal du Nord and Cambrai, 2 September–October 9. Map by Mike Bechthold.

wake of wet and stormy weather, "unable to train" was one of Peck's main concerns.[4] In this regard, proper assimilation of these new troops was a top priority. As one veteran cautiously observed: "Nearly 75% of [the] battn are new men and most N.C.O.'s are new to their work with many new officers. Our battn *looks* alright [*sic*] for we got good men in the last drafts but we are not even acquainted let alone understand one another [emphasis in original]."[5]

"They are to prove themselves as good soldiers as any"

Very high casualties at Amiens, at Arras, and now at the D-Q Line had again raised challenges and concerns about manpower. Reinforcements had flowed rapidly forward, but these men had not come up as quickly or in the quantity that one might have expected. For example, the 1st Division had sustained 3,324 casualties in the recent offensive, but by 7 September, it had received just 1,352 replacements. Nevertheless, more than 9,000 infantry had been sent to the Canadian Corps in the first week of Amiens, and another 12,072 ORs had been dispatched between 26 August and 9 September alone (all but 418 going to Currie's four infantry divisions) – further proof, it would seem, that the CCRC had mastered the complex mechanics of real-time manpower replacement.[6] Indeed, in his dissertation on the reinforcement system, Richard Holt concluded that by 1918 "trained reinforcements [were being provided] in a timely manner." This was mainly due, he observed, to the establishment of a Canadian Corps Railhead Depot (CCRD) closer to the front, which allowed the corps "to speed up the movement" of these men from the CCRC and "to hold [them] as far forward as possible" until required. Other reinforcements, he added, bypassed the CCRC altogether and were "sent directly from the base depot at Étaples to the CCRD," once again illustrating the flexibility that would prove crucial to success in the Hundred Days.[7]

Still, efforts to restore the corps' effective combat strength were hindered by near constant and deadly fire from enemy machine-guns, artillery, and air bombardment, all of which continued to inflict heavy casualties across the front. According to Nicholson's *Official History*, "there were few days when the count of battle casualties fell below 100."[8] Lieutenant-Colonel W.N. Moorehouse's 3rd Battalion, Canadian Machine Gun Corps (CMGC), was especially unlucky. During its mid-morning parade, four days after it had moved back into division reserve at Camp Walrus (about 10 kilometres west of Arras), the battalion suffered a bombing attack by a German aircraft. The subsequent explosion was devastating, inflicting one of the biggest single-event casualty tolls ever experienced by the Canadian Corps. When the acrid smoke cleared, no fewer than 35 ORs were dead and another 35 wounded, 15 of whom would die later at the CCS.

Among this grim total were five conscripts, including Private Charles Darby, a carpenter from Hamilton.[9]

A year later, when he looked back on this tumultuous time, war correspondent J.F.B. Livesay would somberly recall these heavy casualties, the constant flow of reinforcements, and the devastated landscape, but for reasons unknown he also chose to introduce to the narrative – *Canada's Hundred Days* – one of the war's great enduring myths:

> Just about this time the Corps receives for the first time reinforcements who, to make no bones about it, are conscripts, drafts under the compulsory service act passed at Ottawa a year ago, though they are to prove themselves as good soldiers as any. It would seem that these men—many of whom were only held back by family circumstances from voluntary enlistment—had been snubbed and bullied on their training grounds. They meet here a very different reception, for they enter at once the brotherhood of arms. They are welcomed on precisely the same footing as had been the volunteer reinforcements.[10]

Livesay may have been partly correct in his assessment of the reception given to the conscripts on their initial arrival. But his casual reference that this period marked "the first time" that such men had been received by the corps is astonishing, given that conscripts had been fighting and dying in great numbers throughout the Hundred Days to this point – something he should have known. Clearly he had direct access to the corps commander, for his newspaper columns suggest a highly informed view of events. Yet this one passage helped establish an enduring myth about the perceived *late* arrival of Canadian conscripts on the Western Front, one that over time seems to have obscured the valour and sacrifice that these men had already shown at Amiens, at the Scarpe, and at the D-Q Line. Livesay was correct on one important point, however – conscripts did in fact "prove themselves as good soldiers as any."

"I don't believe I ought to let them do it"

Ludendorff would later gravely recall that at this crucial juncture in the war, while the Germans were not yet beaten, there was "no longer any chance of the pendulum swinging in our favour."[11] Indeed, the Germans' fatal spiral accelerated on 12 September when Pershing's First American Army launched a massive assault at Saint-Mihiel, south of Verdun. This impressive attack by the fledgling and largely conscript American army was a key part of Foch's four-part grand offensive strategy, which was meant to deliver successive and coordinated blows along the full length of the Western Front.[12] The Canadian Corps was required to "form a defensive flank facing north-east to protect a major attack by the Third and Fourth Armies." Initially, the Canadians were expected to leap across the Canal du Nord, capture Bourlon Wood and its commanding heights (110 metres), and then establish a crucial protective screen for the left flank of General Julian Byng's Third British Army. But only a week later, this ambitious undertaking was expanded to include "the bridges over the Canal-de-l'Escaut north of Cambrai along with the high ground overlooking the Sensée Valley."[13]

Currie proposed to begin by funnelling lead elements of two divisions through a narrow gap, about 2.5 kilometres wide, opposite the village of Inchy-en-Artois, where the unfinished portion of the canal was relatively dry. These and follow-on forces (initially about 30,000 men) would then fan out north and east in a broad arc nearly 10 kilometres wide. A very risky plan, it required the assembly of all attacking forces in front of a heavily congested chokepoint, one well-known to the enemy and therefore extremely vulnerable to artillery bombardment. Currie had gambled before, though, and had won at Amiens when the corps had escaped detection in Hangar Wood. If he succeeded here, the rewards might be even greater. Still, a successful breach of the canal itself was a big "if." Besides needing to first overcome a "dense barricade of wire," Currie's men would presumably have to withstand the best defence that the machine-gunners and artillery of General Otto von Below's Seventeenth Army could deliver, even before they could begin their advance against the Marquion Line, or for that matter the heights of Bourlon Wood beyond.[14]

Historian Shane Schreiber notes that "once again ... the boldness of Currie's plan disturbed his superiors," in particular General Horne, who believed that the plan could not be executed without "heavy losses."[15] Undaunted by what appear to have been his commander's "grave objections," however, and having already done his usual business-like cost–benefit analysis, Currie resisted all suggestions that he modify it. Consequently, Horne appealed to Haig for further guidance, and it was not until 21 September that Horne finally, and reluctantly, gave his "tentative" approval.[16]

Yet Horne remained skeptical. Later he declared to his chief of staff, "I don't believe I ought to let them do it."[17] Horne, like Haig, was under strong pressure to preserve manpower, and since the 11th British Division would be a key component of this assault, his increasing apprehension is understandable. Currie's audacious plan threatened the lifeblood of the First British Army precisely at a time when, because of an ongoing shortage of trained reinforcements, Horne could ill afford heavy battlefield losses.[18] Horne consulted next with General Byng to ascertain his views regarding the plan, and three days later,

Byng (the former commander of the Canadian Corps) took up the matter directly with Currie. Byng, whose Third Army had fought with mixed results at Cambrai a year earlier, warned Currie that a catastrophe at the Canal du Nord could very well result in him being relieved of command. Nonetheless, Currie remained confident and determined to deliver the goods, secure in the knowledge that even if he were to fail, his beloved corps would survive.[19]

At the Edge of the Abyss

Prior to meeting with General Byng, Currie hosted all of his divisional commanders at a final planning conference on Tuesday morning, 24 September. There he briefed them on a complex two-phase attack that would begin with a full-scale breach of the Canal du Nord, followed by capture of the Marquion (Red) Line, and, after a very brief pause, full investment of the village of Bourlon and its adjacent heights (the Green Line). The corps would then move rapidly east and northeast, another 3.5 kilometres or so, to the Blue Line, its third objective.[20] If the enemy could not be overcome, the corps would pause, regroup, and prepare for the next day's attack – with but one exception. Currie was adamant that the 1st Division continue to press on at least three more kilometres to take the village of Haynecourt, there to "gain observation of the Bantigny Ravine ... probably the Enemy's main line of approach for counter-attack."[21]

The very challenging second phase of this attack, the timing of which could not "be determined beforehand," would be similar in both scope and vision to the original plan for the second day of battle at the Scarpe; it gamely foresaw the corps attacking several kilometres beyond the Blue Line, then seizing "the bridges over the Canal de L'Escaut northeast of Cambrai and establishing the necessary bridge heads, [and] at the same time capturing the high ground overlooking the Sensée Valley."[22] Some Canadian units would actually push forward nearly 10 kilometres on the first day of battle, but a further advance of 4 kilometres in the face of determined resistance was at best a plan, never a realistic objective.

Currie's plan was, without question, his most daring, complex, and elaborate undertaking, and its success would depend heavily on the favourable outcome of a multitude of interlocking events over which Currie's division and brigade commanders had only limited control. Nevertheless, every possible effort would be made to maximize their chances of success, especially in the crucial breaching of the canal itself. Integral to Currie's plan of attack was the significant bridging work to be accomplished by his now heavily reinforced engineer brigades (twelve battalions), the ranks of which had swelled considerably in September with much needed reinforcements, many of them conscripts.[23]

Two formations not committed to this assault were Currie's battered 2nd and 3rd Divisions, which were still deployed in defensive positions along the canal. Their task was to establish strong outposts, deny enemy counter-incursions, and ultimately maintain overall control of "no man's land." The challenge, however, was that the Germans were not the least bit compliant. Efforts by the 26th Battalion to establish one such post resulted in "heavy fighting" and eleven casualties – four dead, two of whom were draftees. One of those killed in this action was Private Percy Morrill, a clerk from Saint John, New Brunswick, who was "shot through the head" while executing "a raid on an enemy post."[24]

The next day was bloodier still for the 25th Battalion, when at about 6:00 a.m. the enemy "put down a heavy barrage ... and started to attack in force." Only after "heavy fighting" were the German raiders "completely repulsed," but not before this unit had sustained another six fatalities and sixteen ORs wounded.[25] Three of these dead were conscripts, including Privates William Day, a carpenter from Hatfield Point, New Brunswick, and Arthur Manuel, a young fisherman from Canso in Guysborough County, Nova Scotia. Both men were wounded in the attack, and both succumbed to their injuries after being evacuated.[26]

Clearly, while the German army had made a defensive withdrawal across the Canal du Nord, it certainly had not withdrawn from the fight. In less than one week of static trench warfare, punctuated by periodic raids, Burstall's deeply wounded formation sustained more than twelve hundred additional casualties, yet another severe blow to any prospect that the 2nd Division might rejoin the offensive any time soon. Nevertheless, its sacrifice had given the 4th Canadian Division the chance for a much-needed rest and crucial time to prepare for what Currie would later describe as "five days of the bitterest fighting we ever experienced."[27]

"The conduct of all ranks was magnificent"

It is often said that great battles are won before the first shot is fired. Thanks to the impeccable planning of the Canadian Corps, the same might also be said of day one at the Canal du Nord. At precisely 5:20 a.m. on 27 September, the stillness of the dawn was shattered, first by the deafening, chest-thumping roar of a great British and Canadian artillery barrage, and shortly thereafter by an even greater tumult not too far to the east, where powerful artillery explosions began to rip across the German lines. The Germans responded in kind, and in short order their guns claimed one of the battle's first victims – Corporal Matthew Fretwell, a Waterdown resident and former pre-med student at the University of Toronto. Fretwell, a conscript then serving with the 2nd Canadian Motor Machine Gun Brigade, had been carrying belts of ammunition to one of the battery's guns when an enemy shell exploded nearby, killing him instantly.

At the same time, leading elements of three Canadian infantry brigades had raced forward to the canal, led at first by just four assault battalions – the 14th, the 4th, the 46th, and the 44th. Remarkably, leading elements of the 4th reached their initial objective in just twelve minutes.[28] The 44th and 46th swept past the enemy's next line of defence – the heavy wire and double-trenches of the Canal du Nord Line – to their final objective, "a sunken road which lay six hundred yards beyond the canal."[29] Both units performed magnificently, but both suffered extraordinary losses.

Apart from an open right flank, the principal challenge for the 44th had been an errant Canadian barrage, which unfortunately landed partly on the canal itself and thus right on top of the attacking troops. Thanks to superb training and discipline, the surviving troops pressed forward resolutely until they ran headlong into the nemesis of the Canadian Corps – heavy fire from enemy machine-guns. Even so, their "steady advance" remained unchecked, and by 6:40 a.m. this battalion was able to report that its final objective, the sunken road, had been reached.[30] The cost was steep. By late that afternoon the 44th, having sustained 184 OR casualties alone, numbered just 356 rifles. Thirteen ORs had been killed outright; ten of those who fell this day or later died of their wounds were conscripts. Among them was Private Harold Mowatt, a young mechanic from St. Stephen, New Brunswick, who had suffered devastating wounds to the "head, legs and arms." The 44th's fighting companies now averaged "65 men each." More important, there was "a serious shortage of trained leaders."[31]

Immediately to the north, the 46th "Suicide" Battalion achieved similar success. Led by their portly but decisive acting CO, Major Jock Rankin, the Saskatchewans fought their way to the sunken road by 6:15 a.m., but at the cost of 214 total casualties, including 21 ORs killed and 9 others missing in action. Seven of the former were draftees, including American-born Private Arngrimur Grandy, a grain buyer from Wynyard in northern Saskatchewan.[32]

To the immediate left, the 1st Brigade's 4th Battalion and the 3rd Brigade's 14th also punched big holes through the Canal du Nord Line. By 7:15 a.m. the Royal Montreal Regiment had reached the Red Line. About an hour later, it captured the adjacent village of Sains-lès-Marquion, but it too "suffered many casualties," in part due to a barrage that was "too slow, difficulty being experienced in keeping the men out of it." Lieutenant-Colonel Worrall hastened to record that his unit's "chain of command" had worked effectively, despite the loss of so many junior leaders: "privates in many cases commanded sections, and in one case a private commanded a platoon." Ultimately, "the conduct of all ranks was magnificent, the men [having shown] wonderful energy and dash."[33] Even so, 209 men had been lost, including 26 killed and 173 wounded and missing – more than one third of the battalion's trench strength. Ten of the soldiers who perished in this battle were draftees, including Private Herman Hawley, a young electrician with the Dominion Textile Company in Magog, Quebec. Among the wounded and missing was Private Walter Turner, a twenty-one-year-old grocer from Hamilton. As it turned out, Turner had been captured, and would be imprisoned at Niederzwehren (south of Kassel) in central Germany, where he died of his wounds on 15 October.[34]

By 8:15 a.m. the 4th Battalion had reached its main objective, the Red Line, right on schedule. It had taken fewer casualties than most attacking units – about 145 officers and men. Among its 18 dead were 13 ORs, including half a dozen conscripts. One of the first of these to fall was Private William Mitchell, a young blacksmith from the small village of York, Ontario, about 35 kilometres south of Hamilton. A runner in the leading assault company, he was "killed by shrapnel from an enemy shell." A week later his platoon commander, Lieutenant A.R. MacKay, wrote to Mitchell's mother to offer words of comfort, describing her son as "cheerful," "well liked," and "very brave." As "a soldier he excelled himself," wrote MacKay, and indeed no higher praise could be offered.[35]

"Falling like ninepins"

By 8:00 a.m., the canal had been thoroughly breached. It was a remarkable feat of arms, perhaps equivalent to what four equally tenacious Canadian infantry battalions would accomplish a generation later when they courageously established a crucial bridgehead at Juno Beach in Normandy. Moreover, while the attacking brigades pushed ahead four more battalions, less than an hour later "the first guns" were also across the ever-expanding gap, charging hard in what soon became one of the decisive engagements of the war.[36]

Following directly behind the 44th Battalion, two companies of the 47th arrived at the sunken road almost at the same time as the men of the 44th. In doing so, the leading platoons sustained "a considerable number of casualties," due in part to "the men's over eagerness taking them into [their] own barrage." Quite likely one of these young men was Private Theodore Caza, a twenty-six-year-old brass buffer from Walkerville, and a Franco-Ontarian by way of Comber, Ontario. Caza had arrived in France on 2 June, along with his younger brother Denny. Both had joined the 47th in the field at Amiens on 14 August. Denny had fallen earlier at the D-Q Line. On this tragic day, after advancing just 100 metres past the canal, Theodore was fatally "hit in the back by a piece of shrapnel." By the time the 47th secured its share of the Red Line, "casualties

Figure 7.1   Private Theodore Caza, 47th Battalion, older brother of Denny, killed in action at the Canal du Nord, 27 September 1918. *Source:* Courtesy of Danielle E. Reaume.

Figure 7.2   Private Frank A. Schefter, 47th Battalion, killed in action at the Canal du Nord, 27 September 1918. *Source:* Courtesy of Clarence Kieffer, Royal Canadian Legion Branch 102.

were quite heavy." In fact, the 47th was nearly crippled in this successful attack by the loss of more than 200 men, including 37 dead. Among them were 9 draftees, including Private Frank Schefter, a factory hand from Walkerton, Ontario. Death came "instantly" that morning for Schefter when he "was shot through the head by a machine gun bullet."[37]

Elsewhere, the 10th Brigade's 50th Battalion became embroiled in a somewhat less difficult though no less dangerous assault. Having jumped past the 46th at about 6:20 that morning, it managed to secure its sector of the Red Line by 7:15 a.m., but not without incurring heavy casualties, particularly at the start of the attack, when Lieutenant-Colonel Page's battalion was savaged by machine-gun fire directly in front of Quarry Wood, where his troops were seen "falling like ninepins." Among the very first of his 125 men to fall was Private Dave Muirhead, a Quaker by faith and a labourer from Pelham Corners near Welland, Ontario, who had been "hit in the chest" by an enemy bullet right at the "'jumping-off' trench."[38]

Farther north, at the centre of the attack and now leading Brigadier-General Griesbach's second-wave assault, was the 1st Battalion. It had quickly leapfrogged the 4th, but in the face of "heavy machine gun fire" found itself in a slow advance to the Green Line, which by 11:00 a.m. it had secured at all points except one. Persistent machine-gun fire, particularly from a "railway embankment" on its right, resulted in about 130 OR casualties, including 20 dead. Among those who perished was Private Joseph Fryer, a twenty-one-year-old farmer and conscript from Acton, Ontario.[39]

Moving in parallel with the 1st was the 13th Battalion, which at the very outset was forced to ford "a stream some three to five feet deep and fifteen to twenty feet across." There, in "water up to their armpits," the Royal Highlanders quickly came "under quite heavy shell and machine gun fire," which resulted in "several casualties."[40] One of them was Private John Shepherd, an electrician from Montreal. Born in Barbados, Shepherd had been "voluntarily" conscripted on 31 October 1917. "Hit by shrapnel in the right leg, right arm and side" during this chaotic crossing, he survived his terrible wounds long enough to be evacuated to No. 30 CCS, where he succumbed two days later.[41]

A bit farther south, at about 10 a.m., Griesbach's 2nd and 3rd Battalions joined the attack, thus initiating a third-wave push to the Blue Line. They too quickly became bogged down at the troublesome railway embankment, where the 2nd Battalion in particular began "to suffer severe casualties" from intense enemy fire. By the time it reached its final objective around 1:00 p.m., the 2nd had sustained nearly 200 OR casualties along with 24 known dead, 11 of whom were conscripts. Among those fatally wounded was Private Clifford Bennett, a medical student from Queen's University in Kingston, Ontario. Ordered initially to "stand fast," the 2nd Battalion had fought its last major engagement of the war.[42]

Lieutenant-Colonel J.B. Rogers's 3rd Battalion, having seized its own share of the Blue Line, was done for the day. It too had just fought its last major engagement as a complete unit. Among 17 dead and 140 wounded ORs were 6 draftees killed and 30 wounded – or about one-quarter of the unit's total losses. They included Privates Joseph Fenech, a Maltese-born labourer from Dunville, Ontario, and Norman Campbell, a craneman from Blind River by way of Tobermory. "Hit in the head and abdomen by enemy shrapnel" while still in the assembly area, Fenech succumbed to these severe wounds at No. 22 CCS in Bucquoy, some 30 kilometres to the rear. Campbell bravely covered 2 kilometres in the battalion's advance before being "hit in the temple by an enemy machine gun bullet." Conscripted in Toronto on 12 April, Private Campbell had not arrived in England until 27 May. After a bit more than thirteen weeks' training, he was dispatched to France in late August and arrived in the field on 6 September. Thus, Campbell's demise on 27 September, in what was his first and only battle, had come exactly four months to the day after his arrival in England – an unenviable record perhaps for the shortest time between a conscript's disembarkation in Liverpool and his death on the Western Front.[43]

"Mort Pour La Patrie"

By this time the 2nd Brigade, now led by Lieutenant-Colonel Gilson, had also entered the fray, first when Major David Philpot's 7th Battalion provided "considerable assistance to the 13th Battalion," and then just prior to noon when this same unit spearheaded the brigade's third-wave attack across the Green Line. The BCR would reach the Blue Line by 2:00 p.m., but by that point it had sustained "200 Other Ranks" casualties, including 36 killed in action, one-third of whom were conscripts.[44] One of these was Private Jim Young, a twenty-six-year-old grocer who had run his own business in Vancouver. Just a few days earlier, he had written his last thoughtful letter home to his mother, reassuring her that he would drop her "a card in a few days," and adding more poignantly, "Don't you worry about me, no news is good news. Even if I become a casualty you will hear right off." A veteran by this time of both Amiens and the D-Q Line, Young and his No. 15 Platoon had been stopped that morning right at the jump-off line by deadly rounds from two German field guns being fired directly at them "over open sights." Three weeks later, Private Young's father, Alfred, a rancher in Chilliwack, would receive this bitter news in a much-dreaded telegram from the Director of Records in Ottawa.[45]

Elsewhere in the 2nd Brigade, the 8th Battalion fought its way past the Green Line and "easily" attained its objective on the Blue Line shortly after 3:00 p.m. The "Little Black Devils" had sustained less than fifty casualties, but most of them appear to have been conscripts. Six of these were initially reported as missing; all were later listed as killed in action. In addition, two other draftees were victims of an air attack: Privates Henri Arnauld, a Franco-Manitoban farmer from Deloraine, and Robert Charmillot, a Swiss-born labourer from Winnipeg. Both were killed instantly "by a bomb dropped from an enemy aeroplane." Arnauld's headstone in Ontario Cemetery would one day read "Mort Pour La Patrie."[46]

As for the 5th Battalion and the "Fighting Tenth," their fourth- and fifth-wave efforts at Haynecourt met with mixed results. Tudor's 5th attacked first at about 3:00 p.m. and managed to reach its final objective, the sunken road east of Haynecourt, with "little difficulty" and on schedule. By this point, 105 ORs had been lost in the assembly and advance, and the battalion found itself enfiladed by machine-gun fire on the right. By the time the 10th Battalion leapfrogged ahead around 5:30 p.m., the 5th's position had become "untenable." In the face of a strong enemy counterattack, it was forced to withdraw nearly

Figure 7.3 Private Jim Young, 7th Battalion, killed in action northeast of Sains-lès-Marquion, September 27, 1918. *Source:* Courtesy of Jim Vallance.

Figure 7.4 Official notification to Alfred Young of his son's death, three weeks after the event. *Source:* Courtesy of Jim Vallance.

CANADIAN PACIFIC R'Y. CO.'S TELEGRAPH
TELEGRAM
FORM T. D. 1

CABLE CONNECTIONS TO ALL PARTS OF THE•WORLD
J. McMILLAN, Manager Telegraphs, Montreal.

```
30nln1bd

                    Ottawa Ont Oct 17 1918

Alfred Young,
   Chilliwack BC.

16686 deeply regret inform you 2020825 Pte James Wellington Young
infantry officially reported killed in action Sept 27th.

                              Director of Records.

1656
```

300 metres to the west of the village, by which time another sixty-three ORs and several officers had fallen. There had been many individual acts of heroism. The "conspicuous bravery" demonstrated by draftee Private James Maguire would be recognized by the award of the Military Medal. Maguire, a store clerk from North Hill Grocery in Moose Jaw, Saskatchewan (by way of Almonte, Ontario), did not live to see it. He died four days later from severe shell wounds to the head and abdomen.[47]

Meanwhile, the 10th had met near disaster. At their jumping-off point east of Haynecourt, Lieutenant-Colonel Eric MacDonald's men encountered stiff resistance and were enfiladed by "several very well placed Batteries of machine guns and field guns" firing at close range. Worse, "two very thick and very wide belts of wire" had to be cut by hand, which delayed progress even further. Fearing the worst, MacDonald halted the advance and sent back an urgent plea that further operations be delayed. Apparently, his plaintive call fell on deaf ears, and the following morning his battalion was ordered to renew the attack. In the meantime, the "Fighting Tenth" had already sustained more than one hundred casualties and at least 20 ORs killed, including 5 conscripts. Among them were 4 American-born draftees, including 2 young farmers: Privates Ben Bunney from Wenham Valley (by way of Missouri), and Carl Haglund from Therien, Alberta, but originally from Minneapolis – both killed by enemy shellfire in this futile and costly attack.[48]

Losses Were Considerable

On the 2nd Brigade's right flank, the 4th Division had not been able to advance much farther than a kilometre or so past the village of Bourlon. First into this key part of the battle had been Lieutenant-Colonel Fred Lister's 102nd Battalion, whose men had swiftly advanced to the Green Line on the edge of Bourlon Wood, only to find that "the Imperials" on their right had been "held up." Shortly thereafter, an enemy shell struck Lister's headquarters, killing his signals officer and several runners and severely wounding both him and his adjutant. In response, Brigadier-General Odlum sent forward Lieutenant-Colonel John Thompson (son of Canada's fourth prime minister) to take command, who promptly moved two companies of the 75th up to reinforce the 102nd just before both units were subjected to a fierce German counterattack. But by late afternoon, Lister's men had achieved their objective, "captured 257 prisoners ... and inflicted heavy casualties." This "great success," however, had come at a high cost, prompting the acting CO, Major E.J. Ryan, to later attribute "failure of the Imperials ... to make good their advance" as the principal cause for the 102nd's heavy losses. Among the battalion's 214 casualties were 44 ORs killed, including 7 conscripts.[49] One of these was Private Norman Markle, a clerk from Hamilton, Ontario, killed "by a shell splinter" at Bourlon Wood. For Alex and Jennie Markle of Galt, Ontario, this devastating news made their worst fears a reality and provided a heartbreaking coda to what had already become a tragic year. Their older son Walter, also a conscript, had died of sickness while in training the previous February. Now Norman was dead as well – on this his twenty-seventh birthday.[50]

Leading the 12th Brigade's third-wave attack on the right was Ralston's 85th Battalion, and on the left Lieutenant-Colonel Stanley Gardner's 38th. Notably, two days earlier the Nova Scotia Highlanders had been dealt a bitter blow. At the train station in Arras, at around 11:30 p.m., an enemy aircraft had dropped a bomb within a few feet of where "C" Company had taken shelter. In the ensuing blast, 9 ORs were killed and 58 wounded. Among them were at least 13 draftees, including Private Archibald March, a twenty-one-year-old sailor, originally from Newfoundland but conscripted in Charlottetown. Struck in the head by shrapnel, March died of his wounds the next day at No. 4 CCS.[51]

By 7:45 a.m. on 27 September, the 85th found itself in position at the Red Line. It soon began a steady push towards Bourlon Village, aided by one section of the 12th Battalion Canadian Engineers. There, while laying "mobile charges," these sappers were savaged by "booby traps and mines."[52] Among their seven casualties was George Schmitt, a twenty-four-year-old butcher from the ethnic German community of Baden, Ontario – killed in this attack when "an enemy shell exploded within a few feet of him." Undeterred, the Highlanders swept through the village largely unopposed and attained the Green Line by 9:45 a.m., eventually sustaining seventy-five OR casualties overall, at least thirty of whom were conscripts. Two of these young men were from PEI – Privates John Davidson, a fisherman from a hamlet 15 kilometres south of Montague, and W.H. Barlow, a twenty-one-year-old farmer from Wellington Station – both killed by shrapnel wounds to the head that fateful morning.[53]

Meanwhile, Gardner's 38th Battalion had made a steady advance to the Green Line and likewise attained its objective, having lost three officers and one hundred other ranks. Among these losses were half a dozen conscripts, including Private Ernest Labrie, a papermaker from Hull, Quebec, who was killed by enemy machine-gun fire.[54] For the 38th, though, its worst day was yet to come.

Leapfrogging Gardner's men at around 10:45 a.m. that morning had been the 72nd Battalion, now led by the newly promoted Lieutenant-Colonel Guy Hamilton Kirkpatrick, who had replaced J.A. "John" Clark on the latter's appointment as the new GOC 7th Brigade. Pushing hard towards the Blue Line without benefit of a barrage, the 72nd quickly encountered deadly "machine gun and point-blank artillery fire [77 mm field guns]." Casualties mounted quickly, but after a fierce all-day assault, the Kilties finally seized the German redoubt at "Pilgrim's Rest Hill" in exchange for "five officers and 228 other ranks" – nearly 38 percent of the unit's trench strength. Among the dead and wounded were at least forty-three draftees. They included Privates Antonio Donatelli, a Canadian-born farmer from Mission, BC, and William Hurley, an "Auto Driver" from Trail, two of the unit's nine conscript fatalities that day.[55]

Elsewhere in the 12th Brigade advance, Kirkcaldy's 78th Battalion had leapfrogged the 85th. By 11 a.m., his hard-charging infantry had "passed through Bourlon Village" and were halfway to the Blue Line when suddenly the Winnipeg Grenadiers found both their flanks fatally exposed. Ultimately the Blue Line would not be taken until 5:00 p.m. By nightfall, having sustained the dreadful loss of 255 men, the unit would be struggling to form two composite companies. One-third of the battalion's forty-seven fatalities were conscripts, including Private William Goodwin, a munitions worker ("Shell examiner") from Orillia. Goodwin had arrived in France in late August after a full twenty-two weeks' training in England and initially had been assigned to the 54th Battalion, only to be fatefully redirected three days later to the 78th.[56]

Kirkcaldy had lost over 43 percent of his men on this first day of the offensive, casualty numbers that were mirrored across the board. Hence, even though this collective sacrifice had produced extraordinary results, Currie's ability to exploit this hard-won success had been seriously compromised. By nightfall on 27 September the Canadian Corps was no longer punching above its weight. Its stunning transit across the heavily fortified Canal du Nord, followed by its explosive advance 6 to 9 kilometres deep into the Hindenburg Line, had unnerved the German high command. But this titanic effort had also savaged the ranks of two Canadian infantry divisions, leaving many units at half strength or less and others reeling from the loss of many junior leaders, men whose experience would be sorely missed in the coming days.

Saturday, 28 September: "The draftees fought well"

Curiously, Currie's "Interim Report" devotes a mere seventy-five words or so to the renewal of the Canadian offensive on 28 September. His personal diary is somewhat more revealing, though, in its mention of his high expectations for taking the Germans' "great distributing centre" at Cambrai "in [just] a few days," which he hoped "might easily mean the fall of Douai," the industrial centre to the north.[57] The actual decision to renew the attack was likely finalized in the afternoon of 27 September, perhaps shortly after Field Marshal Haig and General Horne visited corps HQ, when Haig apparently "told Currie that with [the] Enemy in his present state there was nothing to fear as to his flank!"[58] This remark was undoubtedly a sanguine rejoinder on the part of the C-in-C in response to concerns expressed by Currie about the earlier failure of XVII Corps (on the right) "to keep pace with [the Canadian] advance" and the subsequent exposure of Currie's troops to "severe enfilade Machine Gun fire from the vicinity of Anneux."[59] Nevertheless, zero hour was set for 6 a.m., except for Gilson's 2nd Brigade; its attack was postponed until three hours later so that the 11th British Division on the left and the 4th Canadian Division on the right would have sufficient time to advance and cover Gilson's still open flanks.[60]

From south to north, leading off the renewed Canadian assault were the 9th Brigade under acting commander Lieutenant-Colonel Donald Sutherland, the 7th Brigade under newly promoted Brigadier-General John Clark, and, for the second day in a row, Ross Hayter's "greatly depleted" 10th Brigade.[61] Attacking the prized Marcoing Line (the German army's last organized line of resistance) and the heavily fortified villages of Raillencourt and Sailly early on the morning of 28 September, Hayter's 47th and 50th Battalions straight away encountered deadly enfilade fire from an open flank on their right. "Stiff fighting" followed, but by 11:30 a.m. the 47th had captured its final objective – a crucial section of the railway line east of the Marcoing Line. Losses, however, numbered 71 ORs (out of 409 sent into the attack), and 15 more casualties would be recorded before this unit was relieved the next day, thus bringing the two-day total to 318 other ranks alone. By then, casualties for the month of September had reached an astonishing 77 percent, with 19 OR fatalities in this most recent action. Four of these were draftees, including Private Edwin Frost, a strapping (nearly six foot/181.6 cm) machinist from St. Thomas, Ontario – killed by enemy shellfire on the outskirts of Sailly.[62]

Page's 50th Battalion also fought a pitched battle at the Marcoing Line, suffering 131 casualties and another 17 ORs killed in action before it could claim its own share of the sunken road. Six of its dead were draftees, including Private Dominic Koabel, a twenty-one-year-old dredger from Humberstone, Ontario (near Port Colborne), who was "shot through the chest" at Raillencourt. Later, the CO would note the relatively "small proportion of [men] killed," although in fact, due to cumulative losses, the 50th had also now fought its last major engagement of the war.[63]

Elsewhere, charging hard in the second wave of this attack had been the remnants of Jock Rankin's 46th "Suicide" Battalion, more than two hundred rifles short from the previous day, and on his right, the equally savaged remains of R.D. Davies's 44th Battalion. The 46th had been expected to capture the village of Sancourt, while the 44th had the even more improbable task of advancing nearly 4 kilometres past the jump-off line to seize the village of Blécourt. Neither battalion was aware that the enemy had concentrated its main defences along the Douai-Cambrai (D-C) road, which, as it turned out, proved to be a nearly impregnable barrier. There, "held up by intense machine gun fire" and by a "double belt of wire," Rankin regrouped and prepared for one final assault on the D-C road. And, in another fierce battle with an enemy who "fought extremely well and to the last," the 46th finally established a tentative hold all along this highway, albeit at considerable cost – 100 men, including 17 dead.[64] Among the latter was Private Llewelyn Rushton, a married conscript and farmer from Piapot, Saskatchewan, by way of Cumberland County, Nova Scotia. "Hit in the head by hostile machine gun fire" in front of the Marcoing Line, Rushton died instantly, just one of 370 casualties sustained by the 46th Battalion in two days of bitter fighting. By then the 46th had lost more men in the month of September than at Vimy Ridge and Passchendaele combined. Rankin would later make special note in his after-action report that the "draftees [had] fought well." So they had, and coming from such a seasoned and highly respected veteran, there could be no higher praise.[65]

On the immediate right of this attack, the 44th experienced "heavy resistance ... in Sailly" and also met with "severe M.G. fire from the Douai-Cambrai Road." Counterattacked multiple times in the afternoon, Davies soon found his "companies reduced to the strength of weak platoons," yet the battalion was thrust into the breach *again* later that evening.[66] By 3:00 a.m., a small part of the D-C road belonged to the 44th, although it had been bought at a very high price – 12 officers and 66 ORs dead, and 152 men wounded. This "awful slaughter" had claimed the lives of 20 draftees, including Private Lester Buck, a twenty-one-year-old farmer from Dorchester, New Brunswick. Like its sister battalion the 46th, this unit had lost 711 officers and men in the month of September alone. As a result, while it rested and refitted, the 44th would be out of action for the next three weeks.[67]

Meeting his death "like the splendid man and hero that he was"

On the far right of Currie's battle sector, at the very centre of these three attacking brigades, was the Royal Canadian Regiment led by Lieutenant-Colonel C.R.E. Willets. Dick Willets became an early casualty when an enemy shell struck his dugout shortly after daybreak, severely wounding him and killing his adjutant. Even so, the RCR pressed the attack and made steady progress until it too was temporarily checked by enfilade fire from the village of Raillencourt on its left and by a troublesome open flank on its right. By 12:30 p.m. the RCR had gained command of its share of the Marcoing Line; however, heavy casualties soon forced it to reorganize into three companies. By the time this battle concluded, the ranks of the RCR had been reduced by 272 ORs, from an initial strength of 588. One casualty was Private Herbert Phillips, a twenty-three-year-old fisherman and motor mechanic from Clarke's Harbour, a small village on Cape Sable Island off the southern tip of Nova Scotia. Phillips had been killed by enemy shrapnel, the first RCR conscript to fall in battle.[68]

For the PPCLI, a proud young regiment, this would be a historic day. Tragically, it began with the loss of its beloved CO, Lieutenant-Colonel Charlie Stewart, struck down by enemy shellfire outside Raillencourt early that morning. Nevertheless, the Patricias advanced smartly forward, leapfrogging the RCR and lending much-needed assistance to both it and the 47th Battalion. Early that evening it advanced again in a much larger coordinated attack with the

49th and 116th Battalions. This latter attack proved successful, but the 1 kilometre advance came with very heavy losses. In fact, over just three days the PPCLI sustained no fewer than 380 casualties, including 38 ORs killed in action.[69] Six of their dead and twenty-nine of the wounded were draftees, including Private Frank McGowan, a young munitions worker from Renfrew, Ontario. McGowan's company commander, Lieutenant Ralph MacPherson, would later write to the family to offer his condolences, and recall that their son had been a "willing hand and a cheerful personality" who had earned everyone's "whole hearted admiration for his good work." Young Frank, he added, had met his death "like the splendid man and hero that he was." These kind words would provide scant comfort for the grieving parents, Robert and Matilda McGowan, for only one day later, Frank's older brother, Private Thomas McGowan (a volunteer with the 38th Battalion) would be killed in action as well.[70]

On the 3rd Division's far-right flank, Sutherland's 9th Brigade attacked at 6:00 a.m., and within three hours Lieutenant-Colonel W.K. Chandler's 43rd Battalion had swept through the troublesome German redoubt at Fontaine–Notre-Dame and captured virtually the "entire garrison" therein. On exiting the village to the east, though the Cameron Highlanders ran into "very heavy M.G. fire from the Marcoing Line and further advance had been stopped." Again, casualties were quite heavy – twenty dead by initial estimates, eleven of them conscripts. Among the first of these to fall was Private Andrew Hanson, a logger from Alert Bay, BC, a remote village off the northeastern coast of Vancouver Island. Hanson, a Norwegian by birth, was fatally "hit in the neck and shoulder" by enemy machine-gun fire about 800 metres from the jumping-off trench. Forced to dig in, the 43rd would ultimately suffer 136 casualties over the next twenty-four hours.[71]

For the 52nd and 58th Battalions, hard combat brought even greater casualties than the Camerons had taken. Tasked to "seize the village of St[e] Olle and [more optimistically] the bridgeheads over the Canal [de l'Escaut]," the 52nd quickly found itself pinned down in front of the wire bracing the Marcoing Line, a formidable barrier featuring "two belts of barbed wire twenty-seven metres thick, machine gun posts every nine metres, and a pillbox every eighteen metres."[72] There, the 52nd came "under severe fire and suffered heavily." A second attempt at 4:00 p.m. to continue the advance also failed; the enemy had been strongly "reinforced" and the attacking companies were, by this time, "much depleted in strength." In the carnage that followed, eight conscripts were killed, including Private John Hunter, a thirty-two-year-old carpenter from Winnipeg. Despite having been diagnosed with rheumatism on enlistment, Hunter had found himself in the attack at Ste-Olle when an enemy shell exploded among him and his comrades.[73]

In his after-action report, the 9th Brigade's acting commander, Lieutenant-Colonel Sutherland, cited a number of lessons learned, not the least of which related to poor information flow, principally caused by the "lack of sufficiently trained officers and NCO's." This deficiency, he declared, was compounded by a "short notice" operation that essentially left the remaining "junior officers and N.C.O.'s [with] only a vague idea of what was required of them." For the 52nd Battalion, which had previously suffered more than 275 casualties at the Battle of the Scarpe, the consequences of these shortfalls had been deadly. By the end of this bitterly tumultuous day, the 52nd had bought about 400 metres of additional enemy real estate in exchange for 250 OR casualties.[74]

The 9th Brigade launched one more assault against the ever-strengthening German defences. Shortly after 7:00 p.m. that evening, under cover of a sector-wide barrage, Lieutenant-Colonel Robert "Alex" Macfarlane's 58th Battalion made its own valiant attempt to pierce the Marcoing Line. In the "severe fighting" that followed, one of the two attacking companies was nearly annihilated, although by that time this sector of the German defences had been fully pierced at a cost of 195 men. Sixteen ORs had been killed and seven were missing, the former including Private Nelson Beatty, a conscript and tiremaker from St. Catharines, by way of Kitchener, Ontario, who had just turned twenty-one.[75]

"An attack that should not have been attempted"

Six kilometres to the north, a similar calamity had befallen the 1st Division. Even with a three-hour delayed start, Macdonell's troops could not escape the fury unleashed earlier against Watson and the newly promoted Major-General F.O.W. Loomis and his beleaguered legions in the 3rd Division. The day before, with his flanks dangerously exposed and fearful of "a great wastage of manpower," the 10th Battalion's Lieutenant-Colonel MacDonald had urged that any further advance be "temporarily delayed." But by then, corps HQ had issued orders to resume the offensive the next day, and the 2nd Brigade had tasked the 10th to lead the renewed attack. The creeping barrage, which began at 9:00 a.m., coincided "with the line that the Battalion was holding," thus forcing MacDonald into a scramble to "withdraw [his] forward troops to a place of safety." This artillery error caused "at least 50 unnecessary casualties." The barrage itself, though, was of a "feeble nature" that left the high ground to the north and south in enemy hands. In the words of Dan Dancocks, it was an attack that "should not have been attempted." Indeed, the doomed assault was abandoned, and just one week later MacDonald would cynically describe it as "worse than useless."[76]

Later, this "heroic effort" would be formally recognized by the award of seven Distinguished Conduct Medals (DCMs) and thirty-eight Military Medals, including an MM for Private Charles Michie, a thirty-one-year-old Scottish-born farmer and draftee from Churchill, Alberta. But in the harsh reckoning that followed, it was clear that the 10th Battalion had sustained devastating losses – 38 dead, including 14 conscripts killed outright and another 4 who succumbed to their wounds shortly thereafter. These included British-born Private Edron Anderson and Norwegian-born Private Austin Botnen, both farmers from the Calgary area. Significantly, this unit had lost more than 530 men in the month of September, and post-battle emotions ran very high. One veteran subaltern hotly declared to his CO: "This isn't war, it's murder. It's just pure bloody murder." MacDonald himself was likely inconsolable as well. A week later, after attending a brigade conference, he left for England on leave, not to return until two days after the Armistice. Perhaps his only real consolation was that the 10th had fought its last major engagement of the war.[77]

On the sensitive subject of exposed flanks, here it is useful to recall what the 1st Division commander had to say on this subject thirteen years later: "Flanks would of course, be more or less exposed [wrote Macdonell]; that went with the job, and just as Wellington said, 'People with too nice notions about religion had better keep out of the army,' we felt the same to be true of people with too nice notions about flanks."[78]

As previously noted, the 2nd Brigade's right flank had been left dangerously exposed on the second day at the Canal du Nord, and the 10th Battalion had been left virtually stranded at the apex of this perilous salient. Moreover, despite clear warnings that this tactical situation posed significant risks, the Albertans were still thrust back into the breach. Macdonell may have simply dismissed the protestations of the 2nd Brigade's veteran acting commander, Lieutenant-Colonel Gilson, or possibly Gilson may not have fully conveyed MacDonald's concerns to the GOC – the war diaries are unclear on the matter. But given Macdonell's hard-charging approach and his genuine lack of concern about exposed flanks, it is unlikely that he would have been very sympathetic. In this respect, one cannot avoid the uncomfortable feeling that Macdonell's high confidence in pressing forward against all odds, and his seeming disregard for the attendant risks, had something to do with the fact that neither casualty counts nor significant manpower shortages had yet become one of his primary concerns. As will be seen, Batty Mac would repeat this same tactical error the following day.

The 1st Division's general objective for this second day of battle had been the Canal de l'Escaut, some 9 kilometres to the east, but as Nicholson notes, despite a valiant effort by the 2nd Brigade, "the infantry made no significant advance here."[79] The tactical situation that evening was analogous to the one that had been faced by Currie and Burstall at Vis-en-Artois a month earlier.

Just as German troops had been heavily reinforced at the Fresnes-Rouvroy Line on 27 August, so too had their defences been strengthened all along this part of the Marcoing Line. With the great majority of Canadian infantry battalions now operating at much reduced strengths, the need for an operational pause seemed more urgent than ever. Once again, it was not to be.

A Dangerous Advance Continued

*So it went on for five days, a ding-dong battle, just like two wrestlers in a ring.
When you are locked in a struggle like that you cannot be the one to quit, and
anyway it has never bean [sic] characteristic of the Canadian soldiers to quit.*

– GENERAL SIR ARTHUR CURRIE

Sunday, 29 September: Troops Are Being Used Too Continuously

CURRIE WAS NEVER ONE to quit. The heavily defended high ground northeast
of Cambrai and the prized crossings just beyond along the Canal de l'Escaut
still lay nearly 5 kilometres to the east. Capture of these objectives remained
crucial in order to protect the left flank of the Third Army to the south.
"Convinced ... that each day's attack forestalled a German counter-attack," and
despite earlier "sentimental objections to attacking on the Sabbath," he abandoned
plans for an operational pause and instead struck for a third consecutive day,
then for a fourth and, more surprisingly still, for a fifth.[1] The crucial factor on
this Sabbath – and indeed throughout the titanic struggle that would follow
over two succeeding days – was the overall condition of Currie's thoroughly
exhausted infantry. In his after-action report, the CO of the 42nd Battalion
would write a stinging summary of lessons learned, one that highlighted that
his own troops had not been properly rested, and that sufficient time had not
been made available to properly brief his company commanders or to conduct
essential field reconnaissance. In the end, the assault by this proud Highlander
regiment was deemed a "failure," the source of which is perhaps best summarized by Lieutenant-Colonel Royal Ewing's last and most salient point: "For the
best results the troops are being used too continuously, without an opportunity
to properly reorganize, which is particularly a necessity with regard to N.C.Os,
amongst whom the casualties have been heavy."[2] In this regard, Ewing might
well have been speaking for *all* Canadian infantry battalions engaged in what
soon proved to be a costly and mostly futile effort.

Starting in the south on the inter-corps boundary, Loomis's 3rd Division
planned a three-brigade assault, with the 9th Brigade tasked to "clean up the
Marcoing Line as far south as the Canal [de l'Escaut]." The 8th Brigade was
ordered to capture "the same objectives as were allotted to the 9th Canadian
Inf. Bde the day previous," that is, "the bridgeheads over the Canal." Likewise,

the 7th Brigade was tasked to "advance on the same objectives" that it too had been unable to secure the day before.[3] Zero hour was set for 6:00 a.m.

Attacking the "strongly-held" village of Ste-Olle astride the Arras–Cambrai road for the second day in a row was Major Dougall Carmichael's 116th Battalion, which immediately ran into withering "cross-belts of machine gun fire." Within the hour both leading companies "were practically annihilated," but drawing on effective fire support from a forward battery of 18-pounders, the remaining companies quickly reversed what might have been a complete catastrophe. In one daring attack, Private Williard Woodcock, a thirty-four-year-old draftee from Dwight, Ontario, "volunteered with two others and succeeded in working forward and closing in on [an] enemy gun crew, bombing them out and killing the crew" in the process. For his "fine courage and determination" under fire, Woodcock was awarded the Distinguished Conduct Medal (DCM) – for Other Ranks the Empire's second highest award for gallantry and, without question, a rare honour for any Canadian conscript. Subsequently, the "Umpty-Umps" were able to secure the entire village, albeit at a very steep cost. "A" Company had been reduced to five men, and "B" Company to twenty-five. Fifteen men had been taken prisoner, including two officers and several draftees. Among the latter was Private Norman Dobbs, just twenty years old, who later had a leg amputated at the Göttingen Town Hospital and died just two days before the Armistice.[4] Lost as well in this desperate struggle was Private Oscar Wilde Church, a painter from Hamilton via Woodstock, Ontario, and just one of the battalion's eight conscripts killed in action on this bloody day. Ultimately, the "Umpty-Umps" would fight one more day at Cambrai, but not before the "Band and Bugles" were ordered up to fill the gaping holes in the ranks.[5]

The Most Desperately Fought Engagement of the War

Among the nine Canadian brigades earmarked to force the Canal du Nord, only one had not yet been committed to battle – Dennis Draper's 8th and his four battalions of Canadian Mounted Rifles (CMR), led on this day by the 1st and 2nd CMRs. Both units jumped off at 8:00 a.m. and were stopped almost immediately by heavy machine-gun fire.[6] Eventually, the 1st CMR would seize the crucial junctions of the Arras-Cambrai and the Bapaume-Cambrai roads, but at a high price. For the acting CO, Major W.E. Maxfield, his first taste of battalion command was a bitter one. He lost 9 officers on that day. Also, 73 of his ORs were killed and another 247 wounded – an appalling total of 320. Fourteen draftees were killed outright and about 50 more wounded, including Privates Arnold McQuoid, a schoolteacher from the once-thriving village of Summerberry, and Albert Stephenson, a Methodist minister from Punnichy – both small towns in Saskatchewan. Although born in the United Kingdom,

Stephenson had studied at Mount Allison University before moving west, where he was recruited in early December 1917. The Canadian-born McQuoid originally joined up in March 1916 but was released for reasons unknown, then conscripted in February 1918. Teacher and minister both had been killed in action at Ste-Olle.[7]

The 2nd CMR, led by acting CO Major L.W. Miller, did not fare much better. Besides a misplaced barrage and deadly machine-gun fire from the front and the left flanks, Miller's men had to contend with three "double apron fences" of uncut wire. In their advance to Neuville–Saint-Remy (northwest of Cambrai), they suffered "very heavy casualties," including "most of the officers and many N.C.O.s." Ordered to withdraw late that night, by early the following morning the 2nd CMR had been reduced, "exclusive of Battalion Headquarters," to just "7 Officers and 180 other ranks." In the end, this unit would sustain 281 casualties overall at Cambrai, including 45 ORs killed. Thirteen years later the former CO would describe the action as "the most desparately [sic] fought engagement of the war for our battalion, possibly the most desparate [sic] for the whole corps." Included in this grim tally were twelve conscripts killed and another forty-five wounded.[8]

"Tell all my friends goodbye"

A bit farther north, the left flank of the 3rd Division had been entrusted to Clark's 7th Brigade. The first objective of his 49th Battalion was to capture the village of Tilloy, immediately east of the Douai-Cambrai (D-C) road, where Major A.P. Chattell, the acting CO, had attacked the previous day and had achieved modest gains in exchange for "severe" casualties. "Heavy machine gun fire and gas shelling" overnight had further reduced the ranks, so it was a much-depleted legion that stepped back into the breach at 8:00 a.m. that fateful morning. Due in part to "withering fire from hostile guns on [its open] right flank," it would take three costly hours for the 49th just to reach the D-C road. Then, in the face of strong enemy counterattacks and still well short of Tilloy, the Edmontonians were ordered to "stand fast." By the time the men were relieved two days later, casualties had grown to 320 – fully 50 percent of their initial trench strength. Several draftees were among the dead, including Privates Charles Campbell, a carpenter from Edmonton, and Robert Crowe, a mechanic from Frank, Alberta (on the Crowsnest Pass) by way of Hamilton, Ontario – both "killed by an enemy machine gun bullet."[9]

The 42nd Battalion suffered even more in terms of overall casualties. Their advance was all but doomed by the failure of corps and division artillery assets to blast their way through multiple belts of enemy wire along the D-C road, or to neutralize any of the Germans' deadly machine-gun posts. By the next day,

Lieutenant-Colonel Ewing had lost over half his trench strength – 57 dead and another 263 wounded or missing, including Private Simon Costello, a cashier and draftee from Montreal, via Hawkesbury, Ontario. Badly "wounded by enemy shell fire," Costello was evacuated all the way to Camiers on the coast, only to die of his wounds there some three weeks later.[10]

Farther north still in the centre of Currie's renewed offensive, Major-General Watson again deployed his 12th Brigade despite great uncertainty regarding German efforts to reinforce this sector. Watson's brief diary entries for this day, "so hellish in its intensity," describe clearly what his men endured. Their own barrage was ineffective, the division's flanks were unprotected, enemy aircraft were very active, and enemy shelling took a heavy toll, as did "intense" machine-gun fire. Ultimately, they were forced back by the risk of even greater losses. Yet it might have been much worse. The lead battalions, the 38th on the right and the 72nd on the left, commenced the attack pitifully under strength, with 445 and 373 rifles respectively (headquarters troops included), followed up by the 85th Battalion at 523 ORs and the 78th at only 340 men.[11]

Setting off from its assembly position at zero, the 38th, now led by Major F.A. Rowlandson, crossed the D-C road and straight away came under "intense shell and Machine Gun fire." In fact, nothing had changed in this sector from the day before. "Unable to advance," it was all the Ottawa men could do to hold their positions and await possible reinforcement. One of the first to fall was Private Hector Lalonde, a thirty-five-year-old fireman and draftee from Hull, Quebec, by way of Alexandria, Ontario – "struck in the chest [and killed] by shrapnel." Eventually the 38th was ordered to withdraw "west of the Douai-Cambrai Road," its attack having resulted in no measurable gains.[12] It should not have been a shock to anyone, though, that a severely understrength battalion, making a frontal assault in broad daylight without benefit of surprise, tanks, or an effective artillery barrage, and opposed by a determined and a well-entrenched enemy, should suffer the losses that it did, particularly since so many of its key junior leaders fell at the outset. The real question is whether this particular attack should have been attempted in the first place. Ultimately, over three days, the 38th's casualties would number 368 officers and men – 62 percent of its initial trench strength. Among them were 74 ORs dead or missing, including 22 conscripts.[13]

As for the 78th, now led by its experienced second-in-command, Major John Semmens, and having lost more than 250 men at the Blue Line two days earlier, its anemic numbers would prove no match for these stout German defences. Crossing the D-C road at 1:30 p.m., the 78th encountered "heavy machine gun fire" and was stopped in its tracks. Since "further progress was impossible," the battalion was finally ordered to withdraw to the west side of the road, by which

Figure 8.1 Private Joseph Pleasence, 78th Battalion, killed in action, south of Sancourt, September 29, 1918. *Source:* Chatham-Kent Museum.

time it had sustained sixty casualties. Among the dead were half a dozen reluctant warriors, including Private Joseph Pleasence, a customs officer from Chatham, Ontario. Records show that Pleasence was "instantly killed by concussion from an enemy shell," but other evidence suggests that death did not come so quickly.[14] In early November the *Chatham Daily Planet* published the following poignant letter:

> No doubt you have heard of your son being killed in action long before this reaches you. I did not know him myself but happened to see him and speak to him after he was wounded. It was an attack we Canadians made on the 29th of September. It was a very bad place and I was only speaking to your son for a few minutes, but done all I could for him during that time. I could see that he was badly hit but wasn't in very much pain for he wrote this post card I am enclosing and asked me to send it if I got through all right.
> – PTE T.A. SPINKS H.Q. RUNNER, 78TH BATT. B.E.F.

According to the *Daily Planet* article, the postcard Spinks sent along was "a photograph of Pte. Joseph Pleseance [*sic*]. The handwriting, though distinct, was irregular and appeared to take some effort. It said: 'Don't worry dear Dad and family. Look after Ena. Tell all my friends goodbye. Joe.'"[15]

Among the many other 78th Battalion casualties there is the curious story of Private Alexander Johnston, a thirty-three-year-old Scottish-born handyman from Hamilton, Ontario. Johnston had spent a full six months training in England before joining the 54th Battalion in the field on 23 August. But four days later he was transferred to the 78th, just in time to fight at the D-Q line and in the memorable assault at the Canal du Nord. Then his luck ran out. Private Johnston was "killed by the explosion of an enemy mine ... the evening of 29th September," and after the battle his remains could not be found. For his parents, their only comfort was a thoughtful letter written to them shortly after the battle by Lieutenant Harold Beairsto, a schoolteacher from New Brunswick and commissioned from the ranks, who attempted to console them with a more sanguine view of their son's final moments. "It was hard fighting," he wrote. "The enemy fought stubbornly and well, but before the irresistible dash and doubtless courage of our men he was forced to fall back."[16] Years later, like those of thousands of his comrades, Alex Johnston's sacrifice would be honoured publicly at the Vimy Memorial. As will be shown later in this narrative, though, the search for Canadians missing in battle is a never-ending one, and Johnston's story was not yet complete. In time he too would receive the proper military burial that he rightfully deserved.

Figure 8.2 Private Alexander Johnston, 78th Battalion, killed in action, 29 September 1918. *Source:* Courtesy of Donald Gregory.

"The fiercest scrap the Canadians had had for some time"

Charging well ahead on the left of the 12th Brigade, Lieutenant-Colonel Kirk-patrick's 72nd Battalion initially fared much better in capturing Sancourt, but soon thereafter the Kilties found themselves amidst what one wounded con-script would describe as "the fiercest scrap the Canadians had had for some time."[17] When relieved two days later, the 72nd had been "reduced to 182 all ranks." Among its casualties were two draftees, Privates Joseph DeFerro, an Italian-born teamster from Trail, BC, and G.E. Jones, a Welsh-born "Steam-shovel Cranesman" from Vancouver. DeFerro, just twenty years old in August, had been cut down by enemy shrapnel right at the start of the advance, while Jones, who had joined this unit the previous March, was "wounded in the shoulder, right leg, and testicles by shrapnel from an enemy shell" and "suc-cumbed to his wounds the next day." A dozen more 72nd conscripts made the ultimate sacrifice at Sancourt, 25 were wounded (2 fatally), and 2 were taken prisoner.[18]

Among the 72nd's many wounded was Private Edward Rich, who had won an MM for his actions at the Battle of the Scarpe. Significantly, a fellow draftee would be similarly honoured, when Lance Corporal Orville McKay, a twenty-one-year-old labourer from Westham Island, BC (south of Vancouver), was awarded the Military Medal for his bravery at Sancourt. As for their command-ing officer, the loss of 11 officers and 376 men at the Canal du Nord and beyond undoubtedly weighed heavily on Kirkpatrick's shoulders. Hence, before proceed-ing on "two weeks leave of absence to the United Kingdom," the CO signed off on a candid and provocative report on the "B.W." Operation. "It is an extremely dangerous proceeding to take villages with a very light force," he declared. "Before objectives are allotted to Battalions or Brigades due regard should be given to their strength," something that apparently Watson and Kirkcaldy did not do.[19]

Again, it is puzzling why Currie would have permitted such understrength units to be recommitted so quickly to battle. As historian A.M. Hyatt has noted in his biography of the Canadian Corps commander, Currie "was firmly con-vinced that sending an under-strength unit into battle almost always resulted in greater losses than if that unit had fought under the same conditions at full strength."[20] Therefore, the precise reason why this overarching principle appears to have been abandoned once more on the outskirts of Cambrai remains a troubling mystery. Indeed, while general histories do suggest that the German armies were now in retreat, they were not yet defeated. And so, even though Haig's earlier direction that "operations [were] to be continued without inter-mission" still applied, his strategy also afforded the troops a timely opportunity "to rest." In fact, rest for the troops was something that Currie had clearly anticipated in his own planning. Yet ultimately he did not provide that opportunity after initial successes earlier, either at Arras and at the Canal du Nord.[21]

Ralston and his weary Nova Scotia Highlanders, then facing the full fury of the German defences at Sancourt, would also learn harsh lessons from fighting at such a troop disadvantage. Forced to establish a defensive perimeter around the village, they battled from "exposed positions and [were] under constant fire," prompting the regimental historian to later write that "the story of how they held on that afternoon ... would fill a volume." Over the next two days the 85th Battalion would be reduced to just 224 rifles, having lost over the course of this great battle "sixty-three per cent of its fighting strength." Among its 381 OR casualties were 66 conscripts, including 35 who fell at Sancourt. One of the last of these was Private Manuel Geneau, a farmer from Richmond, PEI. "Wounded in the hip, thigh, and hand by shrapnel from an enemy shell," he received immediate attention, only to die from these wounds three days later at No. 7 Canadian General Hospital in Étaples.[22]

Meanwhile, on the northern edge of this perilous advance, General Macdonell had decided to renew the assault with just one brigade – the 2nd. Lieutenant-Colonel Gilson chose to deploy just one battalion forward – the 8th, which soon discovered that both its flanks were dangerously up in the air, prompting the CO (Lieutenant-Colonel Bug Saunders) to later decry "the full extent to which [his troops] were to reap the fruits of such a hurried affair." Sharp and intemperate words to be sure, but not, it appears, without some substance. Plagued not only by friendly artillery fire that fell catastrophically "short," but also by the same "storm of bullets and shrapnel" that had stopped their sister battalion, the 10th, in its tracks only the day before, Saunders's troops were "forced to withdraw."[23] According to the 2nd Brigade diarist (the Brigade Major), "we had accomplished nothing."[24] Worse, in what would be the 8th Battalion's last major battle of the war, "casualties for this day had unfortunately been heavy." In all, 365 ORs had fallen, including 59 killed in action. Among them was Private Robert Baird, a British-born farmer from Foxwarren, Manitoba. Seriously "wounded in the stomach," Baird succumbed to his wounds the next day at No. 23 CCS – the last of thirty-five conscripts from the 90th Rifles to die over three tumultuous days along this fateful stretch of the Douai–Cambrai road.[25]

Monday, 30 September: "An operation based on false assumptions"

In his "Interim Report," General Currie described the opposition that the corps met on 29 September as "severe," but made no specific mention of the heavy and debilitating losses that the corps had sustained to this point – only that his three attacking divisions had "all made progress." According to the official historian, however, this was another day in which the Canadians had gained little ground. Nevertheless, there does not appear to be any evidence that the commander had any doubts about his next course of action: capture "the bridges over the Canal-de-L'Escaut north of Cambrai and the high ground overlooking the Sensée Valley."[26] But Fergusson's XVII Corps on the right had only just managed to cross the Canal de l'Escaut on 29 September, and his 57th Division would not complete this difficult transit until the following day. So it seems fair to suggest that had Currie taken even a one-day operational pause at this late point, his corps and Fergusson's might well have executed a better prepared and much better coordinated attack on 1 October, one that might have been less costly as well. As Shane Schreiber has sharply noted, "the solution of deliberately building in a pause for battle procedure was for the most part ignored as Currie and his divisional commanders sought to pound their way into Cambrai [for a fourth consecutive day] against an ever-increasing tide of German defenders." Consequently, "as at Amiens and at the D-Q Line, the deadly cycle of diminishing returns began to repeat itself."[27]

According to some historians, the corps commander had no practical alternative – he simply had to press forward.[28] For at least one of Currie's subordinate commanders, though, the lack of a crucial operational pause here, as had normally been done to prepare for previous large-scale Canadian operations, was very much a risky and surprising decision. Watson's 11th Brigade, for example, did not receive official orders to continue the offensive until late on Sunday, thus forcing Brigadier-General Odlum to "conference [his] battalion commanders" late that night (at 11:00 p.m.) for an attack that began at 6:00 a.m. the following morning. In his after-action report, Odlum levelled harsh criticism against his superiors, bluntly asserting that "the failure of the [subsequent] attack was due to the haste in which it was thrown in and the failure to protect the exposed left flank." He went further, declaring that the main reason why "the operation did not go well" was that "it was based on false assumptions, namely that the enemy was beaten and would withdraw." More important, all of Currie's attacking battalions were understrength – some like the 75th severely so – and all would ultimately suffer severe casualties in exchange for extremely limited gains.[29]

A Disastrous Turn

Odlum's brigade major issued final orders for this attack at 2:20 a.m. on 30 September, placing the 75th Battalion in the lead with the 54th following in close support and with the 87th arching to the south towards Eswars. The

Mississauga Battalion, still under the temporary command of Lieutenant-Colonel John Thompson, managed "good progress" early on, but then things took a disastrous turn. About 650 metres east of a railway cutting that had earlier scarred the 78th, 85th, and 38th Battalions, Thompson's men came under "very heavy machine gun fire," from Blécourt to their left front and, more dangerously, from Sancourt in their left rear. In short order this devastating enfilade forced the 75th and 54th Battalions back to the railway itself. In the carnage that followed, the 75th was reduced to just three officers and "about 75 other ranks."[30] By late the next day, 8 officers were dead and 16 wounded, along with 75 ORs killed and another 280 wounded – overall a stunning loss of 379 men. Sixteen of the dead were draftees, including Privates James Wilson and Thomas Squair, both from Toronto. Wilson, a candymaker, had previously served three years with the Queen's Own Rifles (QOR). Private Squair, just twenty-one years old, had worked as a "solderer." A "well known West End athlete" in Toronto, young Squair had excelled in hockey and baseball. Curiously, the records do not reveal precisely how any of these men died, the details having been lost no doubt with the twenty-four officers and countless NCOs who also fell this day.[31]

Similarly, while Lieutenant-Colonel A.B. Carey's 54th Battalion and K.M. Perry's 87th achieved modest success, their small triumphs were bought at a steep price, fate and a run of bad luck having intervened at the outset. Almost immediately after zero hour, the enemy counter-barrage opened up: Carey himself was slightly wounded, and his adjutant killed. Perhaps worse, his deputy CO, Major Ben McDiarmaid, was also killed. It appeared, moreover, that "the Boche was attacking in great strength," and thus the primary objective of the 54th was changed to an all-out effort "to stay this attack in force." By day's end the battalion had sustained 205 total casualties, including 25 dead ORs. Six draftees were among this latter group.[32]

The 87th Battalion's tale was even more tragic. Moving forward at 7:55 a.m. with a fighting strength of 21 officers and 456 other ranks, the Canadian Grenadiers were stopped cold by "heavy shelling and heavy machine gun fire" just 500 metres from the JOL. There Perry's men were "badly cut up" and forced to hunker down for most of the day along a "portion of the Railway Cutting."[33] "Lying out in the open" under heavy fire was a "near calamity" for this deeply wounded unit, which suffered another 312 casualties while able to do "nothing."[34] Among them were 14 conscripts killed or who died of wounds, including Privates Frederick Johnston, a munitions worker from Sherbrooke, Quebec (born in Bombay, India), and T.F. (Thomas) Hilson, a brickmaker from Milton, Ontario.[35] Two days later, Perry would reward about one-quarter of his surviving soldiers for their conspicuous bravery north of Cambrai, recommending no fewer than 31 of them for the Military Medal. Only one went to a conscript – Private Rene Archambault, a twenty-four-year-old painter from Montreal.[36]

"Ordered to attack again – it was suicide"

The heavy Canadian losses in front of Sancourt and Blécourt on this fourth consecutive day of battle would soon be the focus of recrimination and of key lessons learned. Odlum's understrength 11th Brigade had been put to a severe test for precious little gain. Lacking nowhere near the support promised, his attacking battalions had been savaged and had suffered a near decapitating blow across all key leadership positions. All was not lost, however. Leading off the 3rd Division's assault at 6:00 a.m., J.A. Clark's 7th Brigade had attacked for its third consecutive day. Although desperately short of men and low in morale (Corporal Will Bird's mates in the 42nd Battalion thought the attack "suicide"), Clark's intrepid warriors still managed to achieve impressive results in the early going. For example, the PPCLI, led by the acting CO, Captain G.W. Little, and operating at "just a little over single-company strength," had advanced almost all the way through the heavily defended village of Tilloy.[37] But in what David Bercuson has described as "one of the costliest Patricia battles of the war," lack of crucial manpower nearly proved to be the regiment's undoing.[38] Two hours into the fight, casualties began to mount, and soon the PPCLI was compelled to call up a company of the 49th Battalion for support, after which fierce resistance and "heavy casualties" forced the "badly disorganized" Patricias to dig in along the Blécourt-Tilloy road. Among their wounded were another half-dozen draftees, including Private George Skipworth, a twenty-three-year-old express messenger from Lindsay, Ontario, the hometown, it should be noted, of the former militia minister, Sam Hughes, who once had vowed that there would be no place for anyone but volunteers in the CEF.[39]

On the left flank, the RCR, supported by a composite company of the 42nd, had also made a quick albeit costly start. Despite "intense Machine Gun fire ... from both flanks," one of its companies briefly made it 1,500 metres to the east. Among the battalion's "considerable casualties" at this point was Private Clarence Reynolds, a twenty-two-year-old machinist and draftee from Murray Harbour, PEI. "Hit in the heart by an enemy machine gun bullet" near the "railroad West of Tilloy," Reynolds has no known grave. With its north flank utterly exposed, the RCR was forced to fall back a full kilometre, thus bringing to a bitter end the valiant efforts by the 7th Brigade to take the high ground east of the D-C road.[40]

Even now, though, the Canadian Corps was not done with the German army north of Cambrai. Early in the afternoon of 30 September, Currie cancelled phase two of the attack (not yet under way) and decided "to defer any further action" until the next day for what would be one last, five-division assault to secure the corps' elusive objectives.[41] That he convinced himself to take such a perilous course of action, even after acknowledging that the enemy clearly intended to hold its positions "at all costs," remains perhaps Currie's single most troubling and contradictory decision of the war. Indeed, because this fateful choice would spell the near destruction of two of his divisions, it is essential to consider Currie's rationale for pressing ahead, the essence of which he documented in his "Interim Report":

> The tremendous exertions and considerable casualties consequent upon the four days' almost continuous fighting had made heavy inroads on the freshness and efficiency of all arms, and it was questionable whether an immediate decision could be forced in the face of the heavy concentration of troops which our successful and, from the enemy's standpoint, dangerous advance, had drawn against us. On the other hand, it was known that the enemy had suffered severely, and it was quite possible that matters had reached a stage where he no longer considered the retention of this position worth the severe losses both in men and moral [sic] consequent upon a continuance of the defence.[42]

Notwithstanding the successful advances of the first two days of this epic battle, Currie had overwhelming evidence that the enemy was willing to absorb "severe losses" in a "continuance of the defence." As historian W.S. Wallace recorded less than a year later, the tactical situation had completely changed: "The Germans were now fighting with their backs to the wall, and were resisting with the energy of despair. The Canadians moreover, had now been fighting for four days, and were exhausted in strength and depleted in numbers. It would appear that they had achieved all that could reasonably be expected of them."[43]

More significantly still, perhaps, the Canadian Corps (supported by the 11th British Division) would be "the only part of First Army actively engaged on 1st October." In this context, since General Horne did not order the Canadians back into action, it seems clear that had Currie chosen not to attack, or at least directed a temporary pause in operations, Horne likely would have quickly acquiesced.[44] Emboldened, however, perhaps by an ongoing flow of reinforcements and by the implicit support of key subordinates, and encouraged by the return of Burstall's revitalized 2nd Division, Currie dismissed any personal doubts and chose to gamble once more. But as historian Tim Travers points out, Currie and his division commanders "had underestimated the opposition of the German Seventeenth Army." What followed the next day would give rise to much "soul-searching."[45]

Tuesday, 1 October: The Canadian Corps Is Pushed to Its Limits

For many weary soldiers in the Canadian Corps, the decision to fight on for a fifth consecutive day came as quite a surprise. "We expected that the Corps command would call the battle off in view of the stiff opposition," recalled signaller Wilfred Kerr (11th Battery, CFA).[46] Likewise the 13th Battalion "was rather surprised" that it was to make an attack the following morning, having just "moved into Divisional Support."[47] No doubt this same sentiment was held by many others, including Brigadier-General Odlum, who had been "ordered to prepare to attack once more" despite the costly failure of the previous day.[48] Nonetheless, the Canadian Corps would make a synchronized assault at 0500 hours, this time with four divisions attacking "simultaneously" – the 11th British and the 1st, 3rd, and 4th Canadian. A fifth division, Burstall's 2nd, would be prepared to exploit success should the opportunity arise. The "general objective" would remain unchanged: seize the high ground to the north of Cambrai and the canal crossings to the east of the city. As will be seen, success in both endeavours would again depend very heavily on the ability of the 11th Division to protect the left flank of the corps.[49]

This crucial part of the narrative begins then not with a Canadian unit but with a British battalion – the 6th York and Lancaster Regiment – which was operating on the right flank of the 32nd Brigade (11th Division). Its daunting task was to penetrate the Marcoing Line, advance 1,500 metres, and secure the heavily defended railway embankment just north of Abancourt, thus providing crucial flank protection for Griesbach's 1st Brigade. It was not to be. While the "York and Lancs" made good initial progress, a "belt of wire of great thickness" coupled with "intense shell and machine gun fire ... caused heavy casualties." Any "further advance" by the 6th was deemed "impossible," and it was forced to retire.[50] Indeed, this single tactical failure at a critical time and place imperilled not only the advance of the 1st Brigade but, in a domino effect, the fortunes of the entire Canadian Corps as well.

The 1st Brigade's formidable task had been to take the German redoubt at Abancourt and, "if possible," capture the Abancourt Spur, thus giving these men "command" over three key villages to the south – Blécourt, Bantigny, and Cuvillers – which were the principal objectives of Tuxford's 3rd Brigade to the right. To accomplish the former, Griesbach deployed two relatively fresh but understrength battalions in a two-phase assault – the 1st, led by Lieutenant-Colonel Walt Sparling, and the 4th, led by Lieutenant-Colonel Lafayette Harry Nelles. The "Mad Fourth" made a rapid advance early on, but when the York and Lancs faltered on the left, the battle at Abancourt suddenly took a grim and decisive turn. "Large numbers of enemy machine guns" were suddenly turned south in order to "bring a plunging fire to bear on the attacking companies of the 4th Battalion," and shortly thereafter orders were issued "that no further advance was to be made." Nelles's losses eventually totalled almost 180 men. Half a dozen draftees were among the dead or dying, including Private Ralph Crawford, a mechanic from Calgary, but born in Des Moines, Iowa. A veteran in every sense of the word, Crawford had joined the battalion in the field on 22 May and had been slightly wounded in September. On this fateful morning, an enemy bullet "penetrated the side of his skull through his steel helmet, instantly killing him."[51]

Unaware of the tragic drama unfolding to the north, Walt Sparling's 1st Battalion jumped off to an equally good start, despite a supporting barrage that featured "numerous shorts." One company commander would later lament: "There is nothing more demoralizing to troops than to be in the fire of their own guns." Soon thereafter, Sparling's attackers were driven into defensive positions by heavy machine-gun fire from the front (Abancourt) and by enfilade fire from the left (Blécourt). Further "movement of any kind was impossible." When finally relieved at 1900 hours, this unit had lost another 12 officers and 183 men – several to friendly fire. One of the 25 dead ORs likely to have fallen in this friendly barrage was Private Leo Dennis, whose remains were never fully identified. Young Dennis had been drafted the same day as his Windsor, Ontario, neighbour, Private Walter Campeau, also killed in this attack.[52] While the war was not yet over for the 1st Battalion, it too had fought its last major engagement.

Less than one week later, Brigadier-General Griesbach uncharacteristically offered a scathing indictment of those forces that had been tasked to protect his left flank. After acknowledging that the British units had gone "forward with great courage and determination," he sharply added: "They failed for no other reason than that there were not enough of them. The task was entirely beyond them and in my judgement they were most improperly employed."[53] This bitter analysis may have been correct, but given what he and his superiors knew at the time (in particular about the enemy's increasingly fierce opposition in the face of tired and depleted Canadian formations), Griesbach's own planning, not to mention that of Macdonell and Currie, should have carefully taken into account the very low probability that the 11th Division – or for that matter the doomed men of the 1st Brigade – would somehow find a way to succeed that morning. Perhaps a one-day pause to permit the relief of the 11th by the 56th Division might have made a difference in the outcome, but if so, the same could be said for the 1st Division, whose worst ever battlefield reverse would be mirrored elsewhere in the corps.

"Bitter disappointment was felt at having to fall back"

Farther south still, Tuxford's 3rd Brigade had been assigned an equally formidable task – attack eastwards past Sancourt into the "Ravine de Bantigny" and capture Blécourt, Bantigny, and Cuvillers, all of which were, ominously, in the shadow of the crucial heights of Abancourt to the north. To accomplish this difficult task, one that had earlier stymied the 11th and 12th Brigades, Tuxford ordered his 13th, 14th, and 16th Battalions into the fray. Within just three hours, Major Ian Sinclair's 13th had wholly invested the village of Blécourt, but at that point the "Huns had suddenly appeared on [his open] left flank in large numbers" firing "field guns at point blank range." Quickly finding their positions "quite untenable," Sinclair's men were forced to retire to a sunken road on the southwest edge of Blécourt, where they remained until relieved later that night. By that time the Highlanders counted sixteen dead among their ninety casualties, including several draftees.[54]

Meanwhile, Lieutenant-Colonel Worrall's 14th Battalion (375 rifles) had leapfrogged past the 13th about an hour after zero and had captured Blécourt, when suddenly events began to take a decidedly negative turn, both for Worrall's men and for the 16th "Canadian Scottish" then attacking Cuvillers less than half a kilometre away to his right. What followed next might very well have been one of the most chaotic and traumatic episodes in the history of the 3rd Brigade, if not the 1st Division as a whole.[55]

The 16th Battalion had swept through Cuvillers and had quickly pushed forward nearly another kilometre to the east when suddenly the acting CO, Major Roderick Bell-Irving, found himself all but stranded in a tiny salient with both flanks "in the air." Moments later, Bell-Irving was dead – "shot through the head by a rifle or machine gun bullet." Worse still, in the chaotic minutes that followed, a cascading flow of German heavy weapons descended with a vengeance on all Canadian attackers, rolling them back like vertical window shutters rapidly closing with deadly effect. Despite mounting a stalwart defence, the 16th soon found that its "tactical position ... was little short of desperate."[56] Supported by Lieutenant C.G. Warner's J Battery of eight heavy machine-guns (1st Battalion CMGC), the remnants of the Canadian Scottish withdrew about 1,000 metres to the southwest. In the process, Warner's men suffered heavy casualties of their own – six killed or missing, including three conscripts. Among these were two farmers from Saskatchewan: Privates Rupert MacCready and Arthur Gilbert, both of whom had turned twenty-one just the previous month. MacCready, who had had a premonition of his death right after the attack at the Canal du Nord, was "hit in the neck by an enemy shell splinter which severed the jugular vein."[57] Days later a saddened comrade wrote to Rupert's mother with a few words of comfort, telling her that her son had "died as a man, and a

GOOD NOBLE man."[58] As for Private Gilbert, he too suffered a serious shrapnel injury that morning, in his case to "the inner part of the left leg." His sergeant dressed the wound, but, given the worsening situation, "could do nothing to remove him" and was forced to leave the young lad behind. Gilbert was taken prisoner and died of his wounds twelve days later in Göttingen, Germany.[59]

Around this time, the 16th Battalion also came under surprising enfilade fire from behind and, "in the midst of considerable confusion," was forced to withdraw again, this time to a sunken road about another 800 metres farther to the west. By then, the battling Canadian Scottish had been "reduced to three officers and 75 men," at which point their beloved CO, Lieutenant-Colonel Cy Peck, arrived to reassume command.[60] But Tuxford wisely chose to cancel Peck's bold plan to renew the attack – a course of action that must have seemed almost heretical to the division commander, who was then faced with the bleak prospect of his formation's first major tactical defeat since Second Ypres. Seemingly oblivious to mounting losses, Macdonell decided that further attacks must still be made in order to achieve the day's objectives. To his great credit, Brigadier-General Tuxford "advised strongly against" these proposals, and eventually Batty Mac agreed, though it was a bitter pill to swallow. In what General Horne later described as "probably the most severe [fighting] experienced on the First Army front during the whole operations from the battle of Arras to the final capture of Mons," Macdonell's wounded formation was forced to conduct a retirement (i.e., a retreat) under fire, the likes of which the 1st Division had rarely experienced.[61]

Apart from the fact that he had lost two hundred men in this largely futile assault, Lieutenant-Colonel Worrall (14th Battalion) would record that "bitter disappointment was felt at having to fall back." His overall fatalities were relatively low, but half of those dead were draftees, including two young labourers: Privates Frederick Martin from Verdun and Adrien André from Saint-Polycarpe, Quebec. In addition, some of Worrall's men had been taken prisoner, one of whom was Private James Coughlin, also a labourer and draftee from Montreal, who was "presumed to have died" three-and-a-half weeks later "at Fortress Hospital, Cologne." Within a week, however, Worrall's losses would be made up by fresh reinforcements, including "a draft of 171 French Canadians" that arrived on 5 October.[62]

On 2 October the battered 16th moved back into reserve, where Cy Peck retired to his "dug out – sick all day," perhaps due in part to dyspepsia but principally due to the effects of a "gas shell."[63] Given his battalion's very heavy casualties, it is likely that Peck was mentally unnerved as well. Besides having lost his most trusted subordinate (Major Bell-Irving) and a dozen other officers, his unit had suffered the devastating loss of 345 men overall, their worst single day of the war. "The 16th Battalion had [also] fought its last major engagement of the war." Not since Vimy had so many Cameron Scottish died or been wounded in a single day, and never had so many been taken prisoner. Of the battalion's 333 total OR casualties, more than 100 were draftees, including 28 who made the ultimate sacrifice. Among these were two young farmers killed by machine-gun fire near Cuvillers: Privates R.R. Gordon from Glevennah, Alberta, but born in Cayuga, Ontario, and Rosario Grégoire from Bruxelles, Manitoba, but raised in Saint-Isidore, Quebec. And nearly seventy of Peck's men were taken prisoner. More than thirty of these were conscripts, including Privates Kingsley Poole, a storekeeper from Winnipeg, via Cornwall, Ontario, and Sidney Smith, a farmer from Pilot Mound, Manitoba, by way of London, England. Both men had been wounded at Cuvillers; both succumbed to their wounds less than two weeks later while in captivity in Germany.[64]

Not all of the 16th POWs were so unfortunate. Years later, Private Frank Appel, a twenty-two-year-old farmer originally from Clover Valley, BC, would recall that the regimental sergeant major (James Kay) had exhorted his desperate men to save their ammo, "let the enemy get close, and then let them 'have it' with the bayonet" – a spell-binding moment documented in the unit's official history. Unfortunately for Appel, his section "had gone too far," and the men "were being picked off by a sniper." Soon thereafter they were all taken captive. It would then be five gruelling days by train and by forced march – nearly 550 kilometres deep into the heart of Germany – before the Germans even fed the prisoners. Fortunately, the war was in its final phase, and mercifully, Private Appel's stay at the notorious Neiderzwehren POW Camp would be short.[65]

"Just as well as the old fellows"

For Watson and his 4th Division, the challenge posed by this latest short-notice operation had been matched only by the great dilemma of having to select a fresh brigade to lead the renewed assault. Only Odlum's less than half-strength 11th Brigade seemed even modestly capable of taking the lead to capture the canal crossings at Eswars. Odlum, having extracted a solemn (but hollow) promise from Watson that his brigade's left flank would be protected, resigned himself to this near impossible task and ordered the 102nd Battalion (Major John Bailey) to advance 3.5 kilometres east to the Blue Line – a dangerous route running southeast from Cuvillers to Ramillies on the Canal de l'Escaut. After that, the hollow shell of Lieutenant-Colonel Perry's 87th Battalion was to "leap-frog and exploit to the CANAL, capturing ESWARS and establishing a bridgehead."[66]

Jumping off at 0500 hours, south of Sancourt and just east of the deadly "railway embankment," Bailey's two leading companies advanced quickly and within ninety minutes had captured both the Blue Line and a large number of prisoners. Afterwards the 102nd fought off at least four counterattacks, all in exchange for about 150 casualties – 12 ORs killed and at least another 131 wounded or missing.[67] Among them were many "draftees," who, according to one eye-witness, performed "just as well as the old fellows."[68] They included Private George Coulter, a pint-sized labourer (only 156 cm/5'1½" and 51.7 kg/114 lbs) from Novar, Ontario, who had arrived in France on 10 May and was very much a veteran in every respect. Just a month short of his twenty-first birthday, Coulter had been severely wounded in the groin; he was evacuated, but later succumbed to his wounds at No. 30 CCS.[69]

Meanwhile, Perry had reorganized his decimated 87th Battalion into one company of "very tired men," who jumped off at 0530 hours and quickly advanced nearly 3 kilometres. By mid-morning, one patrol had even succeeded in reaching "the outskirts of Eswars" – the deepest penetration of enemy lines across the entire Canadian front this day. At that point, however, the game was up. Limited firepower, heavy opposition, open flanks, and successive German counterattacks all combined to force these troops back nearly 1 kilometre or risk being totally annihilated. By late afternoon the Grenadier Guards had been reduced to a fighting strength of less than eighty men all ranks – a 40 percent casualty rate.[70] Most would be quickly replaced by new men, including one draft of 197, who, as the diarist pointedly noted, "turned out to be almost all French Canadians."[71] They took the place of men like Private Arthur Papillon and Private Albert Miller, both from Quebec City and both wounded near Blécourt on 30 September. Papillon, a twenty-five-year-old butcher by trade, died of his wounds the following day, while Miller, a twenty-one-year-old carter, perished three days later. Even so, just two weeks later the 87th once again marched nearly five hundred men back into the line.

"Faithful unto death"
Elsewhere on this fifth and final day of Currie's Canal du Nord offensive, there remained one other Canadian formation still fully engaged (Loomis's 3rd Division), and one other division still eagerly awaiting its chance to re-enter the fight (Burstall's 2nd). For his part, Lieutenant-Colonel Don Sutherland (9th Brigade) chose to employ all four of his battalions in yet another attempt to capture the high ground overlooking Pont d'Aire and the village of Ramillies some 3 kilometres to the east.[72] Leading off at zero hour (0500 hours), the 52nd Battalion (436 rifles strong and apparently led at this critical point by the adjutant Captain Gerald Rutherford, a barrister in civilian life) made excellent progress early on, and not long thereafter captured the "high ground." But on cresting the ridge and "pressing forward down the reverse slope," the 52nd

suffered "very heavy" losses – more than one hundred OR casualties overall.[73] Among the dead and dying were eight conscripts, including Private Roger Richard, a farmhand from St. Ambroise, but originally from Pigeon Lake, Manitoba. Wounded in the attack, Richard, a "North American Indian," survived the action only to perish three days later at No. 4 Canadian CCS near Duisans, west of Arras.[74]

In the meantime, on the brigade's right flank, Chandler's 43rd Battalion had also got off to a quick start. Seizing the first objective, the village of Tilloy, the battalion halted for fifteen minutes while waiting for the barrage to move up, but in doing so it again suffered a "considerable number of casualties." In fact, by 1000 hours "A" Company had been reduced to just fifteen men. The remainder of the battalion pressed resolutely forward to the high ground overlooking Pont d'Aire before it too was stopped cold by the withering machine-gun fire blistering the reverse slope beyond. Then, as the diarist would chillingly record, around 1500 hours "the whole of the left flank of the Corps was observed moving slowly back, apparently without reason and without leaders." Subsequently, the casualty ledger for the Cameron Highlanders would include another 233 names – 22 dead, 186 wounded, and 25 missing. Twenty conscripts were killed outright; a dozen more were fatally wounded or missing and three of the latter were later declared dead. Among them were Privates David Cook, a Toronto-born "Cowpuncher" from 105 Mile House, BC, and Frank Hook, a British-born farmer from Wide View, Saskatchewan. In time, Cook's father George, a Scot, would add these simple but poignant words to his son's headstone at Mill Switch British Cemetery outside Tilloy: "He Nobly Died." Alice Hook of Maidstone, England, would similarly inscribe her own son's grave marker with the haunting phrase: "Faithful Unto Death."[75]

Elsewhere, the 58th Battalion, having been reduced only two days earlier on the Marcoing Line to three understrength companies (320 rifles), was forced to bring up "29 men drawn from the bands." Then, having passed through the 43rd Battalion, it too descended across the deadly reverse slope, where it straight away ran into the same angry jaws of machine-gun and mortar fire that had stymied its sister battalion. Shortly thereafter, "heavy casualties" and a late afternoon German counterattack forced Macfarlane's men back nearly 1 kilometre from the canal. By then they had sustained the astonishing loss of 366 comrades, including 42 dead ORs, 7 of whom were conscripts.[76]

Further evidence of the impossible task laid before the 9th Brigade is provided in official and other historical accounts of the 116th Battalion, which, despite jumping off last, did not fare any better than the lead assault units. Major Dougall Carmichael himself "was badly wounded in the face" as he crossed the D-C road, and "owing to blood loss" was forced to transfer his command to the next senior officer – Captain E.P.S. Allen. Nonetheless the "Umpty-Umps" made excellent progress early on, until they too crested the villainous ridge above Ramillies, where the tide immediately turned. A rushed assault there by a severely understrength battalion against a "well organized system of enemy defences" once again had predictable and devastating consequences, most notably 140 casualties. Among the dead and dying were another seven draftees, including Private Francis Shannon, a shipbuilder from Collingwood, and Private John Woodcock, a "Bushman" from Dwight in the Muskoka district of central Ontario. Shannon sustained severe shrapnel injuries to the "back and legs" and died of his wounds two days later. As for John Woodcock, his father William had seen two of his sons conscripted the previous February. Williard, the eldest by one year, would return safely home, having been decorated with a DCM for his bravery at Cambrai. Younger brother John, however, lies buried today in the Mill Switch British Cemetery, not far from where he fell and right on the Douai-Cambrai road.[77]

"Situation is not very good"

In a coda to this epic battle, Harry Burstall mistakenly assessed "that the attack on October 1st might progress rapidly." He therefore charged his "commanders to push forward as rapidly as possible" and "to be ready to take chances" – their ultimate and most improbable goal being to seize the distant crossings on the river Erclin south of Iwuy, 7 kilometres to the northeast.[78] But Burstall's optimistic assumptions, particularly with regard to enemy troop dispositions, would prove to be largely false.

The 6th Canadian Infantry Brigade, led since April 1918 by Brigadier-General Arthur Bell – a professional soldier – had been tasked by Burstall to "pass through the 3rd Canadian Division as soon as that Division ha[d] established one or more bridge heads over the canal." In yet another testament to a rushed and heavily compressed staffing process, Bell was unable to meet his COs until 0200 hours; thus, his brigade orders were not issued until 0400 – just one hour before zero.[79] In the event, no bridgeheads would be established this day. Despite reports that the advance of the 1st and 4th Canadian Divisions on his left had been checked, and despite harbouring doubts that the 3rd Division (9th Brigade) "had reached the Canal de L'Escaut," Burstall ordered the 6th Brigade to press forward and "force the crossings." Almost simultaneously, at 1130 hours, the 6th Brigade reported that the "situation [was] not very good," particularly on its worrisome flanks, after which Bell's brigade major flatly informed Division HQ that "it was not deemed advisable to try for the bridges at the present." At that point Burstall finally recognized that the canal could not be forced "without suffering very heavy casualties"; therefore he ordered Bell's troops to "stand fast." Indeed, the GOC's urgent new task was to stem the tide of successive counterattacks from the north and thereby prevent what must then have appeared to be the ever-growing possibility of a major battlefield reverse. Currie's last ditch all-out offensive had reached a tipping point. No longer was this attack simply a battle for the crossings at the Canal de l'Escaut; quite surprisingly, it was fight for the survival of the Canadian Corps itself.[80]

All four of Bell's battalions were engaged this day. The 27th, led by Major Ken Patton, had deployed northeast of Tilloy, where the deadly threat to the north eventually claimed over 110 OR casualties. Among them were several conscripts, including Privates Christman Swanson and Charlie Weber – both farmers, from Glenboro and Virden, Manitoba, respectively.[81] Likewise Alex Ross's 28th Battalion, operating farther north and on Patton's left, had sustained "several casualties" from a hostile left flank as it crossed the Douai-Cambrai road. The frightening spectacle created by "a large number of 1st Canadian Division men ... coming back through our lines" prompted Ross to quickly withdraw his own troops in order to establish a defensive flank for the brigade. This timely manoeuvre no doubt helped stem the German tide, but by then the 28th had sustained another hundred casualties. Among them was Private Arthur Lamoureux, a thirty-five-year-old Quebec-born farm labourer and draftee from Vonda, Saskatchewan, who was "killed by splinters from an enemy high explosive shell."[82]

In the meantime, Ross was summoned to the 6th Brigade headquarters to replace Brigadier-General Bell, who had been wounded in the chest by enemy shellfire. Likely unnerved somewhat by the loss of a tested commander, and by events which seemed to be quickly spiralling out of control, Burstall ordered all 2nd Division units "to dig in and be organized for defence in depth."[83] None too soon it would seem, since most evidence at that moment strongly suggested that the German Seventeenth Army was not done yet. As war correspondent J.F.B. Livesay later recalled, "our losses had been so severe, our reserves so freely drawn upon, that there was anxiety on all hands that night as to whether the morning might not see a last final thrust such as we might be in no condition to fight off."[84]

"The dash and magnificent bravery of our incomparable infantry"

While the planned five-division assault of 1 October may not have been a complete catastrophe for Currie and the Canadian Corps, it was undoubtedly a bitter disappointment, the human cost of which cast a dark shadow over the earlier and extraordinary victory at the Canal du Nord. More importantly, perhaps, the harsh reality was that after three more very costly days, the primary objectives – the canal crossings east of Cambrai at Pont d'Aire and Eswars –

remained beyond the reach of the Canadians. As historian W.S. Wallace observed, "nothing like a German collapse [had] occurred."[85] With his troops totally exhausted and his infantry mostly spent, Currie was finally compelled to accept the obvious: "To continue to throw tired troops against such opposition," he wrote, "without giving them an opportunity to refit and recuperate was obviously inviting a serious failure."[86] But while this much belated decision "to break off the engagement" was welcomed by all, it was in fact General Horne who decided "that no further attack was to be made" and who ordered the Canadians to "reorganize in depth."[87]

Two days later, Currie's "special order" of the day would heap great praise on the Canadian Corps, and in particular on "the dash and magnificent bravery of our incomparable infantry." But while their triumphs had been many, the human cost had been great. As one regimental historian remarked, "defeat had been avoided but victory had escaped the Canadians' grasp."[88] It had also been a very close thing. Consequently, Currie's division commanders heartily welcomed plans for their relief by XXII Corps, but again it was not to be. Instead, the Canadian Corps would be required once more to renew the siege at Cambrai in cooperation with the Third Army.

Over the next week, the entire area remained a seething cauldron of fire. "We had not seen such shelling since Passchendaele," recalled one veteran. Similarly, General Watson would record that the "Bosche planes [were] very active," resulting in one engagement of particular note, the aftermath of which was later summarized in the *Supplement to the London Gazette:*[89]

2129336 Pte. C. McDonald, 27th Bn., Can. Inf.
For conspicuous gallantry and devotion to duty north of Cambrai on 3rd October, 1918. When one of our aeroplanes was crashed in our front line, the pilot being killed and observer badly wounded and the area subjected to heavy fire, he with a display of great personal gallantry crawled over 200 yards to where the wounded officer was lying and succeeded in dragging him to a place of safety. He showed great courage and initiative.[90]

For his selfless act of bravery, Charles McDonald, a thirty-three-year-old Scottish-born farmer and conscript from Deloraine, in southern Manitoba, would be awarded the Distinguished Conduct Medal, further evidence it would seem that those reluctant warriors who by then had filled out the ranks of most battalions in the Canadian infantry corps were, at least in the heat of battle, not much different from their volunteer comrades. It was day sixty-one of the Hundred Days.

Cambrai and Iwuy: "For a time hell was loose"

"Who will last till 1920?"

BY 28 SEPTEMBER, Field Marshal von Hindenburg and General Ludendorff had concluded that the war could no longer be won. The fundamental question of reinforcements had led them to one simple conclusion: the German field armies "were no longer able to cover wastage."[1] Hence, the next day in Spa, Belgium, the Kaiser accepted a government proposal to sue for peace, and thus was set in motion the penultimate chapter of this great conflict, one that would end six weeks later with the signing of the Armistice. But for now there would be no reprieve for the Canadian Corps. A few days later, Haig decided to renew the general offensive, and the much-anticipated relief of the corps was indefinitely postponed. Next up was the capture of Cambrai, a vital German transportation hub, the loss of which "would render the rest of the Hindenburg Line untenable" – and after that, a deadly but long unheralded rendezvous at Iwuy.[2]

Ludendorff was not the only senior leader then wrestling with a shortage of reinforcements. On 3 October, Haig would reply to a recent letter received from Winston Churchill (the munitions minister) in which the latter had expressed the need to conserve "resources 'for the decisive struggles of 1920.'" Reacting to this pessimistic outlook, Haig had privately fumed: "What rubbish. Who will last till 1920? Only America??"[3] Still, Haig remained convinced that the war could be won that autumn or perhaps in early 1919, and with the German armies now seemingly in full retreat there was a real possibility that his own legions might yet possess sufficient strength to deal the enemy a *coup de grâce*.

In reality, manpower shortages and battlefield wastage had become much more vital concerns to senior leaders in the Canadian Corps, which had suffered forty-five hundred casualties per week (on average) over the previous two months. These were Somme-like numbers – arguably the cumulative equivalent to the average trench strength of sixty-eight infantry battalions. Although successive victories had made this campaign very much different than the Somme, clearly this high rate of losses was not sustainable, even for the Canadians. In fact, despite a steady flow of conscripts and other new men to the front (5,000 to the 2nd Division alone since the start of operations in August), there remained alarming gaps in the company strengths of most infantry battalions. By mid-October, Burstall's 2nd Division was short "4200 men" overall, and Watson's 4th, about 2,300.[4]

By then, General Horne had assigned the Canadian Corps a pivotal role in Haig's renewed offensive, one that would require Currie to finally "secure the passage of the Escaut Canal at Ramillies." In response, and in light of the high casualty numbers the week before, Currie "decided that [the still relatively fresh] 2nd Canadian Division would attack by night" – a bold and dangerous initiative, but one that would prove most advantageous.[5]

Wednesday, 9 October: The Capture of Cambrai

Currie's plan for the investment of Cambrai was simple but not without great risk. The main attack by the Canadians would be led by a single division, Burstall's 2nd, whose primary task would be to secure the crossings on the Canal de l'Escaut northeast of Cambrai between Morenchies and Ramillies and then invest the village of Escaudoeuvres on the opposite bank. Thereafter, depending on the ability of XVII British Corps to capture the heights of the Awoingt Spur east of Cambrai, McCuaig's 4th Brigade would punch through the city and join up with the British forces in phase two of the assault. At the same time, Loomis's 3rd Division would secure Burstall's right flank by capturing the railway embankment and slag heap directly north of Cambrai, then cross the canal once their passage had been secured by the 2nd Division. To achieve an essential element of surprise and to maximize stealth and force protection, zero hour was originally set for 2130 hours. By noon on 8 October, however, it had become disappointingly clear that the British would not be able to take Awoingt for at least another day. Currie was therefore faced with a dilemma: he could go that night regardless, he could attack the next morning, or perhaps he could even delay twenty-four hours and risk leaving the left flank of Fergusson's XVII Corps fully exposed. Apparently he did not hesitate. Setting aside some understandable anxiety, Currie reset zero hour for 0130 that night, and the show was on.[6]

Fortune would favour the attackers. In a repetition of a similar withdrawal made in front of the Canadians along the D-Q Line on the night of 2–3 September, the German 18th Division had already executed a hasty retreat, leaving behind only rearguard units at critical points, including at least one small party of men who apparently were "left behind with instructions to set fire to Cambrai."[7] The late-night timing of the assault, however, caught the remaining Germans by complete surprise, with devastating results for them.

First into the breach about ten minutes after zero were the 25th (Nova Scotia) Battalion on the left and the 26th (New Brunswick) on the right. Both had been tasked to seize crossings over the Canal de l'Escaut. Each was assigned large numbers of field engineers for this purpose. Captain Coulson Mitchell, 4th Battalion (Canadian Engineers), and his party of "50 other ranks," supported by a platoon of infantry from the 26th, led the way to the canal at Pont d'Aire in front of the village of Escaudoeuvres. There Mitchell's men found the main bridge – a 23 metre steel girder and stone structure that could easily support all forms of transport – still intact but wired for demolition. Despite the pitched gun battle that ensued, Mitchell's party quickly secured this vital crossing, and by 0230 hours the 2nd Division was in command of its primary objective.[8]

It had not been a bloodless assault. "A" Company of the 25th Battalion recorded that "several casualties were caused by our own artillery which had been dropping short during the whole advance." One of them perhaps was Private Polide Aucoin, a twenty-one-year-old farmer from Cape Breton Island. Aucoin, a native of Chéticamp, suffered a wound "in the right thigh" during the advance and "succumbed to his wounds the same day." A very stubborn defence mounted by German machine-gunners at Pont d'Aire, supported by enemy aircraft, also took its toll. Among the men "instantly killed" in that attack was Private Raymond Dujay, a sailor originally from Amherst, Nova Scotia, one of four conscripts along with eleven other men in this unit to make the ultimate sacrifice that day.[9]

The 26th Battalion advanced rapidly as well. By noon its forward patrols had joined up not only with the 4th CMRs (8th Brigade) coming up hard on the right but also with elements of the 24th British Division. Subsequently, Brigadier-General Tremblay ordered the 25th and 26th to resume the offensive starting at 1700 hours, the next objective being the fortified village of Naves and the high ground some 3.5 kilometres farther to the east. Once again, though, the Canadians had underestimated the Germans' tenacity. Jumping off at zero, the attackers "were soon met with such a hail of machine gun fire" that their advance was quickly brought to a halt. When relieved early the next morning, the New Brunswickers counted another eighty-six casualties. Among them was Private Charles Arbeau, a twenty-one-year-old farmer and draftee from Upper Blackville, New Brunswick, who died after being "severely wounded in the body, legs and head by an enemy shell."[10]

To the north, Major Nelson Spencer's 31st Battalion had moved forward with more than six hundred rifles, although tentatively at first because the 11th British Division had yet to secure the deadly heights adjacent to Abancourt. But by mid-morning it was quite clear that the Germans were in the midst of a full withdrawal; thus, Burstall ordered the 6th Brigade to push farther east at least 4 kilometres to the next bridgehead at Thun-l'Évêque. There, Spencer's men encountered a "severe" artillery barrage along with "deadly enfilade fire" from an open left flank, which quickly claimed six lives and resulted in over two dozen other casualties. Among the dead and dying was a twenty-one-year-old farmer and draftee from Retlaw, Alberta, named Private Howard Pattison. Originally from Buffalo, New York, Pattison had suffered "Gun shot wounds [to the] Right Shoulder and Abdomen." He died later that day at No. 33 CCS.[11]

On the corps' far-right flank, the 8th Brigade (4th and 5th CMR) had met "little or no resistance." In fact, "by 0700 both battalions had reached a line halfway through the city," remarkably without having suffered a single casualty.[12] Just one hour later, as the 3rd Division would record, "Cambrai had been completely captured."[13]

Thursday, 10 October: "Troops who had not slept for three days"

For the next phase of the advance, Burstall attacked with two brigades forward. The 6th, on the left and still astride the canal, would complete its investment of Thun-l'Évêque and then move on to the German redoubt at Iwuy, another 3 kilometres to the east. On the right would be Brigadier-General Eric McCuaig's 4th Brigade, which had gone untested since nearly being wiped out at Vis-en-Artois on 28 August, and which had not had a chance to rest for two days, mainly because it had been tasked with providing close support to the 5th Brigade during its investment of Cambrai.[14] Completely rebuilt over the previous six weeks, this brigade consisted largely of conscripts. The 21st Battalion, for example, had received 414 reinforcements in September, including at least 260 draftees (63 percent of the total) and twenty-five BCRM men. Similarly, the 20th Battalion had taken on 304 reinforcements, including 159 MSA men. Strong in numbers but short on experience, the 4th Brigade now faced multiple trials by fire: the first being to attack across the dangerous open ground in front of Naves and then to capture the high ground about 900 metres to the east. If McCuaig succeeded in all this, his next objectives would be more ambitious still – another ridge 2.5 kilometres to the northeast and then Iwuy itself.[15]

The two lead battalions (the 18th and 19th) did not receive their final orders until about 0330 hours that morning. According to Corporal Deward Barnes, these same troops had not slept "for three days" and were not "told what [they] were going to do until it was near daybreak." Nonetheless, jumping off at 0600 hours in what would be the first of three such attacks that day, the 19th made excellent progress early on. Major Harry Hatch's men passed quickly through Naves and by 0835 had secured the high ground to the east. Initially, casualties were few. Two more successful assaults were then launched, the first at 1400 hours across the Erclin River, and the second at 1715 hours, in the course of which this unit advanced another 1,500 metres to higher ground. Exhausted and spent after having fought "for every foot of ground," the 19th moved into temporary reserve.[16]

Jumping off one hour later, Lieutenant-Colonel L.E. Jones's 18th Battalion was stopped cold in its tracks by "heavy enemy machine gun fire from the left flank." So violent was the German resistance at this point that the battalion remained largely pinned down for the remainder of the day. The 18th counted

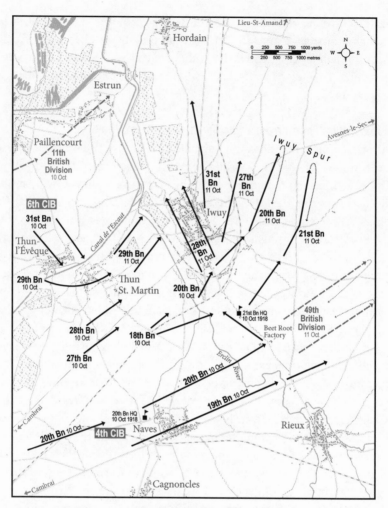

Map 5   Iwuy, 10–11 October 1918. Map by Mike Bechthold.

at least eighty casualties, including six dead, one of whom was Private Leonard Lavelle, a widely known hockey player and former "sporting editor of the Stratford Herald." Lavelle, twenty-four years old, the youngest of three brothers (all conscripts), had been "shot through the body and instantly killed by an enemy bullet."[17]

At the same time, the 21st Battalion, following closely behind in support, had sustained eighteen casualties but just one fatality – a conscript named Private George McGregor. Among the wounded was another reluctant warrior, a tall (5'10½"/179 cm) twenty-two-year-old photographer from Hull, Quebec, by the name of Emile Mousseau. At some point in the action, Private Mousseau had found himself surrounded by dead and dying comrades. Despite the "intense fire" and the effects of several shrapnel wounds, he took over a weapon (likely a Lewis machine-gun) and used it with great effectiveness to defend his position. For his conspicuous bravery, Mousseau was later awarded the Military Medal.[18]

Farther north, Brigadier-General Alex Ross had deployed two battalions (the 28th and 29th) to support this attack, but both failed to reach their jump-off positions in time (i.e., by 0600). Thus, the weary 27th, led by Lieutenant-Colonel Harold Riley (a twenty-nine-year-old Winnipeg lawyer), was forced to advance again, this time to protect the left flank of the 4th Brigade. This it succeeded in doing, although enemy machine-guns claimed many casualties, including Private William Beetham, a Yorkshire-born marine engineer and conscript from Winnipeg, who was killed on a "reconnoitring patrol." In the meantime, ninety minutes after the 31st Battalion captured the crucial bridge-head at Thun-l'Évêque, the 29th secured the adjacent village of Thun-Saint-Martin.[19] There, bombarded by gas shells and stymied by marshy terrain and heavy machine-gun fire, Tobin's Tigers came to a sudden halt. Nevertheless, Burstall ordered both attacking brigades to make good the Erclin River and to capture Iwuy as well. For its part, 4th Brigade would manage to secure the southern perimeter of the village, but the 6th Brigade had gone as far as it could. The 29th Battalion had suffered thirty-two casualties up to this point, including seven killed. Among the latter were two conscripts: Privates Alexander Matheson, a logger from Heriot Bay, BC, but originally from Forest Hill, PEI, and William Irving, a marine fireman from Victoria, by way of Liverpool. Shell-fire had taken both their lives.[20]

11 October: "I Have Fought the Good Fight, I Have Kept the Faith"

The regimental historian for the 20th Battalion would later note that while "the enemy was perhaps giving ground elsewhere ... in front of the 2nd Canadian Division he was, from all accounts, contesting every inch."[21] Even so, early on the evening of 10 October, Burstall boldly ordered the 4th Brigade to advance 5 kilometres and capture the village of Avesnes-le-Sec, and then "move on [another 5 kilometres to] Noyelles and attempt to make good [the] crossings of [the] River Selle." The 6th Brigade was "to clear up the situation at Iwuy" (suggesting perhaps that the remaining opposition there did not pose any great risk), after which it too was to "continue the advance" northeast for another 5 kilometres, first to Hordain and finally to Lieu-Saint-Amand.[22] Except for the capture of Iwuy, an obscure and costly triumph, none of these plans would come to fruition. Burstall's basic plan of attack was clearly flawed, since it was based on at least one major false assumption – that the Germans would not continue to defend this sector with the same determined effort that they had so vigorously exercised over the previous twenty-four hours. In addition, a risky assault in broad daylight did not augur well for Burstall's attackers. As will be seen, the Germans still had at least one other major surprise to mete out to the Canadians.

Among the first Canadian units into this fight was Lieutenant-Colonel Henry Pense's fully replenished 21st Battalion, followed immediately on his left by the 20th, which was led at that moment by the reliable and very experienced Major Charles Ingles. The 21st arrived at its assembly position 1 kilometre south of Iwuy at about 0330 hours, after which it was subjected to intermittent shelling right up to the moment it jumped off. Then, at zero (0900 hours), just as the battalion began to advance to the east towards Avesnes-le-Sec, it quickly came under enfilade fire from the right flank. Likely among the first of those killed in this phase of the assault was Private Gidreau Chartrand, an illiterate "Bushman" originally from Chichester, Quebec, whose headstone conveys a simple, two-word epitaph by his mourning parents – "French Canadian." Ultimately, Pense lost "fifty percent of his officers, N.C.O.'s and Lewis Gunners" in just "the first thirty minutes of this advance." Even so, by mid-morning his exhausted troops had managed to seize the high ground – the Iwuy Spur – some 2.5 kilometres beyond the jump-off point.[23]

There the Canadians were stunned by a second German surprise. At 1100 hours, and just as it appeared that the difficult march towards Avesnes-le-Sec might succeed, the Germans launched a combined arms counterattack directly at the centre of the Canadian and British effort. This deadly thrust "consisted of two German Assault Tank Detachments," eight tanks in total, including "five German designed A7V tanks" and "three captured British Mk IV" models, all of which were supported by the 371st Reserve Infantry Regiment. Not surprisingly, since no Canadian foot soldiers had ever experienced such an attack, the shock of being suddenly confronted by seemingly unstoppable armour had its desired effect. But the British apparently absorbed "the brunt of the tank assault," and, according to Burstall, they were "driven back almost to their 'jumping-off line.'" The impact on the 4th Brigade, though, was not much different. As the imperial troops fell back, so too did the startled infantry of the 21st, who initially were forced to withdraw almost 2 kilometres. By noon, when field artillery and heavy machine-guns were brought to bear against this new threat, heavy casualties had all but halted the 4th Brigade's momentum, prompting Burstall to later record that the attack "had practically failed."[24] In fact, had the 21st Battalion not secured the crucial high ground at the Iwuy Spur, the efforts of the 4th Brigade (and the 146th British Brigade on its right) would have been for naught. For the 21st, however, the day's harsh results had

Figure 9.1   Private Gidreau Chartrand's epitaph, a simple declaration by his mourning parents, speaks to one of the core issues of conscription in Canada. *Source:* Courtesy of Len Scott.

Figure 9.2   Private William Harold Edmiston, 21st Battalion, killed in action at Iwuy, France, 11 October 1918. *Source:* Courtesy of Steve St. Amant.

once again spelled near catastrophe. On this, its second-worst day of the war, Pense's battalion alone sustained a stunning 326 casualties, only slightly fewer than it had suffered on 28 August along the Scarpe.[25]

Among the 21st Battalion's 39 men killed in action, there were no fewer than 19 conscripts. In addition, 6 other draftees later died of their wounds and one other, also wounded, was taken prisoner. Representing the broadest possible spectrum of young Canadian men, they included Privates Wellesley Wesley-Long, a twenty-three-year-old Munich-born divinity student from Saskatoon, and William Edmiston, a twenty-five-year-old cheesemaker from Paris, Ontario. The precise circumstances of these two deaths would go undocumented (there being few surviving witnesses), but we are still left with one enduring testament to Edmiston's sacrifice. The poignant epitaph on his headstone reads: "I Have Fought A Good Fight, I Have Kept The Faith" – a worthy tribute, and one perhaps equally applicable to all his comrades.[26]

On the left of the 4th Brigade, the 20th Battalion had also undergone a trial by fire, first with the enemy's very effective counter-barrage, which quickly claimed "many casualties," including the lives of at least half a dozen conscripts. Then, jumping off "without visible artillery support," the 20th encountered "severe opposition" right from the outset, and in particular "intense M.G. fire" from its open left flank – Iwuy itself. Nonetheless, Ingles's men succeeded in skirting the village on the southeast and pressed forward another 2.5 kilometres to their first objective – a crucial "sunken road five hundred yards due east of the village." Shortly thereafter, the German tank assault brought an abrupt halt to their advance.[27]

Yet unmolested by the 6th Brigade advancing from the south, the Germans concentrated their heavy machine-gun fire on the 4th Brigade to the east side of the village. There Lieutenant Wallace Algie of the 20th Battalion led a small party of "nine volunteers" (including at least one conscript) in a sudden rush against several machine-gun posts, silencing two of the guns and capturing ten defenders in a lightning assault. Ultimately this action paved the way for the unit to advance north another 2 kilometres, but by then it had been reduced to about one full company. When it was relieved at 0300 the next morning, the 20th's losses numbered 330 men, including 29 killed outright. Two-thirds of the dead were conscripts. For Eric McCuaig, who was fighting his first major engagement as a brigade commander, the overall price had been even higher. In just two days he had lost no fewer than thirty-four officers and nearly one thousand men.[28] Thus the 4th Brigade would be *hors de combat* yet again for another month.

The Hardest Fight in the History of the Battalion

The battle for Iwuy itself, once home to nearly four thousand French, was a decidedly different affair. The heavy combat of 10 October had made it clear that the Germans had no intention of giving up this small but tactically important village. But siege warfare this was not. Ross's plan was for an aggressive envelopment of Iwuy; however, Burstall's artillery not only failed to silence in advance the enemy's robust machine-gun defences but also did little to minimize the "devastating barrage" that the enemy subsequently "brought down upon the Canadian formations."[29] Hence the stage was set for another costly battle.

Tobin's Tigers executed an effective diversionary attack to the west, and likewise managed a successful advance to the Erclin River, doing so with relatively light casualties – only eleven fatalities. Three of these men were conscripts, one of whom was Private Sydney Hill, a British-born artist from Vancouver. Apparently a victim of the enemy's initial barrage, Hill suffered multiple shrapnel wounds and died at No. 9 Canadian Field Ambulance.[30]

Unknown to the Canadians, though, Iwuy had "been converted into a formidable fortress." So when three companies of Major G.F.D. Bond's 28th Battalion pushed forward at zero hour, they unexpectedly encountered their "hardest fight" of the war. In the fierce battle that followed, this once-prosperous town, some 2 kilometres in length, was "contested inch by inch." Early losses included Private John Robinson, a draftee and married farmer from Prince Albert, who was gassed during the enemy's counter-barrage. Quickly evacuated, Robinson was then "struck with shrapnel and severely wounded in the back and both legs." He died of these wounds eight days later. Casualties mounted rapidly in the house-to-house fighting that followed, and by the time "the village was finally 'mopped up,'" Bond had lost another 140 men. Among them was Private William Benson, an American-born farmer and draftee of Norwegian descent from Cabri, Saskatchewan. In a classic example of the deadly hazards of urban warfare, Benson, a Lewis gunner in the attack, had been "hit in the back by an enemy bullet and almost instantly killed."[31]

What ultimately saved the 28th was the somewhat belated arrival of the 27th and 31st Battalions. These units had been expected to punch their way through Iwuy after it had been "mopped up," but the Germans simply did not cooperate. In fact, both units were subjected to "terrific shelling with gas and high explosives." Twenty years later, a regimental historian would chillingly describe this horrific barrage: "For a time hell was loose among the men of Alberta. The shells, as they fell, detonated off the trees that covered the Battalion's assembly area, and the wounds caused by the flying shell splinters were terrible."[32] Private Andrew Blake, a surveyor from The Pas, Manitoba, was killed by the concussive effects of an "enemy shell exploding close to him." Private Norman McLeod, a Scottish-born "Smelterman" from the once-thriving mining community of Anyox, BC, died of shrapnel wounds the next day. This hideous bombardment lasted for several hours. Not until noon was Riley's 27th able to press forward and bring much-needed relief to Bond's beleaguered 28th, albeit at some cost and still several kilometres short of the main objective of Lieu-Saint-Amand.[33]

Meanwhile, less than half a kilometre to Riley's left, the 31st Battalion had had to fight its way onto higher ground in the northern part of the village, belying earlier reports that Iwuy had been "cleared of the enemy." Forced to reorganize into two composite companies, Spencer's Albertans engaged in "stiff fighting" but ultimately failed to seize their main objective, Hordain.[34] There were countless acts of bravery, not least of which was the conspicuous gallantry shown by Private Allen McCreery, a thirty-five-year-old shipping clerk from Windsor, Ontario. His citation for the Military Medal reads in part: "This man was in charge of a platoon, and noticing an enemy machine gun was holding up its advance, with utter disregard to personal danger, and in the face of heavy fire, rushed the gun and killed the crew. His conduct throughout the operation set a splendid example to the men of his platoon."[35]

The fact that a conscript with only a few months' combat experience was in charge of a platoon at the time speaks volumes about the phenomenal attrition of junior leaders in front-line battalions. That McCreery performed so well under fire, and in doing so set such a good example for his mates, is likewise a tribute to his solid training and discipline. More important perhaps, his actions underscore yet again how difficult it must have been for all these new men to engage in successive episodes of hard combat, often without the crucial benefit of experienced leadership, which is typically a prerequisite for success on any battlefield. But McCreery's actions were not unique; at least twenty others demonstrated similar courage, including another reluctant warrior, Private Rudolph Weiler, also a clerk in civilian life, whose "coolness and daring" under fire while "in charge of a Lewis Gun Section ... set a fine example to the men of his Section." He soon earned a Military Medal as well.[36] In this context, one is drawn to Major-General Burstall's later assertion that his "new drafts" had been largely helpless in making an effective "advance against enemy machine guns." That simply did not ring true in this case, and arguably was a false conclusion based either on insufficient information, personal bias, or a combination of both, but apparently not supported by actual events on the ground.[37]

By day's end the 31st Battalion had progressed north to within 1 kilometre of Hordain, but serious losses finally forced Spencer to halt the advance and to consolidate once again. When relieved at 0100 the following morning, the Albertans counted 12 dead and 137 wounded among their casualties. Four of those killed outright were conscripts, including Private Herbert Leeder, a twenty-one-year-old farmer from Port Elgin, Ontario, who perished after being "hit in the right side of the head by a piece of shrapnel." Another half-dozen draftees died of their wounds shortly thereafter.[38]

Thus, the battle for Iwuy came to a victorious but bitter end. Forced to withdraw once more, the enemy had yet again made the 2nd Division pay a steep price for what appeared to be modest gains. Outgunned, outnumbered, but arguably not outfought, the Germans had acquitted themselves well in this major rearguard action. Any hope that the enemy could be quickly "mopped up," here or elsewhere on the Canadian front, clearly needed to be abandoned. Nonetheless, very late on 11 October, General Burstall telephoned his two leading brigade commanders to ask if they "could carry on the attack" for a third consecutive day. To their great credit, both Ross and McCuaig, only recently battalion COs themselves, replied emphatically in the negative, declaring not only that their troops were utterly exhausted but also that, given the "large

Figure 9.3 The Leeder brothers, Herbert (left) and Arthur
Iden, both conscripts from Port Elgin, Ontario. Herbert,
31st Battalion CEF, was killed in action 11 October 1918.
Arthur survived the war. *Source:* Bruce County Museum
and Cultural Centre: A991.047.002, Evans Studio.

proportion of inexperienced officers and men [remaining] they would not," in
Burstall's words, "be fit to continue the operations on the following day without
suffering excessive casualties."[39] Indeed, both courageous officers explicitly
reaffirmed what was mistakenly thought to be a crucial lesson already learned
– that to continue to fight understrength units against a determined and desperate foe posed grave risks that Burstall could ill afford to ignore.

The Pursuit to Mons Begins

What would one day be called the "pursuit to Mons" now began to take a distinct
shape, but not with the speed that is commonly ascribed to this historic event.

The Germans were not reeling in defeat (at least not yet), nor were they with-drawing in any kind of disorganized or confused manner. Consequently, the overall progress of First Army slowed considerably.[40] The Canadian Corps, still attempting to recover from heavy losses at the Canal du Nord, Cambrai, and now Iwuy, would make mixed progress over the next few weeks. The great steeltown of Valenciennes lay just 20 kilometres away, but, before the assault could begin there, the corps would first engage in a number of minor but often costly actions that would typify combat in the last month of the war.

At 1200 hours on 12 October, Tremblay's 5th Brigade began the "pursuit" with attacks by the 24th Battalion, first at Hordain and then at Basse Ville (Bouchain) – a key crossing astride the Canal de l'Escaut. Stymied by a horribly misplaced supporting barrage, and brought to a halt by strong enemy fire, Lieutenant-Colonel Charles Ritchie's troops were forced to dig in and then reattack Basse Ville at 0900 hours the next day, a Sunday. Once again, German resistance was stiff. Stopped in their tracks by "very heavy" machine-gun fire, the Victoria Rifles were eventually pushed back all the way to "their original line." When relieved a day-and-a-half later, they counted nearly eighty casualties from this action, including eleven dead. Five of those killed outright were conscripts; several draftees were among the many others who were fatally wounded, in-cluding Private Patrick Derynck, a twenty-two-year-old labourer from Montreal. "Wounded in the right arm, thigh and chest by enemy shell fire," Derynck "suc-cumbed to his wounds" three days later at No. 22 CCS. More tragically still, young Derynck had left his widowed mother Margaret in grief for a second time, her younger son Fred having been killed in action the previous year at Vimy Ridge.[41]

The next day, amidst several reports that "the enemy was retiring North of the SENSEE Canal," Tremblay ordered his old unit, the 22nd Battalion, to "cross the Canal and get in touch" with the retreating Germans. The intelligence proved to be false, and "the enemy was found to be holding the Canal as before." Van Doo "patrols failed to get across" either the Canal de l'Escaut or the Canal de la Sensée, and the unit sustained a dozen casualties in the attempts. Most were conscripts; two were killed outright and five more died within a week.[42]

A "Chinese" Fake Show

Elsewhere in Currie's area of responsibility, the 1st Division had returned to his command on 11 October after passing nearly four days under the direction of XXII Corps. Having suffered heavy losses north of Cambrai, this tired forma-tion was supposed to have gone into corps reserve a week earlier for a well-earned

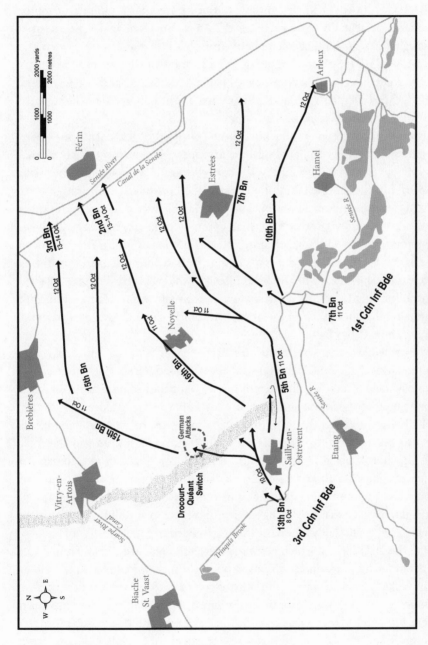

Map 6 Scarpe to the Sensée Canal, 8–14 October 1918. Map by Mike Bechthold.

rest some 25 kilometres to the west. Instead, it had relieved the 4th British Division on 6–7 October, after which Lieutenant-General Alexander Godley (GOC XXII Corps) had straight away issued orders for a number of minor operations, essentially designed to test the strength of German defences in what was believed to be a "quiet" sector of the front.[43] The first of these was "jocularly termed a 'CHINESE' (fake) show," a small feint intended "to cause the enemy to believe that a general advance [was] being undertaken," and also to enlarge a bridgehead over the Trinquis River, south of the heavily wired but lightly held German outpost at Sailly-en-Ostrevent.[44]

Even though the main attacking force consisted of less than one "weak" company (from the 13th Battalion), the first operation was successfully carried out at 0530 hours the next day, 8 October. Within the hour, all of its objectives had been achieved, including the capture of 25 prisoners. Only 4 men were slightly wounded in this action, but another 8 Highlanders fell early that evening (2 dead, 6 wounded) during a German counterattack. One of those killed was a twenty-two-year-old married conscript named William Young. A British-born clerk from North Battleford, Saskatchewan, he had been recruited exactly one year earlier, apparently with the initial intent of sending him to the Army Medical Corps Training Depot. As it turned out, Young's fate was not to be found with a non-combatant branch of the army, but rather where he was needed most, with a line infantry battalion.[45]

Emboldened perhaps by this success, Brigadier-General H.C. Thacker (acting GOC during Macdonell's absence on leave) pushed for stronger patrols, and two days later a second minor operation was launched to once again establish the enemy's dispositions and possibly his intent as well. More ambitiously still, Tuxford ordered the 13th (in cooperation with the 15th Battalion on its left), to "push out battle patrols ... endeavour to capture Sailly," and finally "enter the Drocourt-Quéant Line" itself.[46] Starting at 0200 hours on 10 October, Ian Sinclair's Royal Highlanders encircled Sailly-en-Ostrevent and within two hours had captured the village along with nearly fifty prisoners. Then, just at daylight, disaster struck. Having missed the signal to withdraw, about fifty of Sinclair's men suddenly found themselves isolated in a narrow slice of the now infamous D-Q Line, at which point the Germans launched a counterattack. In short order the Canadians were overrun; eight men were killed and another thirty taken prisoner. Among the latter were a half-dozen conscripts, including two skilled workers from Montreal – Private Charles Houston, a Scottish-born secretary who had previously served three years with the 58th Regiment, Westmount Rifles; and Private John Hughes, an engineer. Overall, casualties from this minor operation totalled at least 145 – a severe blow just ten days after the Highlanders had sustained heavy losses north of Cambrai. As the unit historian would one day lament, though, there did not seem to be any real choice but to push new men into battle without essential leadership, training, or unit indoctrination.[47]

But apparently there *was* an alternative. Evidence suggests that at this late stage of the war, given the widespread German withdrawals across the entire Western Front coupled with robust peace initiatives, adjacent British formations had attempted to strike a balance between exploiting success at a high cost and carrying their advances forward at a more measured and cautious pace. As Shane Schreiber has observed, "no other formation had been tasked with taking part in three major engagements under two different armies in the same span as the Canadian Corps." Indeed, "casualty figures point dramatically to how lopsided the effort truly was." For example, Godley's XXII Corps operating on Currie's left flank "between 27 September and 7 October ... sustained 86 officer and 1,840 other rank casualties," while "the Canadian Corps casualty rate" was seven times higher: "707 officers and 12,913 other ranks."[48] Such figures seem to raise two crucial but unanswered questions: Could Godley have done any more? And could Currie have done any less?

At 1700 on 11 October the 1st Division was transferred back to the Canadian Corps. That night Thacker ordered his 2nd and 3rd Brigades to once again deploy strong patrols along the Canal de la Sensée and attempt "to gain bridgeheads" there the next day. Within an hour of zero (0600), Major David Philpot's 7th Battalion captured the near bank of the canal only to discover that "all bridges had been destroyed" and that the enemy was massing in force "on the East bank." Quite prudently, the 2nd Brigade's newly promoted GOC, Brigadier-General R.P. Clark, decided to forgo any attempt to make a crossing, and the BCRs began to dig in. There they rode out a storm of artillery and sustained forty casualties, including thirteen dead ORs. Four of the dead or dying were conscripts.[49]

Attacking at the same time on the right had been the 10th Battalion, led that Saturday morning by Major Philip Walker (acting CO). With a trench strength of 482, including fifty new men taken on board one or two days earlier, Walker's Albertans had the difficult task of capturing "three strongly wired lines of trenches" at the junction of the Canal du Nord and the Canal de la Sensée," plus the adjacent and strongly garrisoned town of Arleux. "Considerable resistance" was encountered, and it took the entire morning for them to finally declare Arleux clear of the enemy. Yet casualties were low – three ORs killed and fifteen wounded. Among the dead and dying were several draftees, including Private T.L. Kennedy, a mechanic from Calgary by way of Newburgh, Ontario. Kennedy had made it to the edge of Arleux when at "about 9 a.m. ... he was wounded by an enemy machine gun bullet which entered the right shoulder and passed out under his left arm." Despite being evacuated to a nearby "regimental aid post" and later some 40 kilometres to No. 23 CCS, Private Kennedy "succumbed two days later."[50]

To the north, the 3rd Brigade's 16th Battalion made a similar and successful advance to the Canal de la Sensée, although it too met with strong resistance, particularly from the village of Ferin "on the high ground on the opposite side of the canal." Casualties were minimal, but enemy fire combined with a "lack of bridging material" prevented further progress.[51] Subsequent attempts to establish even a temporary bridgehead proved costly and futile. J.B. Rogers's 3rd Battalion alone suffered over thirty casualties on 14 October during a chaotic six-hour battle on the east side of the canal. Among the dead was Private George Potter, a twenty-one-year-old draftee and printer from Owen Sound, Ontario – killed by rifle fire as he crossed the Canal.[52]

The next day General Horne issued orders that "all Corps were to concentrate on re-organization of formations" – essentially an operational pause. The two sides then spent the next few days feeling each other out, exchanging periodic artillery and machine-gun barrages. Typical of this period, losses were relatively light, with Hayter's 10th Brigade suffering just a dozen casualties on 16 October. Among them was Private Alfred De Pew, an American-born farmer from Bow Island, Alberta, who was "hit in the head by shrapnel" and "instantly killed" 5 kilometres west of Féchain. De Pew's courage under fire had previously been recognized when he was awarded the Military Medal, most likely for gallantry displayed nearly three weeks earlier at the Canal du Nord.[53]

He Gave His Life for Others

For Currie, while the Canal de la Sensée represented yet another "serious obstacle" to forward progress, there appeared around this time two even greater challenges that together threatened to slow or even stop the Canadian Corps in its tracks, no matter how determined its efforts. The first was logistics. In their fighting withdrawal, the Germans had destroyed countless roads, bridges, railway lines, and other supporting infrastructure that might have assisted the pursuing armies. For good measure, the enemy had flooded low-lying areas and left behind "many 'booby traps' and delayed action mines," which, according to Currie, had "considerably impeded [the] progress" of his forces.[54]

A second and potentially more deadly menace to the corps was the long-expected arrival in force of a devastating pandemic – the Spanish influenza. This new threat to Currie's plans, which first appeared in strength about four months earlier, had now gathered sufficient lethal momentum to strike a telling blow against all the armies on the Western Front. Over the following year, this debilitating and virtually untreatable disease would infect nearly 46,000

Canadian soldiers overseas and eventually claim close to 800 lives. Among the first of many conscripts at the front to be felled directly by this scourge, or by its "associated condition" of pneumonia, would be Privates William Andrews, a Ceylon-born fireman from Okanagan Landing, BC, who was then serving with the 16th Battalion, and Robert Beach of the 102nd, a farmer from Brookfield, Ontario. Andrews died of "broncho-pneumonia" at No. 14 General Hospital [in] Wimereux" on 14 October ; Beach succumbed to "influenza" two weeks later at No. 4 Canadian CCS in Agnez-lès-Duisans.[55] For the Canadian Corps, these two deaths were just the tip of a very dangerous iceberg.

The real threat posed by the flu epidemic to Currie's operational planning was its potential impact on training establishments in England and therefore on his capacity to replace large numbers of casualties with adequate numbers of reinforcements. For example, in his report for the month of October, Brigadier-General Rennie, then commanding the Canadian Training Division at Bramshott, ominously reported that "the epidemic of influenza which raged during the month seriously interfered with training. The number of admissions to hospital amounted to 2,242, as well as many held within unit lines. Those becoming convalescent were unable to participate in any training except remedial, for a period of at least three weeks. The deaths numbered 142."[56] In the 15th Reserve Battalion alone, no fewer than 43 draftees perished from disease that month, one-third of whom succumbed directly to influenza or to a pneumonia-related illness.[57]

The Canadian army's entire training pipeline was under full assault by this epidemic, from transport ships en route, where "epidemics of influenza" became quite common, all the way back to military bases in Canada, where thousands of draftees were biding their time awaiting passage to the United Kingdom. For many, that interlude proved deadly. Official records indicate that "during the last four months of 1918 ... 11,496 soldiers or 19 per cent of the forces were affected" by the disease, and that "in some districts the percentage rose to 42."[58] Ultimately, in addition to the many thousands of Canadian civilians killed in the epidemic, pneumonia and influenza took hundreds of soldiers' lives, the majority of them being conscripts awaiting transport to Europe or draftees in transit to the west coast to join the Canadian Expeditionary Force (Siberia). Among those fatally stricken at this time was Private Charles Sims, a thirty-five-year-old labourer from Hamilton, Ontario, who had been drafted in August on the same day as his younger brother Malick. Influenza killed Charles on 28 October. Tragically, only three days later, Malick, then serving with the 3rd Reserve Battalion in Bramshott, also died of disease. In time their grieving parents would inscribe the headstone of their older son with the simple but poignant words: "He Gave His Life For Others."[59]

The flu pandemic then confronting the Canadian army was more than just a medical crisis. It had dramatically reduced the flow of conscripts overseas and had significantly interrupted training in England. Likewise, it had reduced the flow to the front of desperately needed reinforcements and placed in jeopardy all of Currie's operational planning. For all that, the primary cause of the latest manpower crisis in the Canadian Corps was not the influenza pandemic, nor was it a faulty training system or a shortage of trained soldiers. Rather, it was a direct consequence of the cumulative effects of more than ten weeks of record attrition. General Turner would point out to Sir Edward Kemp on 28 October that 31,000 men had been sent to France in the previous three months alone and that there were "more than sufficient men at present in training to meet" any expected shortfalls. This sanguine assessment was based on one fundamental assumption, however – that "unforeseen losses" would not "occur in the interval."[60] In this context, it would not be the flu that would seal the fate of the Canadian Corps, but rather the operational tempo set by Currie and the length of time that the German army was prepared to sustain a tenacious defence.

Honour and Duty in the Pursuit to Mons

"Practically all new men and seem to have their heart in the work"

AT THIS CRUCIAL POINT in the Hundred Days campaign, open warfare truly became the *modus operandi* for the Canadian Corps. Yet the next major objective would not be an attack on German forces in the field; rather, it would be on a major urban centre – Valenciennes. This steel production town of 34,000 people had been occupied by the Germans since 1914 and remained a key component of the thinly constructed but still vital Hermann Line, which ran straight through it. Immediately to the south lay the heavily defended Mont Houy, which Schreiber has described as "a more dominating feature than Vimy Ridge."[1] The loss of Valenciennes would be another great blow to the Germans and would likely hasten the final defeat of their army. And 30 kilometres beyond was the city of Mons, still a "critical logistics hub" for the Germans and supplier of "the finest coal in Belgium."[2] As the setting for the BEF's first combat action four years earlier, it had enormous symbolic value. Its capture would coincide with the end of the war; it would also give birth to a bitter legacy and to controversial charges (to be addressed later in this narrative) regarding whether the costly attack at Mons had been necessary at all.[3]

On the morning of 17 October the German army, now at a mere fraction of its former strength, renewed its sullen retirement to the east. The 1st and 2nd Brigades picked up the pursuit and pushed across the Canal de la Sensée, followed later in the day by Ross's 6th Brigade to the south. Re-entering the fight early the next morning, the 2nd Brigade in particular continued to press forward throughout the day, boldly leaving both its flanks exposed for anywhere from 2 to 4 kilometres – a new risk considered wholly justified by Brigadier-General R.P. Clark, given his overriding requirement to maintain contact with the enemy.[4] The Germans, however, were not totally compliant. In fact, they briefly and bravely stood their ground in front of a number of villages, even though at best they could inflict only minor losses on the steadily advancing Canadians. Among this brigade's six casualties there was just one fatality – Private Thomas Douglas, a twenty-three-year-old farmer and conscript from Carman, Manitoba. Caught up in an enemy barrage, Douglas was "hit in the head, throat and elbow by shrapnel." Two days later the battalion diarist recorded that "a Military funeral was given the remains of No. 2327522 [actually 2379502],

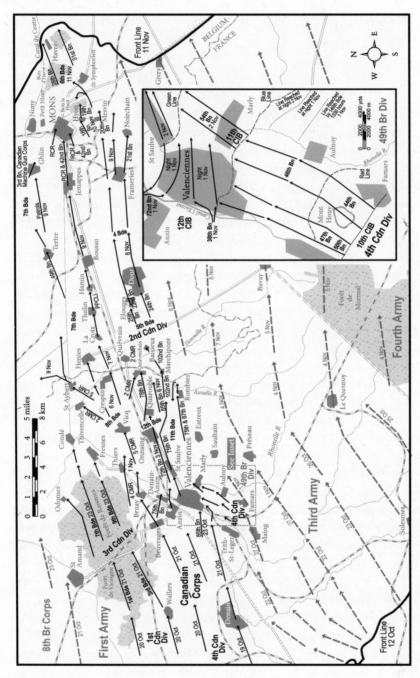

Map 7 Valenciennes to Mons, 23 October–11 November 1918. Map by Mike Bechthold.

Pte. T.W. Douglass [*sic*], killed in action, near here, on the 18th inst."[5] Rarely if ever did the burial of an individual soldier warrant such an entry into any wartime diary of the CEF. Perhaps it reflected a new sensitivity to individual losses, or a greater acceptance of conscripts in this unit, but more likely it represented a return to regimental traditions reluctantly jettisoned over the previous two months of continuous high casualty counts.

Farther north, Griesbach's 1st Brigade had pushed forward another 8 kilometres, and again casualties were astonishingly low in comparison to the recent past – twenty-two other ranks in total, including four dead. Private Frank Belanger was one of the latter, a twenty-one-year-old teamster and conscript from Sudbury, Ontario, killed "by shrapnel from an enemy shell." The performance of the 4th Battalion had been impressive, though, and in the after-action report the acting CO, Major George Blackstock, offered the following simple but noteworthy tribute to his eager troops: "General Behaviour of men –excellent. Practically all new men and [they] seem to have their heart in the work."[6]

Meanwhile, charging hard from south to north were Watson's 10th and 11th Brigades, both of which collided with the 1st Division and were forced to pivot right and advance in an easterly direction. At this point, the grand pursuit appeared to be turning into something of a rout. Early on Saturday afternoon, 19 October, the 44th and 47th Battalions (10th Brigade) leapfrogged ahead virtually unopposed, right into the heart of Denain, a town of about 25,000 on the Canal de l'Escaut. Ultimately, the Canadian Corps pushed forward an astonishing 11 kilometres – "the longest [advance] made by Canadians on any single day of the war."[7] But then, at the eastern end of Denain and all along the canal, both battalions ran headlong into stiff opposition, and just as suddenly their historic march came to an abrupt halt. One 44th man to fall at this time was a "mechanical repairer" and draftee from Sterling, Ontario. Shot in the "left hand, legs and head," Private Clarence Rodgers was evacuated to "No. 53 General Hospital Boulogne," only to contract septicemia and die of his wounds ten days later.[8] Thus, while Dan Dancocks has noted that a general "mood of optimism prevailed among the Canadians," it was clear that the German army was still determined to wage a fierce fight, even as the frequency and intensity of its defence diminished by the day.[9]

That was certainly the case for the 1st Division in the Forêt de Vicoigne northwest of Valenciennes. There, that Sunday morning, Griesbach's 1st Brigade made a cautious 7 kilometre advance towards the villages of Hasnon and Grand Bray, where Blackstock's 4th Battalion alone suffered no fewer than 36 casualties. Among his 10 fatalities were 4 conscripts, including Private Aime Boulet, a twenty-two-year-old Sudbury labourer born in Hull, Quebec, who was struck "in the ankle and back by machine gun bullets" as he advanced down the main

Figure 10.1 Another conscript to fall in the rapid advance towards Denain was Private Frederick Kenny, 47th Battalion CEF, killed in action at Émerchicourt, 18 October 1918. *Source:* Courtesy of Clarence Kieffer, Royal Canadian Legion Branch 102.

street of the village.[10] The next day, the 3rd Battalion pushed another 4 kilometres east into the town of Saint-Amand-les-Eaux, sustaining nineteen casualties. Among them was Private Thomas Naphan, a foreman from Toronto, who was "hit in the head" by a bullet from an enemy sniper. At thirty-five years and seven months, Naphan was one of the oldest Canadian conscripts to die in action; he was also the last to do so in the 1st Division. Late the following morning the division moved into corps reserve: unbeknownst to Macdonell, who had just returned from leave, this proud formation had fought its last engagement of the war.[11]

"A most regrettable though unavoidable incident"

Elsewhere, Currie's 3rd and 4th Divisions had manoeuvred to envelop the city of Valenciennes from the south, the west, and, more impressively, the northwest. This latter action involved a two-brigade effort (the 7th and 9th) to clear the enemy from the Forêt de Raismes starting on 22 October, a difficult two-day advance. The Royal Canadian Regiment made "excellent progress" early on, passing through to the southern end of the Raismes forest by mid-afternoon on the first day and suffering only minimal casualties – one officer wounded, along with three other ranks killed, all of them conscripts, each of whom had fallen to enemy shelling. They included Private Avard Mader, a cook from Halifax, whose commemorative headstone in the Valenciennes Communal

Cemetery today bears the simple but evocative query: "What more can a man do than to lay his life down for his country?" In their advance the next day into the town of Fresnes, about 10 kilometres downstream from Valenciennes, the RCRs sustained two more fatalities. Again, both were conscripts.[12]

At about the same time, more than 20 kilometres to the southwest, Kirkcaldy's 12th Brigade had made its own triumphant march through Denain, having followed directly behind Hayter's 10th Brigade, which had earlier liberated the town. But when the 85th Battalion stopped for dinner just a few kilometres to the east, "a light shell fell among "C" Company, inflicting 7 casualties, 4 of which proved fatal." Three of these men were draftees, including Private Orphila Mondoux, a millwright from Kirkland Lake, Ontario. "Wounded in the thigh by shrapnel, [he] was immediately attended to" before being "evacuated to No. 57 CCS," only to succumb to his wounds 15 days later.[13]

On 23 October, the 85th attacked the southernmost of three bridgeheads on the west side of Valenciennes. The approaches to this all but destroyed bridge were "heavily wired," and in the face of heavy "machine gun and rifle fire," the attackers found it "impossible" to attempt any kind of crossing. By the time the assault was finally terminated, the Highlanders had suffered another fourteen casualties, including Lieutenant-Colonel Ralston – "wounded for the fourth time" since arriving in France in 1917 – and six conscripts.[14] Undeterred, two nights later the 85th made another attempt to capture the crossing, but it too "proved a failure" when the enemy blew up remnants of the bridge just before the Highlanders could cross it. This time the battalion sustained sixteen casualties and five dead, apparently all conscripts.[15] A similar attack the following day resulted in yet another failed effort and fourteen more casualties, including Private Richard Hughes, a twenty-one-year-old barber from Charlottetown. "Severely wounded in the stomach by [enemy] shrapnel," Hughes was evacuated to No. 1 CCS, where he "died the same evening."[16]

A few kilometres farther downstream and opposite the village of Beuvrages, Jock Rankin's 75th Battalion (11th Brigade) had been similarly frustrated. There for an entire week the Mississauga Battalion had boldly conducted cross-canal reconnaissance patrols every night, with one such venture resulting in "a most regrettable though unavoidable incident." On the night of 24–25 October, a fifteen-man patrol led by Lieutenant Henry Hanan had no sooner "crossed over to the Bosche side of the canal" when they were "fired on by a machine gun and about 20 rifles at 40 paces distance." Compelled to withdraw, seven of Hanan's men "attempted to swim back across the Canal instead of making for the bridge." Five of these soldiers did not make it back – a sergeant, two scouts, and two others, both conscripts, including Private S.J. Sauve, a commercial traveller from Toronto, whose "body was recovered from the canal a few days later." Clearly, more robust efforts to secure a bridgehead were in order, and in this respect the corps' grand offensive was about to take another decisive turn.[17]

Valenciennes: Plan of Attack

By Friday, 25 October, the Great War was racing to its grand finale. The following day, General Ludendorff tendered his resignation to the Kaiser in Berlin; to the general's abject disappointment, it was immediately accepted.[18] Two days later, General Horne met with Currie and Godley in Auberchicourt to discuss how best "to force the enemy to evacuate Valenciennes." There it was agreed that beginning on 28 October, Godley's XXII Corps would secure the "high ground west of Aulnoy" and the "wooded height of Mont Houy" (both south of the city), along with "the sunken road north of it." That task complete, in phase two Currie would relieve Godley, and two days later both corps would advance 2.5 kilometres in a northeasterly direction to the steel works in Marly, east of Valenciennes. For phase three, Horne envisioned a multi-corps attack on 1 November that would see the city completely enveloped.[19] All these things would eventually come to pass, but not, as was often the case in the Hundred Days, before the Germans had their own say in how the great battle would unfold.

Lieutenant-General Godley chose to commit his 51st (Highland) Division against Mont Houy on 28 October, rather than his comparatively "fresh 49th Division," and to do so employing "relatively modest fire support." By mid-morning the 4th Battalion of the Seaforth Highlanders had seized most of its objectives at Mont Houy, but with heavy casualties. For some unknown reason, Godley failed to reinforce this remarkable success, and subsequent German counterattacks pushed the British all the way back to the southern slopes of this vital summit.[20] By dusk it was clear to Currie that Horne's original plan of attack required serious modification, one that would result in a simultaneous attack by the Canadian Corps and XXII Corps starting 1 November. Indeed, in Currie's view, the Canadians would also need "to carry out all three phases of the operation against Valenciennes."[21]

For Currie, the main challenge at Valenciennes was how best to employ his much depleted infantry in the most efficient manner possible. Wherever possible, he would substitute more "firepower for manpower" – a wise approach, given that daily casualty counts had continued to mount.[22] For example, on 29 October, Lieutenant-Colonel A.D. Cameron's 38th Battalion had been "heavily shelled by H.E. and Gas," resulting in a handful of casualties, including two French Canadians – Privates Leon Provencher, a farmer from Chicopee, Massachusetts, but originally from Plessisville, and Joseph Pelletier, a labourer from Hull, Quebec. Provencher was killed outright, while young Pelletier suffered "Shrapnel Wounds [to his] Right Thigh" along with fractures to both his leg and his right arm. Evacuated to No.1 CCS, he died from these wounds the next day.[23] Likewise, nearly 9 kilometres farther to the north, the 1st Battalion CMR was being subjected daily to "fairly active" enemy artillery fire. Among the many casualties was Private Gordon Young, an Ontario-born farmer and conscript from Limerick in southern Saskatchewan. Enemy shrapnel fractured Young's left elbow and caused a similar compound fracture to the tibia and fibula just above his left ankle; another piece of shrapnel penetrated his chest. Because of the often-lethal effects of shock, blood loss, and infection, Young's chances of survival were slim. His subsequent treatment, though, demonstrates just how sophisticated the military medical system had become; it also graphically illustrates the painful journey that he and thousands of his wounded mates were forced to undergo.[24]

Evacuated immediately to a regimental aid post, Private Young was next shuttled by No. 10 Canadian Field Ambulance from Valenciennes to Brebières (No. 23 CCS), some 50 kilometres to the west, and from there another 120 kilometres farther west to No. 7 Canadian General Hospital in Étaples. Doctors would save Young's life in Brebières, but not before amputating his left arm 10 centimetres above the elbow and, somewhat hastily, resetting his serious leg fractures. The latter effort ultimately resulted in his left leg being 7 centimetres shorter than his right. On 10 November, Young was moved again, this time to Queen Alexandra's Military Hospital (Millbank) in London, where he underwent two more operations and spent fifteen weeks convalescing before being transferred on 28 February to Granville Canadian Special (Orthopedic) Hospital in Buxton. Finally, on 21 May 1919, Young was invalided home to Canada, there to undergo another eleven months of therapy at the Dominion Orthopedic Hospital in Toronto, where he was finally discharged from the service as "Medically Unfit" on 10 April 1920.[25]

Friday, November 1: "Honour and Duty Came First"

While the initial tactical advantage in any attack almost always belongs to the defender, this principle appears to have been doubly true for the German army at Valenciennes. The enemy, blessed by the previously mentioned high terrain at Mont Houy, was able to field the still formidable remnants of at least five infantry divisions; it was also able to shelter many assets among a large civilian population and, more important, it could take full tactical advantage of the ample cover afforded by a large urban landscape. Besides all this, the lead Canadian formation, Ross's 10th Brigade, was a mere shadow of its former self, with

Figure 10.2 Private Gordon
Alexander Young, 1st Battalion
Canadian Mounted Rifles, on the
mend in 1919, having lost his left
arm and part of his left foot at
Valenciennes. *Source:* Courtesy
of Tex Young and Tracey Bexson.

a trench strength of just "1200 all ranks or about 300 per battalion" – about half
that typically deployed at the outset of such a major engagement. In view of the
failure of an equally determined but understrength British force to hang on
three days earlier at Mont Houy, the prospects for Canadian success were
guarded at best. But as a result of bringing to bear double the number of field
artillery brigades previously employed by Godley, combined with deadly enfilade
fire from no less than twelve machine-gun batteries, the outcome of this assault
would be decided even before the first clash of bayonets. Still, it would be a
hard-won victory.[26]

Stepping off to a thunderous barrage at 0515 hours on that cold and very wet
Friday morning, Keegan's much reduced 47th Battalion advanced 1 kilometre
towards Le Poirier Station, the western end of the "Red Line"; meanwhile, on
the right, Davies's equally understrength 44th Battalion led the rest of the 10th
Brigade in a swift frontal attack on the German redoubt at Mont Houy and on
the adjacent village of Aulnoy. Two minutes after zero hour, the Germans opened
a deadly counter-barrage of their own, predictably catching Ross's two rear
battalions in a maelstrom of "gas and H.E." Among these early casualties were

two draftees from the 46th: the Montreal-born Private Leon Forgue from Howell, Saskatchewan, and Private William Kitchen of Alexis Creek, BC, originally from Hillsdale, Ontario – both "killed by enemy shell fire."[27]

Undeterred, Davies launched two "low strength" companies forward, one "to clear Mont Houy Wood" on the left and the second "direct on Aulnoy." Both met little opposition at first, and in fact within just ninety minutes this New Brunswick regiment had secured all its primary objectives along with a key bridge crossing the Rhonelle River. Even so, some "enemy machine gunners" had offered stiff resistance, and thus the 44th sustained dozens more casualties. Several draftees were among them, including Privates Lucien Papillon, a twenty-one-year-old "Steamship Stoker" from Sorel, Quebec, and Alfred Jodin, a twenty-year-old labourer from Lancaster, Ontario, both killed during the attack.[28]

Similarly, in the "severe fighting" at Poirier Station, while hundreds of German soldiers had quickly laid down their arms, most "did not surrender until many had been killed by the bayonet, or shot down." Thus, Keegan's men had suffered as well. One casualty was Private Stanley Hosey, a twenty-one-year-old labourer from Chatham, Ontario, who died after being "struck on the head by a piece of enemy shrapnel."[29] Notably, upon enlistment Private Hosey's "Complexion" was described as "Dark (negro)." One of a small number of men from Kent County, Ontario, to be described as such, Hosey was also one of less than a dozen to actually see service in a front-line infantry unit.[30] Indeed, his story is part of a much larger narrative that embraces another uncomfortable fact about Canadian society at the time, one that historian Barbara Wilson would one day sum up in this simple observation: "Negro volunteers were not welcome in the Canadian Expeditionary Force."[31]

Figure 10.3 Private Stanley Hosey, 47th Battalion, killed in action at Valenciennes, 1 November 1918. *Source:* Chatham-Kent Museum.

Elsewhere in the 10th Brigade, Lieutenant-Colonel Herbert Dawson had ordered his 46th Battalion to act essentially as moppers-up in their drive north to the Red Line, between Mont Houy and Aulnoy, but because troop strength in the 44th was "very weak," the efforts of the two battalions were rapidly "merged." The "mopping-up" that followed proved to be "deadly work." Private Donald Manson, a farmer from Lillooet, BC, was "hit in the breast and instantly killed by an enemy machine gun bullet," while Private Edward Schnitzler, a garage man and fellow draftee from Bienfait, in southern Saskatchewan, suffered a fractured thigh from shellfire and died of his wounds the next day at No. 42 CCS.[32]

Jumping off a second time shortly after 0700 hours to a renewed barrage, the 46th advanced rapidly up the main road towards Marly and Valenciennes before running headlong into stiff resistance at a crucial road junction just north of Aulnoy. Soon the Saskatchewans began to sustain "severe casualties ... principally from enemy machine guns." One of those who probably fell around this time was Private Russell Long, a twenty-two-year-old farmer and draftee from Kennedy, Saskatchewan (by way of South Gower, Ontario). A member of a "Lewis Gun section," Long was fatally "struck in the head" by machine-gun fire. In fact, dozens of conscripts in the 46th Battalion would fall in action this day, including ten killed outright, plus two more who were fatally wounded. Their sacrifice, along with that of all their comrades, is perhaps best summed up by the poignant phrase inscribed on Private Manson's headstone at the Aulnoy Communal Cemetery, solemn words that seem to speak for all of the fallen on that day: "Honour And Duty Came First."[33]

Later that morning, Dawson's "A" Company, then under the command of Captain R.W. Gyles, fought a seminal engagement at the steel works in Marly. In his after-action report, Gyles was effusive in his praise that "the men did all that was expected of them." But he also sought in the wake of 126 casualties "to specially mention the valuable services throughout the entire operation" of six individuals in particular. Sergeant Hugh Cairns (who won a posthumous Victoria Cross) topped this list, along with Company Sergeant-Major Fred Gibbons. Gyles also made specific note of three other ORs, including Private Edward Slack, who was recommended for an immediate DCM and who no doubt was among a handful of ORs who fought valiantly beside Sergeant Cairns that day. Slack, a twenty-four-year-old farmer and conscript from Springside, a remote village in eastern Saskatchewan, would be denied the DCM, but he too would be awarded a Military Medal for his heroism on this historic day.[34]

"Some very useful killing was also achieved"

Keegan's 47th Battalion on the left had also met very strong opposition in its own successful advance into the southern outskirts of Valenciennes. Although the guns of Brigadier-General Andrew McNaughton (recently promoted to GOC Corps Heavy Artillery) had already sealed their fate, the German defenders mounted a formidable defence, and dozens more southwestern Ontario men fell in this second phase of the attack. Among them were Privates Odiel Deporter, a Belgian-born farmer from the tiny hamlet of Glen Rae (south of Petrolia), and Roy Graham, a railway brakeman from Windsor – just two of seven conscripts in the battalion to make the ultimate sacrifice this day.[35]

Lieutenant-Colonel Page and his 50th Battalion met with equal success. Still, while his second-in-command would chillingly record that "some very useful killing was also achieved," victory came yet again at a high cost. By the time it was relieved the following day, the 50th had lost 127 men. Among their wounded was Private Donald McLeod, a Scottish-born farmer from Big Prairie (Carstens), Alberta, who was gassed during the morning advance. At nearly thirty-six years old, McLeod, who had been drafted just over four months earlier (23 June), was also one of the oldest conscripts in the CEF. When he died three days later at No. 42 CCS, McLeod had the unenviable distinction of being one of the very last of these "late"-arriving conscripts to succumb to wounds sustained at the front.[36]

Thus, in exchange for inflicting a decisive defeat against the German forces opposing him south of Valenciennes, Ross's 10th Brigade alone sustained around five hundred casualties. Moreover, in just one day, and in what would be the brigade's last engagement of the war, this formation had suffered a roughly 40 percent reduction in trench strength.[37]

Yet the battle for Valenciennes still had not been decided. Leading the way across the canal from the west late that morning was Lieutenant-Colonel Alex Cameron's fresh but understrength 38th Battalion, numbering just ten officers and 398 ORs. Cameron wisely chose to forgo the use of a risky cork float bridge; instead he opted to drive his troops rapidly across a nearby damaged bridge. This he successfully accomplished with few casualties between 1145 and 1240 hours. Among them was Private Robert Publow, a liveryman and draftee from Perth, Ontario, who was fatally "struck by a machine gun bullet" as he made his way across the canal. More tragically, particularly for his grieving family back home in Canada, Robert was David Publow's second son to be killed in action – a younger son (Orville) had fallen two months earlier at the D-Q Line.[38]

Farther north, Major James Hamilton, acting CO of the 72nd Battalion, was faced with similar challenges all along his sector of the canal, which was nearly 20 metres wide at this point, "full to overflowing," and heavily defended by German machine-gun posts. In addition, the 72nd's assault would have to be made in broad daylight using "collapsible boats, rafts and a cork float bridge," and by a force of just 371 rifles. Still, the 72nd made short work of the crossing and quickly secured a bridgehead, after which "the kilties flung themselves with ardour against the German posts in the railway yards," and in particular against the "big station building," which was strongly defended. By nightfall, the enemy had been largely routed, at a cost of forty casualties.[39] When a number of awards for bravery were later announced, they included one draftee: Private Gonzaemon "Jack" Niihara, a twenty-eight-year-old Japanese-born "Rancher and Farmer" from Vernon, BC. Niihara, who previously had been wounded on 10 August at Amiens, was in charge of a Lewis gun section at Valenciennes. Having survived the treacherous canal crossing, he found himself quite alone on the opposite bank. Then, according to one eyewitness, Niihara single-handedly continued his attack into the railway yards and apparently "confused" the enemy in the process, who likely were a bit shocked by the sudden appearance of this lone machine-gunner. In the event, his timely and heroic actions enabled his platoon to gain "complete possession of the station." For bravery under fire and for conspicuous gallantry, Private Niihara was awarded the Military Medal.[40]

At dawn the next day the 12th Brigade renewed its assault on Valenciennes. The 38th Battalion advanced virtually unopposed through the centre of the town, while the 72nd raced unchecked across the northern half, at least until one of its cyclist patrols (seven men) ran directly into the path of three German machine-gun nests at the city's northeast corner. There, "unexpected fire at close range told sadly on the cyclists." Among the casualties was Private Joseph Roy, an American-born labourer and draftee from Byng Inlet, Ontario – "killed by a machine gun bullet which hit him over the left eye." Pressing forward another 2 kilometres, the Seaforths drove "the last of the Boches ... from the village of Saint-Saulve" in exchange for 2 more killed (both BCRM men) and 22 wounded, including 14 conscripts.[41]

In the meantime, on the far-right flank of this renewed offensive, Brigadier-General Odlum thrust his 11th Brigade back into the breach, this time at Marly, where his troops soon found that the Germans were much less compliant than those who had abandoned the centre of Valenciennes. In particular, Alfred Carey's 54th Battalion met strong opposition and "considerable street fighting ensued." Casualties mounted quickly.[42] Sent forward around noon to reinforce, Major Edward Ryan's 102nd encountered "considerable enemy machine gun fire." Although his troops eventually prevailed, Ryan would lose five men killed, including two Ontario lads – Privates William Ney from Midland and George Hill from Marshville – both of whom had been conscripted in Hamilton not quite six months earlier. In a noteworthy postscript to the fierce fighting, another draftee, Private James Barlow, a twenty-three-year-old British-born "Roll

Turner" from Hamilton, would be awarded the Military Medal for his gallantry during this final action at Valenciennes.[43]

By the end of the day, the Canadian Corps had killed more than eight hundred of the enemy and captured another eighteen hundred, proving once again that it was a formidable force. Indeed, given the sheer ferocity of the struggle, more than one account suggests that these numbers could have been considerably higher.[44] Similarly, one cannot ignore the fact that in the case of the 10th Brigade, Brigadier-General Ross had successfully accomplished his main task with four seriously understrength infantry battalions, the ranks of which had been brought up to minimum fighting strength by the timely arrival of hundreds of reinforcements, most of them conscripts.

"Completely wiped out by enemy machine gun fire"

Despite what appeared to be a full-scale retreat, Field Marshal Haig remained convinced that "the German Army [was] not yet demoralized," and therefore no let-up in the offensive would be permitted. Accordingly, General Horne directed that First Army continue its "general advance," its far objective initially being set for Maubeuge on the right and for the historic city of Mons on the left.[45] Thus Watson's 11th and 12th Brigades renewed their drive east on 3 and 4 November, only to encounter "strong resistance." The 38th and 72nd Canadian Battalions were stopped cold in their tracks on the outskirts of Onnaing, where both suffered many casualties. Among these were Privates Isidore Godin, a twenty-year-old fisherman from Maisonette, New Brunswick, and Donald McAskill, a twenty-eight-year-old Scottish-born labourer from Sandon, BC. Godin was fatally struck by an "enemy machine gun bullet" during a platoon attack near the brickyards just southeast of Onnaing. McAskill was part of an eight-man patrol that was "completely wiped out by enemy machine gun fire" only 100 metres east of the village.[46]

Both brigades supplied fresh battalions to the assault the following day, augmented in part by the 8th Brigade to the north. Yet all three were stymied again by strong enemy resistance. On the far right, the 75th and 87th Battalions quickly swept past the village of Rombies, but further progress beyond the River Aunelle proved impossible, principally due to concentrated enemy machine-gun fire from a German redoubt near the hamlet of Marchipont. The 87th would lose nearly forty men there; the 75th would fare even worse. Just one unsuccessful platoon-sized frontal attack against Marchipont resulted in fifteen casualties, including Private Robert Andrews, a farmer and draftee from Brampton, Ontario, killed in action one day after his twenty-second birthday. Ultimately ten more conscripts lost their lives this day, during which time "the weather conditions and the heavy strain were almost unbearable." For Jock Rankin and his 75th Battalion, this was their last engagement of the war.[47]

In the centre of this attack, the 12th Brigade sent forward two fresh battalions into the fight – the 78th on the left and the 85th on the right. Both jumped off at 0530 hours on 5 November and quickly captured the village of Quarouble. But the real challenge for the 85th was another 2.5 kilometres east, almost at the Belgian border – a slag heap and fortified German trench called Fosse no. 2, just southwest of the town of Quiévrechain. The first two attempts to take the redoubt were met with "stubborn and costly opposition," resulting in at least a dozen casualties. Among them were several draftees, including Privates Cecil Boutilier, a young lumberman from Boutilier Point, and Joseph Sarty, a fisherman from Parker's Cove, Nova Scotia. Boutilier was killed outright by enemy rifle fire in the initial advance; Sarty was much more fortunate. First wounded during a horrific German air raid at the train station in Arras on 25 September, Private Sarty had recovered just in time to rejoin his unit on 2 November and receive a final albeit survivable blighty at Quiévrechain.[48] As for his battalion, its third and successful attempt to take Fosse No.2 had met with even deadlier results – 1 officer and 16 other ranks killed; 3 officers and 28 other ranks wounded. No fewer than nine of the dead and at least half of the wounded were conscripts, among them Private Clifford Morris, a widower and ship carpenter from Advocate Harbour, Nova Scotia, who was "hit in the body and instantly killed by several enemy bullets."[49]

In summing up the "many incidents of outstanding personal acts of courage" evidenced throughout this hard-fought battle, the 85th's historian, Joseph Hayes, would one day single out the heroics of seventeen ORs – all but two of whom were awarded the Military Medal for conspicuous gallantry. The two exceptions were Private Robert Henry, a twenty-two-year-old tailor and draftee from Halifax who had joined the battalion on 6 September and "was of invaluable assistance to his company in organizing and leading attacks against enemy machine gun posts under heavy fire," and Private William Kurtzweg, a thirty-four-year-old carpenter and conscript from Jacksonboro in Northern Ontario. "Though wounded," Kurtzweg had "volunteered to take back important messages under severe machine gun and artillery fire within short range and direct observation of the enemy."[50] Ultimately, the 85th would not award a Military Medal to any conscript soldier in the Great War, one of nineteen Canadian infantry units to have this same distinction.

Farther north, Dennis Draper's 8th Brigade had provided crucial flank protection for MacBrien's 12th Brigade on the right, but in the face of "considerable opposition" the GOC decided to reorganize and prepare a "set attack" for the next day. Jumping off at 0530 hours on 6 November, Lieutenant-Colonel G.

Chalmers Johnston's 2nd CMRs made a "rapid advance" to the Aunelle River north of Quiévrechain, and then another 400 metres east to the Grande Honelle River at Quiévrain, which, quite fortuitously, helped prevent the Germans from destroying two vital bridges essential for continuing the advance the next day. This was a costly action: the 2nd CMR suffered "40 other ranks casualties," half of which were fatal. And yet the Canadian Corps now had a firm foothold in Belgium, its first in nearly a year. Mons, a nearly impossible objective only five weeks earlier, was now tantalizingly within reach, just 23 kilometres away.[51]

On the far-right flank, Odlum's 11th Brigade had pushed forward a single battalion – the 102nd. Tasked to "clean up the country west of the Grande Honnelle River," Major Ryan's legion did even better than that. By 0700 hours it had disposed of the loathsome enemy redoubt at Marchipont. Then, pressing north to envelop Quiévrechain, it advanced relentlessly eastwards until by 0900 hours it found itself on the banks of the Grande Honnelle, knee-deep and 4.5 metres wide. Seizing the moment, an intrepid party of five, led by Lieutenant R.L. Gale, crossed the river "in the face of heavy machine-gun fire" and quickly established a secure post on the opposite bank – an action that would ultimately lead to "the complete capture of Baisieux." An unexpected but very worthy triumph, this daring attack on an obscure Belgian village resulted in a unique distinction – it would be "the last position taken by the 4th Division." Remarkably, casualties had been "comparatively light"– thirty-seven overall, mostly due to poison gas. Among the wounded was Private Fred Allen, a twenty-two-year-old farmer and draftee from Caistor, Ontario (near Hamilton) who, after suffering a "Gunshot wound [to the] shoulder," died the next day at No. 33 CCS in Denain.[52]

"A second telegram of regret"

Over the next four days (7 to 10 November) the Germans continued their fighting retreat, often yielding large tracts of land without offering any resistance, but at other times throwing up a deadly wall of fire. While overall losses for the 3rd Division were low, such was not the case for Burstall's 2nd Division, which was advancing at the same time and in parallel along the south side of the Mons-Valenciennes road. For Tremblay's 5th Brigade, the capture of Élouges on 7 November came at a stiff price. Lieutenant-Colonel C.J. Mesereau's 25th Nova Scotia Rifles suffered 59 casualties, including "10 O.R. killed and 41 wounded." Similarly, to the north, Henri Desrosier's 22nd "Van Doos" met "a good deal of opposition" before claiming their own share of the village, sustaining thirty-five casualties, including four dead. Among the latter was Private George Blanchette, a labourer from Huntingdon, Quebec, whose older brother Guy, also a conscript with the 24th Battalion, had been killed on the first day of the Battle of Amiens.[53] Their father Frank would now be the recipient of a second telegram of regret.

On Saturday, 9 November, the German peace delegation met with Marshal Ferdinand Foch in his railway car at Compiègne to receive the terms of the armistice; meanwhile, in Germany, a political and military revolution was about to reach its angry climax. Nevertheless, despite a fervent desire among all parties for an immediate ceasefire, Foch concluded that "hostilities [could not] cease before the signing of the Armistice." Hence, the pursuit of the German army would continue across the Western Front, not least for the men of the Canadian Corps, who on this day found themselves just over 3 kilometres from the centre of Mons.[54]

Advancing rapidly to the northeast, McCuaig's 4th Brigade encountered "little or no opposition." Indeed, Harry Pense's 21st Battalion made a triumphant march east to Noirchain before encountering enemy artillery and machine-gun fire that claimed six casualties, including one dead. That soldier was Private Lawrence Sullivan, a twenty-one-year-old lumberman and draftee from Rapides-des-Joachims, Quebec, killed by shellfire during the advance. Remarkably, his death is mentioned specifically in the unit's war diary, once again a nearly unprecedented notation, given that no apparent act of gallantry was involved. The diarist also recorded that Sullivan, who had been on strength since 28 August, "was considered an efficient soldier." But perhaps the real explanation for such an unusual diary entry is the simple fact that Private Sullivan was this battalion's last combat fatality of the war.[55]

Overnight, the corps continued its envelopment of the historic city of Mons, which, like Cambrai, presented the troops with a splendid prize to liberate as well as a perilous obstacle to navigate. By early the next morning, 10 November, it was clear that the city would not be surrendered without a serious fight. As Major-General Loomis later recorded, "the enemy showed that he intended to resist our entry into the town to the utmost" – hence the need for the Canadians to make yet another large-scale Sunday attack.[56] The 3rd Battalion (Canadian Machine Gun Corps), operating 3 kilometres to the northwest in support of the 7th Brigade, suffered some of the first Canadian casualties. At around 1030 hours, one of this battalion's gun limbers was passing through Ghlin when the occupants, two young conscripts among them, were apparently the target of enemy artillery. Mortally wounded in this attack were the brakeman Private William Garvin, a cigarmaker from Hamilton, and likely Private Earl McKenney, an engineer from Welland, Ontario. Garvin, "his right leg ... severed" by the blast, also "received a bad shrapnel wound to the abdomen." Heavy shelling and machine-gun fire prevented his timely removal to a dressing station, and two hours later he was dead. As for Private McKenney, he too

Figure 10.4   Private Clayton
Elmer Underwood, 18th Battalion,
died of wounds 11 November 1918.
Source: Grace Schmidt Room
Digital Collection, Kitchener
Public Library.

suffered "Shrapnel wounds [to the] head, hand, [and left] thigh," the latter of
which had been fractured in the explosion. Evacuated to No. 4 CCS, he perished
from his wounds later that day.[57]

Farther south that morning, and also completing its last combat action of
the war, the 18th Battalion managed to establish outposts on the outskirts of
Hyon, a small village just 1 kilometre southeast of Mons. There it too was forced
to endure "considerable scattered shelling" for most of the day, which resulted
in a number of losses. One soldier, a volunteer named Private John Rowlinson,
was captured by the Germans early in the advance and later executed. Among
the other casualties was Private Clayton Underwood, a draftee from Bridgeport
(Kitchener), Ontario, who died of his wounds the next day. Both men had been
shoemakers before the war.[58]

Leapfrogging the 18th and making the 4th Brigade's primary advance to the
east of Mons on this day were the 19th and 20th Battalions. Almost from the
outset their combined assaults suffered severely, mainly due to near crippling
enemy machine-gun fire from the area's most "dominant and key position," the
Bois la Haut, a heavily wooded area 2 kilometres east of Mons, which rose 107
metres above the surrounding terrain.[59] Pinned down for most of the day just
outside the village of Mesvin, Bert Hooper's 20th Battalion would sustain forty-
two casualties, including eleven ORs killed in action. Among the latter were
Privates Percy Simmons, a painter by trade, and Alfred Dawson, a baker, both
British-born and from Toronto. Simmons had been "shot through the head";

Dawson had suffered a "gunshot wound [to the] abdomen" and was later "Admitted Dead to No. 6 Canadian Field Ambulance."[60]

Meanwhile, Hatch's 19th found itself pinned down by "heavy machine gun fire from houses in Hyon" and by "hostile artillery fire" from the Bois la Haut. Only a heavy artillery barrage on the Bois finally allowed the 19th to occupy Hyon, which it did at 0230 hours the following morning, after sustaining more than fifty casualties. Twelve other ranks were either dead or dying, including six conscripts. Private James Buttimer, an Irish-born cashier from Toronto, was among the latter. A member of a "stretcher bearing party," Buttimer had been traversing "no man's land ... when the enemy opened up machine gun fire instantly killing" him. Two days later, in a poignant postscript, he and his fallen comrades would be initially interred with full military honours at the Hyon Communal Cemetery. There the battalion and a grateful "civilian population" would pay a fitting tribute to the sacrifice of "these brave men."[61]

Farther west, advance patrols of the 42nd Battalion and the RCR crept forward under cover of darkness to the very edge of the city, their aim being to cross over two separate water obstacles – the Canal du Centre in the north and west, also known as the Mons-Condé Canal, and the narrow (6 metre) extension of the river Trouille in the south – and thence into Mons. By 2300 hours, one platoon of the 42nd had crossed the Condé Canal, "passed through the railway yard and entered the city at a point near the station," thereby cutting off the stalwart German defenders then facing a larger group of Canadians preparing to advance from the south.[62] There, one company each from the 42nd and the RCR forced a crossing and soon began to invest the city. At the same time, another company of the RCR stole across the Canal du Centre some 3 kilometres north of the city and captured the village of Nimy, the same area where British and German forces had first clashed in 1914. By "0600 Mons was reported clear of the enemy." The battle was over. Two days of tough fighting, however, had cost the 42nd another thirty-one casualties, while the RCR and PPCLI had sustained an overall loss of seventy-four men, several conscripts among them.[63] Meanwhile, the 6th Brigade began to move yet again to the east, for what would be its own final advance to contact with the enemy.

"The Fighting Is Over"

As Harry Burstall would later write: "November 11th was a fine autumn day, all conditions being most favourable for a rapid advance." Even though an armistice was imminent, Burstall had issued somewhat ambitious orders late the previous evening for Alex Ross's 6th Brigade to march 6 kilometres to the northeast, capture Havré, and seize "the crossings over the Canal [du Centre] north of this village, after which they were to move East." Later that evening, corps headquarters signalled that the 2nd Division's more modest objectives assigned for the previous day remained unchanged: "seize the high ground at Bois la Haut." Nonetheless, given the "general situation," Burstall decided not to cancel 6th Brigade's orders; thus, the attack would begin at 0800 hours. His troops were fresh and the Germans were clearly on the run; at that moment the men of his 2nd Division remained the only Canadians still in the fight.[64]

At about 0400 hours the 28th and 31st Battalions began a forced march from Frameries to St. Symphorien, a memorable and circuitous route march in "pitch darkness" that covered 16 kilometres in less than four hours, highlighted by "large numbers of civilians [who] flocked into the streets and received the men with scenes of remarkable enthusiasm." Then, just as these units were arriving at their JOL (0730 hours), the 6th Brigade received notification from Division HQ that hostilities would "cease at 1100" and "that troops will stand fast on the line reached at that hour." However, war diaries reveal that neither battalion received this crucial information until 0900, one hour *after* they began their attack. Apparently, given no change in tasking from the night before, Ross had simply ordered his "attacking Battalions ... to push on with all possible speed in order to gain as much territory as possible before 1100 hours."[65]

Jumping off on the right at 0800, Spencer's 31st made excellent progress, at least "for the first hour," despite "considerable machine gun fire" coming from the south side of the Bois d'Havré. Then, after another successful 3 kilometre advance, the Albertans ran headlong into "concentrated fire from ten or twelve machine gun nests," after which the enemy suddenly let loose a final salvo, wounding one officer and five other ranks. Immediately thereafter, in what surely must have been a stunning scene, "the enemy put up the white flag, shot up white flares, about sixty of them ... emptied the water out of their machine guns and marched away in formation."[66] Retiring in apparent defeat but having fought with great determination right to the bitter end, these soldiers provided final proof, if any was really needed, that Currie and the Canadian Corps had faced a formidable enemy to the last.

Farther to the north, Major A.F. Simpson's 28th Battalion also "made extremely rapid progress," encountering only minor opposition in the Bois d'Havré. Thereafter, despite "somewhat increased resistance," this unit captured the village of Havré and crossed the Canal du Centre another kilometre to the east. Notably, the total tactical advance for the "North West" Battalion on this day had been nearly 7 kilometres – the farthest east that the Canadian Corps penetrated during the entire war – all at the cost of a single fatality.[67] That soldier was Private George Price, the twenty-five-year-old Nova Scotian and farm labourer from Saskatchewan mentioned in this volume's Introduction. According to the official Circumstances of Death report signed by his Commanding

Figure 10.5 Sapper Roy Neilson (centre) and comrades with Belgian family who billeted the men at the end of the war. *Source:* Courtesy of Dr. Peter Neilson.

Officer, Private Price was "killed by [an] enemy sniper at three minutes to eleven," which made him the last Canadian to die in battle during the Hundred Days.[68] His remains were interred in the St. Symphorien Military Cemetery, where today he rests, not far from the grave of the first British soldier killed more than four years earlier – Private John Parr of the Middlesex Regiment.[69]

The tragedy of Price's untimely death aside, the Great War on the Western Front had come to an abrupt end. The suddenness of the ceasefire and the eerie quiet that descended across the battlefield initially left most eyewitnesses in stunned disbelief. Nearly half a century later, the regimental historian for Tobin's Tigers would recall that "for the first time in its history, the 29th Battalion appeared to be at a complete loss. No one seemed to know what to do" – a sentiment likely shared by most other Canadian infantry units.[70] For most troops, confirmation of the Armistice came "as a great surprise – almost an incredible relief," but for many others, the news was "mixed with disappointment" at the thought of not being able "to have another 'go' at the Boche."[71] Echoing this latter sentiment, Sapper A. Roy Neilson's diary entry for this historic day read, "Armistice signed and Hostilities cease at 11 A.M. much to the *Sorrow*? [*sic*] of the Troops."[72]

In this historical context, the notion that the Canadians might still have enough manpower to pursue the enemy in such an aggressive fashion was rooted in one fundamental and defining reality: unlike the British army as a whole, the Canadian Corps still enjoyed a crucial and steady (albeit reduced) flow of trained reinforcements. The British on the other hand, according to Sir Philip Gibbs (an official war correspondent at the time), "could not have gone on much farther after November 11th ... The pace could not have been kept up."[73]

Even as the headlines back home proclaimed that "The Fighting Is Over," another sharp reality quickly emerged: the great triumphs of the Canadian Corps had come at an enormous cost in battle casualties, especially during the Hundred Days.[74] Thus, while soldiers throughout the corps paused to mourn their fallen comrades, a grateful nation solemnly reflected on the many great sacrifices that had been made.

As for the Canadian conscripts who had fought throughout the corps' final campaign – neither slackers, nor shirkers, nor malingerers – these brave men could take some comfort in having made their own special mark on the battle-fields of France and Belgium. They had done so in significant numbers and ultimately had provided the Canadian Corps with a crucial manpower resource just when it was needed most. These were Canada's reluctant warriors – reluctant to embrace a cause that they and most of their draft-age comrades had largely refused to accept, but warriors too, thousands of whom, once compelled to fight, had distinguished themselves remarkably in combat, just as their volunteer comrades had done before them. Subsequent efforts to secure some measure of that hard-won legacy would last nearly a century and prove mostly futile. Nevertheless, as Laurence Binyon once declared in his iconic lament:

At the going down of the sun and in the morning
We will remember them.[75]

11
The Equal of the Best

But the kind, common ones that I despised
(Hardly a man of them I'd count as friend),
What stubborn-hearted virtues they disguised!
They stood and played the hero to the end,
Won gold and silver medals bright with bars,
And marched resplendent home with crowns and stars.

– SIEGFRIED SASSOON, "CONSCRIPTS"

"All the Lights Are On Again in England"

THE DAY AFTER THE Armistice, it was clear to one and all in the Canadian Corps that the killing was finally over. But, as many families back in Canada would tragically learn, the dying had a way to go. At least a dozen Canadian soldiers succumbed to combat wounds that day, and many more the next, including several conscripts. Among them was Private Emerson Cascaddan, a farmer from Shedden, Ontario, who had fallen in action two weeks earlier from "Gunshot wounds [to the] chest and right arm." Three days later his fellow draftee, Private Edgar Houle, a Quebec-born munitions worker and "Van Doo" from Toronto, also perished after suffering "Gun shot wounds" and the amputation of his left leg. In the weeks and months to come, many others would fail to recover from their terrible wounds. One of these later fatalities was Private Reginald Howell of the 50th Battalion, a storekeeper from St. Catharines, Ontario. Howell had been "severely wounded in the left thigh by a splinter from an enemy shell" during the attack near Cambrai on 28 September, and his leg amputated "at the thigh." Eight weeks later he expired at No. 20 General Hospital in Camiers.[1] Others met a similarly tragic end. For those whose fate had been sealed by the debilitating effects of gas poisoning, it might be several years before the inevitable outcome. Moreover, in the weeks after the Armistice, just as the Canadian army was about to make its advance to the Rhine, another more perilous threat re-emerged – the pernicious influenza virus.[2]

On 18 November 1918, the 1st and 2nd Divisions began an epic march that eventually took them across the Rhine to Germany on 4 December – a 250 kilometre odyssey – their ranks having been swelled by even greater numbers of new men.[3] It would be a brief sojourn. One month later, Currie's forces were withdrawn to Belgium, though not before many of his men witnessed the safe return of their remaining prisoner-of-war comrades. Among the latter was Private Ernest Hanson of the 31st Battalion, who the previous June had been the first of ninety-three conscripts to be captured. Joining Hanson was Private Eric Hedin of the 21st, who had been wounded in the foot and leg by shrapnel before he too was taken captive during his unit's attack at Iwuy.[4] For many others, though, this short tour in Germany was the very end of the line. Private Patsy Anile, a thirty-five-year-old Sicilian labourer from Windsor, Ontario, serving with the 18th Battalion, was one of those. Anile, who had joined the colours in mid-November 1917, fell victim to "Pneumonia and Influenza" in Bonn and died nearby at No. 1 CCS on 18 January 1919. Buried initially at the Poppelsdorfer Friedhof south of the city, his remains, like those of many of his comrades, were reinterred in the Brussels Town Cemetery some ten months later.[5]

In the meantime, Currie's 3rd and 4th Divisions had been "transferred to the IV Corps, Fourth Army," to take up duties as garrison troops in Belgium. For some veteran soldiers, no doubt this was a bitter blow. "To us who had set our hearts on entering *Allemagne* as victors after four years of war," wrote Victor Wheeler (50th Battalion), "now to be denied that satisfaction was very hard to accept."[6] For others, this decision, along with a general postwar malaise, likely helped sow more than a few kernels of discontent among the troops. Consequently, on 23 November, General Currie summoned all available "divisional commanders and brigadiers" to his headquarters in Mons, first to ascertain "the truth or otherwise of the rumours concerning a certain spirit of unrest amongst the troops; and secondly, [their views] as to demobilization." With regard to the latter, Currie was pleased to have general support for his proposal "to send the troops home by complete battalions," as opposed to "first over, first back."[7] Currie later recorded in his diary that "there is no doubt that some of those who have joined as a result of the Military Service Act have not acquired the proper *esprit de corps*"[8] – a rather vague albeit damaging allegation that was clarified somewhat in a letter written later in the day to Sir Edward Kemp: "We are having some troubles with the drafts who have recently joined us, that is men who have had no previous service in France, and I write to ask you that no more of these men be sent."[9]

Clearly, the primary focus of Currie's correspondence was on MSA men who had not been blooded. Three weeks later at a meeting with Lieutenant-Colonel H.S. Cooper (officer commanding the 1st Divisional Wing, Canadian Corps

Reinforcement Camp), Currie discussed "some trouble they were having there with draftees" and the need, in Currie's view, to send these men "to their divisions as soon as possible."[10] Thus, a wider and perhaps more sinister perception of conscripts appears to have emerged among the senior leadership of the Canadian Corps, principally as a result of developments after the end of the fighting. For example, having attended Currie's conference, Brigadier-General Griesbach noted the "general dissatisfaction with conscripts" and the fact that the "conference agreed no more MSA men are to be sent over."[11]

How thousands of conscripts were suddenly perceived in such a negative light remains a troubling mystery. Moreover, by deflecting attention away from the real source of dissatisfaction among many volunteers in the corps, and equally away from those soldiers who were actually fomenting the unrest, General Currie appears to have lost a crucial opportunity to seize control of what would soon become a major problem. Perhaps worse, at the same time he also put in place the foundations for the popular myth that conscripts were postwar troublemakers. This myth would do much to obscure the great achievements and sacrifices of Canadian draftees on the battlefield and to imperil their historical legacy. Moreover, it would not be long before Currie's own apparent antipathy towards conscripts would burst its banks.

"The draftees are not a well-disciplined body"

The catalyst for Currie's next *cri de coeur* came on 11 December, when, after spending a full month in Mons, Brigadier-General John Clark's 7th Brigade marched in "full kit" nearly 25 kilometres east to La Hestre, and the next day advanced in the cold and rain another 15 kilometres northeast to Nivelles. It appears that at this point, long-simmering antagonisms towards the GOC combined with general resentment towards objectionable military regulations to create what quickly became a dangerous cocktail of ill-disciplined and poorly led troops. Heavy casualties at the Canal du Nord and Cambrai had robbed these four battalions of many key leaders – a deficit that was never made up – while subsequent losses during the approach to Mons on the eve of the Armistice had become a source of bitter and lingering resentment. In this poisoned and highly charged climate, "several hundred men" gathered the next day (13 December) in Nivelles "to discuss their grievances" and later to present their list of demands to Clark – a list that he apparently refused to accept. The next morning, large numbers of angry troops broke into the brigade guardrooms and released the prisoners, after which the vast majority of men returned to their units. This tension-filled episode was a mighty shock, both to Major-General Loomis and to General Currie each of whom soon perceived the alleged role played by conscripts in this disturbance from quite different perspectives.[12]

Writing shortly afterwards "to his immediate superior, the GOC 4th British Corps," Loomis asserted that the men's complaints were "trivial" and that "the whole matter was one of discipline, training and efficient Officers and Non-Commissioned Officers. It was not," he added, "a condition of recent growth" – that is, the result of the 7th Brigade taking on board large numbers of new troops, especially conscripts.[13] In this respect, Loomis had drawn the opposite conclusion to Currie, who a few weeks earlier had warned the overseas minister that "our discipline [problem] is of recent growth; it has not been bred in the bone." At that same time, Currie had declared that the only way men, who "had not even heard a shot fired ... a great many [of whom were] enlisted in Canada because [of the] Military Service Act," could be "controlled" would be to maintain the "present organizations." For Currie, the conscripts were a threat to "good discipline," one that could be properly managed only by adhering to his demobilization plan. Thus, with respect to the latter, he made one last emotional appeal to Kemp: "For God's sake do not play with it for you are playing with fire."[14]

One week after the disturbance at Nivelles, Currie sent a "preliminary report" to Sir Edward Kemp in which he declared that "professional agitators [were] the cause of the trouble." Had the corps commander stopped right there he would have been perfectly correct, especially when one considers that among all his twelve infantry brigades, the 7th appears to have taken on strength the fewest number of conscript reinforcements. But in an awkward and somewhat startling attempt to perhaps better focus Kemp's attention on what he genuinely believed to be the core issue, he then added:

As I have written to you before, the draftees are not a well-disciplined body, and had the war gone on, we should have had a lot of trouble with them; although I do not intend for a minute to convey the impression that they are all bad. What I do say, is that there are a great many bad men amongst them, while many of them were hurried across to France with very little training.[15]

Once again, Currie was painting all draftees with a single brush and in a highly negative manner, and conveying these false impressions to an uninformed minister of the Crown, who no doubt was compelled to accept this biased assessment at face value. Then, in what appears to have been another not so subtle attempt to deflect attention from any involvement in the disturbances by volunteers, he immediately followed up this missive with a lengthier report to general headquarters that offered an even stronger indictment of conscripts: "all the trouble we have had in any unit, comes from the draftees." Those draftees, he added, "declare openly that they never wanted to come to the war, and that they want to have nothing to do with anything of a military character ... They have not fought with their units long enough to get a proper 'esprit de corps.'"[16] This assessment, however, was directly at odds with the government's official view on the subject, not to mention with the views of hundreds of junior leaders at the platoon and company levels, who knew differently. Yet to a certain extent, it has prevailed in the historiography. Indeed, Currie's evident lack of a wider view of conscripts, coupled with his apparent dismissal of positive evidence of their field discipline and their remarkable battlefield performance, clearly deserves further study.

With respect to the general unrest among the troops between November 1918 and June 1919, G.W.L. Nicholson observed that Canadian troops were involved in no less than "thirteen instances of riots or disturbances" in England alone, the "most serious [having] occurred at Kinmel Park on 4 and 5 March 1919." Although there is scant evidence that any draftees were at the centre of those events, resentment at the early repatriation to Canada of some conscripts – men whom Nicholson described as having "comparatively little service" – was cited as a contributing factor.[17] But in fact it was Currie's insistence that the Canadian Corps be repatriated as organized units, coupled with other major irritants in the Canadian "concentration camps" at Kinmel Park – widespread sickness, bad weather, poor food, crowded and poorly heated quarters, lack of pay, and, most important, lengthy delays in the assignment to Canada of suitable transports to carry the men home – that combined to fuel the worst riot in Canadian military history. In its immediate aftermath, five soldiers died and twenty-three were wounded.[18]

Currie would later record "that the troublemakers were men of the Forestry Corps and railway troops." Even so, as Tim Cook points out, Currie "blamed the riots on conscripts" and on those other "men who had not been part of the corps." Hence another distortion of the official record would emerge to detract yet again from the hard-won recognition these reluctant warriors had so fleetingly earned on the battlefield.[19]

"Whip the poor devils into line"

Back in Canada, the roughly 26,000 conscripts who had not yet been sent overseas were released from service shortly after the end of hostilities. However, the sudden Armistice did not end the pursuit by authorities of thousands of men who had ignored the call to report (i.e., defaulters).[20] Not until more than a year later, on 20 December 1919, did the Governor General finally sign an Order in Council that proclaimed a "general amnesty" for all of those who had committed offences under the MSA. This decision quickly resulted in the "release of all Canadians imprisoned for offences under the Military Service Act, and the suspension of all proceedings against others" – an official pardon of sorts that went a long way to help "restore peace" in a deeply divided country.[21]

But there was another group of conscripts, smaller but important, who were still very much under arms. For these draftees, soon destined to form a large part of the Canadian Expeditionary Force (Siberia), the Great War was far from over. Their remarkable story captures the harshest aspects of what Nicholson sharply described as "an aggressive enterprise," one that he equally declared to be "a complete failure." After Russia and Germany had signed the Treaty of Brest-Litovsk on 3 March 1918, the Allied powers feared the possible German exploitation of Russia's vast resources and its Far Eastern ports, which soon prompted open support by the Western allies for the anti-Bolshevik forces. In mid-July, Sir Robert Borden agreed to a War Office request for "the dispatch of a small Canadian force to Siberia." From the very start, though, the precise tasking for this force was obscure. While Russia had been a strong ally in the war up until 1917, its descent into Bolshevism had been alarming enough that Canada and twelve other countries were persuaded to offer some assistance and perhaps protection to the White Russian forces. Hence, the CGS immediately began to organize a composite brigade under the command of Major-General J.H. Elmsley (previously GOC 8th Brigade), which rapidly began to take shape at camps in New Westminster, Coquitlam, and Victoria, BC.[22]

The initial call for CEFS volunteers met with only partial success, so in early August the militia minister directed that gaps in the brigade's ranks be filled "with men obtained under the Military Service Act." Conscripts drawn principally from Ontario and Quebec provided nearly 40 percent of the force's overall strength (1,653 of 4,210 soldiers), including more than 50 percent of the 260th Battalion and nearly two-thirds of the men in the 259th. But by the time these soldiers arrived on the west coast in late October 1918, the war in Europe was nearly over. And, shortly after the Armistice, both the press and the public began to question the military rationale for the entire enterprise, not to mention the legality of sending conscripts overseas in support of a mission that did not appear to be aimed at contributing to the defence of Canada per se.[23] Even so, the prime minister decided to stay the course. Thus, the stage was set for another dark chapter in the history of Canadian conscripts, and the creation of one more myth that would further damage a hard-won legacy.

Early on the morning of 21 December 1918, the soldiers of the 259th Battalion began a 6 kilometre route march from Willows Camp to their troopship, the SS *Teesta* in Victoria harbour. According to eyewitness accounts, about halfway into the march a number of riflemen from the two French Canadian companies refused to go any farther, so the commanding officer, Lieutenant-Colonel Albert E. "Dolly" Swift, "drew his revolver and fired a shot over their heads." Afterwards, "the other two companies from Ontario were ordered to take off their belts and whip the poor devils into line," which apparently "they did with a will."[24] Some forty soldiers were subsequently arrested and summarily tried for their participation in this act of defiance. In addition, starting on 25 January 1919, ten soldiers – all conscripts and all French Canadians – were paraded before a Field General Court Martial in Vladivostok. All but one were found guilty on mutiny-related charges. The four ringleaders received the harshest punishments, varying from one to three years' imprisonment; the remainder escaped with less severe sentences ranging from twenty-eight days of Field Punishment No. 1 to six months' detention with hard labour.[25] If nothing else, good order and discipline had been restored among the ranks.

Elmsley's force, however, never did see any action. In February 1919, Borden decided to withdraw the Canadian contingent, and in late April the first returning troopship set sail for Victoria. But the scars from this ill-fated affair would take a long time to heal. French Canadian conscripts had rightfully challenged the legality of this deployment but had fatally compromised their position with an unacceptable mutiny. The spectacle of English Canadian conscripts then beating their comrades was an ugly metaphor for the divisive, deeply rooted, and widespread prejudices of the time. In the end, twenty-one fatalities were attributed to this untidy mission, including seven conscripts – none, thankfully, in the streets of Victoria.[26]

"The equal of the best sent over since the war began"

The return to Canada of Elmsley's force that June was yet another milestone in the closing days of the CEF, for with the arrival from Europe that month of Watson's 4th Division, the vast majority of Canadian soldiers were finally home. There began a long, cathartic process of national accounting for the sacrifices and achievements of the war. This included the tabling in Parliament of several official government reports that summarized the nation's accomplishments. Among the first of these was *European War Memorandum No. 5*, the Department of Militia's report on its major activities between 1 January and 31 October 1918. In the very first paragraph, Parliament was informed that "final victory was due, in part, to the fact that Canadian units went into action with full ranks, and with an abundant supply of reinforcements ready to replace casualties." As revealed earlier, this assessment was not entirely accurate. Nonetheless, conscripts did provide the greater part of infantry reinforcements, at least during the Hundred Days, and reports of their service prompted the Militia Department to conclude that "the recruits obtained under the Military Service Act are a fine body of men, physically and mentally – the equal of the best sent over since the war began. They show keen interest in their work, and make astonishing progress. Young and uniform of age, they constitute a reserve of the very best quality."[27]

Next, on 6 May, Lieutenant-Colonel Harold Machin's report on *The Operation of the Military Service Act, 1917* was tabled in the House by the Honourable Arthur Meighen. To some extent a self-serving document, it extolled the merits of the MSA but also highlighted at least one enduring controversy. Statistics on the large number of exemptions initially granted in November 1917, coupled with Machin's response to widespread criticism regarding "the issuance to draftees of harvest leave and compassionate leave," would in the long run help fuel the debate about the fairness with which the act had been applied. Nevertheless, as Machin recorded, a net total of 113,461 men had been "made available for military service,"[28] prompting G.W.L. Nicholson to observe decades later that "there seems no doubt whatever that had the demand persisted, the objective of sending 100,000 draftees overseas would have been achieved."[29] Machin also noted that "in the fall of 1917 recruiting by the volunteer system ... had almost completely stopped" and that "casualties were increasing rapidly and had actually passed the numbers being recruited." Because the MSA had been "successful in overcoming [both these] difficulties," he declared, "an absolutely irrefutable argument [had been made] for the necessity of enacting the Military Service Act."[30] Of course, "necessity" in this context was and continues to be interpreted in many different ways. But in this case, it presumes one overriding factor: the unequivocal decision made by the prime minister in May 1917, and later endorsed by his Cabinet, for Canada to maintain four full infantry divisions in the field (48 battalions) along with all other divisional and corps troops.

Less than one week after Parliament received Machin's account, Sir Edward Kemp submitted his own *Report of the Ministry, Overseas Military Forces of Canada, 1918*. Tabled in the House of Commons on 12 May, it was, in Kemp's words, simply a "general survey of many matters" pertaining to his ministry. But it also included General Currie's seminal postwar document: his "Interim Report on the Operations of the Canadian Corps during the Year 1918." Significantly, neither Kemp nor Currie made any special mention of the contribution made by conscripts to the final campaign of the war, or even to the role played by the MSA in furnishing thousands of reinforcements, even though high casualty rates during the Hundred Days had decimated the ranks of the infantry.[31] Still, the following excerpt seems to reflect Sir Edward's basic understanding of the reinforcement issue, and likewise illustrates in part how General Currie was able to sustain his great offensive drive:

During the year 1918 the demand for reinforcements was extremely heavy on account of the continued activity at the front ... In order to be better able to follow up every success gained, the experiment of reinforcing Infantry Units actually in action, without withdrawing them from the Line, was put into effect for the first time in warfare and proved successful, as Battalions withdrew from the fight at practically the same strength as they entered.[32]

Kemp's point is important for at least two reasons: first, this "experiment" most likely would not have been possible without the availability of large numbers of conscripts; and second, the official text confirms that many of these reinforcements (both draftees and BCRM men) were rushed into the firing line without the usual benefit of unit-level assimilation, a crucial and time-honoured process designed not only to extend the useful life of newly arrived riflemen but also to provide some small measure of assurance for their veteran comrades, whose survival might soon depend on these trained but inexperienced soldiers.

Decades later, Nicholson's *Canadian Expeditionary Force 1914–1919: Official History of the Canadian Army in the First World War*, first published in 1962, would equally omit any specific contribution made by conscripts to the war effort. However, Nicholson did provide a confirmation of Machin's earlier assessment as well as his own unequivocal judgment on the results of the MSA: "It must be concluded that while the administration of the Military Service Act was often inefficient and attended by many gross malpractices, the Act itself was neither a failure nor ineffective. Statistics show that it did produce the military results which it was designed to produce."[33]

Private accounts, on the other hand, such as *Canada's Hundred Days* by J.F.B. Livesay (1919), did mention the conscripts' combat role. But these references were not made explicit, as evidenced in this eyewitness account, which simply noted the steady flow of reinforcements to front-line units:

In many a regiment and many a battle, thirty, forty and fifty per cent were casualties in a single day, and reinforcements would come so rapidly that in two days the battalion again would be in full strength. It is only right that those at home should know that much of the success that came to Canada last year was due to the stream of reserves in the months of August, September and October.[34]

Indeed, the substance of what conscripts contributed to the campaigns of 1918 would be detailed only in occasional snippets, just as it was in most battalion war diaries. The real nature of the conscripts' battlefield legacy would remain mostly hidden, even though it could still be found in the same place where all such sacrifice is documented – in the CEF's official casualty records. These include details of all those killed in action or died of wounds; when combined with lists of others wounded and missing in action (in Part II orders and appended to the honour rolls of most regimental histories), they provide unquestionable evidence of the great sacrifice made by conscripts.[35] Yet because these difficult-to-find statistics were subsumed within all other CEF casualties, the documentation of conscripts in combat, or for that matter of the actual manpower contribution of the MSA to the Hundred Days campaign, remained scanty at best.

"What stubborn-hearted virtues"

Conscripts returning to Canada in 1919 from the battlefields of France and Belgium had many things in common with their comrade volunteers, starting with their rapid demobilization. All received a numbered and cherished Wartime Service Badge "For Service At The Front," the British War Medal for serving overseas, and the Victory Medal for having served with a unit in a theatre of war. All told, fifty-six received the Military Medal, which for some was belated recognition for their acts of conspicuous bravery.[36] But soon the memory of their shared triumphs and sacrifices began to fade.

With respect to demobilization, itself a somewhat disorienting "final experience of military administration," each of these men was suddenly transformed from a trained soldier into an independent civilian, and each became a full-time participant in a new struggle, one that historians Desmond Morton and Glen Wright would call *Winning the Second Battle*. Some would qualify for a disability pension, but most would not. Moreover, thousands who had been wounded and "ostensibly cured would, for the rest of their lives, find in their wartime service the source of debility, pain, sickness, and personal failure."[37] Others would never recover. For example, Private Ken Fraser of the 16th Battalion, who was shot through the leg at Cambrai and subsequently spent a year in England attempting to recover from the effects of his terrible wounds, was transferred to Deer Lodge Hospital in Winnipeg, Manitoba, in the summer of 1919, only to die of renal failure there on 16 January 1920. His comrade and fellow conscript, Private Harold Wrench, who was captured north of Cambrai at Cuvillers on 1 October and released on 24 November, was repatriated to Canada in early April 1919. After returning to his birthplace in Frodsham, Cheshire, he succumbed to nephritis on 21 January 1921. His death was attributed to service-related causes. And then there was Private Leo Buote, who had suffered a gunshot wound to the head on 29 September 1918, when his 85th Battalion was savaged at Sancourt. Miraculously he survived, and after an eight-month recovery period he returned to Canada, where he was demobilized in late June

1919, his "general health and physical condition" at the time being described as "very good." Disfigured, though, with a 10-centimetre-wide facial scar and a small depression on his left forehead caused by the loss of "frontal bone," Buote, a fireman from Summerside, PEI, was plagued by headaches that ultimately claimed his life. After suffering a "cerebral thrombosis" at Camp Hill Hospital in Halifax, he died on 26 October 1921, at age twenty-seven. His death, too, was declared "attributable to service."[38]

Tragic as these stories are, many other conscripts fared much better. Most, all things considered, achieved some measure of recovery. Private Frank Appel (16th Battalion) was released from Neiderzwehren POW Camp on 3 December and quickly repatriated to Canada. Eventually he settled in Agassiz, BC, where, blessed with a large family, he lived a long and prosperous life. Private Hilaire Dennis of the 18th, who had been shot "below the left kidney ... through the big hip bone" on the third day of the battle at Arras, made a remarkable recovery. Thanks to what he described as a "very strong constitution" and some excellent medical care, he safely returned to Canada to marry and raise a family. "Those three months [in France] are worth all the rest of my Life," he later declared.[39] Despite painful wounds that festered periodically throughout his life, he became a proud member of both the Great War Veterans' Association and later Branch 12 (Ontario) of the Canadian Legion in Walkerville. Twenty-five years later, like many of his comrades, this once-reluctant warrior watched anxiously as his own son went to war as a volunteer with the RCAF, and then rejoiced in that son's safe return, luck and fate having once again joined forces to secure a happy outcome.[40]

Private Gordon Young of the 1st Battalion CMRs, who had suffered severe leg wounds at Valenciennes and the amputation of his left arm, would make an even more notable recovery. Permanently disabled, in constant pain and unable to walk without a cane, Young lived a long and productive life and became a father to eight children. Moreover, while he never spoke of the war, he still displayed strong pride in his military service and attended Remembrance Day ceremonies every year, each time proudly wearing his wartime medals, his beret, and his 1st CMR armband, right up until March 1964, when he died of leukemia at age seventy-two.[41]

Private "Jack" Niihara of the 72nd Battalion, a Japanese-born conscript from Vancouver, joined some of his chums in Vernon, BC, soon after his discharge and worked for many years clearing forests and building roads. "Seriously injured twice while logging and ... paralyzed in the legs," he was forced "to learn [how] to walk again." Later, after settling in the picturesque village of Lumby some 25 kilometres east of Vernon, Jack became the popular caretaker of the Community

Park, where long-time resident Eileen Wejr fondly recalls that he "loved all the kids who played there" and, in return, was "respected and loved by everyone in the village." Indeed, two years before he died of cancer at age seventy-seven in 1961, this "Hero of World War I" was presented to the Queen on her Royal Visit. And upon his death a funeral service with "full legion honours" was conducted at the Legion Hall, after which Private Jack Niihara was carried to his grave by six veterans – all volunteers. Never married, but remembered still, this reluctant warrior and winner of the Military Medal rests today with many of his comrades in the Canadian Legion plot in Lumby.[42]

"The results obtained justified what we did"

General Sir Arthur Currie also experienced a somewhat difficult transition to civilian life. Returning to Canada in August 1919, a hero to most people but reviled by some, Currie never did receive the honour of a full vote of government thanks – at least not in his lifetime.[43] Promoted to the rank of full general and appointed Inspector-General (IG) of the Militia, largely a ceremonial post, Currie endeavoured to preserve a large part of that army, but his efforts were overshadowed by the reality that only "peacetime conscription" could possibly satisfy the huge manpower bill required to support it. In this respect, Currie quickly recognized that the nation did not have the stomach for "universal training," no matter how strong the rationale. Nor did there appear to be much political support for even a modicum of the funding that would be essential "to the restructuring of the Militia. Deeply disappointed, he resigned from the Militia effective 31 July 1920 to accept a new appointment as the Principal and Vice-Chancellor of McGill University.[44]

What retirement did not allow Currie to do was leave behind once and for all the fractious debate over Canadian losses during the Hundred Days, nor for that matter a lingering controversy about the precise role that conscription and conscripts had played in that final campaign. At the beginning of 1919, just prior to the opening of Parliament, Sydney Mewburn, the militia minister, anticipating there would be "lots of criticisms regarding the Military Service Act," wrote to Currie asking him to confirm that "the results obtained justified what we did," and to provide a statement "showing that through [the Government's] efforts the Corps was able to maintain its strength."[45] When Currie replied six weeks later on 17 March, his principal focus was on "demobilization," the recent troop riots at Kinmel Park near Rhyl, and slanderous accusations recently made against him in Parliament by Sir Sam Hughes. Only one short paragraph was offered in response to Mewburn's principal query; it is quoted here in its entirety:

When August 8th came we had never been as strong in numbers, as well organized, as well Staffed, or as well trained, nor had we as many reinforcements in the
Depot. We had one hundred extra men per Battalion, while our Engineer reorganization had been completed as had our Machine Gun re-organization. In
the last month, of course, we had quite a number of Military Service Act men.
These had not quite as much training as one would have liked, but still they
rendered most excellent service, and what the Corps accomplished fully justified
the steps you took in Canada to get the men.[46]

Currie's tardy and perfunctory response is most revealing, since he did not
directly confirm any specific contribution made by MSA men *before* "the last
month" of the war. Likewise, Currie did not acknowledge that his ability to
recover from the heavy losses at Passchendaele, from the eight subsequent
months of normal but significant battlefield wastage, and from the widespread
impacts of significant organizational changes, had anything to do with the steady
flow of reinforcements provided by MSA men, thousands of whom had arrived
in France beginning in the spring of 1918. He would only concede that "quite a
number of Military Service Act men" appeared in "the last month" of the war,
the implication being that they had missed most of the major battles, and that
even then they had not been trained "as one would have liked." Nonetheless,
Currie did acknowledge the "most excellent service" of conscripts, and conceded
that "what the Corps accomplished fully justified the steps [Mewburn] took in
Canada to get the men."[47] By itself this latter assertion seems to have provided
the Union Government with ample military justification for implementing the
Military Service Act, but truncated as it was by the "last month" comment and
the lack of any detail, this was a tepid offering.

Currie and MSA Men on the Firing Line

As noted in the Introduction, in the summer of 1926 Currie responded to a
request from Smeaton White (publisher of Montreal's *Gazette*), who was seeking
clarification about the role that conscripts had played in the Great War. The
Liberals under William Lyon Mackenzie King had used the controversies over
conscription against Arthur Meighen, Borden's successor as Conservative leader,
in the general elections of 1921 and 1925, and they would likely do so again in
the forthcoming election. White had recently learned from "several people,"
that "none of the men enlisted by authority of [the MSA had] ever actually
reached the firing line, although many of them may have been in France and
possibly in the reserve battalions." This assertion was contradicted by "officers
in the Department [of National Defence]," whose "opinion" it was "that many
of the men so enlisted actually did reach the firing line, some being killed and

a number wounded." But these officers also acknowledged that "no special re-port of the performance of these men [had been kept] after they reached Great Britain."[48]

It seems a good bet that the staff at National Defence Headquarters were well aware that large numbers of conscripts had arrived at "the firing line." Likewise, Currie must have been acutely aware of this flow in 1918, and he could easily have deduced a general rate of casualties for MSA men. At this point, though, Currie seemed willing to modify his views only slightly. Rather than reassert his position of seven years earlier, he offered his "impression" that "very few conscripted men reached France before September, 1918" – that is, that conscripts had not factored significantly into any of the corps' major battles before the Canal du Nord. In fact, Currie would never yield on this position.

"Old wounds that are better forgotten"

The following year, however, Currie would be forced to revisit the overall issue of casualties during the Hundred Days in a very public way, when a press report covering a memorial ceremony at the Hôtel de Ville in Mons on 12 June 1927, struck a negative chord with at least one small newspaper back in Canada. Lieutenant-General Sir Harry Burstall had unveiled a large plaque that day on behalf of the "Canadian Battlefield Memorial Commission," one that simply acknowledged that "here was fired the last shot of the Great War." The "impres-sive oration" that followed, given by the Honourable "Rodolphe Lemieux the speaker of the Canadian House of Commons," recalled the men who had fallen "in the fighting for the town" and marvelled at the difficult but triumphant advance of the corps in the "closing weeks of the war."[49] In response, Frederick W. Wilson, publisher of the *Port Hope Evening Guide*, and an associate W.T.R. Preston, agreed that the public needed to be offered an alternative view of this perceived paean to Currie – one which suggested that perhaps the capture of Mons should be "very much regretted rather than glorified." The following day, an "unsigned editorial" appeared on the front page of that evening's paper, arguing that the attack at Mons should never have taken place, and that Currie was guilty of a "deliberate and useless waste of human life."[50] For Currie, this insult was the last straw. Rather than ignore yet another scurrilous attack on his reputation, he decided to risk all and sue for libel. In April 1928, during what Dan Dancocks has described as "one of the most dramatic court cases in Canadian history," Currie's exercise of command was subjected to sometimes painful scrutiny.[51]

In some respects, General Currie was the catalyst for his own agony. Somewhat disingenuously, he declared on the witness stand that he had "never ordered an attack on Mons at all," or at least "not on Mons as a unit."[52] Technically, he was correct. But his later assertion that his men did not fall "in the fighting for the town" was clearly a more perilous argument, and for the dozens of officers and men killed and the hundreds wounded in this final advance, it was also a shameful obfuscation. Nevertheless, the defendants failed utterly to prove their case that there had been a "deliberate and useless waste of life" at Mons. The six-man jury ruled in Currie's favour and awarded him $5,000 in damages – not the $50,000 he had claimed. Moreover, at a banquet that evening to celebrate his courtroom triumph, Currie was visibly moved when he read aloud a telegram he had received earlier in the day. The sender had offered him his "humble hope" for success "in bringing to justice those responsible" for this painful affair, adding sombrely that these were "old wounds that are better forgotten." It was signed by James Price, the "father of [conscript] George Lawrence Price, the only Canadian killed on Armistice Day."[53]

"Last Post"

Private George Price may very well have been the only Canadian killed in action that day, but as noted earlier, a premature death would come as well to many of his wounded comrades in the days, weeks, and months and even in the years to come. Who is to say that General Currie's own untimely death at age fifty-seven, due to stroke and complications from pneumonia, was not also directly attributable to the aging effects of combat and to the strains of command over four tumultuous years? For Currie, though, there would be a state funeral in Montreal on 5 December 1933, the likes of which would rival anything seen before in the history of the young Dominion. For thousands of other veterans there would be little or no ceremony, especially for those whose bodies have no known grave, but whose names are etched forever in stone on the Menin Gate in Ypres and on the Vimy Memorial. Yet there would be some exceptions, and in the case of one of Price's fellow conscripts, there would be quite a different ending to this story.

Almost seventy-five years after General Currie was laid to rest, French construction workers digging at an industrial site about 1 kilometre northeast of Sailly-lez-Cambrai in France unearthed the remains of a Canadian soldier, along with some of his uniform insignia. Over the next three years, DNA testing and other extensive research and analysis collectively identified him as Private Alexander Johnston. He had been listed as missing and presumed dead after the 78th Battalion had fought a costly action across the Douai-Cambrai road south of Sancourt on 29 September 1918. And so, on 25 October 2011, some ninety-three years after the mine explosion that had claimed Johnston's life, relatives of this Scottish-born conscript were joined by numerous dignitaries

Figure 11.1 Headstone,
Private Alexander
Johnston, 25 October
2011. *Source:* Courtesy
of Donald Gregory.

at the nearby Cantimpré Canadian Cemetery where, once again, a grateful nation paid a solemn and moving tribute to a young man's sacrifice. Laid to rest that day with full military honours and in the presence of the Canadian Ambassador to France, Private Johnston also received one other final and special farewell. Corporal Ann Gregory, a trumpeter with the Governor General's Foot Guards in Ottawa and a great-grandniece of this reluctant warrior, played the "Last Post" and "Reveille" for her long-lost relative. That day her sombre notes echoed over a freshly dug grave and a newly carved headstone, one that now bears Johnston's last and perhaps most poignant message: "Finally At Rest With His Comrades."[54] Thus, the journey that began for Alexander Johnston when the Governor General first signed into law the Military Service Act in late August 1917 had come to a bittersweet end. As of this writing, he is the last of nearly three thousand Great War conscripts to have found a final resting place after dying in the service of his country.

Conclusion:
Evidence Has a Way of Dissolving Theories

Canadians refused to recognize the existence of alternative interpretations of the events of 1914–18, insisting instead that such interpretations were inaccurate, misleading and untrue. Notably this stout defence of the received version was not always made in defence of truth. Strict adherence to historical fact was desirable, but only if such facts did not contradict myth. It was myth, not fact, that was paramount; it had to be safeguarded against anything, even an indisputable truth, that threatened to undermine it.

— JONATHAN VANCE, *DEATH SO NOBLE*

A Forgotten Sacrifice – A Legacy Renewed

THE STORY OF THE Great War is often told from a macro-view – the vast movement of armies and corps. An alternative view is one which simply acknowledges that all the war's land battles, including Canada's, were fought at the most basic level, that of the individual soldier fighting as a member of a rifle section in one of four platoons in each infantry company, whose individual actions are the stuff of victory or defeat on the battlefield. Contrary to popular myth, by the end of the war conscripts constituted about half the trench strength of most infantry battalions in the Canadian Corps and had emerged as a pivotal force in every line infantry company. Although it had taken one full year for this historic evolution to take place, with more than eight months having passed since the first conscript had landed in France, the intervening months had seen these reluctant warriors not only forge a solid reputation at the front, but also develop into the Corps' principal source of reinforcements (replacements actually), not late in the war as myth would have it, but right from the start of the Hundred Days campaign. In the case of the 2nd Canadian Division, this transformation had begun in late April and early May of 1918. Thus, it is quite clear that Amiens was not, as Dan Dancocks once noted, "the last great battle fought by the Canadian Corps as an all-volunteer force" – that particular distinction rests soundly with the corps' immense efforts at Passchendaele some nine months earlier.[1] Nor is it true that "compulsory military service ... came too late to have a significant military impact," or that only a relatively small number of conscripts made it to France in a timely manner.[2] Indeed, it is only when the lens of history is shifted from the broader view of the Canadian Corps at war in 1918, and is focused more sharply on the key issue of manpower and the corps' critical need for infantry reinforcements, that one can fully appreciate how evidence does have "a way of dissolving theories" and why a number of long-held myths about the imagined role of Canadian conscripts on the Western Front must be put to rest.[3]

But myth, as Jonathan Vance tells us, is a powerful force – a curious "combination of invention, truth and half-truth that characterizes Canada's memory of the war." Over the past century, Canada's myth and memory of the Great War has evolved into a widely accepted "textbook mythology of war," one in which myth and half-truths feature prominently in the national narrative.[4] In particular, with respect to Canadian conscripts it appears that crucial evidence documenting their battlefield performance has generally been overlooked, resulting in an official and popular historiography that is incomplete and sometimes wholly inaccurate. Nevertheless, a detailed analysis of earlier research coupled with a more in-depth review of casualty records has revealed that the actual role played by conscripts in the Hundred Days was much more significant than previously thought.

In fact, nearly half the three thousand conscripts whom Veterans Affairs Canada has listed as having given their lives during the Great War were killed in action, died of their wounds, or succumbed later for reasons attributable to their service at the front. That is nearly 16 percent of all Canadian other ranks fatalities during the Hundred Days. In addition, 459 draftees died in England or en route at sea, mostly from disease, while 970 others are recorded as having perished in Canada without ever having served overseas.[5] As for the wounded, the numbers are considerably higher. During the Hundred Days, more than four soldiers were wounded for every enlisted soldier killed.[6] Thus, at least six thousand conscripts were likely wounded in action. When this figure is then added to known conscript battle-related fatalities, it is apparent that about seventy-five hundred Canadian conscripts became casualties, all as a direct result of service at the front. Since the official historian of the CEF has noted that 24,132 "draftees" were "taken on strength [in] units in France," it appears therefore that in less than six months of combat, approximately 31 percent of all conscripts who served in fighting units in France or Belgium became casualties of the Great War. But for many infantry battalions the casualty rate for draftees was closer to 50 percent. This should not be all that surprising, though, since more than half the 42,065 reinforcements the Canadian Corps received during the Hundred Days were conscripts.[7]

That none of these remarkable statistics appears to have been tabled for discussion during the plethora of national debates on conscription attests to one simple fact: the legacy of Canadian conscripts in the Great War has, for better or worse, lain largely undisturbed for nearly a century – an anomaly of sorts in Canadian military history, best illustrated by the following summary of six long-standing myths.

Myth: Conscripts Were Slackers, Shirkers, and Malingerers

"Under national service 'conscript' has no invidious meaning," declared the Military Service Council in October 1917: "It is expunged from the language ... The new regiments to go forward under the Military Service Act will perform deeds of valor equal to any that have glorified Canadian arms."[8] But, despite such high-minded pronouncements, the word conscript *did* have an invidious meaning, one that was synonymous with the equally negative labels of slacker, shirker, and malingerer, and one that has long resisted all attempts to expunge it from the language. Canada, a nation that for almost three years had refused to conscript its citizens, finally relented under enormous pressures imposed by parliamentarians, the church, and the press, as well as by returning soldiers who had already paid the price. Collectively, these highly vocal proponents of conscription succeeded in obtaining the necessary legislation to legally compel draft-age Canadian men to submit themselves for military service against their will. Thereafter these men, who in the parlance of the times had to be "fetched," were publicly slandered. As such their destiny was fatefully intertwined with a stunning transformation in Canada's social and political landscape, the militia minister having abjured earlier in the war the requirement for anyone but volunteers to serve in the CEF and, as noted in chapter 1, the prime minister having flatly declared that "there has not been, [and] there will not be, compulsion or conscription."

Many of the conscripts who eventually did make it to the battlefields of Europe would arrive at the front having been hardened by a long narrative of insults against their lack of patriotism and loyalty to country, and even against their manhood. Once blooded, though, these men appear by most accounts to have performed their duties in a resolute and courageous manner. The "draftees['] loyalty ... their willingness to fight and sacrifice once in khaki, was certain," declared one hardened veteran – "their prowess as first rate infantrymen and front line soldiers was equal to that of their fellow comrades-in-arms."[9] Indeed, as historian W.S. Wallace confirmed shortly after the war, "the draftees called up under [the MSA] proved to be a fine upstanding class of men." More importantly, "the part they played in the final successes of the Canadian Corps showed them capable of achieving results scarcely less splendid than the volunteers who had preceded them."[10]

In this respect, a number of relevant conclusions arise in response to a related question: Who were these draftees? For starters, they came from every province

(Appendix 3). Most of them were Canadian-born, but a number were British or American, while a few were Italian, Japanese, Norwegian, or Russian. Others were Austro-Hungarian, and some were ethnic German. The average age on recruitment of those killed in action or died of wounds was 25.7 years, compared with 26.3 for the typical recruit in the CEF.[11] In addition, the declared place-of-birth percentages for conscripts appear to be generally comparable with historical data cited by Chris Sharpe in his recent study on enlistment in the CEF – for example, 40.07 percent of deceased conscripts being from Ontario compares with 39.2 percent of total enlistments from Ontario.[12] Moreover, conscripts came from every segment of Canadian society – farmers, factory workers, fishermen, urban and rural folk (Appendix 4). Many had initially been rejected for service because of physical ailments or deficiencies that were entirely overlooked in the later conscription process. Others, such as farmers, whose absence from the fields in larger numbers could have seriously jeopardized wartime food production, were legitimately employed in critical occupations and industries directly supporting the war effort. Most of these men were neither slackers nor shirkers. Rather they were part of the *majority* of young Canadian men who either did not embrace the principal case for the war or who simply deferred military service for other valid reasons.

Myth: Conscripts Did Not Arrive in England to Be Well Enough Trained When They Were Wanted

"Well enough trained for what?" is the first question that might come to mind. "Compared to whom?" is a close second. For example, first contingent soldiers fighting at Ypres were once described as being "for the most part, untrained and amateur soldiers." Still, even though the fledgling Canadian Division had "almost ceased to exist" by the end of that historic battle, these largely inexperienced soldiers made a successful defence there. In addition, as historian Ken Radley reminds us, of the "50,000 Canadians who reached France between April 1915 and October 1916, almost half were only partially trained."[13]

Notably, an analysis of Training Division documents and hundreds of relevant personnel files reveals that most of these conscripts were not rushed to the front in the late spring of 1918 without essential training. At least two-thirds benefited from a delayed dispatch to the front and were held at the CCRC, thus allowing them to complete, in most cases, more than the required fourteen weeks' training before joining their units in the field. In general, these new men were arguably better trained upon first arrival at their field units than most of their volunteer comrades, due in no small part to the fact that the standard training syllabus they followed had been regularly modified to include numerous lessons learned over the previous three years.

As for General Currie's long-held conviction that the conscripts "did not arrive in England ... when they were wanted," the clear implication is that they were too late to meet his operational needs. That stance, though, is not supported by historical evidence.[14] Currie's first manpower crisis of 1918 was in fact a direct consequence of the lingering fallout from the high casualties his men had sustained at Passchendaele, after which the corps had been very slow to reconstitute itself. That testy problem was subsequently solved, at least in the short term, by the break-up of the 5th Division in early February 1918 and by the subsequent transfer of more than 7,000 infantry to the corps in France.

The second manpower crisis evolved much more slowly, throughout the first seven months of 1918. Although the corps was not committed to major combat during this time, the cumulative impact of ongoing wastage became significant: apart from non-battle casualties, which averaged 100 per day, other losses from March to July alone included "2,135 killed and 8,254 wounded."[15] These totals, coupled with the additional troops required to meet the demands of Currie's reorganization of the corps (one hundred more infantry per battalion, fifty more to compensate for the men removed from each of these units to augment the Machine Gun Corps, and several thousand more soldiers required to fill the ranks of newly formed engineer brigades), stressed the reinforcement pool to its limit. Initially, to compensate for these losses and transfers, Currie was able to draw on a large, mixed cadre of volunteers, BCRM men, and a few thousand conscripts, all of whom collectively allowed the corps to once again return nearly to full strength.

The third manpower crisis faced by Currie in 1918 was created by the high losses sustained at Amiens and afterwards at Arras. In this case, successive offensives left no time for the manpower system to react other than to dispatch all trained reinforcements to the front in order to replace some twenty thousand casualties. In-depth analysis of available regimental histories, combined with hard casualty data, reveals that most of the infantry reinforcements were conscripts. Thus, by that point draftees had become the primary source of manpower for the corps, and they would remain so throughout the final ten weeks of the war.

In this context, one can only speculate how Currie might otherwise have reinforced the corps at the moment of its greatest need had these same conscript reinforcements arrived much earlier (i.e., in early 1918), assuming that they had been dispatched to England soon after the MSA received Royal Assent in late August 1917. Most likely an earlier infusion of conscripts would have helped preserve the 5th Division largely intact and thus salvaged the OMFC's original plan to field a Canadian army of two, albeit weaker, corps. In that case, though, it is likely that a larger Canadian army would have been directly committed to help actively counter the German spring offensive (*Michael*), no doubt resulting in much higher casualty counts than those actually experienced by the corps during this period, and thus placing even greater pressure on the reinforcement system.

A stronger argument can be made (and indeed *was* made by Currie himself) that two smaller corps would have advanced much more slowly and that each would have sustained more casualties in their efforts than a single robust corps. In short, by not getting his wish for early conscripts (i.e., "when they were wanted"), Currie was able to create a single, more robust and powerful Canadian Corps, and when casualties inevitably mounted, as they did in the summer of 1918, he was similarly able to call upon a deep reservoir of reinforcements, men who arrived in force and apparently did so at the exact moment when he needed and "wanted" them most.

Myth: Only 24,000 Conscripts Saw Service at the Front

This common refrain, one that implies *too few*, is one of those half-truths that has greatly helped perpetuate the myth that overall conscript numbers were insufficient to make any significant difference in Canada's contribution to the Hundred Days campaign.[16] Since over 97 percent of conscripts were infantry, and at most the forty-eight infantry battalions had just over 1,000 men each, the impact of conscripts on the trench strength of these units *was* significant. Specifically, using Currie's goal of having six hundred rifles on the fire step at the start of each offensive, this sharp end of the corps typically numbered about 29,000 men. So even if there were on average "only" 8,000 to 10,000 draftees spread across the infantry corps at the height of the Hundred Days (i.e., from the Drocourt-Quéant line to the Canal du Nord), then one might reasonably conclude that these soldiers represented up to 25 percent of the front-line infantry (one infantry company per battalion) at that time alone.[17] Thus, when placed in operational context, the diminutive "only," which is sometimes misleading but almost universally associated with every description of the number of conscripts who made it to the front, is largely muted, and the vital role played by these thousands of conscripts comes more sharply into focus.

As noted earlier, the number of MSA men believed to be in France was "24,132," a figure that has long been a matter of some dispute. Indeed, Nicholson himself acknowledged that this number was "only an approximation," based principally on "a painstaking survey of Part II Orders" that counted "soldiers serving in the field [who] bore regimental numbers appearing in either the 3,000,000 or 4,000,000 series of numbers." Furthermore, "it was assumed that [both] these blocks had been set aside for the exclusive use of draftees," which, in the case of the former (i.e., the 3000000 series), proved to be partly false. Complicating the issue even further, the official historian noted as well that "there were instances of volunteers' receiving numbers from these blocks and of draftees' being given numbers appearing in other series of regimental numbers." Nonetheless, Nicholson declared that "these exceptions tended to cancel out each other," and concluded that "it seems safe to assume that this figure [24,132] would not greatly differ from one obtained by an examination of every service document."[18] In this respect he appears to have been quite correct. While an "examination of every [conscript] service document" is well beyond the scope of this monograph, the preponderance of evidence obtained, drawn from a detailed analysis of the nominal rolls and the honour rolls from twenty-eight battalions, coupled with relevant documentation from all forty-eight infantry battalions, strongly suggests that Nicholson's figure of 24,132 MSA men who "served in the field" is still fairly accurate – if anything, it is a bit low.[19]

Based on a detailed examination of casualty figures and of killed and wounded ratios in 1918, it is clear that at least 24,000 conscripts must have been deployed to the field in order to account for the total number of dead and wounded draftees during the Hundred Days. In addition, apart from verifying that a significant number of conscript casualties were assigned regimental numbers in the 3000000 and 4000000 series, this study confirms that a large group of dead and wounded MSA men were given regimental numbers from the 2000000 series. More remarkable still, hundreds of others were assigned six-digit regimental numbers starting with a "2" or "3," such as Private George Price (256265) and Gunner John Quinn (339792). When all these casualties are then added to another small but important group that featured seven-digit regimental numbers starting with a "1," the rationale for Nicholson's original "approximation" becomes even more tenable. Thus, supported as it is by additional empirical data evidenced throughout this study, Nicholson's fact-based assumption appears to be valid, and will likely stand the test of further scrutiny as Archives Canada brings online all the personnel files of the nation's Great War veterans.

Myth: Conscripts Were Unreliable in Battle

The genesis of this particular myth is difficult to pinpoint, but appears to be rooted in a general antipathy for the non-volunteer, and has been nurtured as well by misconceptions about the level of training these men received. Absent any proof to the contrary, it would lead J.L. Granatstein to cautiously observe that "we have no firm sense of whether these unwilling soldiers performed well in action."[20] But, as documented throughout this text, soldiers who actually fought alongside the draftees – junior leaders and ordinary infantrymen alike

– were in general well-satisfied with their performance on the battlefield. "Such of those I met were definitely good material," Private E.W. Russell wrote. Lieutenant Don Goudy would likewise recall that his 21st Battalion, "largely seeded by new drafts," had performed surprisingly well at Arras.[21] In fact, these men performed valiantly in battle: they fought to the death in support of their comrades on either side of them, and many were cited for courageous acts in combat.

Myth: Conscription Was Not a Military Necessity

This is another half-truth. To look at this issue objectively, one must first set aside the fact that conscription was an extremely contentious political and cultural issue, one that dangerously divided the young nation as never before. Second, one must equally acknowledge that Canadian conscripts were not "necessary to win the war," as historian Jack Hyatt has so eloquently pointed out. Consequently, the principal counter to this controversial myth depends entirely on the acceptance of one fundamental imperative – the overriding requirement for the Canadian Corps to be sustained in the field with all four of its infantry divisions fully intact, itself a *sine qua non* for Currie, who firmly believed that conscription was essential to do just that. More importantly, Currie was similarly convinced "that sending an under-strength unit into battle"– a tactical outcome he was sworn to avoid – "almost always resulted in greater losses than if that unit fought under the same conditions but at full strength."[22] It follows that the new drafts *were* necessary to sustain the Canadian Corps throughout its costly but victorious drive during the Hundred Days, and it is within this framework that one is inevitably drawn to the conclusion that conscription *was* a "military necessity." As noted in the Introduction, A.M. Willms first made this point in 1956. Dan Dancocks reached a similar conclusion thirty years later when he declared that "the Corps could not have contributed so impressively during the remaining months of the war [post Amiens] without the conscripted soldiers who filled the ranks."[23] And in 2015, Chris Sharpe, in his updated study "Enlistment in the Canadian Expeditionary Force 1914–1918 – A Re-evaluation," confirmed that "conscripts provided the great bulk of the corps' reinforcements during [the] critical period" of the Hundred Days, and therefore concluded that "conscription was necessary."[24]

Myth: The Military Service Act Was a Failure

According to Nicholson's *Official History*, at the end of the war there were 99,651 MSA men on the strength of the CEF, including "16,296 draftees on *unexpired* [sic] harvest or compassionate leave of absence without pay." This essentially left 83,355 such men in uniform, including 47,509 who had already proceeded overseas.[25] Thus by war's end Prime Minister Borden had delivered nearly half of the 100,000 MSA men he had originally promised, and the remaining number were already en route or were to be mobilized and deployed in early 1919. Nonetheless, given more than 400,000 "Class 1 registrations" and the fact that ultimately 55 percent of these were "granted exemption on various grounds," while another 24,139 "defaulted and were not apprehended," it is commonly thought that the program was so deeply flawed that it has to be judged a failure. As noted earlier, Nicholson disagreed, declaring that the MSA "was neither a failure nor ineffective."[26] The *Toronto Globe* seems to have taken a similarly informed view when in December 1919 it declared:

> The object for which the [Union Government] Coalition had been formed was achieved when during the historic Hundred Days ... the sixty thousand casualties incurred by the Corps in its splendid advance were made good largely by draftees who proved themselves to be fine fighting men and stout Canadians in the field, but who would not have been available for the reinforcement of the Corps had the Military Service Act not been enforced.[27]

The interesting part about both these public pronouncements, separated as they are by forty-three years, is that both "contradict myth" – the myth that the Military Service Act was a failure, one that in the words of Jonathan Vance "had to be safeguarded against anything, even an indisputable truth, that threatened to undermine it." Still, another four decades would pass before J.L. Granatstein dramatically modified his views on this complex subject, and a few years more before he directly challenged this particular myth. MSA "reinforcements kept units up to strength," he declared; more importantly, they "allowed the Canadian Corps to function with great effectiveness and efficiency in the final battles of the Great War, and helped to minimize casualties."[28]

Conscripts and Currie

Conscripts, the principal product of the MSA, were directly employed by General Currie and by his subordinate commanders in the spring of 1918 and throughout the Hundred Days. Therefore, no analysis is complete without taking into account tactical decisions made by Canadian commanders in employing these reinforcements. At the same time, there is a need to juxtapose the extraordinary success of the Canadian Corps with the harsh fact that the corps sustained an unprecedented number of casualties over a relatively short period (ninety-six days) – nearly forty-six thousand in battle (all ranks) and an additional eighty-five hundred in "Sick Wastage."[29] But precisely how the virtual non-stop replacement of these casualties directly influenced the decision-making of General Currie and his subordinate commanders remains largely an untilled field of study, and one that clearly merits further and serious critical analysis. New evidence presented in this study suggests a number of preliminary conclusions, though, which should inform the debate and perhaps also provide some important clues as to the way ahead.

Foremost in this analysis are conclusions related to the central postwar issue of high casualties during the Hundred Days, inasmuch as General Currie has long been credited with having done everything in his power to minimize battle-field losses. Indeed, Hyatt has described the Canadian Corps commander as a "natural tactician," one who "never stopped trying to reduce casualties" and who "continually sought victory at the lowest possible cost in lives."[30] As Currie himself acknowledged, however, "you cannot have war without the inevitable price."[31] In this regard, there is considerable evidence that on at least two occasions Currie does not appear to have sought victory at the *lowest* possible cost. Over time he occasionally succumbed, like most senior military commanders, to a flawed but universal standard of relative success, one based almost exclusively on the number of yards gained, enemy killed or captured, and enemy weapons captured or destroyed. Solid in every respect except one, this tree-top view of the battle sphere features one glaring fault: its marginalization of the "blood-tax" paid with the lives of thousands of one's own soldiers for what might come to pass but is never certain – victory on the battlefield.[32]

While historian Tim Cook has described Currie as "one of the finest generals of the war," he was quick to add that Currie "was not without his faults," although these "failures" did "not tarnish his reputation" but rather revealed "merely that he was human."[33] To be truly objective, then, one is compelled to turn the lens on those decisions that Currie made that were less than stellar. And in fact, it is this latter analysis that provides this subject with a new and intriguing element of clarity, chiefly with respect to the role played by Canadian conscripts.

As this study reveals, Currie's willingness in the summer of 1918 to assume greater and greater risks was not simply a measured response to the favourable turn in Allied fortunes on the Western Front; it also took directly into account the immense advantage that the corps then enjoyed over all other British forces – a constant stream of trained reinforcements, forecasted to last well into 1919. The natural temptation was to push the battlefield envelope beyond an individual formation's breaking point, in the knowledge that the resources necessary to repair those breaks were immediately at hand.

Currie appears to have surrendered to such temptation on at least two crucial occasions during the Hundred Days campaign. First, on 28 August at the Second Battle of Arras, the 2nd Division and to a lesser extent the 3rd Division were both extended well beyond their operational limits for little tactical or operational gain, even though Currie had foreseen the need for an operational pause at precisely the moment that he subsequently chose to ignore. Then, a month later, after achieving an overwhelming victory at the Canal du Nord and at Bourlon Wood, Currie once again appears to have pushed too far and for too long. After the third day of fighting on 29 September, more than half of the offensive's planned objectives had been achieved. While an operational pause (again, one that Currie had originally envisioned) would have temporarily relieved pressure on the German defenders and allowed them to resupply, it equally could have provided his own desperately exhausted divisions crucial time to reorganize and reconstitute for the important battles that lay ahead. Instead, Currie recommitted his much-fatigued forces to a fourth straight day of attacks against superior enemy forces, incurring in that deadly process substantially higher casualties for yet again limited operational gains. Moreover, when presented once more with overwhelming evidence that he should finally order a tactical pause the next day, Currie decided otherwise. He threw his exhausted and heavily depleted infantry into the fight, risking all on a furious fifth day of offensive operations, one that ultimately saw many of them so badly mauled that they never fought another engagement in the Great War.

Hence a key question arises: Why would Currie, arguably Canada's best fighting general, take such enormous risks, violating in the process his own well-founded principles about not sending weakened formations against formidable obstacles and determined opponents? The answer would seem to be "reinforcements" – mostly conscripts but also BCRM men. Currie had more of these replacements than anyone save the American commander General John J. Pershing; he knew that no matter the risk or the battle's outcome he could rapidly reconstitute the Canadian Corps and fight on. But again, in abandoning a proven battlefield *modus operandi*, Currie and his subordinate commanders gambled heavily and successively, taking heretofore unimaginable risks.[34] Like most great commanders, though, Currie succeeded. Nonetheless, the symbiotic relationship between the high costs of that success and an unprecedented flow of reinforcements is clearly one area of the Canadian campaign that demands further study.

In this regard, new evidence shows that high Canadian casualty counts during the Hundred Days were, in part, directly attributable to the introduction of large numbers of conscript reinforcements to the Canadian Corps. Unshackled from previous manpower constraints, Currie conducted a singular campaign of near continuous, large-scale, high-intensity operations, apparently without any undue concern about shortfalls in trained replacements. It would seem therefore that Currie should not be judged, as history has generally done, simply by his many victories. Rather, as Professor Hyatt suggests, a more balanced examination should reveal the full complexities of this esteemed commander, and perhaps at the same time give Canadians a new and enhanced understanding of all those tactical decisions taken during the Hundred Days that may have been influenced, *inter alia*, by the timely arrival of more than 24,000 conscript reinforcements.

Currie's Subordinate Commanders and Conscripts

If Currie was guilty on occasion, as historian Shane Schreiber notes, of "simply pushing too hard" and of "creating greater casualties," it must also be said that his divisional commanders were equally at fault for not pushing back on occasion, and not demanding sufficient time for "proper coordination" and preparation of the battlefield.[35] All four of his subordinate commanders are accountable in this regard. For example, Major-General Burstall had ample justification to seek a battle pause at Arras that restless night of 27 August when both his lead attacking brigades (the 4th and the 5th) had just suffered severe and debilitating losses. Burstall knew that his troops were very tired, that the enemy was reinforcing against his sector, and that resistance was rapidly mounting. Nevertheless, he appears to have unconditionally accepted the order to attack the next day, with what turned out to be disastrous results – his division was rendered incapable of participating in the offensive for another month. Thus, the question that comes immediately to mind is how exactly did the prospect of continuous reinforcements impact the ever-zealous Burstall in his decision not to demand a crucial one-day pause to regroup? Similarly, Major-General Macdonell, who prided himself on not being overly concerned about his "flanks," and who would chastise the "stickiness" of anyone so inclined, would appear to have exercised a similar lapse in judgment on 30 September, when he too failed to insist on an operational pause north of Cambrai despite overwhelming evidence that his formation was then operating at a severe disadvantage. The next day he saw his 1st and 3rd Brigades thoroughly savaged.

In this regard, the impact that a steady stream of replacements had on these key decision-makers once again warrants deeper analysis. The near-constant flow of reinforcements appears to have provided additional means for Currie's subordinate commanders to press forward and, on occasion, to do so without having first engaged in essential preparation and planning for the battle. Indeed, the brigade and battalion war diaries are rich with accounts of infantry units being rushed into action at this time. Brigadier-General Odlum, for example, was furious with Watson's decision to abruptly press his 11th Brigade back into the assault on 30 September, asserting that "the failure of the attack was due to the haste in which it was thrown in."[36] But while some may argue that Odlum's subsequent losses would have occurred regardless, the correlation of extremely heavy casualties with the arrival of large numbers of conscripts remains an unsettling coincidence, and one most worthy of broader investigation.

Conscripts and the Price of National Forgetting

The arrogant line of cleavage drawn by volunteers between themselves and "conscripts" was and is much to be deprecated.[37]

Victory over the German army brought a bittersweet ending to a long and painful struggle. Bitter because during the Hundred Days so many draftees died or were wounded in countless ways, but sweet because most of these reluctant warriors proved that they were not cowards after all, and that when their democratic choice *not* to serve had been legally removed, they had faithfully answered their nation's call. Yet bitter too because in the subdued but joyous aftermath of the war, their crucial role in the Hundred Days seems to have been forgotten – this despite the overriding but unacknowledged fact that in the midst of Amiens, the Canadian Corps, having expended nearly 400,000 Canadian soldiers, found itself almost totally dependent (at least as far as the infantry was concerned) on the timely flow of conscripts to the front. Indeed, without them it would have been virtually impossible to effectively sustain the corps' remarkable drive. But if this somewhat disturbing reality ever became more widely acknowledged, no doubt it would have resulted in a number of uncomfortable conclusions, few of which would likely have been very compatible (politically or militarily) with the received wisdom about many of the subsequent achievements of the Canadian Corps.

In time, then, the valuable battlefield contribution of conscripts faded in memory and was subsumed by a much larger, more heroic, and less controversial narrative. Innocently enough, it also appears that this exercise in forgetting occurred through a sort of mutual but unspoken agreement between the volunteer and the conscript, and between the historian and the individual regiments. Nevertheless, when a nation forgets or chooses not to remember the sacrifice of any of its citizens, there is often another price to pay. In Canada's case, that promissory note came due nearly a quarter-century later when Canadians, having chosen to confront Nazi tyranny, were forced to decide once again whether compulsory service should be the law of the land.

This renewed debate on conscription seemingly had the benefit of two historical facts: first, the previous iteration had clearly divided the nation in a perilous manner and therefore needed to be approached with due caution; second, despite the great political and social schism created a generation earlier, a considerable force of conscripts had in fact been sent to France and had arrived just in time to sustain the Canadian Corps in its final campaigns of the war. At the Scheldt in late 1944 and on the Rhine in early 1945, however, the infantry of General Crerar's First Canadian Army did not enjoy Currie's manpower advantages, in part because even though Canadians vividly recalled the political lessons of conscription in the Great War, somehow they had managed to forget the military lessons.[38] The latter of course had been buried so deep, and therefore the past contribution of conscripts to the battlefield calculus was so obscure, that it was quite impossible to offer Canadians any tangible proof that conscription had once been a military necessity. In this context, the old lament "lest we forget" had another meaning entirely. That Canada did forget and conceivably might do so again is yet another rationale for an even more comprehensive account of the actual role played by conscripts in this polarizing national undertaking.[39]

Canadian Conscripts: A Modern Legacy

Niall Ferguson has written that "the First World War was nothing less than the greatest error of modern history."[40] In this respect, those who opposed conscription in Canada were perhaps more prescient than they were given credit for. Still, once conscripts went off to war and performed their required duties on the battlefield, there appears to have been little or no national reconciliation, no healing of any sort, nor does there seem to have been any desire to set aside earlier prejudices. In time, any historical detail on conscripts at war would become very difficult to find, due in no small part to the fact that many regimental histories contain large gaps in their narratives in this regard. Similarly, it appears that a number of official and semi-official accounts addressed the subject either superficially or inaccurately, and thereby tended to minimize the contribution made by conscripts. One direct result was that the much more controversial political legacy of conscription survived intact.

As historian Daniel Byers has observed, "after 1939, every political decision related to manpower would be framed around trying to avoid what conscription had done to Canada during the earlier conflict."[41] Moreover, when this divisive issue raised its Hydra-like head later during the Second World War, it quickly became evident that old animosities had been handed down to a new generation of Canadians. Regrettably, some of the original Great War antipathy for the non-volunteer – what some might call the demonization of conscripts – continues today.[42] It is as if the act of rejecting what was believed to be a specious argument for Canada waging its part in the Great War was, and still is, entirely unforgiveable, no matter how valid the original counter-arguments may have been, then or now. In this troubling sense, the legacy of Canadian conscripts appears to have been constructed, not always from facts – from what conscripts actually did in battle – but rather from myth, and from what conscripts did not do as a consequence of not serving (like many volunteers) until the last year of the war.[43]

As for Canada's national Great War mythology, it is deeply rooted in the sacrifice of the loyal, patriotic volunteer – a tragic and profound loss that in time would permeate and disturb all levels of Canadian society. Perhaps with the exception of Amy Shaw's *Crisis of Conscience*, that narrative has rarely provided a place for those who rejected the war's fundamental raison d'être, or for those thousands of others who, when compelled to fight, had forsaken their principles only to fall in battle. Yet if one accepts the fundamental premise that the Great War "made Canada a nation,"[44] then the evidence documented here seems to suggest that Canada's reluctant warriors can take their own rightful place alongside their volunteer comrades in the pantheon of national heroes – soldiers who also sacrificed so much to help forge this young nation.

In summary, official records clearly show that Canadian conscripts fought a war that was profoundly different than the one waged by their volunteer comrades in the first three years of the conflict, and that they did so across a broader space of time, in more battles and in far greater numbers than perhaps ever previously thought. Most performed admirably, sometimes magnificently; they provided Currie not only with the requisite infantry reinforcements necessary to support the creation of a more powerful corps, but also with the key ingredient for sustaining his controversial but often brilliant battlefield strategy. More importantly, and beyond the overarching issue of sustainability, it is equally clear that without the critical mass provided by these reluctant warriors, and their sacrifice, there would never have been a "Hundred Days" for the Canadian Corps.[45]

Today, one hundred years after the great convulsion of 1917–18, Canada like the world around it is entirely transformed. But throughout the past century one common societal theme has prevailed – armed conflict. Indeed, who knows what forces might conspire to once again threaten the core values that all Canadians cherish and how, in the face of real or apprehended threats, Canada might once again compel its citizens to fight. One hopes that should such a calamitous situation ever arise again, the national debate that perforce must follow will more faithfully address all relevant aspects of this controversy, to include a balanced consideration of both the military justification for conscription and specifically what conscript soldiers might ultimately bring to the fight – and at what cost.

If nothing else, the crucial role once played by Canadian conscripts in the Great War is a cautionary tale for future generations. For this hard-won legacy likewise recalls that a nation is shaped not only by its past but also by the manner in which it remembers that past, and sometimes by its capacity both to set aside myth and ultimately to embrace historical fact. Hence, the precious freedoms these young men once surrendered, and the sacrifices they so courageously made in battle, might not be forgotten after all. And perhaps, for the more than two million Canadians who count themselves today as direct descendants of those men who were summoned to the colours in 1918, and especially for the one in three of these who likely had a family member serve in France or Belgium, future acts of remembrance will feature a new and enlightened focus.[46] Not simply a poignant poem or a colourful parade, this modern memory of war will instead dutifully recall another powerful lesson from the Great War – that the freedom of the individual Canadian citizen is ultimately neither sacred nor free, not even in Canada.

Appendices

Appendix 1: Excerpts from the Military Service Act, 1917

Classes

Class 1. Those who have attained the age of twenty years and were born not earlier than the year 1883 and are unmarried, or are widowers but have no child.*

Class 2. Those who have attained the age of twenty years and were born not earlier than the year 1883 and are married, or are widowers who have a child or children.

Class 3. Those who were born in the years 1876 to 1882, both inclusive, and are unmarried, or are widowers who have no child.

Class 4. Those who were born in the years 1876 to 1882, both inclusive, and who are married, or are widowers who have a child or children.

Class 5. Those who were born in the years 1872 to 1875, both inclusive, and are unmarried, or are widowers who have no child.

Class 6. Those who were born in the years 1872 to 1875, both inclusive, and are married, or are widowers who have a child or children.

* Only men in Class 1 were conscripted. The effective date for the MSA was 13 October 1917, when the Royal Proclamation was published throughout the country. *Note:* "any man married after the sixth day of July, 1917" was "deemed to be unmarried."

Exemptions

National Grounds of Exemption:

No. 1. – *Present occupation –* ... continuance of which is in the national interest ... [e.g.,] maintenance of the supply of food, with particular reference to fish, wheat and meat, of coal, steel and certain kinds of metal, and of timber of certain kinds ... [as well as] certain manufactured products and of the operation of railways, steamships, telegraphs, telephones, light, heat and power plants [and the] machinery of finance.

No. 2. – Prospective Employment. – [per above in work] of national importance.

No. 3. – Education and Training – must be manifest to the tribunal that the education or training of the individual concerned is designed to qualify him for service which will increase the national strength for war purposes, or which will be necessary for the maintenance and upholding of the social fabric of the nation and its stability during and after the war.

Personal Grounds of Exemption:

No. 4. – Financial Obligations – men who have undertaken such heavy financial obligations that their withdrawal for military service would involve grave hardship.

No. 5. – Business Obligations – men ... upon whom depends the prosperity or even the existence of a business.

No. 6. – Domestic Position – may have relation to the financial support the man in question has been in the habit of providing for relatives or others who would as a result of his withdrawal for military service be in want ... [or] personal considerations connected with the mental and physical health or the age (at both extremes) of individuals in respect of whom the man in question stands in some special personal relation ... [or] the extent to which voluntary enlistment from the family of the man in question has already taken place.

No. 7. – Ill Health or Infirmity – the man is clearly incapable of any kind of military duty by reason of his condition being such as to incapacitate him from many civil occupations.

No. 8. – Conscientious Objection – the man himself should have a conscientious objection to undertaking combatant service, and it is also necessary that he should in good faith belong to an organized religious denomination which was existing and well recognized in Canada on the 6th of July, 1917, and by the tenets and articles of faith ... combatant service was prohibited.

No. 9. – Disfranchisement under the War-time Elections Act – Every naturalized British subject who was born in an enemy country and naturalized subsequent to the 31st day of March, 1902 ... [or] whose natural language, otherwise described as "mother tongue," is a language of an enemy country, and who was naturalized subsequent to the 31st day of March, 1902.

Source: *Military Service Act, 1917, Manual for the Information and Guidance of Tribunals in the Consideration and Review of Claims for Exemption*, 22–23, 10–16, 18.

Appendix 2: Awards for Gallantry to Canadian Conscripts

Distinguished Conduct Medal

2129336	Private Charles McDonald	27th Battalion
3106766	Private Willard Thomas Woodcock	116th Battalion

Military Medal

3320458	Private Robert Lindsay Alexander	2nd Battalion	WIA
3155139	Lance Sergeant René Joseph Archambault	87th Battalion	
2378506	Lance Corporal William Alexander Barclay	43rd Battalion	WIA
2128930	Private William Barker	78th Battalion	
3108909	Private James Wesley Barlow	102nd Battalion	
4040227	Private Eugène Beaulieu	22nd Battalion	
3230862	Private Thomas Henry Bethell	20th Battalion	
1263581	Private Francois Xavier Cardinal	14th Battalion	WIA
3320987	Private Henri Carrière	44th Battalion	
3159276	Corporal Arthur Champagne	87th Battalion	
4080038	Private Walter Chisnall	29th Battalion	WIA
3106311	Private Harry Clark	54th Battalion	WIA
3033089	Lance Corporal Michael John Cole	75th Battalion	
3206718	Private Milford Cole	50th Battalion	
3231121	Private William Patrick Coyne	4th CMR	
3033485	Private George Dennis Dalton	19th Battalion	
1263585	Private Sam Maud Dayton	52nd Battalion	
4020088	Private Francois Xavier Delarosbil	21st Battalion	
3206693	Private Alfred Steel De Pew	50th Battalion	
256718	Private George Crosley Duck	52nd Battalion	
3081502	Lance Corporal Walter Elmer Dustin	87th Battalion	
3082159	Private Joseph Thomas Fahey	43rd Battalion	
3080591	Private Charles Edward Frost	5th CMR	
3314316	Private George Walter Garrett	116th Battalion	
2383444	Private John Garrett	43rd Battalion	
2129133	Private Hugh P. Gilbert	78th Battalion	
3031490	Private James Green	75th Battalion	
3107265	Corporal Louis Henry Guidi	21st Battalion	
3256187	Private George Timothy Haughan	44th Battalion	
257184	Private James Johnston	50th Battalion	
3131396	Private John Ernest Jolie	18th Battalion	
3310459	Private Thomas Lamont	50th Battalion	

3108499	Private Robert Leckie	5th CMR	
2129125	Private Herbert Booth Lorimer	43rd Battalion	
258400	Private James Patrick Maguire	5th Battalion	DOW
257507	Private William Ross Masters	28th Battalion	
3106807	Private Walter McAleer	116th Battalion	
3130529	Private Allen Norval McCreery	31st Battalion	
2137925	Lance Corporal Orville Albert McKay	72nd Battalion	
3320103	Private Donald McDonald	21st Battalion	WIA
3205025	Private Charles Edward Michie	10th Battalion	
3130288	Private William Thomas Mott	31st Battalion	
4020272	Private Emile Sylvio Mousseau	21st Battalion	WIA
2020445	Private Gonzaemon "Jack" Niihara	72nd Battalion	WIA
3205264	Lance Corporal Ernest Thomas Parkinson	50th Battalion	
3310207	Private Harry Ramsdale	116th Battalion	
2021355	Private Edward William Rich	72nd Battalion	WIA
2128984	Private William James Roche	43rd Battalion	
3033796	Private Walter Earl Ryder	2nd Battalion	
3205130	Lance Corporal James Scaife	50th Battalion	
3056217	Lance Corporal Clifton Charles Shultz	38th Battalion	
257761	Private Edward Norman Slack	46th Battalion	
3321013	Private John Struthers	38th Battalion	
3205528	Private William Rudolph Weiler	31st Battalion	
3205743	Private Ernest Aubrey White	50th Battalion	
3032058	Private Orloff Nicholls Whitney	4th Battalion	

Source: This list is drawn mainly from a survey of regimental histories and war diaries at http://www.bac-lac.gc.ca/eng/discover/military-heritage/first-world-war/Pages/war-diaries.aspx, and from relevant *Supplements to the London Gazette* (1919) available at https://www.thegazette.co.uk/.w

Appendix 3: Selected Demographics – Age and Origin

Conscripts killed in action, died of war-related wounds, accident, or disease, or missing – by province or country of birth and age on recruitment.

Province or country of birth	#	%	Average age
Prince Edward Island	15	1.05	23.96
Nova Scotia	52	3.62	23.75
New Brunswick	54	3.76	24.01
Quebec	172	11.99	25.20
Ontario	575	40.07	25.00
Manitoba	144	10.03	25.38
Saskatchewan	113	7.87	26.55
Alberta	69	4.81	25.83
British Columbia	120	8.36	26.53
Subtotal Canadian-born	1,314	91.56	25.13
United Kingdom	61	4.25	27.07
United States	30	2.09	24.88
Other	30	2.09	25.14
Total	1,435	99.99	25.70

Source: RG 150, Accession 1992–93/166 Personnel Records, Canadian Expeditionary Force, and Edward H. Wigney, *The C.E.F. Roll of Honour.*

Appendix 4: Selected Demographics – Occupation

Conscripts killed in action, died of war-related wounds, etc., by occupation.

Principal occupations	#	%
Farmers	399	27.80
Labourers	200	13.94
Fishing, hunting, and forestry	56	3.90
Subtotal	655	45.64
Tradesmen	357	24.88
Munitions workers	22	1.53
Mining, iron, steel	46	3.21
Transport, railway workers, shipping	153	10.66
Manufacturing	20	1.40
Shipbuilding	10	0.70
Merchants and sales	36	2.51
Clerical and postal	80	5.57
Professional	56	3.90
Total	1,435	100

Note: The much smaller number of fatal casualties among miners, munitions workers, and other industrial workers suggests that these men were, perhaps, more *essential* to the war effort at home, and therefore likely benefited from higher exemption rates – another area worthy of further study. For more detailed statistics on eligible industrial workers, see Richard Holt, "Filling the Ranks," 231.
Source: RG 150, Accession 1992–93/166, Personnel Records, Canadian Expeditionary Force.

Notes

Introduction: Slackers, Shirkers, and Malingerers

EPIGRAPH: The chapeau verse comes from a British recruiting poster [n.d.] quoted in Ilana R. Bet-El, *Conscripts: Lost Legions of the Great War* (Guildford: Sutton, 1999), 190.

1 Official records for (256265) Private George Lawrence Price and for all other conscripts cited in this text are available online at Library and Archives Canada [hereafter LAC], Records Group [RG] 150, Accession 1992–93/166, http://www.bac-lac.gc.ca/eng/discover/military-heritage/first-world-war/personnel-records/Pages/search.aspx. Additional documentation is drawn from LAC, Circumstances of Deaths Registers [CDR], at http://www.bac-lac.gc.ca/eng/discover/mass-digitized-archives/circumstances-death-registers/Pages/circumstances-death-registers.aspx#b, and from Veterans Affairs, The Canadian Virtual War Memorial [hereafter CVWM], http://www.veterans.gc.ca/eng/remembrance/memorials/canadian-virtual-war-memorial.

2 The "Hundred Days" typically refers to the closing military campaign of the First World War beginning with the Allied attacks at Amiens commencing on 8 August 1918.

3 See Kathryn M. Bindon, *More Than Patriotism* (Don Mills: Thomas Nelson and Sons, 1979), 156; David Bercuson, *The Fighting Canadians* (Toronto: HarperCollins, 2009), 185; and Andrew Theobald, *The Bitter Harvest of War* (New Brunswick: Goose Lane, 2008), 92.

4 Telephone interview with Mr. George Barkhouse, nephew and namesake of Private Price, 3 September 2014. Years later, Florence Price (mother of George) would recall the day the war ended and "celebrating the Armistice on the school grounds," only to return home and learn the shocking news of her brother's death.

5 G.W.L. Nicholson, *Canadian Expeditionary Force, 1914–1919: Official History of the Canadian Army in the First World War* [hereafter Nicholson, *Official History*] 2nd printing (corrected) (Ottawa: Queen's Printer, 1964), 551, 553.

6 J.L. Granatstein and J. Mackay Hitsman once wrote that "only 24,132 conscripts got to France, a very small number indeed." See *Broken Promises* (Toronto: Oxford University Press, 1977), 98, 24.

7 Tim Cook, *Shock Troops* (Toronto: Viking, 2008), 612–13.

8 LAC, RG 24, vol. 1820, file GAQ 5–14, "Overseas Military Forces of Canada 1914–1919: Details of Strength, Casualties and Captures."

9 At 10 percent, battlefield "wastage" was highest in the infantry and the machine gun corps. See *Report of the Ministry: Overseas Military Forces of Canada 1918* [hereafter *Report of the Ministry*] (London: HMSO, 1919), 59.

10 On conscription, see Granatstein and Hitsman, *Broken Promises*; on reinforcements, see Richard Holt, "Filling the Ranks: Recruiting, Training, and Reinforcements in the Canadian Expeditionary Force 1914–1918" (PhD diss., University of Western Ontario, 2011).

11 See A.M. Willms, "Conscription, 1917: A Brief for the Defence," *Canadian Historical Review* 37, 4 (December 1956): 338, 349–50; and A.M.J. Hyatt, "Sir Arthur Currie and Conscription," *Canadian Historical Review* 50, 3 (September 1969), 285–86, 294.

12 See J.L. Granatstein, *The Greatest Victory* (Toronto: Oxford University Press, 2014), 80; and Chris Sharpe, "Enlistment in the Canadian Expeditionary Force 1914–1918: A Re-evaluation," *Canadian Military History* 24, 1 (Winter–Spring 2015): 46.

13 Willms, "Conscription, 1917," 349, 338.

14 Desmond Morton, *When Your Number's Up* (Toronto: Random House, 1993), 69–70; and *Fight or Pay* (Vancouver: UBC Press, 2004), 209.

15 Cook, *Shock Troops*, 595.

16 In noting one soldier's assertion that "the conscripts [he] knew who got sent over were not much good anyway," Andrew Theobald states "that this should not have been a surprise" given "the little training that conscripts received before reaching the front." See *The Bitter Harvest*, 92.

17 See Agnes Laut, "The Slacker," *Maclean's Magazine*, November 1917, 27. Likewise, in *When Your Number's Up*, 244, Morton writes: "Unlike the Australians, though, Canadians were content to fill their ranks with conscripted 'slackers' if it brought victory closer and improved their own chances of survival."

18 See Jeffrey A. Keshen, *Propaganda and Censorship* (Edmonton: University of Alberta Press, 1996), 67; and Benjamin Isitt, *From Victoria to Vladivostok* (Vancouver: UBC Press, 2010), 85, 95.

19 Ian Miller, *Our Glory and Our Grief* (Toronto: University of Toronto Press, 2002), 94–95, 100–102. See also Paul Maroney, "'The Great Adventure': The Context and Ideology of Recruiting in Ontario, 1914–1917," *Canadian Historical Review* 77, 1 (March 1996): 96.

20 A. Fortescue Duguid, *Official History of the Canadian Forces in the Great War 1914–1919*, [hereafter Duguid, *Official History*], vol. 1 (Ottawa: J.O. Patenaude, 1938), vi–vii.

21 Morton adds, "People who bury their history for convenience or to avoid embarrassment pay a price." See *Silent Battle* (Toronto: Lester, 1992), x–xi.

22 Tim Cook, "'Literary Memorials,'" *Journal of the Canadian Historical Association / Revue de la Société historique du Canada* 13, 1 (2002): 175, 180.

23 With respect to the British "Myth of Participation in the War," Bet-El notes that the acclaimed BBC television series *The Great War*, first broadcast in 1964, drew upon "memories" of only those veterans "who had served on any front up to the end of 1915" – that is, before conscription was implemented. See *Conscripts*, 14, 203–5.

24 Notable exceptions are Willms, "Conscription"; and Dan Dancocks, *Spearhead to Victory* (Edmonton: Hurtig Publishers, 1987). In addition, a quarter-century after *Broken Promises*, in his essay "Conscription and My Politics," *Canadian Military History* 10, 4 (Autumn 2001): 37–38, J.L. Granatstein provided a remarkable counter-balance to his earlier views on this subject, one he developed much further in "Conscription in the Great War," in *Canada and the First World War: Essays in Honour of Robert Craig Brown*, ed. David Mackenzie (Toronto: University of Toronto Press, 2005), 62–75. More recently, Tim Cook's *Shock Troops* and Chris Sharpe's "Enlistment," have echoed these sentiments.

25 Some responses to requests for information by the author elicited strong negative sentiments, both against the act of conscription itself and against the conscripts themselves who had been compelled to fight.

26 LAC, Currie fonds, MG30 E100, vol. 27. Letter from Currie in response to Smeaton White (publisher of Montreal's *Gazette*) 2 August, 1926.

244 Notes to pages 9–16

27 Granatstein, *Greatest Victory*, 141, 195.

28 In addition, more than 1,500 digitized conscript files and nearly 3,000 CVWM postings were analyzed.

Chapter 1: "The Blood Dimmed Tide"

NOTE: Chapter title from William Butler Yeats, "The Second Coming," *W.B. Yeats: Selected Poetry,* Ed. A. Norman Jeffares (London: Macmillan, 1971) 99–100.

EPIGRAPH: Margaret Levi, "The Institution of Conscription," *Social Science History* 20, 1 (Spring 1996): 133–167.

1 Granatstein and Hitsman, *Broken Promises*, 9–10.
2 See James Wood, *Militia Myths* (Vancouver: UBC Press, 2010), 3–7.
3 Richard Holmes, *The Western Front* (London: BBC Worldwide, 1999), 22–23.
4 Michael S. Neiberg, *Dance of the Furies* (Cambridge, MA: Harvard University Press, 2011), 145.
5 Herbert Asquith, "Address to Parliament Announcing the War on 6 August 1914," quoted in *Source Records of the Great War,* vol. 1, ed. Charles F. Horne, (New York: The National Alumni, 1923), 404.
6 Neiberg, *Dance,* 140; Marc Ferro, *The Great War 1914–1918,* trans. Nicole Stone (London: Routledge and Kegan Paul, 1973), 27.
7 "Canada to Send Large Force If Needed," *The Toronto World,* 31 July 1914, 1; Duguid, *Official History,* 2.
8 Duguid, *Official History, Chronology, Appendices and Maps* [hereafter *Chronology*], Appendix 16, 14.
9 John Herd Thompson, *The Harvests of War* (Toronto: McClelland and Stewart, 1981), 22.
10 G.R. Stevens in "Part II: Canada Answers the Call," *Flanders' Fields: Canadian Voices from WWI* [DVD-Audio] December 1964 (Canadian Broadcasting Corporation, 2006); and Canada, *Debates of the House of Commons (Special War Session)* [hereafter *Debates*], 19 August 1914, 19.
11 *Debates,* 19 August 1914, 8–9.
12 See John Lewis, "Canada at War," in *Canada in the Great War,* vol. 2 (Toronto: United Publishers, 1920), 31. See also Desmond Morton, *Canada and War: A Military and Political History* (Toronto: Butterworth, 1981), 54, 76–81.
13 See Robert Craig Brown and Donald Loveridge. "Unrequited Faith: Recruiting the CEF 1914–1918," *Revue Internationale d'Histoire Militaire* 51 (1982): 56–57.
14 Robert Rutherdale, *Hometown Horizons* (Vancouver: UBC Press, 2004), 47. Note: Andrew Iarocci argues there was "no typical recruit." See *Shoestring Soldiers* (Toronto: University of Toronto Press, 2008), 19–20.
15 Thompson, *The Harvests of War,* 23.
16 Duguid, *Official History,* 18.
17 Duguid, *Chronology,* "Extract from *Montreal Gazette,* 16th August, 1914," Appendix 57, 42.
18 *Debates, Special War Session,* 22 August 1914, 95.
19 Duguid, *Chronology,* "P.C. 2080," Appendix 48, 36.
20 Ibid., Sam Hughes, "Where Duty Leads," Appendix 149, 122–23.
21 Ibid., Appendix 98, 66.
22 Ibid., 65.
23 A fundamental flaw in Canada's troop planning was that "there were no provisions for replacements and reinforcements," a crucial oversight that led to the "conscription crisis." See Stephen J. Harris, *Canadian Brass* (Toronto: University of Toronto Press, 1988), 141–42.

24 Duguid, *Official History*, 103–4.
25 Unless otherwise noted, all figures for enlistments are drawn from Nicholson, *Official History*, Appendix C, 546.
26 "Out of a total strength of 1098, 1049 had been with the Colours," but only "10 per cent ... were of Canadian origin." See Ralph Hodder-Williams, *Princess Patricia's Canadian Light Infantry*, vol. 1 (London: Hodder and Stoughton, 1923), 10.
27 LAC, RG 9, series III-D-3, Militia and Defence fonds [digitized online], War Diaries, [hereafter WD], at http://www.bac-lac.gc.ca/eng/discover/military-heritage/first-world-war/Pages/war-diaries.aspx. See WD, PPCLI, 7 January, 31 March, and 8 May 1915.
28 See Iarocci, *Shoestring Soldiers*, 97–180.
29 Duguid, *Chronology*, Appendix 847, 433; Nicholson, *Official History*, 546.
30 Tim Cook, *At the Sharp End*, vol. 1 (Toronto: Viking, 2007), 214–15.
31 Duguid, *Chronology*, "P.C. 1593," Appendix 733, 367; Gwatkin to Loring Christie, 25 June 1915, cited in Harris, *Canadian Brass*, 108.
32 Nicholson, *Official History*, 108, 127.
33 Duguid, *Chronology*, Appendix 8, 4.
34 Ibid., 7, 4.
35 Robert Borden, *Robert Laird Borden: His Memoirs*, ed. Henry Borden, 2 vols. [hereafter Borden, *Memoirs*] (Toronto: Macmillan of Canada, 1938), vol. 1, 528–29; Duguid, *Chronology*, Appendix 8, 7.
36 Richard A. Preston and Sydney F. Wise, *Men in Arms*, 2nd rev. ed. (New York: Praeger Publishers, 1970), 266.
37 A direct connection between conscription and "Haig's attrition strategy" is suggested in Michael Neiberg, *Fighting the Great War* (Cambridge, MA: Harvard University Press, 2005), 296.
38 Wood, *Militia Myths*, 225–27. See also Nic Clarke, *Unwanted Warriors* (Vancouver: UBC Press, 2015), 105, 114–16; Miller, *Our Glory and Our Grief*, 43, 114; and R. Matthew Bray, "'Fighting as an Ally': The English-Canadian Patriotic Response to the Great War," *Canadian Historical Review* 61, 2 (1980): 149, 153–54.
39 James Kirkcaldy, quoted in Jim Blanchard, *Winnipeg's Great War* (Winnipeg: University of Manitoba Press, 2010), 107.
40 See Jonathan Vance, *Death So Noble* (Vancouver: UBC Press, 1997), 112–13.
41 Nicholson, *Official History*, 546.
42 Brown and Loveridge, "Unrequited Faith," 60–61.
43 J.T. Copp and T.D. Tait, *The Canadian Response to War* (Toronto: Copp Clark, 1971), 27, noted that "all major newspapers with the exception of *Le Devoir* exhorted their readers to volunteer." For more on the "nationalistic stance" taken by Canadian papers, see Bray, "Fighting as an Ally," 149–50.
44 Russell G. Hann, "Introduction," in *The Great War and Canadian Society*, ed. Daphne Read (Toronto: New Hogtown Press, 1978), 26.
45 J. Castell Hopkins, *Canada at War: 1914–1918* (Toronto: The Canadian Annual Review, 1919), 77. Also see Miller, *Our Glory and Our Grief*, 74–75.
46 Copp and Tait, *The Canadian Response*, 29.
47 See Matt Baker, "The List of the Nation's Heroes, Voluntary Enlistment in Chatham, Ontario 1914–1916," *Canadian Military History* 24, 1 (Winter–Spring 2015): 162–63.
48 Copp and Tait, *The Canadian Response*, 29–30.
49 *Veteran*, December 1917, 19.
50 Hann, *The Great War and Canadian Society*, 31. Also see Blanchard, *Winnipeg's Great War*, 112. On 14 April 1916, Judge Mathers of Winnipeg told Prime Minister Borden that "it is

absurd to speak of enlistment at the present day as voluntary. In the cities of the west the man who is not in uniform is made to feel that he is a sort of social outcast. No man who joins the ranks today does do voluntarily. He does so because he can no longer resist the pressure of public opinion."

51 Hopkins, *Canada at War*, 78.
52 Debbie Marshall, *Give Your Other Vote to the Sister* (Calgary: University of Calgary Press, 2007), 250; see also Barbara M. Wilson, ed., *Ontario and the First World War* (Toronto: University of Toronto Press, 1977), lxxxv, who noted that while "most women supported their country's war effort wholeheartedly, some hung back ... [in part] from fear of the fate which might befall their husbands and sons."
53 Judge P.A. Macdonald, quoted in Blanchard, *Winnipeg's Great War*, 108.
54 Nicholson, *Official History*, 154, 198.
55 Sir Robert Borden, "Appeal for national service," 23 October 1916. See LAC, http://www.collectionscanada.gc.ca/primeministers/h4-4069-e.html.
56 Miller, *Our Glory and Our Grief*, 102, 85; and Granatstein and Hitsman, *Broken Promises*, 39.
57 Hugh Urquhart, *The History of the 16th Battalion* (Toronto: Macmillan, 1932), 189.
58 Vera Brittain, *Testament of Youth* (London: Weidenfeld and Nicholson, 2009), 556; Hew Strachan, *The First World War* (New York: Viking Penguin, 2004), 247.
59 Ferro, *The Great War*, 83.
60 LAC, MG 27 II D23, Garnet Hughes papers, vol. 14, folder 7, draft "Canada's Fifth Division: A History, January 1917–March 1918," 2–4 and 4a, letter from Borden to G. Hughes, n.d.
61 Tim Cook, *Shock Troops*, 144, notes that "April 9, 1917, was the single bloodiest day of the entire war for the Canadian Corps."
62 Ibid., 167.
63 Sir Robert Borden, Speech, Canadian Club Halifax, 18 December 1914. See LAC, http://www.collectionscanada.gc.ca/primeministers/h4-4043-e.html.
64 Borden, *Memoirs*, vol. 2, 617.
65 New Zealand's "Military Service Act [hereafter MSA] was passed in August 1916 and implemented in November." See Margaret Levi, "The Institution of Conscription," *Social Science History* 20, 1 (Spring 1996), 143, 152.
66 Note: "Universal military training for Australian men aged 18 to 60 had been compulsory since 1911." The first referendum, which "if carried, would have extended this requirement to service overseas," was held in October 1916 and "was defeated with 1,087,557 in favour and 1,160,033 against." A second referendum was defeated in December 1917. See National Archives of Australia, http://www.naa.gov.au/collection/fact-sheets/fs161.aspx; and George Q. Flynn, *Conscription and Democracy* (Westport, CT: Greenwood Press, 2002), 38.
67 See LAC, MG 27 II D 9, Albert Edward Kemp papers [hereafter KP], vol. 118, file 12, Memos: Mewburn to Kemp, "Canadian Defence Force," "Report on Progress" and "Suggestions for Compulsory Method of Enrolment in the Active Militia," 25 April 1917.
68 LAC, KP, vol. 118, file 12, Letters, Bennett to Kemp, 26 April 1917, and S. Masten to Kemp, 7 May 1917.
69 "Have Done with Puttering," *Toronto World*, 1 May 1917, 5; LAC, KP, vol. 118, file 12, "The Military for Enforced Service," *Winnipeg Telegram*, 2 May 1917.
70 "Time to Act," *Ottawa Journal-Press*, 3 May 1917, 4.
71 *Saturday Night*, 19 May 1917, quoted in A.M. Willms, "Conscription," 347–48.
72 Robert Craig Brown, *Robert Laird Borden, A Biography*, vol. 2: *1914–1937* (Toronto: Macmillan, 1980), 84; *Debates* 18 May 1917, 1540–42.
73 *Debates*, 1542.

74 Editorial, *Toronto Globe*, 18 May 1917; "The Only Way," *Gazette*, 19 May 1917, 12.

75 Elizabeth Armstrong, *The Crisis of Quebec, 1914–1918* (Toronto: McClelland and Stewart, 1974), 174, 194–96. *La Patrie*, 24 May 1917, 8, agreed that Germany needed to be defeated, but posed this vital question: "La nation Canadienne, la province du Québec sont-elles prêtes à aller jusqu'au bout?"

76 More extreme views were heard from one speaker who charged "that the government [should] 'put a revolver to the head of the fit man who refuses to go.'" See Miller, *Our Glory and Our Grief*, 137.

77 LAC, KP, vol. 120, file 26, Letter, Gwatkin to Kemp, 5 June 1917.

78 Laurier to Aylesworth, 15 May 1917, Laurier Papers, vol. 708, file 195527a-b-c, quoted in James Crowley, "Borden: Conscription and Union Government" (PhD diss., University of Ottawa, 1958), 132, http://www.ruor.uottawa.ca/handle/10393/20873.

79 Borden and Laurier met on 25 and 29 May, and again on 4 and 6 June, 1917. See Borden, *Memoirs*, vol. 2, 720–27; and Brown, *Borden*, 84–90.

80 *Debates*, 11 June 1917, 2278, 2280–82.

81 Ibid., 2283. Those eligible for the draft included "every male British subject ... (a) ordinarily resident in Canada; or (b) [who] has been at any time since the fourth day of August, 1914, resident in Canada." One important caveat in the draft text regarding marital status specified that "any man married after the eleventh day of June, 1917, shall be deemed to be unmarried."

82 Ibid., 2286–88.

83 Nicholson, *Official History*, 284.

84 Hyatt, "Sir Arthur Currie and Conscription," 285.

85 Daniel Dancocks, *Sir Arthur Currie* (Toronto: Methuen, 1985), 122. See also "Currie Urges Imperative Necessity of Early Reinforcements," *Toronto Globe*, 25 June 1917.

86 Currie to F.A. Mackenzie, 19 June 1917, quoted in J. Castell Hopkins, *The Canadian Annual Review War Series: 1917* [hereafter *CAR 1917*] (Toronto: The Canadian Annual Review, 1918), 520.

87 Hopkins, *CAR 1917*, 338, 342. On the demographics of Canada's "Manpower Pool," see Holt, "Filling the Ranks," 228–31, 234, 283. For more on resistance to conscription by industrial and farm workers, see Daniel Byers, *Zombie Army* (Vancouver: UBC Press, 2016) 26–28.

88 *Debates*, 18 June 1917, 2397; "Discussion of Conscription Ends in Vote at Early Morning Hour," *Toronto Globe*, 6 July 1917, 1. Note: Henri Bourassa, who referred to "conscription" as a "blood tax," was a key catalyst for this "cleavage." See Béatrice Richard, "Henri Bourassa and Conscription: Traitor or Saviour," *Canadian Military Journal* 7, 4 (Winter 2006–7): 76.

89 *Debates*, 24 July 1917, 3723, 3729.

90 Ibid., 3733–34; Borden, *Memoirs*, vol. 2, 705. Note: early postwar scholarship suggested that Quebec was largely responsible for this "cleavage" over conscription. See O.D. Skelton, *Life and Letters of Sir Wilfrid Laurier*, vol.2, ed. David M.L. Farr (Toronto: McClelland and Stewart, 1965); and H. Blair Neatby, *Laurier and a Liberal Quebec: A Study in Political Management*, ed. Richard T. Clippingdale (Toronto: McClelland and Stewart, 1973 [1956]). More recent scholarship, however, reveals that opposition to conscription was in fact a national phenomenon. See Thompson, *The Harvests of War*; John English, *The Decline of Politics: The Conservatives and the Party System 1901–1920* (Toronto: University of Toronto Press, 1977); and J.L. Granatstein, *Canada's Army: Waging War and Keeping the Peace*, 2nd ed. (Toronto: University of Toronto Press, 2011).

91 "Military Service Bill Carried," *Toronto Globe*, 25 July 1917, 1; *Debates*, 3736.

92 Borden "found uneven support from French-Canadians, organized labour, and farmers across the nation." See Curtis Mainville, *Till the Boys Come Home* (Fredericton: Goose Lane, 2015), 15, 55. Likewise, in *Unwanted Warriors*, 35, Nic Clarke notes that "a significant number of eligible Canadian men of military age ... had little or no enthusiasm for the war."

93 LAC, KP, vol. 124, file 40, Adjutant-General to Kemp, "Memo as to Recruiting Organization in the United States," 28 May 1917.

94 LAC, KP, vol. 120, file 23, *European War – Memorandum no. 5*, Department of Militia and Defence, Ottawa, 1 January 1919, 12.

95 Richard Holt, "British Blood Calls British Blood: The British-Canadian Recruiting Mission of 1917–1918," *Canadian Military History* 22, 1 (Winter 2013): 33.

96 "Liberals Suggest Three Improvements," *Toronto Globe*, 9 July 1917, 5. Note: the bill in question addressed a "reciprocal convention between the United States and Great Britain"; it permitted conscription of each other's citizens for military service and was ratified on 30 July 1918. See Holt, "British Blood," 34.

97 *Toronto Globe*, 9 July 1917, 1.

98 This 12th Parliament was expected to last five years. However, neither party was inclined to contest an election in 1916. Thus on 8 February, the Commons agreed to a one-year extension, which subsequently required an amendment (by the British Parliament) to the British North America Act.

99 Borden, *Memoirs*, vol. 2, 748, 742.

100 See Currie diary entry 15–18 August 1917, in Mark Humphries, ed., *The Selected Papers of Sir Arthur Currie* (Waterloo: Laurier Centre for Military, Strategic and Disarmament Studies and Wilfrid Laurier University Press, 2008), 48–49.

101 The Military Voters Act enfranchised any British subject, male or female, who had gone on active service with either Canadian military forces or select British forces. It also permitted military voters to assign their vote to any riding in which they had previously been domiciled, or allowed their preferred party to assign their vote to the riding where it would be most useful. See *The Canada Year Book 1918* (Ottawa: J. De Labroquerie Taché, 1919), 641–42.

102 The Wartime Elections Act disenfranchised large groups of voters, including "all new Canadians from enemy countries who had arrived in Canada since [31 March] 1902"; it also "enfranchised the immediate female relatives of members of the armed forces." In time this latter group, "the mothers, wives and sisters of the men in the overseas forces," were heavily pressured to vote Union. See Grace Morris Craig, *But This Is Our War* (Toronto: University of Toronto Press, 1981), 130.

103 Tim Cook, *Warlords: Borden, Mackenzie King, and Canada's World Wars* (Toronto: Allen Lane, 2012), 110.

104 Brown, *Borden*, 100–1.

105 "Parliament Prorogues on Eve of 6th Anniversary," *Toronto Globe*, 21 September 1917, 1.

Chapter 2: "Canada's New Fighting Forces"

EPIGRAPH: *Toronto Daily Star*, 20 September 1917, 10.

1 H.A.C. Machin, *Report of the Director of the Military Service Branch on the Operation of the Military Service Act, 1917* [hereafter *MSB Report*], (Ottawa: J. De Labroquerie Taché, 1919), 5. Other members of the Military Service Council were Machin; O.M. Biggar, Edmonton; John H. Moss, K.C., Toronto; and L.J. Loranger, K.C., Montreal.

2 Canada, Department of National Defence [hereafter DND], Directorate of History and Heritage [hereafter DHH], Edwin Pye fonds 74/672, box 4, folder 14, "The Military Service Act," 69.

3 *Toronto Daily Star*, 11 September 1917, 4.

4 Machin, *MSB Report*, 34, 44.

5 See Brown, *Borden*, 51–54. "In 1912 the Ontario Department of Education issued Instruction 17," which directed that "instruction in Ontario Schools was to be in English." This controversial decision may have been on the minds of many Franco-Ontarians when the first call to report came in October 1917.

6 Royal Proclamation, *Toronto Daily Star*, 13 October 1917, 16.

7 *Manual for the Information and Guidance of Tribunals in the Consideration and Review of Claims for Exemption* [hereafter *Manual*] Military Service Council (Ottawa: J. De Labroquerie Taché, 1918), 100.

8 Ibid., 11–16.

9 Vance, *Death So Noble*, 121.

10 Hopkins, *CAR 1917*, 351.

11 *Manual*, 6.

12 Ibid., 5.

13 Machin, *MSB Report*, 9; and Miller, *Our Glory and Our Grief*, 148–49.

14 Amy J. Shaw, *Crisis of Conscience* (Vancouver: UBC Press, 2009), 37. Note: According to Granatstein and Hitsman, *Broken Promises*, 98, Justice Duff "burned" all related tribunal documents. Official records, however, preserved by Lieutenant Émile Vaillancourt, show that one tribunal in Montreal exempted English and French Canadians in almost equal numbers. My thanks to Molly Ungar for "Saving the Past: Evidence from Military Tribunal 330, October 1917," unpublished conference paper, Military History Colloquium, Wilfrid Laurier University, 1999.

15 Wilson, ed., *Ontario and the First World War*, lvi.

16 Hopkins, *CAR 1917*, 351. See also "Eighteen Unfit, Given Exemption," *Gazette*, 30 November 1917, 4.

17 Machin, *MSB Report*, 42, 46. In Nova Scotia, 92 percent requested exemptions; in New Brunswick, 92 percent; in PEI, 94 percent; in Quebec, 98 percent; in Ontario, 92.9 percent; in Manitoba, 89.4 percent; in Saskatchewan, 95.1 percent; in Alberta, 90.4 percent; and in British Columbia, 83 percent.

18 Agnes C. Laut added: "Is their kind wanted? Does it do any good? Does it justify being alive?" See "The Slacker," *Maclean's Magazine*, November 1917, 27.

19 LAC, (2204524) George Edward Jones.

20 *For the Defence of Canada* (Ottawa: Military Service Council, 1917), 19.

21 Bill Rawling, *Surviving Trench Warfare* (Toronto: University of Toronto Press, 1992), 143.

22 Dancocks, *Currie*, 109; Cook, *Shock Troops*, 309–66. Cook notes "16,404" total casualties but an official report indicating "12,403" actual battle casualties.

23 See Lieutenant-General Sir Arthur Currie, "Interim Report on the Operations of the Canadian Corps during the Year 1918," in *Report of the Ministry Overseas Military Forces of Canada 1918* [hereafter "Interim Report"] (London: HMSO, 1919), 107.

24 Note: While in November 1917 the 5th Division remained a potential source of reinforcements, Currie still saw implementation of the MSA as his next key source of manpower.

25 W.R. Plewman, "The War Reviewed," *Toronto Daily Star*, 13 December 1917, 2.

26 Daniel Dancocks, *Legacy of Valour* (Edmonton: Hurtig Publishers, 1986), 226.

27 Dancocks, *Currie*, 122, 125.

28 Letters from Currie to Lieutenant-Colonel John Creelman and Dudley Oliver, 30 November 1917, quoted in Humphries, ed., *The Selected Papers*, 61–63; and Iarocci, *Shoestring Soldiers*, 30, 162.

29 Hyatt, "Currie and Conscription," 286–87.
30 Dancocks, *Currie*, 123; "First Duty to Support Troops," *Toronto Globe*, 7 December 1917, 9.
31 Letter, Currie to Perley, 7 December 1917, quoted in Hugh Urquhart, *Arthur Currie* (Toronto: J.M. Dent and Sons, 1950), 190; "Gen. Byng and Gen. Currie," *Toronto Daily Star*, 8 December 1917, 10.
32 "Have an Ulterior Motive," *Toronto Daily Star*, 14 December 1917, 23; lead editorial in the *Toronto Globe*, 7 November 1917, 6.
33 C.G. Williams, "Report of Lieut. Col. (Rev.) Cecil Grosvenor Williams, Chief Recruiting Officer for Canada," [hereafter Williams, *Report*]. LAC, KP, vol. 124, file 42, 30, n.d. [August 1917].
34 John Becker, *Silhouettes of the Great War* (Nepean, ON: CEF Books, 2001), 133–34.
35 LAC, James Layton Ralston fonds, MG 27 III B11, vol. 2, letter Ralston to parents, 15 July 1917.
36 Canon Frederick G. Scott, *The Great War As I Saw It* (Ottawa: CEF Books, 1999), 165; R.B. Fleming, ed., *The Wartime Letters of Leslie and Cecil Frost 1915–1918* (Waterloo: Wilfrid Laurier University Press, 2007), 202.
37 Canadian War Museum [hereafter CWM], 20050041–003, 58A 1 217.31, Albert Blount, letter to John Loye, 30 November 1917.
38 J.L. Granatstein, *Hell's Corner* (Vancouver: Douglas and McIntyre, 2004), 110.
39 Sandra Gwyn, *Tapestry of War* (Toronto: HarperCollins, 1992), 413.
40 LAC, KP, vol. 150, file M-9, Kemp to Borden, 2 April 1918, with letter from Major F. Gibson.
41 *Berwick Register*, 9 February 1918, letter MacKinlay to father, 3 December 1917.
42 "Canada Votes Union," *Toronto Globe*, 18 December 1917, 1. Weeks later, CEF polling results reversed the outcome in fourteen ridings – all in favour of the Unionists, thus providing a decisive seventy-one seat majority. See Desmond Morton, "Polling the Soldier Vote," *Journal of Canadian Studies* 10, 4 (November 1975): 52.
43 Borden, *Memoirs*, vol. 2, 765.
44 Machin, *MSB Report*, 6, 44.
45 "Bugle Calls Up Draftees," *Toronto Globe*, 3 January 1918, 1; Morton, *A Military History of Canada*, 156.
46 "Canada's New Fighting Forces," *Toronto Globe*, 3 January 1918, 4.
47 For examples, see LAC, (3232014) Robert Adams; (3034780) Norman Finley Campbell; (3317149) Joseph Patrick Dillon; (3106793) Frank Xavier Rioux; and (3285570) Joseph Barrette.
48 See LAC, (3107203) Olivier Charlebois; and (3032685) Roy Wesley Geach.
49 "Ottawa Is Silent Concerning the Draft," *Windsor Record*, 10 January 1918, 5; "Les Mobilises – Pas de Chiffres Officiels," *La Patrie*, 7 January 1918, 1.
50 "Doesn't Seem Quite Right," *Windsor Record*, 7 January 1918, 4.
51 Machin, *MSB Report*, 22–24.
52 "Nemesis of Slackers Wins Chief's Thanks," *Windsor Record*, 3 January 1918, 3.
53 "Canada and United States to Round Up and Conscript Slackers; Drag-Net Closing," 5 January 1918, 1; "Draft Evaders Held in Armories," *The Windsor Record*, 24 January 1918, 9.
54 "Seeking British Recruits in Detroit," *Windsor Record*, 10 January 1918, 6; "First Class Will Yield about 70,000 Draftees," *Toronto Daily Star*, 14 February 1918, 1.
55 One press report stated: "The new men are of a very good type indeed. The discipline among them has been equal to that of any unit yet mobilized." See *Windsor Record*, 21 January 1918, 5.

56 LAC, (256172) Harold Edwin Earnshaw; (3131552) Albert Edward Brooks; and ancestry. ca, War Graves Registers, Circumstances of Casualty. For more on the "ice-box," see "Officers With Real War Experience Will Train Draftees At Base Camp," *The Windsor Record*, 14 January 1918, 2.

57 This fact is derived from an analysis of all applicable entries in Edward H. Wigney, *The C.E.F. Roll of Honour* (Winnipeg: Bunker to Bunker Books, 1996), and applicable personnel records at LAC.

58 Personal Diary [hereafter PD], (3132264) Albert Roy Neilson, 4–7 March 1918. I am grateful to Neilson's grandson, Dr. Peter Neilson, for the loan of this diary. For more on "Physical Standards" and requirements, see Clarke, *Unwanted Warriors*, 27–34, and Appendix A, 162–70.

59 LAC, RG24-c-1-a, vol. 2554, Perley to Kemp, 12 October 1917, re: Lieutenant-General Turner's Memo Scheme for Training Conscripts, 29 August 1917.

60 Ibid., Mewburn memo to the Minister's private secretary titled "Reinforcements – Training and Despatch from Canada," 19 September 1917.

61 The National Archives (hereafter TNA), Cabinet Records (hereafter CAB), 24/151/15, Western and General Report no. 65, "Diversion of Shipping," 24 April 1918.

62 "First Draftees from the Coast Crossing Continent," *Abbotsford Post*, 22 February 1918.

63 "Draft of 500 Men Bid Good-Bye to London 'Ice-Box,'" *The Windsor Record*, 1 February 1918, 1.

64 See Humphries, ed., *The Selected Papers*, 70; and Tim Cook, *Shock Troops*, 372–73.

65 LAC, KP, vol. 157, R-3, War Office to Kemp, 121/Overseas/5296. (S.D.2), 11 January 1917.

66 Ibid., Kemp to Borden, draft cable 14 January 1918; Urquhart, *Arthur Currie*, 198–99.

67 See W.A. Willison, "Holding the Line," in *Canada in the Great War*, vol. 5, 62; and LAC, KP, vol. 142, F-2, Kemp to Prime Minister, 26 January 1918.

68 LAC, KP, vol. 142, F-2, Borden to Kemp, 1 February 1918.

69 Mewburn had cabled Kemp on 6 February 1918, noting that while "13,599 [men] are due to embark," he could give "no guarantee as to numbers subsequently available." LAC, KP, vol. 157, R-3.

70 LAC, KP, vol. 142, F-2, Currie to Kemp, 7 February 1918.

71 Ibid., Kemp to Borden, "*Reorganization of the Canadian Corps,*" 8 February 1918; KP, vol. 157, R-3, Mewburn to Kemp, "Reinforcements Available in Canada," 6 February 1918.

72 LAC, MG 27 II D23 vol. 14, folder 7, Garnet Hughes Papers, "Canada's Fifth Division," 12–13; Hyatt, "Currie and Conscription," 296.

73 Terry Copp, "The Military Effort 1914–1918," in *Canada and the First World War*, ed. David Mackenzie, 55.

Chapter 3: The First Canadian Conscripts in Combat

1 The Halifax Memorial commemorates military personnel who lost their lives at sea and have no known grave. Panels One and Two (for 1918) commemorate 168 soldiers and 14 nursing sisters, including 67 conscripts and 9 BCRM men.

2 While the *Report of the Ministry*, 10–11, states that the period of confinement was "normally 28 days," further analysis reveals that four weeks were not the norm but rather the exception, particularly in the spring of 1918 when it appears that two weeks or less segregation typically met the requirement.

3 Turner directive, quoted in Nicholson, *Official History*, 351.

4 See "They're Volunteers of '18," *Toronto Daily Star*, 21 March 1918, 17; Michael O'Leary, "Punishment," www.regimentalrogue.com/misc/researching_first_world_war_soldiers_part16.htm.

5   The Canadian Letters and Images Project, www.canadianletters.ca [hereafter CLIP], William George Calder, letter 10 January 1918; John Row, Jr., letter 10 March 1918; Bertram Howard Cox, letter 17 June 1918.

6   Ben Wagner, quoted in Daphne Read, ed., *The Great War*, 108–9.

7   WD, Assistant Director of Medical Services [hereafter ADMS], Bramshott, 31 March 1917, and 17–19 February, 1918.

8   See Desmond Morton, *Report no. 98* – "The Command of the Overseas Military Forces of Canada in the United Kingdom, 1914–1918" (Ottawa: DHH, n.d. [1962]), 108; and OMFC, *Report of the Ministry*, 9.

9   For details on the fourteen-week training syllabus, see Kenneth Radley, *We Lead, Others Follow* (St. Catharines: Vanwell, 2006), 283; see also Cook, *Shock Troops*, 52.

10 Hostilities between Germany and Russia initially ceased on 15 December 1917. Mindful of the relentless build-up of American forces, Ludendorff subsequently reduced his divisions in the east by thirty-eight and increased those in the west by forty-three. See David Stevenson, *1914–1918: The History of the First World War* (London: Penguin Books, 2012 [2005]), 399; and General [Erich] Ludendorff, *My War Memories, 1914–1918*, vol. 2 (London: Hutchinson, 1919), 510–11, 588.

11 Ibid., Ludendorff, 596–99; Malcolm Brown, *1918: Year of Victory* (London: Pan Books, 1999), 48–51.

12 Currie, "Interim Report," 108.

13 Wilfred Kerr, *Arms and the Maple Leaf* (Ottawa: CEF Books, 2005), 66.

14 Denis Winter, *Haig's Command* (London: Penguin, 2001) 173–74; Brown, *1918*, 70. Also see J.P. Harris, *Douglas Haig and the First World War* (New York: Cambridge University Press, 2009), 447–60.

15 WD, General Staff Canadian Troops, Witley, March 1918.

16 Ibid.

17 Brigadier-General Alex Ross thought that Currie's faulty rhetoric "left the troops cold." See Dancocks, *Currie*, 133–34.

18 LAC, KP, vol. 150, M-5, Kemp to Mewburn, 26 March 1918.

19 Nicholson, *Official History*, 348.

20 Brown, *Borden*, 132.

21 LAC, KP, vol. 150, M-9, Currie to Kemp, 27 March 1918, quoted in Kemp to Borden, 2 April 1918.

22 Martin F. Auger, "On the Brink of Civil War," *Canadian Historical Review* 89, 4 (2008): 508.

23 Nicholson, *Official History*, 347–48; Borden, *Memoirs*, vol. 2, 786–87.

24 Armstrong, *The Crisis of Quebec*, 228; Borden, *Memoirs*, vol. 2, 788.

25 PD, Neilson, 1–2 April. See also Auger, "On the Brink," 533n79, 538.

26 Auger, "On the Brink," 532n75, 534n83.

27 Nicholson, *Official History*, 349.

28 Granatstein and Hitsman, *Broken Promises*, 90–91.

29 British diplomats observed: "Canada is the first of the Dominions to hold a secret session of Parliament." See TNA, CAB, 24/151/15, Western and General Report No. 64, 17 April 1918; http://www.nationalarchives.gov.uk/; "Germany Must Be Defeated," *Toronto Globe*, 18 April 1918, 1.

30 Borden, *Memoirs*, vol. 2, 800.

31 "Both Houses Endorse Measure of Conscription," *Toronto Globe*, 20 April 1918, 4.

32 Brian Douglas Tennyson, *Canada's Great War* (Lanham, MD: Rowman and Littlefield, 2014), 106, 108.

33 Haig, quoted in Harris, *Douglas Haig*, 469, 419–20. Note: The British were not short of trained reinforcements per se. Evidence suggests that the War Cabinet had been "rationing Haig's manpower" since April 1917.

34 *Times*, 19 April 1918. For more on the MSA in the United Kingdom, see Bet-El, *Conscripts*, 11–13.

35 See WD, General Staff Canadian Troops Witley, March 1918, memorandum HQ OMFC to "Headquarters Canadians, Bramshott, Witley, Seaford and Shorncliffe," 25 March 1918.

36 WD, HQ Canadians Bramshott, "Memorandum ... for Month of March, 1918"; General Staff Canadian Troops Witley, March 1918.

37 WD, "Memorandum – Canadian Training Division, for Month of April 1918," 7 May 1918.

38 WD, HQ Canadian Troops Witley, 11 August 1918; LAC, (3107292) Austin Kempffer.

39 While even "fourteen weeks" appear hardly sufficient to prepare a soldier for combat, as late as 1917 the Chief Recruiting Officer for Canada reported that "three months training" appeared to be "sufficient" to make a soldier "fit for any duties that he may be called upon to perform." See Williams, *Report*, "Training in England," 76–77. For examples of training duration see LAC, (256389) Thomas Alkers – thirteen weeks; (2129301) George Edward – nearly sixteen weeks; and (2137864) Arthur Freeman – seventeen weeks.

40 WD, General Staff Canadian Troops Witley, June 1918, Appendix 5, 29 June 1918, and July 1918, Appendix 2, 13.

41 WD, HQ Canadians Bramshott, "Memorandum Canadian Training Division – for July 1918," 6 August 1918.

42 Notably, in his "Narrative of Operations, from March 13th to November 11th, 1918," 22 (hereafter, WD, 2nd Division, Report), Major-General Harry Burstall declared that about half of his "two thousand odd reinforcements" at Arras (August, 1918) "were only partially trained." Likewise, Currie gave this myth added traction when he asserted that "many [conscripts] were hurried across to France with very little training." See CWM, CP, 58A 1 60.6, Currie to Kemp, "preliminary report," 22 December 1918, and CP, 58A 1 61.5, Currie to Mewburn, 17 March 1919.

43 Tim Cook, *Shock Troops*, 375.

44 Nicholson, *Official History*, 383.

45 Bill Rawling, "A Resource Not to Be Squandered," in *1918: Defining Victory*, ed. Peter Dennis and Jeffrey Grey (Canberra: Army History Unit, 1999), 48.

46 More than 600 conscripts likely underwent engineer training in England (1.3 percent of 47,509 conscripts who "proceeded overseas"). See LAC, KP, vol. 120, file 23, *European War – Memorandum no. 5*, 10; and Nicholson, *Official History*, 551.

47 Currie, "Interim Report," 112.

48 H.C. Singer and A.A. Peebles, *History of Thirty-First Battalion* (Calgary: [privately printed], 1939), 313. For more precise casualty figures, see WD, 2nd Canadian Division, Report, 2.

49 WD, 7th Battalion, April 1918; LAC, (2020341) Alexander Bey; (2020370) Werner Olaf Magnos Olson; (2020458) Niels Peter Pedersen; and Nominal Roll, 7th Battalion, British Columbia Regiment (BCR) Archives, Vancouver, BC, courtesy of Colonel Keith Maxwell, OMM, CD (Retired).

50 WD, 7th Battalion, April 1918, Appendix 5, "7th Battalion Orders April 26th, 1918," 3; 85th Battalion, May 1918, Appendix I; LAC, (2655641) Archibald Delaney Forbes; Joseph Hayes, *The Eighty-Fifth in France and Flanders* (Halifax: Royal Print and Litho, 1920), 112.

51 WD, 18th Battalion, 10 June 1918; LAC, (3130373) George Henry Allsop.

52 See Captain Robert N. Clements, M.C., *Merry Hell*, ed. Brian Douglas Tennyson (Toronto: University of Toronto Press, 2013), 202.

53 A.J. Lapointe, *Souvenirs et impressions de ma vie de soldat* (St-Ulric: [privately published], 1919), 88–91; WD, 22nd Battalion, 8 June 1918, and "Special Report on Enemy Attempted Raid."
54 See WD, 6th Canadian Infantry Brigade, June 1918; and 31st Battalion, 24 June 1918.
55 WD, 31st Battalion, 28 May 1918; LAC, (3130259) William James Laidlaw; (3131406) Ernest Dan Laforet. Note: The term "instantly killed" was often used as an all-encompassing euphemism to describe a sudden but not always *instant* or painless death.
56 LAC, (3130464) Ernest Edward Hanson. See also Edward H. Wigney, *Guests of the Kaiser*, ed. Norm Christie (Ottawa: CEF Books, 2008), 61.
57 WD, 27th Battalion, June 1918, Appendix F.
58 Tim Cook, *The Madman and the Butcher* (Toronto: Allen Lane, 2010), 244.
59 Personal Letters, (3130875) Hilaire Dennis, 12 May 1918.
60 Ibid. In writing that his "life is not worth ten cents," Dennis underscored how little value was attached to the life of the common soldier, and perhaps alluded to the fact that soldiers then "overseas" received an additional ten cents a day field allowance.
61 PD, Neilson, 11–12 and 15–16 May 1918.
62 Ibid., 20 and 22–23 May 1918.
63 All fatalities but one were infantrymen with Company B of the 58th Regiment. See Blackwell-Frazier American Legion Post #142, https://www.americanlegion142.org/memories/andrew-blackwell/the-sinking-of-the-rms-moldavia.
64 PD, Neilson, 24 May 1918. Note: Nielson spent ten days in "quarantine" before being released into the main camp.
65 LAC, KP, vol. 157, R-3, Wilson to Kemp, 12 June 1918.
66 Ibid., Kemp to Wilson, 21 June 1918.
67 See Brown, *Borden*, 137; and Borden, *Memoirs*, vol. 2, 809–13.
68 Brian Douglas Tennyson, *Percy Willmot* (Sydney: Cape Breton University Press, 2007), 180.
69 See Scott, *The Great War*, 193, 106–9, 165.
70 Larry Worthington, *Amid the Guns Below* (Toronto: McClelland and Stewart, 1965), 134.
71 Kim Beattie, *48th Highlanders of Canada* (Toronto: 48th Highlanders of Canada, 1932), 307.
72 R.C. Fetherstonhaugh, *The Royal Montreal Regiment 14th Battalion* (Montreal: Gazette Printing, 1927), 212; WD, 14th Canadian Infantry Battalion, 16–19 June 1918.
73 WD, 4th Canadian Field Ambulance, 18 June 1918; Peter Bick, ed., *The Diary of an Artillery Officer* (Toronto: Dundurn Press, 2011), 88.
74 Andrew Macphail, *Official History of the Canadian Forces in the Great War 1914–19: The Medical Services* (Ottawa: King's Printer, 1925), 266; Rawling, "A Resource Not to Be Squandered," 52.

Chapter 4: Conspicuous Gallantry at Amiens
EPIGRAPH: Ralf Frederic Lardy Sheldon-Williams, *The Canadian Front in France and Flanders* (London: A. and C. Black, 1920), 6.
1 Ferdinand Foch, quoted in Terraine, *To Win A War* (Garden City, NY: Doubleday, 1981), 122.
2 J.P. Harris with Niall Barr, *Amiens to the Armistice* (London: Brassey's, 1998), 16–19.
3 Churchill, *The World Crisis*, vol. 4 (New York: Scribner's, 1927), 232, 216.
4 Currie, "Interim Report," 128.
5 Harris, *Douglas Haig*, 487; Gary Sheffield and John Bourne, *Douglas Haig: War Diaries and Letters 1914–1918* (Chatham: BCA, 2005), 438.

6   Roland Hill, "On the Eve of a Great Battle," in *Canada in the Great War*, vol. 5, 127.
7   Worthington, *Amid the Guns Below*, 135.
8   Ludendorff, *Memories*, vol. 2, 640.
9   Currie, quoted in Roland Hill, "On the Eve of a Great Battle," 132.
10 WD, Canadian Corps, Administrative Branches of the Staff [A.A. and Q.M.G.], August 1918, Appendix H, "Memoranda," 2.
11 Ibid., 4 August 1918.
12 Borden, *Memoirs*, vol. 2, 837.
13 James McWilliams and R. James Steel, *Amiens* (Toronto: Dundurn Press, 2001), 7–9.
14 WD, 21st Battalion, 29 July–5 August, 1918.
15 "What Happened on the Night of August 5th–6th Near Amiens," *21st Battalion Communique* [*sic*] 7, 1 (January 1938), 9; WD, 21st Battalion, 5 August ; LAC, (3320178) Patrick Thomas Belanger; (3320437) Arthur Brabant.
16 Brereton Greenhous, *The Battle of Amiens* (Toronto: Balmuir Books, 1995), 13.
17 LAC, Major-General David Watson fonds, microfilm reel M-10, diary entry 7 August 1918 (hereafter Watson Diary).
18 According to Greenhous, *The Battle of Amiens*, 15, "the operational planning for the battle left much to be desired."
19 See Shane Schreiber, *Shock Army of the British Empire* (St. Catharines: Vanwell, 2005), 40.
20 Note: The *Llandovery Castle* was a "Canadian hospital ship ... torpedoed and sunk by U-86" on 27 June 1918. There were 234 lives lost, including 14 Canadian nurses. See McWilliams and Steel, *Amiens*, 31.
21 Nicholson, *Official History*, 395–96.
22 S.F. Wise, "The Black Day of the German Army," in *1918 Defining Victory*, ed. Peter Dennis and Jeffrey Grey (Canberra: Army History Unit, 2001), 16–19.
23 Watson Diary, 8 August 1918; Robert John Renison, "A Story of Five Cities – a Canadian Epic of One Hundred Days," in J. Castell Hopkins, *Canada at War: A Record of Heroism and Achievement 1914–1918* (Toronto: Canadian Annual Review, 1919), 367.
24 See Harris with Barr, *Amiens*, 93.
25 WD, 20th, 18th, 19th and 21st Battalions, 8 August 1918; LAC, (3032485) Gus Izzo; (3130239) William Isaac Hudson; (3032342) Dewart Keir; (3320489) David Barr; (3055348) Wilford Keith Barr. My thanks to Evelyn Rose, Keir's niece, for sharing the contents of this letter of condolence dated 12 September 1918. She adds that her uncle, originally from Baldwin, Ontario, was engaged to be married at the time he was conscripted.
26 WD, 7th Brigade and 49th Battalion, 8 August 1918; LAC, (3205832) William Henry Powell.
27 WD, 1st Division, "Narrative – August 8th, 1918" and "Observations and Lessons Learned"; LAC, (3155395) Guy Blanchette.
28 WD, 5th Brigade, August 1918, Appendix 4, 2, "Narrative of Operations – Aug. 8th."
29 R.C. Fetherstonhaugh, *The 24th Battalion* (Montreal: Gazette Printing, 1930), 226; LAC, (3155152) Joseph Biron.
30 WD, 5th Battalion, 8 August 1918; LAC, (256827) Herbert Fahrenkopf.
31 WD, 2nd Brigade, Appendix 15, Narrative ... August 8th/9th 1918," 14; LAC, (3205651) Vincent Rawlins.
32 Ludendorff, *Memories*, vol. 2, 679. See also Dancocks, *Spearhead*, 57.
33 Ralf Frederick Lardy Sheldon-Williams, *The Canadian Front in France and Flanders* (London: A. and C. Black), 6.
34 Currie, quoted in Urquhart, *Arthur Currie*, 237.
35 Dancocks, *Spearhead*, 60–61, 63. Note: Major-General Archibald Montgomery (Fourth Army Chief of Staff) reversed a commitment that General Rawlinson had made the

previous afternoon to take the 32nd British Division out of reserve and assign it to the Canadian Corps for operations the following day.

36 See Robin Prior and Trevor Wilson, *Command on the Western Front* (Barnsley: Pen and Sword, 2004), 328–30, 332.

37 According to Prior and Wilson, "sixteen attacking brigades employed thirteen different start times." See *Command*, 330.

38 WD, 29th Battalion, Appendix 9, "Scout Officer's Report ... August 9th, 1918"; LAC, (4080123) Frederick Bennett.

39 Singer and Peebles, *History of Thirty-First Battalion*, 359; WD, 31st Battalion, 9 August 1918.

40 WD, 31st Battalion, September 1918, Appendix B4; LAC, (3130288) William Thomas Mott and 31142 *Supplement to the London Gazette*, 24 January 1919, 1245. For a full list of MMs awarded to Canadian conscripts, see Appendix 2.

41 Singer and Peebles, *History of Thirty-First Battalion*, 357; LAC, (4100708) Arthur Henry Barley.

42 See CWM, Major-General Henry Edward Burstall Papers – maps showing "German Order of Battle" at Amiens on 4 August 1918, and 9–12 August 1918.

43 WD, 8th Battalion, August 1918, Appendix 5, "Narrative of Events no. 2"; Bruce Tascona and Eric Wells, *Little Black Devils* (Winnipeg: Frye, 1983), 112–13; LAC, (2378762) John Gibson; (2378702) George Christy.

44 See WD, 1st Brigade, August 1918, Appendix 8.

45 WD, 4th Battalion, 9 August 1918; LAC, (3231491) Thomas Alton McMinn. Note: A first-hand account of this action is found in James Pedley, *Only This* (Ottawa: CEF Books, 1999), 224–31.

46 Patrick Brennan, "From Amateur to Professional: The Experience of Brigadier General William Antrobus Griesbach," in *Canada and the Great War: Western Front Association Papers,* ed. Briton C. Busch (Montreal and Kingston: McGill–Queen's University Press, 2003), 86.

47 See WD, 8th Brigade, 10 August 1918.

48 WD, 2nd CMR, 8–10 August 1918; CVWM and LAC, (3032001) Frederick John Wood.

49 Lt.-Col. G. Chalmers Johnston, *The 2nd Canadian Mounted Rifles in France and Flanders* (Ottawa: CEF Books, 2003), 68, 163–65.

50 Bernard McEvoy and Captain A.H. Finlay, *History of the 72nd Canadian Infantry Battalion* (Vancouver: Cowan and Brookhouse, 1920), 118–20; LAC, (2021278) John McPhail.

51 See WD, 50th Battalion, "Operations ... 10-8-18 to 13-8-18"; LAC, (3205549) David Paterson.

52 LAC, (3055853) Gordon Beall; also see Ken Reynolds, http://www.38thbattalion.blogspot.ca/2007/04/private-gordon-percy-beall.html.

53 WD, 78th Battalion, "Statement by: – no. 2129142 Private Slater, Howard Esli 'C' Company"; "Tabulated Statement of Exact Casualties," 10–11 August 1918; WD, 50th Battalion, August 1918, Appendix 11.

54 Tim Travers, *How The War Was Won* (Barnsley: Pen and Sword, 2005), 130–31.

55 WD, Canadian Corps, Administrative Branches of the Staff [A.A. and Q.M.G.], August 1918, Appendix H, "Memoranda," 3. Lacking the restorative powers of conscript reinforcements, the Australian Corps would manage to stay more or less in the fight until mid-September. But by then the trench strength in its 4th Division battalions averaged only 405 men, while its 1st Division battalions could muster only 339 rifles. See C.E.W. Bean, *Official History of Australia in the War of 1914-1918*, vol. 6, *The Australian Imperial Force in France During the Allied Offensive 1918* (Sydney: Angus and Robertson, 1942), 896.

56 WD, 7th Battalion, 8 and 14–15 August 1918. Correlation of conscript numbers and re-inforcements on these dates was made possible by examining the 7th Battalion, "Nominal roll, 1918," courtesy of the BCR Museum, Vancouver. For similar data on the 72nd Battalion, see McEvoy and Finlay, *72nd Battalion*, 231–90.

57 See Urquhart, *Arthur Currie*, 241, Letter, Currie to Rawlinson, 13 August 1918.

58 Nicholson, *Official History*, 418.

59 Brigadier-General Sir James E. Edmonds, *Military Operations: France and Belgium, 1918*, vol. 4 (London, HMSO, 1947), 163.

60 Schreiber, *Shock Army*, 55.

61 WD, 42nd Battalion, 12 August 1918 and Appendix 2, "Report ... 12th, 13th, 14th and 15th of August, 1918." See also "Forty-Twa, 'Parvillers,'" *The Legionary* 3, 4 (September 1928), 18.

62 WD, 49th Battalion, 13–16 August 1918; PPCLI, August 1918, Appendix 1, "Narrative – August 11th/15th 1918; LAC, (3206362) Cecil Dalbert Kirkpatrick.

63 WD, 52nd Battalion, 14–15 August 1918; Appendix 7, "Operations in Front of Damery"; LAC, (2379103) Horace Llewellyn Mallinson; (2379141) William Alexander Sibbald; (2379033) Roy Curtis Hand.

64 WDs, 2nd Division and 1st Canadian Divisional Artillery, 16 August 1918, the latter of which states that "lack of progress is due to strict orders regarding 'not to engage in battle.'"

65 WD, 9th Brigade, 16 August 1918; 43rd Battalion, August 1918, Appendix B, "Narrative – 15th/16th August, 1918"; 58th Battalion, 16 August 1918.

66 LAC, (2129416) Homer Roy Cronk; (2129209) William James Bawdon; CVWM and (2128966) James Alfred Reid.

67 WD, 4th Brigade, Appendix 24, "Narrative – 16th August 1918"; LAC, (3231312) William Taylor; (3032305) Carmelo Grech.

68 WD, 2nd Brigade and 7th Battalion, 17 August 1918.

69 LAC, (2020922) Charles Beattie Reid; (2021459) William Knowles.

70 WD, 2nd Canadian Divisional Trench Mortar Group, 17 August 1918; LAC, (336157) Morris John Mills; (2601898) Alexander Victor Noble.

71 LAC, (2378341) John Louis Knox.

72 LAC, (2020484) James Austin Fox; (4030002) James Hugh Hooppell; (3205092) Jesse Barmby; (2655629) Evan William Pugh. Notably Pugh, barely twenty-one years old, had been born in Newfoundland.

73 See WD, 12th Brigade, 24 August 1918; 78th Battalion, 13–24 August 1918.

74 McEvoy and Finlay, *History of the 72nd Battalion*, 124.

75 CVWM and LAC, (2378773) Stuart James Grigg.

76 Currie, "Interim Report," 141.

77 See Nicholson, *Official History*, 419; J.F.B. Livesay, *Canada's Hundred Days* (Toronto: Thomas Allen, 1919), 93.

78 Shane Schreiber notes that the first day at Amiens "cost only 500 casualties per mile of advance," while action on 9–11 August yielded about "1000 per mile." See *Shock Army*, 61.

Chapter 5: "Draft Men" and the Battle of the Scarpe, 1918

1 Letters, Currie to Kemp and to Brigadier-General F.W. Hill, 15 August 1918, quoted in Humphries, ed., *The Selected Papers*, 104–6.

2 Ibid., Currie Diary entry 22 August 1918, 109.

3 Haig to Army Commanders, 22 August 1918, quoted in Harris with Barr, *Amiens*, 145.

4 Two notable Canadian exceptions are the writings of Shane Schreiber and Tim Cook. Both have critically examined Currie's risk-taking during the Hundred Days.

5 See Currie, "Interim Report," 144–46; and Schreiber, *Shock Army*, 74.

6 Rawling, *Surviving Trench Warfare*, 206; and Nicholson, *Official History*, 426.

7 See D.J. Corrigall, *The Twentieth Canadian Battalion* (Toronto: Stone and Cox, 1935), 231–35.

8 Hill, "Breaking the Drocourt-Queant Line," in *Canada in the Great War*, vol. 5, 172.

9 James McWilliams and R. James Steel, *The Suicide Battalion* (Edmonton: Hurtig Publishers, 1978), 184.

10 D.M. Goudy, "The M.S.A. Sent Us Good Men," *21st Battalion Communique* 7, 2 (July 1938): 14.

11 Personal letters, Hilaire Dennis, 23 August 1918.

12 Ibid.

13 Haig, quoted in Dancocks, *Spearhead*, 93.

14 Burstall warned of the "short time available for the Battalions and Artillery concerned to make the necessary plans and preparations." See WD, 2nd Division, Report, 24.

15 See Currie, "Interim Report," 146.

16 WD, 8th Brigade, 25 August 1918.

17 WD, Canadian Corps – Administrative Branches, August 1918, Appendix J, "Special Order," 3–4.

18 "We take our objective or die." Excerpt from the unpublished diary of (3159481) Armand Thérien, in Michel Litalien, *Écrire sa guerre* (Outremont: Éditions Athéna, 2011), 175.

19 Personal letters, Hilaire Dennis, 28 October 1918.

20 GHQ had requested that "zero" be changed to "dawn" to synchronize Canadian efforts with Third Army. Currie did not agree, but it was his BGGS, Brigadier-General Ox Webber, who is alleged to have said to the emissary from GHQ (Lieutenant-Colonel John Dill, a future field marshal): "All we want from General Headquarters is a headline in the *Daily Mail* the morning after the attack reading 'The Canadians in Monchy Before Breakfast.'" See Urquhart, *Currie*, 245.

21 LAC, (3033685) William Douglas Johnson; Norm Christie, *For King and Empire*, vol. 5 (Nepean, ON: CEF Books, 1997), 83–84. My thanks to Ruth Holz, Bracebridge Public Library, for sharing an article on Private Johnson from the *Muskoka Herald*, 12 September 1918.

22 WD, 21st Battalion, 26 August 1918; LAC, (3056275) Archie McDonald. Note: "Trench strength" referred to the actual combat power at the sharp end of an infantry battalion. While the reported strength of a battalion was always much higher, men "on command," left out of battle, or otherwise engaged tended to significantly reduce that number.

23 Schreiber, *Shock Army*, 74.

24 Dancocks, *Spearhead*, 98; Ludendorff, *Memories*, vol. 2, 695.

25 WD, 2nd Division, Report, 27–29.

26 Before the attack began, Currie acknowledged that there were "three main systems of defense to penetrate [Monchy, Fresnes-Rouvroy Line, and the D-Q Line] ... which will mark definite stages in the advance, as it will probably be necessary to pause for 24 hours in front of each while fresh brigades and Tanks are brought up and artillery moved forward." See Currie, "Future Policy of Operations – 25 August 1918," quoted in Schreiber, *Shock Army*, 73–74.

27 WD, Canadian Corps Administrative Branches, August 1918, Appendix J.

28 WD, 2nd Division, Report, 28–29.

29 See WD, 2nd Division, 26 August 1918.

30 WD, 52nd Battalion, August 1918, Appendix 9, "Narrative of Events," 2; LAC, (2378737) Reginald William Edwards.

31 WD, 58th Battalion, 27 August 1918.

32 LAC, (2383442) Archie Blanchard; MG 30 E32, Diary (693265) Corporal Albert C. West, hereafter West Diary, 38; WD, 43rd Battalion, Appendix C, "Narrative – August 26th–29th 1918," 2.

33 WD, 4th Brigade, Appendix 31, "Narrative of Operations ... August 1918," 4.

34 Personal Letters, Hilaire Dennis, 28 October 1918.

35 WD, 4th Brigade, Appendix 31, 4.

36 Sandy Antal and Kevin Shackleton, *Duty Nobly Done* (Windsor, ON: Walkerville, 2006), 286; LAC, (3130556) Frederick Readhead.

37 WD, 19th Battalion, Appendix 6, "Operations ... August 25th–29th 1918," 8; CVWM and LAC, (3033824) Lorne Douglas Cox.

38 Stephen Nichol, *Ordinary Heroes* (Almonte, ON: [privately published], 2008), 191; LAC, (3055348) Wilford Keith Barr.

39 WD, 5th Brigade, Appendix 8, "Narrative of Operations – Aug 19th to 29th 1918," 3–5. Note: On 9 August, Lieutenant-Colonel Thomas Louis Tremblay was CO of the 22nd Battalion. On that date he replaced Brigadier-General J.M. Ross, who had been wounded by enemy shelling near Wiencourt.

40 WD, 22nd Battalion, 27 August 1918; LAC, (4040257) Jean Baptiste Degagné.

41 WD, 24th Battalion, 27 August 1918; CVWM and LAC, (4040076) Joseph Brochu. For more on the "dead man's penny," see http://www.greatwar.co.uk/memorials/memorial -plaque.htm.

42 WD, 2nd Division, Report, 31–32; Dancocks, *Spearhead*, 101.

43 Currie, "Interim Report," 149.

44 Between 26 August and 9 September, 2nd Division sustained 3,896 battle casualties at Arras compared to 2,940 in the 3rd Division. See LAC, RG 24, vol. 1821, file GAQ 11–5.

45 Dancocks, *Spearhead*, 101. See also Schreiber, *Shock Army*, 76. In addition, Tim Cook acknowledges that "Currie rarely made mistakes, but he should have pulled his tired divisions from the front at this point, or postponed the operation." See Cook, *The Madman and the Butcher*, 255.

46 WD, 9th Brigade, August 1918, Appendix 28, "Narrative – August 25th to 30th," III.

47 WD, 52nd Battalion, August 1918, Appendix 9, "Narrative of Events," 3.

48 Ibid., 28–29 August 1918; LAC, (2383479) Thomas Byron Fraser; (2378389) William Frank.

49 WD, 5th CMR, August 1918, Appendix 9, "Summary," 6–8; LAC, (3155220) Rosario Larivière.

50 WD, 43rd Battalion, Appendix C, "Narrative – August 26th – 29th 1918, 3; LAC, (2129310) William Carruthers Hamilton.

51 WD, 2nd Canadian Motor Machine Gun Brigade, Appendix 8, "Report – August 28/29th –30/31st 1918."

52 Lieutenant-General Sir Archibald Macdonell, "The Old Red Patch," *Canadian Defence Quarterly* 4, 4 (July 1927): 391–92. For more on Macdonell, see Ian McCulloch, "'Batty Mac': Portrait of a Brigade Commander of the Great War, 1915–1917," *Canadian Military History* 7, 4 (Autumn 1998): 11–18.

53 WD, 2nd Division, Report, 32–35 and 28 August 1918.

54 Corrigall, *The Twentieth*, 241–43; LAC, (3031292) John Bratti; (3032853) Walker Patterson.

55 See Antal and Shackleton, *Duty Nobly Done*, 286–87; and WD, 18th Battalion, 28 August 1918.

56 Letter, (3130549) Private Harold George Penwarden to Mr. and Mrs. John F. Penwarden, *St. Thomas Times-Journal*, 30 September 1918, in Jeffrey Booth, ed., *Opened by Censor* (Aylmer: Aylmer Express, 2008), 203–4.

57 Personal letters, Hilaire Dennis, 21 September and 28 October 1918.

58 LAC, (3130949) Lloyd James Claus; (3130907) Leslie Allison.

59 Goudy, "The M.S.A. Sent Us Good Men," 14–15.

60 Nichol, *Ordinary Heroes*, 192–94.

61 LAC, (4020901) Jack Bevis; (4020887) John Lober.

62 WD, 19th Battalion, Appendix 6, Captain J.A. Linton, O.C. "D," report to C.O., 8.

63 Ibid., Linton, 9; Bruce Cane, ed., *It Made You Think of Home* (Toronto: Dundurn Press, 2004), 245–48.

64 WD, 19th Battalion, Appendix 6, "Operations ... August 25th–29th," 3; LAC, (3032687) Robert Francis Pickens; (3231327) Harry John Walker.

65 Fetherstonhaugh, *The 24th Battalion*, 241–42.

66 LAC, (3080916) Joseph Ernest Field; (3155673) Arthur Daigle.

67 Clark-Kennedy was awarded the Victoria Cross. See Fetherstonhaugh, *The 24th Battalion*, 243.

68 WD, 22nd Battalion, 28 August and September 1918; LAC, (4035039) Alfred Maher; (3155125) Arthur Lamarche. Note: Georges Vanier served as Canada's Governor General from 1959 to 1967.

69 Humphries, ed., *The Selected Papers*, 24 August 1918, 111.

70 Christie, *For King and Empire*, vol. 5, 34.

71 See Travers, *How The War Was Won*, 146; and Dancocks, *Spearhead*, 103.

72 On August 27, General Ludendorff noted the impact of the German army's "unfavourable reinforcement situation" on any proposed "retirement into ... the Hindenburg Position." See Edmonds, *Military Operations: France and Belgium, 1918*, vol. 4, 312.

73 Harris with Barr, *Amiens*, 157.

74 CWM, 58A 1 241.3–16, Private William Shaw Antliff Letters, mother to Will, 29 August 1918.

Chapter 6: The Hardest Single Battle: The Drocourt-Quéant Line

1 Harris, *Douglas Haig*, 500; Nicholson, *Official History*, 434.

2 Cook, *Shock Troops*, 498; Lieutenant-Colonel Andy McNaughton, quoted in Dancocks, *Spearhead*, 108. For details of Currie's "four phase" attack plan, see Nicholson, *Official History*, 435.

3 Dancocks, *Spearhead*, 109–10.

4 WD, 1st Division, August 1918, "Arras Operations" Section II, 1–2.

5 WD, 1st Brigade, Appendix 23, "report ... for the 29th, 30th and 31st August," 2–3.

6 W.W. Murray, *The History of the 2nd Canadian Battalion* (Ottawa: Mortimer, 1947), 285; LAC, (4020253) George Alexander McLaren.

7 D.J. Goodspeed, *Battle Royal* (Toronto: Charters, 1962), 247; WD, 1st Brigade, August 1918, Appendix 23, 3.

8 LAC, (3230473) Kilby Vicars Hickling; WD, 4th Battalion, 30 August 1918.

9 Currie needed this postponement to permit the artillery to effectively reduce the uncut wire in front of the D-Q Line. See Schreiber, *Shock Army*, 79; and WD, 8th Battalion, August 1918, Appendix 13, "Narrative of Events Phase 1."

10 WD, 14th Battalion, 1 September 1918, Appendix 4, "Report on Operations," 1–2.

11 George B. McKean, *Scouting Thrills* (Ottawa: CEF Books, 2007), 111; LAC, (3081022) Alexander Niven.

12 WD, 5th Battalion, 1, 4 September 1918, and Appendix 3, "Narrative."

13 Harris with Barr, *Amiens*, 165.

14 Cook, *Shock Troops*, 483.

15 LAC, MG30 E134, Cyrus Wesley Peck fonds, personal diary, 2 September 1918 [hereafter Peck Diary]; (2129147) Henry Simpson; (2129508) Norman Mark Kirk.

16 WD, 14th Battalion, September 1918, Appendix 5, "Report on Operation of September 2nd."

17 WD, 3rd Brigade, Appendix 3, "Report ... Sept. 2nd, 1918, 9."

18 LAC, (3155873) Aquilas Côté; (3317046) Haviland Hewitt Harris Hunking. See also (1263581) Francois Xavier Cardinal; and 31173 *Supplement to the London Gazette*, 11 February 1919, 2128.

19 WD, 4th Battalion, 2 September 1918; 1st Brigade, September 1918, Appendix 7, "Report," 5.

20 LAC, (3033602) Clifford Joseph Lockley; CVWM, *Toronto Daily Star*, 27 September 1918.

21 See Captain W.L. Gibson, *Records of the Fourth Canadian Infantry Battalion* (Toronto: Maclean, 1924), Nominal Roll, 31–229; and LAC, (3231052) John Edwards.

22 WD, 7th Battalion, 2 September 1918; LAC, (2021284) John Ralph Michell.

23 WD, 10th Battalion, September 1918, Appendix 4, "Narrative," 2–5; Daniel G. Dancocks, *Gallant Canadians: The Story of the Tenth Canadian Infantry Battalion, 1914–1919* (Markham, ON: Penguin Books, 1990), 182.

24 LAC, (3205077) Harvey Driscoll; (3205571) Frederick Kane Steele. For more on Steele, see CVWM, *Toronto Daily Star*, 19 September 1918; and *Calgary Daily Herald*, 24 September 1918, 12.

25 Watson Diary, 29 August 1918.

26 WD, 72nd Battalion, September 1918, Appendix B, "Scarpe Operation" 1–2; LAC, (2138357) William Alfred Moul; (2021296) Arthur Francis Sellwood.

27 LAC, (1263625) Myles James Russell; WD, 11th Brigade, September 1918, Appendix 2, "Narrative ... [to] Sept 5th, 1918."

28 WD, 85th Battalion, September 1918, Appendix "Scarpe," 5, and "Casualty Report," 1–5; Hayes, *The Eighty-Fifth*, 150–51, 154; LAC, (2655616) Howard MacPherson.

29 For more on Ralston and conscription, see Daniel Byers, "J.L. Ralston," *Canadian Military History* 22, 1 (Winter 2013): 11–13.

30 WD, 38th Battalion, September 1918, Appendix 1, "Report on Scarpe Operations," 3–4.

31 LAC, (3056307) Orville Francis Publow; CVWM and (3320221) Robert Oliver Publow. See also *Perth Courier*, 20 September and 11 October 1918; and Christine M. Spencer, http://www.rootsweb.ancestry.com/~onlanark/NewspaperClippings/Spencer/WW1_15.htm.

32 LAC, (2020541) Alexander Price; (2020739) John Ballantyne Price.

33 WD, 12th Brigade, September 1918, Appendix 14, "Scarpe Operation," 4; LAC, (4080007) Henry Gilbert Heslop.

34 WD, 72nd Battalion, September 1918, Appendix B, "Scarpe Operation," 7.

35 LAC, (2021355) Edward William Rich; 31227 *Supplement to the London Gazette*, 13 March 1919, 3449.

36 WD, 47th Battalion, September 1918, "Report ... 1st September to 4th September, 1918, inclusive," 2, 5.

37 LAC, (3130407) William Denny Caza; (3130945) Ernest Raymond Charbonneau; (3131578) Albert Edward Eberly.

38 WD, 50th Battalion, 1–2 September 1918; Appendix IVa, "Report," 4.

39 Victor Wheeler, *The 50th Battalion* (Calgary: Comprint, 1980), 327.

40 LAC, (3205370) Hubert Fournier; (3205978) Alphonse Garnier.

41 WD, 46th Battalion, September 1918, Appendix 20, "Report on Operations"; McWilliams and Steel, *Suicide Battalion*, 161–69; LAC, (256444) Ole Botten; (257859) William Otto Walberg.

42 E.S. Russenholt, *Six Thousand Canadian Men* (Winnipeg: De Montfort Press, 1932), 177, 179.

43 Ibid., 177; LAC, (2378817) John James McAuliffe; (3255766) Arthur Ernest McKeeve.

44 For Hayter's other salient points, see WD, 10th Brigade, September 1918, Appendix D, 17.

45 WD, 11th Brigade, September 1918, Appendix 2, "Narrative," 2.

46 WD, 54th Battalion, September 1918, Appendix 1, "Narrative," 6; CVWM and LAC, (3106349) Charles Elroy Clarkson; (3106305) William Samuel Lane.

47 WD, 75th Battalion, 2 September 1918; 11th Brigade, Appendix 2, "Narrative," 4.

48 LAC, (3033067) Joseph Alphonse Allaire; (3033242) Herbert Keith Devine; (3033148) Thomas James Dinning.

49 WD, 87th Battalion, September 1918, Appendix 4, "Report ... Sept. 1/2nd to midnight Sept. 4/5th."

50 WD, 11th Brigade, September 1918, Appendix 2, [sub] Appendix "B," "Casualties"; LAC, (3155447) Joseph Dubé; (3155649) Louis Philippe Bourgeois; (4035370) Charles Alarie.

51 WD, 102nd Battalion, 2 September 1918, and Appendix D, "Narrative," 2–3; LAC, (3317289) James Dick.

52 WD, 11th Brigade, September 1918, Appendix 2, 7–8 and [Sub]-Appendix B, 2.

53 WD, 4th Division, September 1918, Appendix 1, "Report on Operations" (Article III, 6); Watson Diary, 3 September 1918.

54 Humphries, ed., *The Selected Papers*, 115; Currie, "Interim Report," 153.

55 See LAC, RG 24, vol. 1821, file GAQ 11–5, "General Statistics ... rendered by A.A.G. 3rd. Echelon, France," compiled by Captain G.W. Cragg, Canadian War Narrative Section, Ottawa, April 1920. These records indicate that in just one month the Canadian Corps sustained 29,288 casualties overall – 26,024 battle and 3,214 sick wastage.

Chapter 7: The Canal du Nord and the Brotherhood of Arms

1 Major-General Sir W.H. Anderson, "The Breaking of the Quéant-Drocourt Line," *Canadian Defence Quarterly* 3, 2 (January 1926), 127.

2 WD, 2nd Battalion, Appendix II/2, "Report ... [to] Sept. 5th, 1918"; 47th Battalion, 3 September 1918; LAC, (3056609) Arthur Bruce Bailey.

3 Dancocks, *Spearhead*, 128.

4 Peck Diary, 9 September 1918; WD, 16th Battalion, August and September 1918.

5 West Diary, 41.

6 See LAC, RG 24, vol. 1821, file GAQ 11–5, "General Statistics" Arras; and WD, Canadian Corps, Administrative Branches of the Staff [A.A. and Q.M.G.], August 1918, Appendix H, "Memoranda," 2.

7 Holt, "Filling the Ranks," 472, 537–38.

8 WD, 1st Division, August 1918, Arras Operations, Section V, Administrative Arrangements, "Casualties," 25 and 30; Nicholson, *Official History*, 441.

9 WD, 3rd Battalion CMGC, 24 September 1918; LAC, (3314541) Charles Henry Darby.

10 Livesay, *Canada's Hundred Days*, 190.

11 Ludendorff, *Memories*, vol. 2, 702.

12 See David Stevenson, *With Our Backs to the Wall* (Cambridge, MA: Harvard University Press, 2011), 129–30, 246. Note: Overall, "72 per cent" of US soldiers were drafted.

13 Currie, "Interim Report," 156.

14 Nicholson, *Official History*, 442–43.

15 Schreiber, *Shock Army*, 98.

16 Urquhart, *Arthur Currie*, 251–53.

17 Bovey, "General Sir Arthur Currie," 378.

18 Lord Milner, Secretary of State for War, had recently warned Haig "that if the British Army is used up now there will not be one for next year." See Sheffield and Bourne, *Douglas Haig: War Diaries*, 21 September 1918, 463.

19 See Cook, *The Madman and the Butcher*, 258. Note: In September, the CCRC took in 15,244 other ranks and dispatched a total of 17,220 reinforcements. See WD, CCRC, 30 September 1918.

20 Dancocks, *Spearhead*, 134–35.

21 WD, 1st Division, September 1918, "Report on Canal du Nord," Appendix A, "Operations Orders," Appendix B, "B-W" Instructions no. 2, 4.

22 LAC, RG 9 III-C-3, vol. 4033, G. 709–8, 1st Brigade, 24 September 1918, "'B.W.' Instructions."

23 PD, Neilson, 14 August and 5 September 1918. Notably, of the 144 reinforcements sent to Neilson's unit in September, 31 percent were draftees. See WD, 8th Battalion, Canadian Engineers, 7 September 1918.

24 LAC, (3255443) Percy Emery Morrill; WD, 26th Battalion, 24 September 1918.

25 WD, 25th Battalion, 25 September 1918.

26 LAC, (3256341) William Colwell Day; (3180782) Arthur James Manuel.

27 WD, 2nd Division, Report, 41; Humphries, ed., *The Selected Papers*, 146.

28 LAC, (3310085) Corporal George Matthew Fretwell; 4th Battalion, September 27, 1918.

29 See McWilliams and Steel, *Suicide Battalion*, 172–74.

30 WD, 44th Battalion, September 1918, Appendix B, "Report," 2.

31 LAC, (3255274) Harold Henry Mowatt; Russenholt, *Six Thousand*, 191.

32 McWilliams and Steel, *Suicide Battalion*, 176; WD, 10th Brigade, September 1918, Appendix 32, "Administrative Report," 2; LAC, (1263678) Arngrimur Grandy.

33 WD, 14th Battalion, September 1918, Appendix 13, "Report on the Bourlon Wood Operation," 1–2.

34 WD, 3rd Brigade, September 1918, Appendix 15, "Narrative," 8; LAC, (3080625) Herman Elvett Hawley; (3106320) Walter Turner; Wigney, *Guests*, 129.

35 WD, 1st Brigade, September 1918, Appendix 17, "Report ... Canal du Nord," 6; LAC, (3033577) William Alfred Mitchell; CVWM, letter to Mrs. Mitchell from Lieutenant A.R. MacKay, October 4, 1918.

36 Cook, *Shock Troops*, 517.

37 WD, 47th Battalion, 27 September 1918; LAC, (3130864) Theodore Caza; (3131709) Frank Anthony Schefter.

38 WD, 50th Battalion, 27 September 1918; Wheeler, *The 50th Battalion*, 349; LAC, (3314172) Dave Muirhead. Note: Muirhead was the only Canadian Quaker killed in action. See Amy J. Shaw, *Crisis of Conscience*, 21, 29–31, Table 1.

39 WD, 1st Brigade, September 1918, Appendix 17, "Report ... Canal du Nord," 3–6; LAC, (3130005) Joseph John Fryer; http://www.miltonhistoricalsociety.ca/military/first-world-war/wwi-soldier-details.

40 R.C. Fetherstonhaugh, *The 13th Battalion* (Montreal: [privately printed], 1925) 275–80.

41 LAC, (3080279) John Shepherd.

42 WD, 2nd Battalion, September 1918, Appendix II/11, "Report"; LAC, (3055143) Clifford Wesley Bennett.

43 WD, 3rd Battalion, September 1918, Appendix 2, "Narrative, September 27th"; LAC, (3032186) Joseph Fenech; (3034780) Norman Finley Campbell.

44 WD, 2nd Brigade, 27 September 1918; 7th Battalion, 27 September 1918, and October 1918, Appendix C, "Narrative."

45 LAC, (2020825) James Wellington Young; http://www.jimvallance.com. Jim Vallance is a great-nephew of Private Young. He cowrote the lyrics for "Remembrance Day" with singer Bryan Adams in 1986.

46 WD, 8th Battalion, September 1918, Appendix 3, "Narrative"; LAC, (2381052) Henri Arnauld; (2380589) Robert Charmillot. Headstone translation: "Died For His Country."

47 WD, 5th Battalion, September 1918, Appendix 3, "October 4th, 1918"; LAC, (258400) James Patrick Maguire; 31430 *Supplement to the London Gazette*, 3 July 1919, 8347.

48 WD, 10th Battalion, September 1918, Appendix 11, "Narrative," 1–3; Dancocks, *Gallant Canadians*, 188–90; LAC, (3206526) Ben Craten Bunney; (3206446) Carl Leroy Haglund.

49 WD, 102nd Battalion, 27 September 1918; L. McLeod Gould, *From B.C. to Baisieux* (Victoria: Thos. R. Cusack, 1919), "Nominal Roll of Other Ranks."

50 LAC, (3106377) Norman Alexander Markle.

51 Hayes, *The Eighty-Fifth*, 152–55; LAC, (3204044) Archibald Emanuel March.

52 WD, 12th Battalion Canadian Engineers, 27 September 1918; Hayes, *The Eighty-Fifth*, 157.

53 WD, 85th Battalion, October 1918, Appendix "Cambrai," 2–3; LAC, (3132449) George Hamel Schmitt; (3204214) John Russell Davidson; (3204048) William Harry Barlow.

54 WD, 12th Brigade, October 1918, Appendix 10 [Appendix no. 7], 38th Battalion, "Report," 2; LAC, (3320018) Ernest Labrie.

55 McEvoy and Finlay, *History of the 72nd Battalion*, 142–44; LAC, (2021582) Antonio Donatelli; (2138163) William James Hurley.

56 WD, 12th Brigade, October 1918, Appendix 10 [Appendix no. 7], 78th Battalion "Report"; LAC, (3310606) William John Goodwin.

57 Currie, "Interim Report," 160; Humphries, ed., *The Selected Papers*, 119.

58 Sheffield and Bourne, *Douglas Haig: War Diaries*, 27 September 1918, 465.

59 Currie, "Interim Report," 159.

60 See Nicholson, *Official History*, 450.

61 Hayter's brigade suffered 751 total casualties on 27 September. See WD, 10th Brigade, September 1918, Appendix 32, "Administrative Report."

62 WD, 47th Battalion, 28 September 1918 and "Report on Operations," "Casualty Report"; LAC, (3131591) Edwin Wesley Frost.

63 WD, 50th Battalion, 28 September 1918; LAC, (3314080) Dominic Otto Koabel.

64 See WD, 46th Battalion, September 1918, Appendix 31, "Report," 4–6; 10th Brigade, Appendix E, "Narrative," 6.

65 Ibid., 46th Battalion, 6; LAC, (257731) Llewelyn Rushton; McWilliams and Steel, *Suicide Battalion*, 181.

66 WD, 44th Battalion, September 1918, Appendix B, "Report," 3–5.

67 Russenholt, *Six Thousand*, 193–99; LAC, (3255033) Lester Joseph Buck.

68 WD, RCR, September 1918, Appendix 9, "Narrative"; LAC, (3180566) Herbert Cecil Phillips. For more on RCR conscripts, see Michael M. O'Leary, "Not All Were Volunteers," www.regimentalrogue.com/rcr_great_war_soldiers/rcr_and_the_msa.html.

69 WD, PPCLI, September 1918, Appendix C, "Operations ... to October 1st, 1918"; 7th Brigade, 30 September 1918, "Casualties for Bourlon Wood Operation."

70 LAC, (3056372) Francis William McGowan and CVWM; *Renfrew Mercury*, 25 October and 22 November 1918. For more on PPCLI conscripts, see James S. Kempling, "Birth of a Regiment: Princess Patricia's Canadian Light Infantry 1914–1919" (MA thesis, University of Victoria, 1978), 38, http://www.collectionscanada.gc.ca/obj/thesescanada/vol2/BVIV/TC-BVIV-3826.pdf.

71 WD, 43rd Battalion, 28–29 September 1918; Appendix M, "Narrative," 1–2; LAC, (2138860) Andrew Levord Hanson.

72 Kevin Shackleton, *Second to None* (Toronto: Dundurn Press, 2002), 266.

73 WD, 52nd Battalion, 28 September 1918; LAC, (2379279) John Patton Hunter.

74 WD, 9th Brigade, September 1918, Appendix 7, Section 5, "Lessons Learnt." Note: A physician by profession, starting in 1930 Sutherland would serve four years as Minister of National Defence.

75 WD, 58th Battalion, 28 September 1918; LAC, (3314127) Nelson Beatty.

76 WD, 10th Battalion, September 1918, Appendix 11, "Narrative," 2–3; Dancocks, *Spearhead*, 152–53. Note: Major-General Loomis replaced Major-General Lipsett on 13 September 1918, when the latter was transferred to command the 4th British Division. See Nicholson, *Official History*, 441.

77 Lieutenant Joseph Sproston, quoted in Dancocks, *Gallant Canadians*, 191. See also LAC, (3205025) Charles Edward Michie and 31430 *Supplement to the London Gazette*, 1 July 1919, 8348; (3205057) Edron Anderson; (3205365) Austin Botnen.

78 Macdonell, "'The Old Red Patch,'" *Canadian Defence Quarterly* 9, 1 (October 1931): 12. See also William Stewart, "Attack Doctrine in the Canadian Corps, 1916–1918" (MA thesis, University of New Brunswick, 1998), 197, who points out that resistance to the idea of "ignoring one's flanks" was well entrenched.

79 Nicholson, *Official History*, 450.

Chapter 8: A Dangerous Advance Continued

EPIGRAPH: Sir Arthur Currie, "The Last Hundred Days of the War," 29 August 1919 (Toronto: The Empire Club of Canada, 1920), 303–317; and http://speeches.empireclub.org/60222/data?n=4.

1 Currie, "Interim Report," 156, 144; Nicholson, *Official History*, 451.

2 See Lieutenant-Colonel C. Beresford Topp, *The 42nd Battalion* (Montreal: Gazette Printing, 1931), 275; and WD, 42nd Battalion, September 1918, Appendix 6, "Narrative," 7.

3 WD, 3rd Canadian Division, "Report ... Sept. 27th to Oct. 10th 1918," 7.

4 WD, 9th Brigade, September 1918, Appendix 7, Section 8, "116th Battalion, Narrative," 1–2; LAC, (3106766 misfiled as 3706766) Williard Thomas Woodcock, and 31168 *Supplement to the London Gazette*, 2 December 1919, 14905; (3106727) Norman Dobbs; Wigney, *Guests*, 45.

5 The Adjutant, *The 116th Battalion in France* (Toronto: Hunter-Rose, 1921), 84; LAC, (3106344) Oscar Wilde Church.

6 WD, 8th Brigade and 1st CMR, 29 September 1918.

7 See LAC, RG150–1, 1st CMR Daily Orders Part II, 30 September–25 October inclusive; (1263716) Arnold Boyne McQuoid; (256287) Albert Edward Stephenson.

8 WD, 2nd CMR, September 1918, Appendix E, "Report"; Johnston, *The 2nd Canadian Mounted Rifles*, 70.

9 WD 49th Battalion, September 1918, Appendix A, "Report," 1, 3, 5; LAC, (3205485) Charles Alexander Campbell; (3205661) Robert Allan Crowe.

10 WD, 42nd Battalion, 26–30 September, 1918; LAC, (3155174) Simon Peter Costello.

11 See Watson Diary, 29 September; WD, 12th Brigade, October 1918, Appendix 10, "Report," 5.

12 WD, 38th Battalion, 29 September 1918; LAC, (3320091) Hector Lalonde.

13 WD, 12th Brigade, October 1918, Appendix 10 [Appendix no. 6], Casualties.

14 Ibid., [Appendix 7], 78th Battalion "Report," 4; LAC, (3132554) Joseph Wilfrid Pleasence.

15 *Chatham Daily Planet*, 7 November 1918. I am indebted to Mr. Jerry Hind, curator http://www.gatheringourheroes.ca, for sharing extensive archival notes on conscripts from the Chatham–Kent, Ontario, area.

16 Lieutenant H.K. Beairsto, letter to Mr. William B. Johnston, 9 October 1918, generously shared by Alex's great-nephew, Don Gregory, Ottawa, Ontario; LAC, (3106416) Alexander Johnston.

17 (2021523) Alfred Ainsworth Kinsley in *Letters From the Front* (Toronto: Southam Press, 1920), 300.

18 McEvoy and Finlay, *History of the 72nd Battalion*, 149 and "Nominal Roll," 231–90; LAC, (2137956) Joseph DeFerro; (2204524) George Edward Jones. Note: One-third of the 72nd Battalion's 66 dead at Canal du Nord/Sancourt were conscripts and about 20 percent of the wounded.

19 LAC, (2137925) Orville Albert McKay and 31338 *Supplement to the London Gazette*, 13 May 1919, 6053; WD, 72nd Battalion, October 1918; Appendix B, "Report," 7 and Sub-Appendix A, Statement of Casualties.

20 According to Hyatt, "In June 1917 ... in a letter to the leader of the Ontario Liberal party," Currie wrote, "'I attribute a great deal of our success to our fighting organization. If our units are not up to strength that organization breaks down, and success cannot be expected in the same measure.'" A.M.J. Hyatt, *General Sir Arthur Currie* (Toronto: University of Toronto Press, 1987), 92–93.

21 On Haig, see Sheffield and Bourne, *War Diaries*, 25 August, 450. Note: Historians Shane Schreiber, Tim Travers, and Tim Cook have all been critical of Currie for not implementing planned operational pauses. Indeed, why Currie felt compelled to attack with battalions at much reduced strengths, clearly warrants additional study.

22 Hayes, *The Eighty-Fifth*, 161–64, 260–362; WD, 85th Battalion, October 1918, Appendix "Casualties"; LAC, (3204332) Manuel Geneau.

23 WD, 8th Battalion, September 1918, Appendix 3, "Narrative of Events," 3–4.

24 WD, 2nd Brigade, October 1918, Appendix 13, "Narrative of Operations," 16–17.

25 WD, 8th Battalion, September 1918, Appendix 3, "Narrative," 4; LAC, (4070262) Robert Baird.

26 Currie, "Interim Report," 160, 156; Nicholson, *Official History*, 450.

27 See Schreiber, *Shock Army*, 105–6, who notes the serious impacts caused by an increasing breakdown in "battle procedure." J.P. Harris also argues: "It seems possible that Currie would have gained at least equal results at lower cost had he adopted a somewhat more deliberate approach, pausing for a day or so, to bring up artillery, and to restore communications, between major attacks." See Harris with Barr, *Amiens*, 231.

28 For example, see Dancocks, *Spearhead*, 159.

29 WD, 11th Brigade, February 1919, Appendix 1, "Narrative," 4–5. See also Travers, *How the War Was Won*, 163–65, for more on Canadian "haste and disorganization" at Cambrai.

30 WD, 75th Battalion, 30 September 1918, and Appendix C, "Commanding Officer's report," 2.

31 LAC, (3034660) James Alexander Wilson; CVWM, *Toronto Daily Star*, 25 and 26 October 1918; (3230800) Thomas Alexander Squair.

32 WD, 54th Battalion, September 1918, Appendix 1, "Narrative of Operations," 16–17.

33 WD, 87th Battalion, 29–30 September 1918.

34 Colonel A.F. Duguid, *History of the Canadian Grenadier Guards* (Montreal: Gazette Printing, 1965), 209–10.

35 LAC, (3081385) Frederick Charles Johnston; (3314330) Thomas Frederick Hilson; http://www.miltonhistoricalsociety.ca/military/first-world-war/wwi-soldier-details.

36 WD, 87th Battalion, 2 October 1918; (3155139) Rene Archambault, 31338 *Supplement to the London Gazette*, 13 May 1919, 6050. Note: The number of draftees killed or died of wounds suggests that conscripts probably numbered about 20 percent of Perry's attacking

force, so perhaps several more MMs might have been justified. But typically, the Adjutant recommended the most senior men first. Indeed, between 6 September and 2 October, 53 ORs were recommended for the MM; only one was a conscript.

37 Corporal Will Bird recalled that his comrades thought "it was impossible that we had been ordered to attack again, that it was suicide." See Ian McCulloch, "The 'Fighting Seventh'" (MA thesis, Royal Military College of Canada, 1997), 215, http://www.nlc-bnc.ca/obj/s4/f2/dsk2/ftp04/mq22774.pdf.

38 David Bercuson, *The Patricias: The Proud History of a Fighting Regiment* (Toronto: Stoddart, 2001), 119.

39 WD, PPCLI, September 1918, Appendix C, "Operations," 2; LAC, (3057425) George Leon Skipworth. Note: Borden had dismissed Hughes in November 1916. For details, see Cook, *The Madman and the Butcher*, 160–79.

40 WD, RCR, September 1918, Appendix 9, "Narrative"; LAC, (3180329) Clarence Crandle Reynolds.

41 See Watson Diary, "Monday 30th Septr."

42 Currie, "Interim Report," 161.

43 W.S. Wallace, "Canada in the Great War," in *Pictorial History of the Great War*, 5th ed. (Toronto: John A. Hertel, 1919), 118.

44 See Edmonds and Maxwell-Hyslop, *Military Operations*, vol. 5, 152; and WD, First Army, "Report on First Army Operations 26th August–11th November, 1918," Part 3, 34.

45 Travers, *How the War Was Won*, 165.

46 Kerr, *Arms and the Maple Leaf*, 112.

47 WD, 13th Battalion, 1 October 1918.

48 WD, 11th Brigade, February 1919, Appendix 1, 5.

49 Dancocks, *Spearhead*, 162. Note: orders had recently been issued directing that effective 1 October, the British armies "adopt the 'Continental System of Time,'" meaning that the "conventional '12-hours' A.M. and '12-hours' P.M. system" had been replaced by the 24-hour clock (e.g., 1800 hours rather than 6:00 p.m.). See Wheeler, *The 50th Battalion*, 352.

50 TNA WO 95/1809/05, WD, 6th York and Lancaster Regiment, October 1918.

51 WD, 4th Battalion, October 1918, Appendix 1, "Narrative," 2–5; LAC, (3205009) Ralph Joe Crawford; (3033842) Joe Lane; Gibson, *Records*, 67, 134.

52 LAC, RG 9 III-C-3, vol. 4033, "Report on Battalion Operations of Oct. 1st by Capt MacLaren," 2–3; LAC, (3130876) Leo Dennis; (3130861) Walter Joseph Campeau.

53 WD, 1st Brigade, October 1918, Appendix 3, G.778–8, "The Attack on Abancourt," 4–5.

54 Urquhart, *The 16th Battalion*, 303; WD, 13th Battalion, 1 October 1918.

55 See WD, 14th Battalion, 1 October 1918, and Appendix 1, "Report," 2; 3rd Brigade, 1 October 1918, and Appendix 4, "Narrative," 4.

56 Urquhart, *The 16th Battalion*, 304–6; CVWM and LAC, CDR, Major Roderick Bell-Irving.

57 WD, 1st Battalion CMGC, October 1, 1918; LAC, (256301) Rupert Elswood MacCready.

58 CVWM, letter Private H.T. Halvorson to Mrs. A.S. MacCready, 11 October 1918.

59 LAC, (256286) Arthur Frank Gilbert.

60 Urquhart, *The 16th Battalion*, 306–7; WD, 16th Battalion, October 1918, Appendix A, "Narrative of Action at Cuvillers."

61 WD, 3rd Brigade, 1 October 1918, and Appendix 4, "Narrative of Events," 6–8; First Army, "Operations...", 1 October, 34.

62 See WD, 14th Battalion, 5 October 1918, and Appendix 1, "Report," 3; 3rd Brigade, Appendix 4, "Narrative," 11; LAC, (3080567) Frederick Clarence Martin; (3155138) Adrien André; (4030112) James Matthew Coughlin.

63 Peck Diary, 2–5 October, 1918.
64 See Urquhart, *The 16th Battalion*, 311, 407 and Nominal Roll 475–847; LAC, (256960) Roy Richard Gordon; (2129591) Rosario Grégoire; (2379354) Kingsley Poole; (2379862) Sidney James Smith; Wigney, *Guests*, 106, 120. Note: by 2–3 October, one-third of Currie's infantry battalions were *hors de combat*.
65 Urquhart, *The 16th Battalion*, 309; LAC, (2021790) Frank Joseph Appel; Wigney, *Guests*, 18. Note: Appel's daughter Patricia revealed that her father, who died in 1983, "suffered all his life." Quotes from his war experiences were generously shared with the author by her and by her sister Mollie, both of Agassiz, BC, as well as by Appel's grandson, Leslie Sand, of Chilliwack.
66 WD, 102nd Battalion, September 1918, Appendix I, "Operation Order no. 142."
67 Ibid., Appendix H, "Narrative of Operations," 3–4.
68 See "Men Never Wavered in Heaviest Barrage," for this quote from a letter by "a Toronto officer with the 11th Canadian Light Trench Mortar Battery," *Toronto Daily Star*, 9 November 1918, 5.
69 LAC, (3317163) George Henry Coulter.
70 Dancocks notes: "It is odd that this unit was asked to undertake an attack in such a weakened condition." See *Spearhead*, 165; WD, 87th Battalion, 30 September and 1 October 1918; and 11th Brigade, February 1919, Appendix 1, Sub-Appendix D, 87th Battalion, "Narrative," 3–4.
71 See WD, 87th Battalion, 9 October; LAC, (4040411) Arthur Papillon; (4040199) Albert Miller.
72 WD, 9th Brigade, September 1918, Appendix 12, Operations Order 202.
73 52nd Battalion, 1 October 1918.
74 LAC, (2379844) Roger Vic Richard; Wigney, *The C.E.F. Roll of Honour*, 635. Note: Despite the fact that Treaty Indians were legally exempt from military service, conscription "initially included Indians." An Order in Council (P.C. 111) on 17 January 1918, however, made them all exempt. See Timothy C. Winegard, *For King and Kanata* (Winnipeg: University of Manitoba Press, 2012), 10, 90–109; and James W. St. G. Walker, "Race and Recruitment in World War I: Enlistment of Visible Minorities in the Canadian Expeditionary Force," *Canadian Historical Review* 70, 1 (1989): 18–19.
75 WD, 43rd Battalion, September and 1 October 1918, Appendix M, "Narrative," 3–4; LAC, (2138863) David Cook; (257092) Frank William Hook.
76 WD, 58th Battalion, 30 September and Appendix 5, "Narrative," 3, and 1 October 1918. See also Shackleton, *Second to None*, 269–73.
77 The Adjutant, *The 116th Battalion*, 84–87; LAC, (3310648) Francis Raymond Shannon; (3106755) John Oliver Woodcock.
78 WD, 2nd Division, Report, 41.
79 WD, 2nd Division, September 1918, Appendix 50, "Operation Order 270"; 6th Brigade, 1 October 1918.
80 WD, 2nd Division, 1 October 1918, and "Narrative," 42.
81 WD, 27th Battalion, 1 and 6 October 1918; LAC, (2128901) Christman Swanson; (2128946) Charles Weber.
82 WD, 28th Battalion, 1 October 1918; LAC, (4090319) Arthur Lamoureux.
83 WD, 2nd Division, 1 October 1918, and "Narrative," 60.
84 Livesay, *Canada's Hundred Days*, 272.
85 Wallace, "Canada in the Great War," 118.
86 Currie, "Interim Report," 162.
87 WD, First Army, "Report," Part III, 35.

88 WD, 9th Brigade, September 1918, Appendix 7, Section 7, "Special orders"; Fetherstonhaugh, *The 13th Battalion*, 284.
89 Kerr, *Arms and the Maple Leaf*, 113; Watson Diary, "Friday, 4th October."
90 See Private Charles McDonald in 31668 *Supplement to the London Gazette*, 2 December 1919, 14899.

Chapter 9: Cambrai and Iwuy

1 Ludendorff, *Memories*, vol. 2, 722–25.
2 Dancocks, *Spearhead*, 128; Harris with Barr, *Amiens*, 237.
3 See Haig's reply and note to Churchill's letter of October 1, quoted in Sheffield and Bourne, *Douglas Haig: War Diaries*, 468.
4 Between 8 August and 10 October the corps sustained 40,923 casualties all ranks. See LAC, RG 24, vol. 1821, file GAQ 11–5, "General Statistics"; and WD, 2nd Division, Report, 61.
5 See WD, First Army, "Report," Part V, 44–45; and Currie, "Interim Report," 164–65.
6 For more on Currie's rationale, see WD, First Army, "Report," Part V, 45.
7 Harris with Barr, *Amiens*, 239–40; WD, 2nd Division, Report, 49.
8 The crossing at Pont d'Aire (Pont d'Erre) was of incalculable value. For bravery under fire, Captain Mitchell was awarded the Victoria Cross, the only Sapper to receive this honour in the First World War. See WD, 26th Battalion, October 1918, Appendix B1, "Report ... 'A' Company."
9 WD, 25th Battalion, October 1918, Appendix C, "Narrative ... 'A' Company"; LAC, (3180061) Polide Aucoin; (3255629) Raymond Dujay.
10 WD, 26th Battalion, Appendix B5, "History ... October 9th 1918"; LAC, (3255106) Charles Burt Arbeau.
11 Singer and Peebles, *History of the Thirty-First Battalion*, 404–6; LAC, (3206141) Howard Wesley Pattison.
12 WD, 8th Brigade, 9 October 1918.
13 WD, 3rd Division, September 1918, "Report," 12. Note: Crossings of the canal were aided immensely by the 7th and 8th Battalions, Canadian Engineers, the ranks of the latter having been augmented by dozens of conscripts.
14 WD, 4th Brigade, October 1918, Appendix 8, "Report on Operations," 2–3.
15 WD, 2nd Division, Report, 50–51; and statistical data courtesy of Dr. Richard Holt, Western University. Overall the 21st Battalion received a total of 783 reinforcements between June and October 1918 – 512 conscripts, 242 volunteers, and 29 BCRM men.
16 Cane, ed., *It Made You Think of Home*, 259; WD, 4th Brigade, Appendix 8, "Report," 4.
17 Antal and Shackleton, *Duty Nobly Done*, 296; LAC, (3131642) Leonard Stanslau Lavelle; CVWM, *Toronto Daily Star*, 26 October 1918.
18 LAC, (3320243) George Earl McGregor; (4020272) Emile Sylvio Mousseau, 31388 *Supplement to the London Gazette*, 14 May 1919, 6053; http://www.21stbattalion.ca/tributemn/mousseau_es.html.
19 WD, 6th Brigade, 10 October 1918; LAC, (2379688) William James Beetham.
20 WD, 29th Battalion, October 1918, Appendix 1, "Narrative," 4–5; LAC, (2138493) Alexander Matheson; (2137525) William Irving.
21 Corrigall, *The Twentieth*, 256.
22 WD, 2nd Division, 10 October 1918.
23 WD, 21st Battalion, 11 October 1918; LAC, (4021569) Gidreau Chartrand, whose epitaph is meant perhaps as a subtle reminder of opposition by most Québécois to conscription. Yet this "French Canadian," with a fiancé (Leda Villeneuve) in Mattawa, Ontario, had paid the ultimate price, and had done so serving in an English Canadian battalion.

24 Nichol, *Ordinary Heroes*, 201–3; WD, 2nd Division, Report, 54.

25 WD, 21st Battalion, 12 October 1918.

26 LAC, (1263566) Wellesley Tylney Wesley-Long; (3108133) William Harold Edmiston. This gravestone invocation comes from *The New Testament*, II Timothy 4, 7–8. See also LAC, (3057627) Russell Crarey (Figure 3.1) killed in this same action.

27 WD, 20th Battalion, 11 October 1918; Corrigall, *The Twentieth*, 260.

28 Corrigall, *The Twentieth*, 262–65; WD, 4th Brigade, October 1918, Appendix 8, "Report," 6. Note: Algie's heroism was recognized with a posthumous Victoria Cross. The conscript was (2020941) William Forsyth, who died that day of wounds received in this action.

29 Singer and Peebles, *History of the Thirty-First Battalion*, 410–11.

30 WD, 29th Battalion, October 1918, Appendix 1, "Narrative," 5–6; LAC, (2020771) Sydney Pridmore Hill.

31 Roland Hill, "Cambrai to Valenciennes," in *Canada in the Great War*, vol. 5, 209; WD, 28th Battalion, October 1918, Appendix H, "Narrative," 2; LAC, (257631) John Harold Robinson; (258949) William Jasper Benson.

32 Singer and Peebles, *History of the Thirty-First Battalion*, 411.

33 WD, 27th Battalion, October 1918, Appendix M, "Narrative," 3–4; LAC, (2138758) Norman McLeod; (2129481) Andrew Blake.

34 WD, 31st Battalion, October 1918, Appendix B-8, "Narrative," 3; Singer and Peebles, *History of the Thirty-First Battalion*, 411–13.

35 WD, 31st Battalion, November 1918, Appendix B-1, awards of the "Military Medal on 7th to 11th Oct. 1918"; LAC, (3130529) Allen Norval McCreery and 31430 *Supplement to the London Gazette*, 3 July 1919, 8346.

36 LAC, (3205528) Rudolph William Weiler and 31430 *Supplement to the London Gazette*, 3 July 1919, 8354.

37 WD, 2nd Division, Report, 53.

38 WD, 31st Battalion, 11 October 1918 and Appendix B-7, Casualties; LAC, (3131414) Herbert Nicholas Leeder.

39 WD, 2nd Division, 11 October 1918 and Report, 55.

40 Harris with Barr, *Amiens*, 241.

41 Fetherstonhaugh, *The 24th Battalion*, 259–61; WD, 24th Battalion, 12–13 October 1918; LAC, (3082155) Patrick Derynck.

42 WD, 5th Brigade and 22nd Battalion, 14 October 1918.

43 See Nicholson, *Official History*, 465–67; WD, 1st Division, 7 October 1918.

44 WD, 13th Battalion, 7–8 October, 1918; 3rd Brigade, Appendix 6, "Operation Order no. 283."

45 Fetherstonhaugh, *The 13th Battalion*, 287–88; LAC, (2476581) William Young.

46 WD, 3rd Brigade and 13th Battalion, 9–10 October 1918.

47 Fetherstonhaugh, *The 13th Battalion*, 291; LAC, (3081162) Charles William Houston; (3082260) John Joseph Hughes; Wigney, *Guests*, 68.

48 See Schreiber, *Shock Army*, 107, 109–10.

49 WD, 1st Division, 12 October 1918; 2nd Brigade, Appendix 14, "Memo of Events," 2–3; 7th Battalion, 12 October 1918.

50 WD, 10th Battalion, October 1918, Appendix 16, "Narrative," 1; LAC, (3205278) Thomas Leo Kennedy.

51 Urquhart, *The History of the 16th Battalion*, 317.

52 WD, 3rd Battalion, October 1918, Appendix 2, report; LAC, (3036173) George Albert Potter.

53 WD, First Army, "Report," Part V, 50; 46th and 50th Battalions, 16 October 1918; LAC, (3206693) Alfred Steel De Pew and 31338 *Supplement to the London Gazette*, 13 May 1919, 6051.

54 Currie, "Interim Report," 171, 173–75; Schreiber, *Shock Troops*, 117. Note: The work of building bridges, repairing roads, and clearing mines was a deadly business. For example, on 30 October, Sapper Joseph Bartle, a "Plasterer" and draftee from Halifax serving with the 7th Battalion, CE, was killed while "filling in craters on the [Thiers] road." See WD, 7th Battalion Canadian Engineers, 31 October 1918; and LAC, (3182120) Joseph Henry Bartle.

55 Macphail, *Official History ... Medical Services*, 266; LAC, (2021976) William Andrews; (3109206) Robert Nelson Beach.

56 WD, Headquarters, Canadian – Bramshott, October 1918, "Memorandum. Canadian Training Division – October 1918."

57 Overall, more than 400 draftees died at training camps in England, mostly due to influenza or pneumonia. See Wigney, *The C.E.F. Roll of Honour*.

58 See Macphail, *Official History ... Medical Services*, 267, 316–17, 319–20. More than 800 conscripts died in Canada in 1918, most of them from influenza, pneumonia, or both. In addition, at least 67 conscripts perished from disease aboard troopships and were buried at sea. For all names and additional data see Wigney, *The C.E.F. Roll of Honour*.

59 LAC, (3040524) Charles Dixon Sims; (3040528) Malick Sims.

60 LAC, KP, vol. 157, R-3, Turner to Kemp, 28 October 1918.

Chapter 10: Honour and Duty in the Pursuit to Mons

1 Schreiber, *Shock Army*, 121.

2 Cook, *Shock Troops*, 572; Nicholson, *Official History*, 480.

3 See Robert J. Sharpe, *The Last Day, The Last Hour: The Currie Libel Trial* (Toronto: University of Toronto Press, 2011), xi–xii; and Cook, *Shock Troops*, 573–74.

4 WD, 2nd Brigade, October 1918, Appendix 15, "Memorandum of Events," 1.

5 WD, 8th Battalion, 20 October; LAC, (2379502) Thomas Wesley Douglas.

6 WD, 4th Battalion, October 1918, Appendix 2, "Report," 5; LAC, (3231249) Frank Belanger.

7 Nicholson, *Official History*, 469.

8 LAC, (2378320) Clarence Delbert Rodgers.

9 Dancocks, *Spearhead*, 183. For more evidence of German resistance, see LAC, WD, 47th Battalion, 18 and 21 October 1918; (3130253) Frederick Harold Kenny.

10 WD, 1st Brigade, October 1918, Appendix 16, Report, 2; LAC, (3231347) Aime Boulet.

11 WD, 3rd Battalion, October 1918, Appendix 1, "Report"; LAC, (3034102) Thomas Naphan.

12 WD, 7th Brigade, 22–23 October 1918; LAC, CVWM and (3181461) Avard Reginald Mader. My thanks to Captain Michael O'Leary (Ret.), former Adjutant with the RCR, for providing insights on the documentation of RCR casualties.

13 Hayes, *The Eighty-Fifth*, 182; LAC, (3107336) Orphila Mondoux.

14 Hayes, *The Eighty-Fifth*, 183–84.

15 WD, 85th Battalion, October 1918, Appendix IX.

16 Ibid., Appendix "Casualties"; Hayes, *The Eighty-Fifth*, 185; LAC, (3204010) Richard Milo Hughes.

17 WD, 75th Battalion, 24 October 1918; LAC, (3230596) Samuel Joseph Sauve.

18 Ludendorff, *Memories*, vol. 2, 763.

19 WD, First Army, "Report," Part V, 58.

20 Harris with Barr, *Amiens*, 267.

21 Currie, "Interim Report," 177.

22 Harris with Barr, *Amiens*, 269.

23 WD, 38th Battalion, 29 October 1918; LAC, (4021563) Leon Provencher; (3320908) Joseph Pelletier.

24 WD, 1st CMR, 29–30 October 1918; LAC, (1263572) Gordon Alexander Young.

25   I am grateful to Gordon Young's grandson, Warrant Officer Tex Young (RCAF), for providing a copy of his grandfather's service file along with additional family background.

26   WD, 10th Brigade, November 1918, Appendix C, "Narrative," 11.

27   The 47th Battalion began this attack with a trench strength of 17 officers and 381 men. See WD, 47th Battalion, 1 November 1918; 46th Battalion, November 1918, Appendix 1, "Report on Operation," 3; LAC, (1263674) Leon Forgue; (2138516) William Douglas Kitchen.

28   WD, 44th Battalion, November 1918, Appendix A, "Report," 2; LAC, (4025143) Lucien Papillon; (4025163) Alfred Jodin.

29   WD, 47th Battalion, November 1918, Appendix 1, "Report," 1; LAC, (3131622) Stanley Hosey.

30   A DHH historian has determined that at least 283 black conscripts served in the CEF (about two-thirds of them overseas). Just ten, however, are known to have been assigned to infantry battalions. My thanks to Major Mathias Joost for sharing his ongoing research in this area.

31   In Hosey's case, apparently after being found guilty of stealing two cases of whisky from a CPR freight shed, a judge dispatched him directly to the infantry depot in London. My thanks to Mr. Jerry Hind of the "Gathering Our Heroes" project for providing additional background on this subject. For more on black soldiers, see Wilson, ed., *Ontario and the First World War*, cviii–cix; Calvin W. Ruck, *The Black Battalion* (Halifax: Nimbus, 1987), 7–13; and Tennyson, *Canada's Great War*, 99–100.

32   WD, 46th Battalion, November 1918, Appendix 1, "Report," 3; LAC, (2021685) Donald Arthur Manson; (257712) Edward Schnitzler.

33   Ibid.; LAC, (258807) Russell William Long; Manson headstone inscription from photo by Eric Reid.

34   WD, 46th Battalion, Appendix 1, "'A' Company's Report," 3; LAC, (257761) Edward Norman Slack, and 31430 *Supplement to the London Gazette*, 1 July 1919, 8352.

35   WD, 47th Battalion, November 1918, Appendix 1, "Report"; LAC, (3130963) Odiel Deporter; (3131378) Roy Everett Graham. Note: Out of a trench strength of 381 ORs, the battalion counted 17 dead among its 130 casualties.

36   WD, 50th Battalion, November 1918, Appendix 4, "Report," 2; LAC, (3206424) Donald McLeod.

37   Many historical accounts, including Currie's "Interim Report," 178, typically cite fewer than 400 casualties at Valenciennes. The 10th Brigade, however, reported losses of 471 men for the first day alone. That figure does not account for 12th Brigade casualties, nor does it include engineers, artillerymen, cyclists, and so on, who were killed or wounded in this battle.

38   WD, 12th Brigade, November 1918, Appendix 18, 38th Battalion "Report," 2; CVWM, *Perth Courier*, November 22; LAC, (3320221) Robert Oliver Publow.

39   McEvoy and Finlay, *History of the 72nd*, 160–64.

40   "Jack Niihara Was Hero of World War I," *Vernon News*, 17 April 1961. My thanks to Barbara Bell, archivist at the Greater Vernon Museum and Archives, and to Ms. Eileen Wejr and Ms. Georgie Hay of the Lumby and District Museum, for generously providing additional background on Private Niihara. See LAC, (2020445) Gonzaemon Niihara and 31430 *Supplement to the London Gazette*, 1 July 1919, 8349.

41   McEvoy and Finlay, *History of the 72nd*, 165–66; LAC, (3106743) Joseph Elias Roy.

42   WD, 54th Battalion, November 1918, "Narrative of Operations," 1–3.

43   Gould, *From B.C. to Baisieux*, 118, and "Nominal Roll of Other Ranks"; WD, 102nd Battalion, 2 November 1918; LAC, (3109002) William Marshall Ney; CVWM and CDR, (3109260) George Hill; WD, 102nd Battalion, December 1918, Appendix A, (3108909) James Wesley Barlow and 31430 *Supplement to the London Gazette*, 1 July 1919, 8337.

44 Brigadier-General J.M. Ross recorded that the "miserable enemy could expect and certainly received no quarter." See WD, 10th Brigade, Appendix C, "Narrative of Operations," 12. As General Currie himself noted in Humphries, ed., *The Selected Papers*, 131, "it was not the intention of our fellows to take many German prisoners."

45 Sheffield and Bourne, *Douglas Haig: War Diaries*, 1 November 1918, 484; WD, First Army, "Report," Part V, 65.

46 WD, 72nd Battalion, November 1918, Appendix B, "Report on Operations," 8; LAC, (4021676) Isidore Godin; (2138850) Donald John McAskill.

47 WD, 87th Battalion, November 1918, Appendix 2, "Report," 2–3; 75th Battalion, 5 November 1918; LAC, (3034979) Robert Oscar Andrews.

48 Hayes, *The Eighty-Fifth*, 195–96, 348; LAC, (3180646) Cecil Melvin Boutilier; (3180692) Joseph Sarty.

49 WD, 85th Battalion, 6 November 1918, and Appendix XII, "Casualties"; LAC, (3181322) Clifford Colen Morris.

50 Hayes, *The Eighty-Fifth*, 198–202; LAC, (3180868) Robert Henry; (3108183) William Kurtzweg.

51 WD, 2nd CMR, November 1918, Appendix B, "Statement of Operations," 1–2.

52 See Gould, *From B.C. to Baisieux*, 119–20; LAC, (3107787) Frederick Oliver Allen.

53 WD, 25th and 22nd Battalion, 7 November 1918; LAC, (3155106) George Blanchette.

54 Foch quoted in Terraine, *To Win a War*, 222; WD, 7th Brigade, 9 November 1918.

55 WD, 4th Brigade and 21st Battalion, 9 November 1918; LAC, (3320034) Lawrence Sullivan.

56 WD, 3rd Division, October 1918, "Report on Operations," 9.

57 LAC, (3310498) William Franklin Garvin; (3314010) Earl Colman McKenney.

58 Antal and Shackleton, *Duty Nobly Done*, 303–4; LAC, (3131734) Clayton Elmer Underwood.

59 Corrigall, *The Twentieth*, 277.

60 WD, 20th Battalion, 10 November 1918; LAC, (3230347) Percy Clarence Simmons; (3031460), Alfred Simmonds Dawson.

61 WD, 19th Battalion, November 1918, Appendix 2, "Report"; LAC, (3231310) James Clarence Buttimer.

62 WD, 42nd Battalion, November 1918, "Narrative," 2.

63 WD, 7th Brigade, PPCLI and 42nd Battalion, 10–11 November 1918; RCR, November 1918, Appendix 2, "Summary," 2.

64 WD, 2nd Division, 11 November 1918, and Report, 66, 68.

65 Singer and Peebles, *History of the Thirty-First Battalion*, 427–30; WD, 6th Brigade, 11 November 1918.

66 WD, 31st Battalion, November 1918, Appendix C, "Narrative of Operations."

67 WD, 28th Battalion, 12 November, and Appendix F, "Narrative," 2. Note: Apart from Private Price, at least ten other Canadian soldiers died on 11 November as a result of wounds received earlier. Among these were two conscripts, one of whom was (3320394) Joseph Nedon (PPCLI), who suffered "[s]hrapnel wounds [to the] Chest [and a] Fractured Left Humerus]" the day before outside of Mons and perished at no. 4 CCS.

68 Just before expiring, Price apparently gave a young Belgian girl a small cloth depicting flowers, which had been hand-crocheted by his fiancé. Remarkably, 73 years later, Price's nephew and namesake, Mr. George Barkhouse, made his first visit to the site to attend a dedication ceremony for a new footbridge at Ville-sur-Haine. There the once-young "Belgian girl" presented George with the same cloth that had been given to her by his uncle over seven decades earlier. (Telephone interview with Mr. Barkhouse, 3 September 2014.)

69 Norm Christie, *Canadian Cemeteries of the Great War*, vol. 1: *Belgium* (Ottawa: CEF Books, 2010), 183.

70 Henry Clyne, *Vancouver's 29th* (Vancouver: Tobin's Tigers Association, 1964), 91.

71 J.S.B. Macpherson, "Chapter XI – From Mons to the Rhine," in *Canada in the Great War*, vol. 5 (Toronto: United Publishers of Canada, 1920), 230.

72 PD, Neilson, 11 November 1918.

73 Sir Philip Gibbs, *Now It Can Be Told* (Garden City, NY: Garden City Publishing, 1920), 504.

74 *Toronto Daily Star*, 11 November 1918, 1.

75 Laurence Binyon, "For the Fallen," *Times*, 21 September 1914, 9.

Chapter 11: The Equal of the Best

EPIGRAPH: *Siegfried Sassoon*, "Conscripts," in *War Poems of Siegfried Sassoon* (Mineola, New York: Dover Publications, 2004), 31. With permission of Dover Publications.

1 The subtitle here is taken from a letter by (3136613) James Knight to his mother, 11 November 1918, in Booth, ed., *Opened by Censor*, 229. See also LAC, (3130111) Emerson Cascaddan; (3031789) Edgar Houle; (3314125) Reginald Arthur Howell.

2 See Macphail, *Official History ... Medical Services*, 391.

3 See Chris Hyland, "The Canadian Corps' Long March – Logistics, Discipline and the Occupation of the Rhineland," *Canadian Military History* 2 (Spring 2012): 5–20; and Currie, "Interim Report," 187–92. Note: on 13 November, the 7th Battalion alone received 112 reinforcements.

4 LAC, (3130464) Ernest Edward Hanson; (2021909) Eric Johan Hedin. See also http://www.21stbattalion.ca/tributehl/hedin_ej.html; and Wigney, *Guests*, 61, 64.

5 LAC, Commonwealth War Graves Registers, (3130045) Patsy Anile.

6 Wheeler, *The 50th Battalion*, 389.

7 Dancocks, *Sir Arthur Currie*, 184–85.

8 Humphries, ed., *The Selected Papers*, 142.

9 CWM, 19801226 – 277, CP, 58A 1 60.6, Currie to Kemp, "no more drafts be sent," 23 November 1918. Note: This appears to be the first of two letters that Currie sent to Kemp this day.

10 Humphries, ed., *The Selected Papers*, 159. For more on Cooper, see Radley, *We Lead*, 250, 260.

11 LAC, GAQ 5–15, W.A. Griesbach, handwritten notes "1918 1st C.I.B. – 15th Aug.–30 Nov."

12 Ian McCulloch, "Crisis in Leadership: The Seventh Brigade and the Nivelles 'Mutiny,' 1918," *Army Doctrine and Training Bulletin* 3, 2 (Summer 2000): 36, 44.

13 Ibid., 45.

14 CWM, CP, 58A 1 60.6, Currie to Kemp, "views on demobilization," 23 November 1918; and Dancocks, *Spearhead*, 226.

15 CWM, CP, 58A 1 60.6, Currie to Kemp, "preliminary report," 22 December 1918.

16 Ibid., Currie to Canadian Section, G.H.Q, 22 December 1918.

17 Nicholson, *Official History*, 531–32. See also Howard G. Coombs, "Dimensions of Military Leadership: The Kinmel Park Mutiny of 4/5 March 1919," Canadian Forces College (October, 2004), http://docplayer.net/34985544-Dimensions-of-military-leadership-the-kinmel-park-mutiny-of-4-5-march-1919.html

18 See Desmond Morton, "'Kicking and Complaining': Demobilization Riots in the Canadian Expeditionary Force, 1918–1919," *Canadian Historical Review* 61, 3 (1980): 344–60; and William F. Stewart, *The Embattled General: Sir Richard Turner and the First World War* (Montreal and Kingston: McGill–Queen's University Press, 2015), 255.

19 Humphries, ed., *The Selected Papers*, 187; Cook, *Shock Troops*, 595.
20 Machin, *MSB Report*, 88; and "No Amnesty for Defaulters," *Toronto Globe*, 9 December 1918, 14.
21 "Orders in Council Nearly All Repealed January 1," *Toronto Globe*, 22 December 1919, 1–2.
22 For more on the rationale for Canada's mission and force composition, see Isitt, *From Victoria to Vladivostok*, 62, 72–73; Nicholson, *Official History*, 519; and Ian Moffat, "Forgotten Battlefields – Canadians in Siberia, 1918–1919," *Canadian Military Journal* 8, 3 (Autumn 2007): 73–83.
23 See Isitt, *Victoria to Vladivostok*, 73–75, 83–85, 89–95, 106; and "The Siberian Expedition," *Toronto Globe*, 28 December 1918, 6.
24 Letter to "wife" from unnamed lieutenant in the 259th Battalion, quoted in Isitt, *Victoria to Vladivostok*, 96–97.
25 Ibid., 101–4.
26 Ibid., 155, 175, and Appendix J, "Deaths," 184. For more, see Moffat, "Forgotten Battlefields."
27 LAC, KP, vol. 120, file 23, *European War – Memorandum no. 5*, 4, 10. Note: Data from this report show that of 465,984 volunteer enlistments, about two-thirds (307,322) were dispatched to the infantry, whereas about 97 percent of the MSA recruits (80,805 out of 83,355) were assigned to the infantry.
28 See Machin, *MSB Report*, 33, 74; and "Service Act Secures Men," *Toronto Globe*, 7 May 1919, 7.
29 Nicholson, *Official History*, 353.
30 Machin, *MSB Report*, 88.
31 "Their Renown Will Endure," *Toronto Globe*, 13 May 1919, 3.
32 Kemp, *Report of the Ministry*, 297.
33 Nicholson, *Official History*, 353.
34 Renison, "A Story of Five Cities," 390.
35 For deaths in the CEF, see LAC, Circumstances of Death Registers; and Wigney, *The C.E.F. Roll of Honour*.
36 Given the large number of conscript infantry soldiers engaged throughout the Hundred Days, and the number of medals awarded, it does not appear that draftees received fair recognition for their efforts. Indeed, between August 1918 and July 1919 a total of 6,519 "Medals and Bars" were awarded the CEF, but the conscript share of that total was less than 1 percent. See Harry Abbink, *The Military Medal: Canadian Recipients, 1916–1922* (Calgary: Alison, 1987), Table 1.
37 Desmond Morton and Glenn Wright, *Winning the Second Battle: Canadian Veterans and the Return to Civilian Life* (Toronto: University of Toronto Press, 1987), 112–14, 130.
38 LAC and CVWM, (2379736) Kenneth James Fraser; (257962) Harold Wrench; LAC, Veterans' Death Cards; (3180411) Leo Francis Buote.
39 Personal letters, Hilaire Dennis, 28 October 1918.
40 As noted in the acknowledgments at the beginning of this book, that RCAF veteran was the author's father.
41 LAC, (1263572) Gordon Alexander Young.
42 *Vernon News*, 17 April 1961; telephone interview with Eileen Wejr, Lumby and District Museum, Lumby, B.C., 12 May 2014.
43 See Urquhart, *Arthur Currie*, 279–80; Cook, *The Madman and the Butcher*, 283–84.
44 Harris, *Canadian Brass*, 143, 148–49. See also Dancocks, *Sir Arthur Currie*, 203–4.
45 CWM, 19801226–282, CP, 58A 1 61.5, Mewburn to Currie, 3 February 1919.

46 Ibid., Currie to Mewburn, 17 March 1919. Note: On 4 March 1919, Sam Hughes had accused Currie of "needlessly sacrificing the lives of Canadian soldiers." See Cook, *The Madman and the Butcher*, 274–76.

47 Ibid.

48 LAC, Currie fonds, MG 30 E100, vol. 27, letter, Smeaton White to Currie, 30 July 1926.

49 "Canada Lives Again in Historic Mons in Plaque Unveiling," *Toronto Globe*, 13 June 1927, 1–2.

50 From the editorial "Mons" in the *Port Hope Evening Guide*, quoted in Sharpe, *The Last Day*, 10. W.T.R. Preston was a seventy-six-year-old "politician, journalist and author." See Sharpe, 60–66.

51 Dancocks, *Sir Arthur Currie*, 236. Note: The trial took place in Cobourg, Ontario, 16 April to 1 May 1928.

52 In his speech on 29 August 1919, titled "The Last Hundred Days of the War," Currie told his audience that "Mons was never assaulted." See http://speeches.empireclub.org/60222/data?n=4; and Sharpe, *The Last Day*, 186–87, 191.

53 Sharpe, *The Last Day*, 196–98, 226.

54 Thanks to Ms. Laurel Clegg, formerly the Casualty Identification Co-ordinator with DHH in Ottawa, for providing additional information on the recovery and identification of Private Johnston's remains. Johnston was identified through mitochondrial DNA testing traced to his great-nephew Don Gregory, whose maternal grandmother was Johnston's sister. Gregory participated in the internment ceremony along with his daughter Corporal Ann Gregory, local dignitaries, and Marc Lortie, Canada's Ambassador to France.

Conclusion: Evidence Has a Way of Dissolving Theories

EPIGRAPH: Vance, *Death So Noble*, 163.

1 Dancocks, *Spearhead*, 86.

2 Daniel Byers, "Mobilising Canada," *Journal of the Canadian Historical Association / Revue de la Société historique du Canada* 7, 1 (1996): 175; Granatstein and Hitsman, *Broken Promises*, 98. See also Wood, *Militia Myths*, 252.

3 Morton, *When Your Number's Up*, ix.

4 Vance, *Death So Noble*, 8; Hann, "Introduction," in *Great War and Canadian Society*, ed. Daphne Read (Toronto: New Hogtown Press, 1978), 25.

5 Total conscript fatalities are derived primarily from Wigney, *The C.E.F. Roll of Honour*, supplemented by LAC, RG 150, Accession 1992–93/166, Personnel Records, and from Veterans Affairs Canada, "Canadian Virtual War Memorial." Note: Veterans Affairs uses 30 April 1922, as a "cutoff date" for documenting the deaths of soldiers "who died of their war wounds." See Cook, *Shock Troops*, 618.

6 LAC, GAQ 11–5, "Consolidated Report," reveals that between 8 August 8 and 11 November, 43,457 enlisted soldiers became "battle casualties," including 6,155 killed and 2,782 missing.

7 The 31st Battalion received 913 reinforcements between 22 May and 11 November, including 430 conscripts (47 percent). Of these, 27 were listed as fatalities and 185 wounded – a total of 212, or about 49 percent of all draftees who served with this battalion. See Singer and Peebles, *History of the Thirty-First*, Appendix 8, Nominal Roll, 459–515. Likewise, the 20th Battalion received 820 reinforcements between 7 May and 4 November 1918, including 443 conscripts (54 percent). Of this latter number, 41 were killed in action or died of wounds, while another 149 were wounded in action, a total of 190 casualties or nearly 43 percent. See Corrigall, *The Twentieth Canadian Battalion*, Appendix IV, Nominal Roll, 232–55.

8 *For the Defence of Canada* (Military Service Council, 1917), 19.

9 Wheeler, *The 50th Battalion*, 204. Historian Kenneth Radley agrees; in *Get Tough, Stay Tough: Shaping the Canadian Corps, 1914–1918* (Solihull, England: Helion, 2014), 286–87, he writes that while "Late-comers, including conscripts were the source of resentment ... in the main, [they] proved good soldiers."

10 W.S. Wallace, "Canada in the Great War," 44.

11 See Appendix 3 and Morton, *When Your Number's Up*, 279.

12 Chris Sharpe, "Enlistment," Appendix, Table III, 53.

13 Radley, *We Lead*, 257.

14 Humphries, ed., *The Selected Papers*, 128.

15 Ibid., 101.

16 See Morton, *A Military History of Canada*, 158; Gwyn, *Tapestry of War*, 418; Theobald, *The Bitter Harvest of War*, 92.

17 For example, the 20th Battalion took on 107 conscripts before Amiens and another 14 prior to Arras – about 20 percent of its trench strength. Similarly, the 2nd CMRs had 127 conscripts on strength before Amiens and added dozens more before the fight at Cambrai. The 85th Battalion had only 18 conscripts at Amiens but added another 157 before Canal du Nord – at least 25 percent of its trench strength.

18 See Nicholson, *Official History*, 551, 553.

19 For further validation of this figure see Wigney, *The C.E.F. Roll of Honour*, and nominal rolls from various regimental histories cited in the bibliography. Note: These collective findings contrast sharply with those of Michel Gravel, *Tough As Nails: The Epic Story of Hillie Foley* (Ottawa: CEF Books, 2006), 159, 162, whose analysis of late war recruiting for the 14th Battalion led him "to assume that an important majority (possibly as high as 50%) of the 24,132 conscripts mentioned [in Nicholson's *Official History*], were actually volunteers recruited in the USA." Notably, in "British Blood Calls British Blood," 33, Richard Holt estimates that "17,000 [BCRM] men were taken on strength" in France, of whom only "7,100, were infantrymen." In this context, though, and based on evidence presented in this monograph, the latter figure is one separate and distinct from the number of "24,132" conscripts.

20 See Granatstein, "Conscription in the Great War," 73.

21 Private E.W. Russell, quoted by Cook, *Shock Troops*, 403; Goudy, "The M.S.A. Sent Us Good Men," 14.

22 Hyatt, "Sir Arthur Currie and Conscription," 294; and *General Sir Arthur Currie*, 93.

23 Willms, "Conscription, 1917," 339; Dancocks, *Spearhead*, 86.

24 Sharpe, "Enlistment," 46, 18. For Sharpe's earlier work, see *Journal of Canadian Studies* 18, 4 (Winter 1984): 15–29.

25 Nicholson, *Official History*, 551, 553.

26 Ibid., 353.

27 "An Election the Way Out," *Toronto Globe*, 18 December 1919, 6.

28 See Granatstein, "Conscription and My Politics"; "Conscription in the Great War," 74.

29 Total battle casualties and sick wastage for the Hundred Days resulted in a net loss of 54,352 all ranks. See LAC, GAQ 11–5, "Consolidated Report."

30 A.M.J. Hyatt, "The Military Leadership of Sir Arthur Currie" in *Warrior Chiefs: Perspectives on Senior Canadian Military Leaders*, ed. Lieutenant-Colonel Bernd Horn and Stephen Harris (Toronto: Dundurn Press, 2001), 48, 51.

31 Currie, "The Last Hundred Days of the War," http://speeches.empireclub.org/60222/data?n=4.

32 "The Great War levied a blood tax on almost every family in the country." See "Introduction" by H.V. Nelles in Craig, *But This Is Our War*, ix.

33   Cook, *The Madman and the Butcher*, 375–76.

34   During the period 24 August to 11 November, General Horne's First British Army (I Corps until 20 September, VIII Corps, XXII Corps, and the Canadian Corps) sustained 57,749 casualties (all ranks), including 34,090 in the Canadian Corps. Thus Canadian losses were fully 59 percent of this total, a number that does not include the 11,822 Canadians who fell with Rawlinson's Fourth Army at Amiens. See WD, First Army, "Report," Appendix 5.

35   See Schreiber, *Shock Army*, 78.

36   WD, 11th Brigade, February 1919, Appendix 1, "Narrative," 4–5.

37   A.H. Young and W.A. Kirkwood, eds., *The War Memorial Volume of Trinity College, Toronto* (Toronto: Printers Guild, 1922), xvi.

38   Minister of Defence Ralston did not forget those lessons. As CO of the 85th Battalion he had witnessed first-hand the crucial role played by conscripts during the Hundred Days. When faced with a similar manpower crisis in late 1944, he did everything in his power to reintroduce conscription. Ultimately his contrarian views resulted in his dismissal from Cabinet. For more, see Byers, *Zombie Army*, 217–22.

39   The intent here is not to advocate in favour of conscription. It is noteworthy, however, that except for Great Britain, most of Canada's key NATO allies retain legal provision for conscription; many practise it to this day.

40   Niall Ferguson, *The Pity of War* (New York: Basic Books, 1999), 462.

41   For more on the legacy of conscription in Canada, see Byers, *Zombie Army*, 13, 34, 28–32.

42   As noted in the endnotes to this book's Introduction, the author encountered several responses to requests for information about conscripts that were sharply dismissive of these "late"-arriving reinforcements.

43   It appears that only Canada and Great Britain have compartmentalized the sacrifices of each nation's youth between two disparate groups: volunteers and conscripts.

44   Strachan, *The First World War*, 335.

45   Doubtless the corps would have prevailed at Amiens without conscript reinforcements, at least for the first five days, but given 13,000-plus other ranks casualties (11,127 battle casualties, 1,936 sick wastage), it is highly unlikely that Currie could have followed up immediately with a similar effort at Arras or at the D-Q Line. As with the Australians, the subsequent role that Canadians played in the Hundred Days would have been significantly reduced. For details of casualties at "Amiens," see LAC, GAQ 11–5.

46   To calculate an approximate number of direct descendants resulting from the 83,355 conscripts on strength with the CEF in November 1918, the author has drawn on basic fertility rates published by the Government of Canada for the period 1926 to 2011. See http://www.statcan.gc.ca/pub/11-630-x/11-630-x2014002-eng.htm. Assuming generations born in the 1920s, 1950s, 1980s and early 2000s, and successive fertility rates of 3.3, 3.9, 1.5, and 1.7, it appears that roughly 2.36 million Canadians are alive today who can trace their family lineage to a Canadian conscript. My thanks to Dr. Marc Kilgour of Wilfrid Laurier University for his assistance in constructing a basic statistical model to help illustrate one possible connection to their past of which many Canadians may not be aware.

Bibliography

Archival Sources

Canadian War Museum Archives – Ottawa
–. Major-General Henry Edward Burstall Papers.
–. General Sir Arthur Currie Fonds.
–. Lieutenant-Colonel C.W. Peck, V.C. Personal Diary, 1918.
–. Letters, Private William Shaw Antliff.
–. Letters, Private Albert Blount.

Library and Archives Canada – Ottawa
–. *An Act Respecting Military Service* (the Military Service Act), 7–8 George V, Chapter 19, Statutes of Canada 1917.
–. *Canada's War Effort 1914–1918*. Director of Public Information. Ottawa: J. De Labroquerie Taché, 1918.
–. *Debates, House of Commons*, 1914 and 1917.
–. *European War – Memorandum No. 5 Respecting Work of the Department of Militia and Defence, From January 1, 1918, to October 31, 1918*. Ottawa, 1919.
–. *European War – Memorandum No. 6. Respecting Work of the Department of Militia and Defence, From November 1, 1918, to October 31, 1919*. Ottawa, 1919.
–. *For the Defence of Canada*. Ottawa: Military Service Council, 1917.
–. *The Military Service Act, 1917, Manual for the Information and Guidance of Tribunals in the Consideration and Review of Claims for Exemption*. Military Service Council. Ottawa: J. De Labroquerie Taché, 1918.
–. *Report of the Military Service Council on the Administration of the Military Service Act*. Ottawa: J. De Labroquerie Taché, 1919.
–. *Report of the Ministry Overseas Military Forces of Canada 1918*. London: HMSO, 1919.
–. *The Canada Year Book 1918*. Ottawa: J. De Labroquerie Taché, 1919.
–. *The Military Voters Act*, 7–8 George V, Chapter 34, Statutes of Canada 1917.
–. *The War-time Elections Act*, 7–8 George V, Chapter 39, Statutes of Canada 1917.
–. *The War Measures Act*, 5 George V, Chapter 2, Statutes of Canada 1914.
–. Sir Henry Edward Burstall fonds, MG 30 E6.
–. Arthur William Currie fonds, MG 30 E100.
–. Garnet Burk Hughes, MG 27 II D23.
–. Albert Edward Kemp fonds, MG 27 II D 9.
–. Archibald Cameron Macdonell collection, MG 30 E20.
–. Cyrus Wesley Peck fonds, MG30 E134.
–. George Halsey Perley fonds, MG 27 II D12.
–. James Layton Ralston fonds, MG 27 III B11.
–. David Watson fonds, Microfilm Reel M-10.

–. Albert C. West fonds, MG 30 E32.
–. RG9, Series III-D-3, Militia and Defence fonds, War Diaries of the Canadian Corps, Canadian Infantry Divisions, Infantry Brigades and Infantry Battalions in the C.E.F.
–. RG 24, Records of the Department of National Defence.
–. RG 150, Accession 1992–93/145–238, Circumstances of Death Registers, First World War.
–. RG 150, Accession 1992–93/314, Commonwealth War Graves Registers, First World War.
–. RG 150, Accession 1992–93/166, Personnel Records, Canadian Expeditionary Force.
–. Veterans Death Cards, First World War.

National Defence, Directorate of History and Heritage (DHH) – Ottawa
–. Army Headquarters Reports (AHR) 1948–1959.
–. Edwin Pye fonds 74/672.

Unpublished Sources
Dennis, H., Private Letters, 1918.
Nominal Roll, 7th (British Columbia) Battalion.
Neilson, A.R., Personal Diary, March–November 1918.

Newspapers, Magazines and Newsletters
21st Battalion Communique
Abbotsford Post
Border Cities Star
Calgary Daily Herald
Chatham Daily Planet
Hamilton Spectator
Legion Magazine
La Patrie
London Gazette
Maclean's Magazine
Muskoka Herald
Ottawa Journal-Press
Perth Courier
Renfrew Mercury
St. Thomas Times-Journal
Gazette (Montreal)
Veteran – Official Organ of the Great War Veterans' Association of Canada
Toronto Daily Star
Toronto Globe
Toronto World
Walkerton Telescope
Waterdown Review
Windsor Record
Winnipeg Telegram
Vancouver Sun
Vernon News

Online Sources

Memorial University of Newfoundland
The Diaries of Sir Robert Borden, 1912–18:
http://www.research.library.mun.ca/2428/

The National Archives, Kew, Richmond, Surrey, United Kingdom
War Office (WO) 95 – British Army War Diaries 1914–22
Cabinet Records (CAB) 24 – Western and General Reports:
http://www.nationalarchives.gov.uk/

National Archives of Australia
http://www.naa.gov.au/

Vancouver Island University
The Canadian Letters and Images Project: http://www.canadianletters.ca

Veterans Affairs Canada
The Canadian Virtual War Memorial: http://www.veterans.gc.ca/eng/remembrance/
memorials/canadian-virtual-war-memorial

Other Sources

Abbink, Harry. *The Military Medal: Canadian Recipients, 1916–1922*. Calgary: Alison, 1987.

Adjutant, The [E.P.S. Allen]. *The 116th Battalion in France*. Toronto: Hunter-Rose, 1921.

Anderson, Major-General Sir W. Hastings, K.C.B. "The Breaking of the Quéant-Drocourt Line by the Canadian Corps, First Army, 2nd–4th September, 1918." *Canadian Defence Quarterly* 3, 2 (January 1926): 120–27.

Antal, Sandy, and Kevin R. Shackleton. *Duty Nobly Done: The Official History of the Essex Scottish Regiment*. Windsor, ON: Walkerville, 2006.

Armstrong, Elizabeth. *The Crisis of Quebec, 1914–1918*. Toronto: McClelland and Stewart, 1974.

Asquith, Herbert. "Address to Parliament Announcing the War on 6 August 1914." In *Source Records of the Great War*, vol. 1, ed. Charles F. Horne, 398–404. New York: The National Alumni, 1923.

Auger, Martin F. "On the Brink of Civil War: The Canadian Government and the Suppression of the 1918 Quebec Easter Riots." *Canadian Historical Review* 89, 4 (2008): 503–40.

[Bailey, John Beswick]. *Cinquante-Quatre 1914–1919: Being a Short History of the 54th Canadian Infantry Battalion*. Ottawa: CEF Books, 2003.

Baker, Matt. "The List of the Nation's Heroes, Voluntary Enlistment in Chatham, Ontario 1914–1916," *Canadian Military History* 24, 1 (Winter–Spring 2015): 141–80.

Bean, C.E.W. *The Official History of Australia in the War of 1914–1918*, vol. 6: *The Australian Imperial Force in France during the Allied Offensive 1918*. Sydney: Angus and Robertson, 1942.

Beattie, Kim. *48th Highlanders of Canada: 1891–1928*. Toronto: 48th Highlanders of Canada, 1932.

Becker, John Harold. *Silhouettes of the Great War: The Memoir of John Harold Becker 1915–1919, 75th Canadian Infantry Battalion (Mississauga Horse) Canadian Expeditionary Force*. Nepean, ON: CEF Books, 2001.

Bennett, S.G. *The 4th Canadian Mounted Rifles 1914–1919*. Toronto: Murray Printing, 1926.

Bercuson, David. *The Fighting Canadians*. Toronto: HarperCollins, 2009.

–. *The Patricias: The Proud History of a Fighting Regiment*. Toronto: Stoddart, 2001.

Bet-El, Ilana R. *Conscripts: Lost Legions of the Great War*. Guildford: Sutton, 1999.

Bick, Peter Hardie, ed. *The Diary of an Artillery Officer: The 1st Canadian Divisional Artillery on the Western Front, Written by Major Arthur Hardie Bick, DSO*. Toronto: Dundurn Press, 2011.

Bindon, Kathryn M. *More Than Patriotism: Canada at War 1914–1918*. Toronto: Thomas Nelson and Sons (Canada), 1979.

Blanchard, Jim. *Winnipeg's Great War: A City Comes of Age*. Winnipeg: University of Manitoba Press, 2010.

Booth, Jeffrey, ed. *Opened by Censor: A Collection of Letters Home from World War I Veterans from Elgin County*. Aylmer, ON: Aylmer Express, 2008.

Borden, Robert. *Robert Laird Borden: His Memoirs*, vols. 1 and 2, ed. Henry Borden. Toronto: Macmillan of Canada, 1938.

Bovey, Lieutenant-Colonel W., O.B.E. "General Sir Arthur Currie: An Appreciation." *Canadian Defence Quarterly* 3, 4 (July 1926): 371–79.

Bray, R. Matthew. "'Fighting as an Ally': The English-Canadian Patriotic Response to the Great War." *Canadian Historical Review* 61, 2 (1980): 141–68.

Brennan, Patrick. "From Amateur to Professional: The Experience of Brigadier General William Antrobus Griesbach." In *Canada and the Great War: Western Front Association Papers*, ed. Briton C. Busch, 78–92. Montreal and Kingston: McGill–Queen's University Press, 2003.

–. "Byng's and Currie's Commanders: A Still Untold Story of the Canadian Corps." *Canadian Military History* 11, 2 (Spring 2002): 5–16.

Brittain, Vera. *Testament of Youth: An Autobiographical Study of the Years 1900–1925*. London: Weidenfeld and Nicholson, 2009.

Brown, Malcolm. *1918: Year of Victory*. London: Pan Books, 1999.

Brown, Robert Craig. *Robert Laird Borden, A Biography*, vol. 2: *1914–1937*. Toronto: Macmillan of Canada, 1980.

Brown, Robert Craig, and Donald Loveridge. "Unrequited Faith: Recruiting the CEF 1914–1918." *Revue Internationale d'Histoire Militaire* 51 (1982): 53–79.

Byers, Daniel. "Mobilising Canada: The National Resources Mobilization Act, the Department of National Defence, and Compulsory Military Service in Canada, 1940–1945." *Journal of the Canadian Historical Association / Revue de la Société historique du Canada* 7, 1 (1996): 175–203.

–. "J.L. Ralston and the First World War: The Origins of a Life of Service." *Canadian Military History* 22, 1 (Winter 2013): 3–16.

–. *Zombie Army: The Canadian Army and Conscription in the Second World War*. Vancouver: UBC Press, 2016.

Cane, Bruce, ed. *It Made You Think of Home: The Haunting Journals of Deward Barnes, Canadian Expeditionary Force 1916–1919*. Toronto: Dundurn Press, 2004.

Christie, Norm. *Canadian Cemeteries of the Great War*, vol. 1: *Belgium*. Ottawa: CEF Books, 2010.

–. *For King and Empire*, vol. 5: *The Canadians at Arras and the Drocourt-Queant Line August–September 1918*. Nepean: CEF Books, 1997.

Churchill, Winston S. *The World Crisis*, vol. 4. New York: Charles Scribner's Sons, 1927.

Clarke, Nic. *Unwanted Warriors: Rejected Volunteers of the Canadian Expeditionary Force*. Vancouver: UBC Press, 2015.

Clements, Captain Robert N., M.C. *Merry Hell: The Story of the 25th Battalion (Nova Scotia Regiment) Canadian Expeditionary Force 1914–1919*, ed. Brian Douglas Tennyson. Toronto: University of Toronto Press, 2013.

Clyne, H.R.N., M.C. *Vancouver's 29th*. Vancouver: Tobin's Tigers Association, 1964.

Cook, Tim. "'Literary Memorials': The Great War Regimental Histories, 1919–1939." *Journal of the Canadian Historical Association / Revue de la Société historique du Canada* 13, 1 (2002): 167–90.

–. *The Madman and the Butcher: The Sensational Wars of Sam Hughes and General Arthur Currie*. Toronto: Allen Lane, 2010.

–. *At the Sharp End: Canadians Fighting the Great War*, vol. 1: *1914–1916*. Toronto: Viking, 2007.

–. *Shock Troops: Canadians Fighting the Great War*, vol. 2: *1917–1918*. Toronto: Viking, 2008.

–. *Warlords: Borden, Mackenzie King, and Canada's World Wars*. Toronto: Allen Lane, 2012.

Coombs, Howard G. "Dimensions of Military Leadership: The Kinmel Park Mutiny of 4/5 March 1919." Canadian Forces College (October 2004). http://docplayer.net/34985544-Dimensions-of-military-leadership-the-kinmel-park-mutiny-of-4-5-march-1919.html.

Cooper, Major J.A. *Fourth Canadian Infantry Brigade: History of Operations, April, 1915, to Demobilization*. London: Charles and Son, 1919.

Copp, J.T., and T.D. Tait. *The Canadian Response to War: 1914–1917*. Toronto: Copp Clark, 1971.

Copp, Terry. "The Military Effort 1914–1918." In *Canada and the First World War: Essays in Honour of Robert Craig Brown*, ed. David Mackenzie, 35–61. Toronto: University of Toronto Press, 2005.

Corrigall, Major D.J., D.S.O., M.C. *The Twentieth Canadian Battalion (Central Ontario Regiment) Canadian Expeditionary Force in the Great War, 1914–1918*. Toronto: Stone and Cox, 1935.

Craig, Grace Morris. *But This Is Our War*. Toronto: University of Toronto Press, 1981.

Crowley, James A. "Borden: Conscription and Union Government," PhD diss., University of Ottawa, 1958.

Currie, Lieutenant-General Sir A.W., G.C.M.G., K.C.B. "Canadian Corps Operations during the Year 1918: Interim Report." In *Report of the Ministry Overseas Military Forces of Canada 1918*, 101–92. London: HMSO, 1919.

Dancocks, Daniel G. *Gallant Canadians: The Story of the Tenth Canadian Infantry Battalion, 1914–1919*. Markham: Penguin Books, 1990.

–. *Legacy of Valour: The Canadians at Passchendaele*. Edmonton: Hurtig Publishers, 1986.

–. *Sir Arthur Currie: A Biography*. Toronto: Methuen, 1985.

–. *Spearhead to Victory: Canada and the Great War*. Edmonton: Hurtig, 1987.

Dennis, Patrick. "A Canadian Conscript Goes to War – August 1918, Old Myths Re-examined." *Canadian Military History* 18, 1 (Winter 2009): 21–36.

Duguid, Colonel A. Fortescue. *History of the Canadian Grenadier Guards 1760–1964*. Montreal: Gazette Printing, 1965.

–. *Official History of the Canadian Forces in the Great War 1914–1919: From the Outbreak of War to the Formation of the Canadian Corps August 1914–September 1915*. General Series, vol. 1 and *Chronology, Appendices and Maps*. Ottawa: J.O. Paternaude, 1938.

Edmonds, Brigadier-General Sir James E. *Military Operations: France and Belgium, 1918*, vol. 4: *8 August–26 September, the Franco-British Offensive*. London: HMSO, 1947.

Edmonds, Brigadier-General Sir James E., and Lieutenant-Colonel R. Maxwell-Hyslop. *Military Operations: France and Belgium, 1918*, vol. 5: *26th September–11th November, The Advance to Victory*. London: HMSO, 1947, and Nashville: Battery Press, 1997.

English, John. *The Decline of Politics: The Conservatives and the Party System 1901–1920*. Toronto: University of Toronto Press, 1977.

Ferguson, Niall. *The Pity of War*. New York: Basic Books, 1999.

Ferro, Marc. *The Great War 1914–1918*, trans. Nicole Stone. London: Routledge and Kegan Paul, 1973.

Fetherstonhaugh, R.C., ed. *The 13th Battalion Royal Highlanders of Canada 1914–1919*. Montreal: [privately printed], 1925.

–. *The 24th Battalion, C.E.F., Victoria Rifles of Canada, 1914–1919*. Montreal: Gazette Printing, 1930.

–. *The Royal Montreal Regiment 14th Battalion C.E.F. 1914 –1925*. Montreal: Gazette Printing, 1927.

Flanders' Fields: Canadian Voices from World War I. CBC Radio, December 1964, 17 parts. J. Frank Willis, Narrator/Director, Frank Lalor, editor. CBC DVD-Audio, 2006. Transcript available at Canadian War Museum, Ottawa.

Fleming, R.B., ed. *The Wartime Letters of Leslie and Cecil Frost 1915–1918*. Waterloo: Wilfrid Laurier University Press, 2007.

Flynn, George Q. *Conscription and Democracy: The Draft in France, Great Britain, and the United States*. Westport, CT: Greenwood Press, 2002.

Forty-Twa. "Parvillers." *The Legionary* 3, 4 (September 1928): 18–20.

Frost, Leslie M. *Fighting Men*. Toronto: Clarke, Irwin, 1967.

Fussell, Paul, *The Great War and Modern Memory*. New York: Oxford University Press, 2000.

Gagnon, Jean-Pierre. *Le 22e bataillon (canadien-français) 1914–1919, Étude socio-militaire*. Québec: Les Presses de l'Université Laval, 1986.

Gibbs, Sir Philip. *Now It Can Be Told*. Garden City, NY: Garden City Publishing, 1920.

Gibson, Captain W.L. *Records of the Fourth Canadian Infantry Battalion in the Great War 1914–1918*. Toronto: Maclean, 1924.

Goodspeed, D.J. *Battle Royal: The History of the Royal Regiment of Canada 1862–1962*. Toronto: Charters, 1962.

–. *The Road Past Vimy: The Canadian Corps 1914–1918*. Toronto: Macmillan, 1969.

Goudy, Donald M. "The M.S.A. Sent Us Good Men." *21st Battalion Communique* 7, 2 (July 1938): 14–15.

Gould, L. McLeod. *From B.C. to Baisieux, Being the Narrative History of the 102nd Canadian Infantry Battalion*. Victoria: Thos. R. Cusack, 1919.

Granatstein, J.L. *Canada's Army: Waging War and Keeping the Peace*. 2nd ed. Toronto: University of Toronto Press, 2011.

–. "Conscription and My Politics," *Canadian Military History* 10, 4 (Autumn 2001): 35–38.

–. "Conscription in the Great War." In *Canada and the First World War: Essays in Honour of Robert Craig Brown*, ed. David Mackenzie, 62–75. Toronto: University of Toronto Press, 2005.

–. *The Greatest Victory: Canada's One Hundred Days, 1918*. Toronto: Oxford University Press, 2014.

–. *Hell's Corner: An Illustrated History of Canada's Great War 1914–1918*. Vancouver: Douglas and McIntyre, 2004.

Granatstein, J.L., and J. Mackay Hitsman. *Broken Promises: A History of Conscription in Canada*. Toronto: Oxford University Press, 1977.

Gravel, Michel. *Tough as Nails: The Epic Story of Hillie Foley, DCM and bar, MM, C de G, 1914–1918*. Ottawa: CEF Books, 2006.

Greenhous, Brereton. *The Battle of Amiens, 8–11 August 1918*. Toronto: Balmuir Books, 1995.

Gwyn, Sandra. *Tapestry of War: A Private View of Canadians in the Great War*. Toronto: HarperCollins, 1992.

Hann, Russell G. "Introduction." In *Great War and Canadian Society*, ed. Daphne Read, 9–38. Toronto: New Hogtown Press, 1978.

Harris, J.P. *Douglas Haig and the First World War*. New York: Cambridge University Press, 2009.

Harris, J.P., with Niall Barr. *Amiens to the Armistice: The BEF in the "Hundred Days" Campaign, 8 August–11 November 1918*. London: Brassey's, 1998.

Harris, Stephen J. *Canadian Brass: The Making of a Professional Army, 1860–1939*. Toronto: University of Toronto Press, 1988.

Hayes, Lieutenant-Colonel Joseph, D.S.O. *The Eighty-Fifth in France and Flanders*. Halifax: Royal Print and Litho, 1920.

Hill, Roland. "Chapter V – On the Eve of a Great Battle." In *Canada in the Great War*, vol. 5: *Triumph of the Allies*, 126–36. Toronto: United Publishers of Canada, 1920.

–. "Chapter VI – The Battle of Amiens," 137–71.

–. "Chapter VII – Breaking the Drocourt-Queant Line," 172–94.

–. "Chapter IX – Cambrai to Valenciennes," 205–20.

Hodder-Williams, Ralph. *Princess Patricia's Canadian Light Infantry 1914–1919*, vol. 1: *Narrative*; vol. 2: *The Roll of Honour and Appendices*. London and Toronto: Hodder and Stoughton, 1923.

Holmes, Richard. *The Western Front*. London: BBC Worldwide, 1999.

Holt, Richard. "British Blood Calls British Blood: The British-Canadian Recruiting Mission of 1917–1918." *Canadian Military History* 22, 1 (Winter 2013): 27–37.

–. "Filling the Ranks: Recruiting, Training, and Reinforcements in the Canadian Expeditionary Force 1914–1918." PhD diss., University of Western Ontario, 2011.

Hopkins, J. Castell, F.S.S., F.R.G.S. *Canada at War: A Record of Heroism and Achievement 1914–1918*. Toronto: Canadian Annual Review, 1919.

–. *The Canadian Annual Review War Series: 1917*. Toronto: The Canadian Annual Review, 1918.

Horn, Lieutenant-Colonel Bernd, and Stephen Harris, eds. *Warrior Chiefs: Perspectives on Senior Canadian Military Leaders*. Toronto: Dundurn Press, 2001.

Humphries, Mark, ed. *The Selected Papers of Sir Arthur Currie: Diaries, Letters, and Report to the Ministry, 1917–1933*. Waterloo: Laurier Centre for Military, Strategic and Disarmament Studies, Wilfrid Laurier University Press, 2008.

Hyatt, A.M.J. "Sir Arthur Currie and Conscription: A Soldier's View." *Canadian Historical Review* 50, 3 (September 1969): 285–96.

–. *General Sir Arthur Currie: A Military Biography*. Toronto: University of Toronto Press, 1987.

–. "The Military Leadership of Sir Arthur Currie." In *Warrior Chiefs: Perspectives on Senior Canadian Military Leaders*, ed. Lieutenant-Colonel Bernd Horn and Stephen Harris, 43–56. Toronto: Dundurn Press, 2001.

Hyland, Chris. "The Canadian Corps' Long March – Logistics, Discipline, and the Occupation of the Rhineland." *Canadian Military History* 2 (Spring 2012): 5–20.

Iarocci, Andrew. *Shoestring Soldiers: The 1st Canadian Division at War, 1914–1915*. Toronto: University of Toronto Press, 2008.

Isitt, Benjamin. *From Victoria to Vladivostok: Canada's Siberian Expedition, 1917–1919.* Vancouver: UBC Press, 2010.

Johnston, Lieutenant-Colonel G. Chalmers, D.S.O., M.C. *The 2nd Canadian Mounted Rifles (British Columbia Horse) in France and Flanders.* Ottawa: CEF Books, 2003.

Kempling, James S. "Birth of a Regiment: Princess Patricia's Canadian Light Infantry 1914–1919," MA thesis, University of Victoria, BC, 1978.

Kerr, Wilfred. *Arms and the Maple Leaf, 1918.* Ottawa: CEF Books, 2005.

Keshen, Jeffrey A. *Propaganda and Censorship during Canada's Great War.* Edmonton: University of Alberta Press, 1996.

Lapointe, Arthur J. *Souvenirs et impressions de ma vie de soldat.* Saint-Ulric: [privately published], 1919.

Laut, Agnes C. "The Slacker." *Macleans's Magazine,* November 1917, 27–28, 99.

Letters From the Front – Being a Record of the Part Played by Officers of the Bank in the Great War 1914–1919, vol. I. Toronto: Southam Press, 1920.

Levi, Margaret. "The Institution of Conscription." *Social Science History* 20, 1 (Spring 1996): 133–67.

Lewis, John. "Canada at War." In *Canada in the Great War,* vol. 2: *Days of Preparation.* Toronto: United Publishers of Canada, 1920.

Litalien, Michel. *Écrire sa guerre, Témoignages de soldats canadiens-français (1914–1919).* Outrement: Éditions Athéna, 2011.

Livesay, J.F.B. *Canada's Hundred Days, with the Canadian Corps from Amiens to Mons, Aug. 8 – Nov. 11, 1918.* Toronto: Thomas Allen, 1919.

Ludendorff, Erich. *My War Memories, 1914–1918.* 2 vols. London: Hutchinson, [1919].

Macdonell, Lieutenant-General Sir Archibald K.C.B., C.M.G., D.S.O., LL.D. "'The Old Red Patch.' The 1st Canadian Division at the Breaking of the Canal du Nord Line." *Canadian Defence Quarterly* 9, 1 (October 1931): 10–26.

–. "'The Old Red Patch' at the Breaking of the Drocourt-Quéant Line, the Crossing of the Canal du Nord and Advance on Cambrai, 30th August–2nd October, 1918." *Canadian Defence Quarterly* 4, 4 (July 1927): 388–96.

Machin, H.A.C. *Report of the Director of the Military Service Branch to the Honourable Minister of Justice on the Operation of the Military Service Act, 1917.* Ottawa: J. De Labroquerie Taché, 1919.

Mackenzie, David, ed. *Canada and the First World War: Essays in Honour of Robert Craig Brown.* Toronto: University of Toronto Press, 2005.

Macphail, Sir Andrew. *Official History of the Canadian Forces in the Great War 1914–19: The Medical Services.* Ottawa: F.A. Acland, King's Printer, 1925.

Macpherson, J.S.B. "Chapter XI – From Mons to the Rhine." In *Canada in the Great War,* vol. 5: *Triumph of the Allies,* 230–64. Toronto: United Publishers of Canada, 1920.

Mainville, Curtis. *Till the Boys Come Home: Life on the Home Front, Queen's County, NB, 1914–1918.* Fredericton: Goose Lane Editions, 2015.

Maroney, Paul. "'The Great Adventure': The Context and Ideology of Recruiting in Ontario, 1914–1917." *Canadian Historical Review* 77, 1 (March 1996): 62–98.

Marshall, Debbie. *Give Your Other Vote to the Sister.* Calgary: University of Calgary Press, 2007.

McCulloch, Ian. "'Batty Mac': Portrait of a Brigade Commander of the Great War, 1915–1917." *Canadian Military History* 7, 4 (Autumn 1998): 11–18.

–. "Crisis in Leadership: The Seventh Brigade and the Nivelles 'Mutiny,' 1918." *Army Doctrine and Training Bulletin* 3, 2 (Summer 2000): 35–46.

–. "The 'Fighting Seventh:' The Evolution and Devolution of Tactical Command and Control in a Canadian Infantry Brigade of the Great War." MA thesis, Royal Military College of Canada, Kingston, 1997. Ottawa: National Library of Canada, [1998 – microfiche].

McEvoy, Bernard, and Captain A.H. Finlay. *History of the 72nd Canadian Infantry Battalion – Seaforth Highlanders of Canada.* Vancouver: Cowan and Brookhouse, 1920.

McKean, George B. V.C., M.C., M.M. *Scouting Thrills: The Memoir of a Scout Officer in the Great War.* Ottawa: CEF Books, 2007.

McWilliams, James, and R. James Steel. *The Suicide Battalion.* Edmonton: Hurtig Publishers, 1978.

–. *Amiens: Dawn of Victory.* Toronto: Dundurn Press, 2001.

Miller, Ian Hugh Maclean. *Our Glory and Our Grief: Torontonians and the Great War.* Toronto: University of Toronto Press, 2002.

Moffat, Ian C.D. "Forgotten Battlefields – Canadians in Siberia, 1918–1919." *Canadian Military Journal* 8, 3 (Autumn 2007): 73–83.

Morton, Desmond. *Canada and War: A Military and Political History.* Toronto: Butterworth, 1981.

–. *Fight or Pay: Soldiers' Families in the Great War.* Vancouver: UBC Press, 2004.

–. "'Kicking and Complaining': Demobilization Riots in the Canadian Expeditionary Force, 1918–1919." *Canadian Historical Review* 61, 3 (1980): 334–60.

–. *A Military History of Canada.* Edmonton: Hurtig, 1985.

–. "Polling the Soldier Vote: The Overseas Campaign in the Canadian General Election of 1917." *Journal of Canadian Studies* 10, 4 (November 1975): 39–58.

–. *Report no. 98, Historical Section (G.S.) Army Headquarters.* "The Command of the Overseas Military Forces of Canada in the United Kingdom, 1914–1918." Ottawa: Department of National Defence, Directorate of History and Heritage, [1962].

–. *Silent Battle: Canadian Prisoners of War in Germany 1914–1919.* Toronto: Lester, 1992.

–. *When Your Number's Up.* Toronto: Random House of Canada, 1993.

Morton, Desmond, and J.L. Granatstein. *Marching to Armageddon: Canadians and the Great War 1914–1919.* Toronto: Lester and Orpen Dennys, 1989.

Morton, Desmond, and Glenn Wright. *Winning the Second Battle: Canadian Veterans and the Return to Civilian Life.* Toronto: University of Toronto Press, 1987.

Murray, Col. W.W. *The History of the 2nd Canadian Battalion (Eastern Ontario Regiment) Canadian Expeditionary Force in the Great War, 1914–1919.* Ottawa: Mortimer, 1947.

Neatby, H. Blair. *Laurier and a Liberal Quebec: A Study in Political Management,* ed. Richard T. Clippingdale. Toronto: McClelland and Stewart, 1973 [1956].

Neiberg, Michael S. *Dance of the Furies: Europe and the Outbreak of World War I.* Cambridge, MA: Harvard University Press, 2011.

–. *Fighting the Great War: A Global History.* Cambridge, MA: Harvard University Press, 2005.

Nichol, Stephen J. *Ordinary Heroes: Eastern Ontario's 21st Battalion C.E.F. in the Great War.* Almonte, ON: [privately published], 2008.

Nicholson, G.W.L. *Canadian Expeditionary Force, 1914–1919: Official History of the Canadian Army in the First World War.* 2nd printing (corrected). Ottawa: Queen's Printer, 1964.

O'Leary, Michael M. "Not All Were Volunteers: The RCR and the Military Service Act." Originally published in *Pro Patria 2006 Regimental Journal of the Royal Canadian Regiment,* Issue 88, 2007. See also "The First World War Non-Commissioned Officers and Soldiers of The Royal Canadian Regiment." *The Regimental Rogue*. www. regimentalrogue.com/rcr_great_war_soldiers/rcr_and_the_msa.html.

Pedley, Lieutenant James H., M.C. *Only This: A War Retrospect, 1917–1918*. Ottawa: CEF Books, 1999.

Preston, Richard A., and Sydney F. Wise. *Men in Arms: A History of Warfare and Its Interrelationship with Western Society*. 2nd rev. ed. New York: Praeger Publishers, 1970.

Prior, Robin, and Trevor Wilson. *Command on the Western Front: The Military Career of Sir Henry Rawlinson, 1914–1918*. Barnsley: Pen and Sword Military Classics, 2004.

Radley, Kenneth. *Get Tough, Stay Tough: Shaping the Canadian Corps, 1914–1918*. Solihull, England: Helion, 2014.

–. *We Lead, Others Follow: First Canadian Division, 1914–1918*. St. Catharines: Vanwell, 2006.

Rawling, Bill. "A Resource Not to Be Squandered: The Canadian Corps on the 1918 Battlefield." In *1918: Defining Victory*, ed. Peter Dennis and Jeffrey Grey, 43–71. Canberra: Army History Unit, 1999.

–. *Surviving Trench Warfare: Technology and the Canadian Corps, 1914–1918*. Toronto: University of Toronto Press, 1992.

Read, Daphne, ed. *The Great War and Canadian Society: An Oral History*. Toronto: New Hogtown Press, 1978.

Renison, Robert John, D.D. "A Story of Five Cities – a Canadian Epic of One Hundred Days." In J. Castell Hopkins, *Canada at War: A Record of Heroism and Achievement 1914–1918*. Toronto: The Canadian Annual Review, 1919.

Richard, Béatrice. "Henri Bourassa and Conscription: Traitor or Saviour." *Canadian Military Journal* 7, 4 (Winter 2006–7): 75–83.

Ruck, Calvin W. *The Black Battalion – 1916–1920 – Canada's Best Kept Military Secret*. Halifax: Nimbus, 1987.

Russenholt, E.S. *Six Thousand Canadian Men; Being the History of the 44th Battalion Canadian Infantry 1914–1919*. Winnipeg: De Montfort Press, 1932.

Rutherdale, Robert. *Hometown Horizons: Local Responses to Canada's Great War*. Vancouver: UBC Press, 2004.

Sassoon, Siegfried. *War Poems of Siegfried Sassoon*. New York: Dover, 2004.

Schreiber, Shane. *Shock Army of the British Empire*. St. Catharines: Vanwell, 2005.

Scott, Canon Frederick G., C.M.G., D.S.O. *The Great War As I Saw It*. Ottawa: CEF Books, 1999.

Shackleton, Kevin. *Second to None: The Fighting 58th Battalion of the CEF*. Toronto: Dundurn Press, 2002.

Sharpe, Chris. "Enlistment in the Canadian Expeditionary Force 1914–1918: A Re-evaluation." *Canadian Military History* 24, 1 (Winter–Spring 2015): 17–60.

Sharpe, Robert J. *The Last Day, The Last Hour: The Currie Libel Trial*. Toronto: University of Toronto Press, 2011 [1988].

Shaw, Amy J. *Crisis of Conscience: Conscientious Objection in Canada during the First World War*. Vancouver: UBC Press, 2009.

Sheffield, Gary, and John Bourne. *Douglas Haig: War Diaries and Letters 1914–1918*. Chatham: BCA, 2005.

Sheldon-Williams, Ralf Frederic Lardy. *The Canadian Front in France and Flanders*. London: A. and C. Black, 1920.

Singer, H.C., and A.A. Peebles. *History of Thirty-First Battalion C.E.F. from Its organization November 1914 to Its Demobilization June 1919*. Calgary: [privately printed], 1939.

Skelton, O.D. *Life and Letters of Sir Wilfrid Laurier,* vol. 2, ed. David M.L. Farr. Toronto: McClelland and Stewart, 1965.

Snell, Colonel A.E., C.M.G., D.S.O., B.A., M.B. *The C.A.M.C. With the Canadian Corps During the Last Hundred Days of the Great War.* Ottawa: F.A. Acland, 1924.

Stevenson, David. *1914–1918: The History of the First World War.* London: Penguin Books, 2012 [2005].

–. *With Our Backs to the Wall: Victory and Defeat in 1918.* Cambridge, MA: Harvard University Press, 2011.

Stewart, William Frederick. "Attack Doctrine in the Canadian Corps, 1916–1918," MA thesis, University of New Brunswick, 1982.

–. *The Embattled General: Sir Richard Turner and the First World War.* Montreal and Kingston: McGill–Queen's University Press, 2015.

Strachan, Hew. *The First World War.* New York: Viking Penguin, 2004.

Tascona, Bruce, and Eric Wells. *Little Black Devils: A History of the Royal Winnipeg Rifles.* Winnipeg: Frye, 1983.

Tennyson, Brian Douglas. *Percy Willmot: Cape Bretoner at War 1914–1919.* Sydney: Cape Breton University Press, 2007.

–. *Canada's Great War, 1914–1918: How Canada Helped Save the British Empire and Became a North American Nation.* Lanham, MD: Rowman and Littlefield, 2014.

Terraine, John. *To Win a War: 1918, The Year of Victory.* Garden City, NY: Doubleday, 1981.

Theobald, Andrew. *The Bitter Harvest of War: New Brunswick and the Conscription Crisis of 1917.* New Brunswick: Goose Lane Editions, 2008.

–. "Une Loi Extraordinaire: New Brunswick Acadians and the Conscription Crisis of the First World War." *Acadiensis* 34 (September 2004). https://journals.lib.unb.ca/index.php/acadiensis/article/view/10651/11307.

Thompson, John Herd. *The Harvests of War: The Prairie West, 1914–1918.* Toronto: McClelland and Stewart, 1981.

Topp, Lieutenant-Colonel C. Beresford. *The 42nd Battalion, C.E.F. Royal Highlanders of Canada.* Montreal: Gazette Printing, 1931.

Travers, Tim. *How the War Was Won: Command and Technology on the Western Front, 1917–1918.* Barnsley, England: Pen and Sword Books, 2005.

Ungar, Molly. "Saving the Past: Evidence from Military Tribunal 330, October 1917." Unpublished conference paper presented to the Canadian Historical Association, Annual Meeting, Sherbrooke, and Military History Colloquium, Wilfrid Laurier University, 1999.

Urquhart, H.M. *Arthur Currie: The Biography of a Great Canadian.* Toronto: J.M. Dent and Sons, 1950.

–. *The History of the 16th Battalion (The Canadian Scottish) Canadian Expeditionary Force in the Great War, 1914–1919.* Toronto: Macmillan, 1932.

Vance, Jonathan. *Death So Noble: Memory, Meaning, and the First World War.* Vancouver: UBC Press, 1997.

–. "Provincial Patterns of Enlistment in the Canadian Expeditionary Force," *Canadian Military History* 17, 2 (Spring 2008): 75–80.

Walker, James W. St. G. "Race and Recruitment in World War I: Enlistment of Visible Minorities in the Canadian Expeditionary Force." *Canadian Historical Review* 70, 1 (1989): 1–26.

Wallace, W.S. "Canada in the Great War." In *Pictorial History of the Great War.* 5th ed. Toronto: John A. Hertel, 1919.

Wheeler, Victor. *The 50th Battalion in No Man's Land*. Calgary: Comprint, 1980.

Williams, C.G. "Report of Lieut.-Col. (Rev.) Cecil Grosvenor Williams, Chief Recruiting Officer for Canada," at Library and Archives Canada, Alfred Edward Kemp fonds, MG 27 II D 9, n.d. [August, 1917].

Wigney, Edward H. *The C.E.F. Roll of Honour: Members and Former Members of the Canadian Expeditionary Force Who Died as a Result of Service in the Great War 1914–1919*. Winnipeg: Bunker to Bunker Books, 1996.

–. *Guests of the Kaiser*, ed. Norm Christie. Ottawa: CEF Books, 2008.

Willison, W.A. "Holding the Line." In *Canada in the Great War*, vol. 5: *Triumph of the Allies*. Toronto: United Publishers of Canada, 1920.

Willms, A.M. "Conscription, 1917: A Brief for the Defence." *Canadian Historical Review* 37, 4 (December 1956): 338–51.

Wilson, Barbara M., ed. *Ontario and the First World War 1914–1918: A Collection of Documents*. Toronto: University of Toronto Press, 1977.

Winegard, Timothy C. *For King and Kanata: Canadian Indians and the First World War*. Winnipeg: University of Manitoba Press, 2012.

Winter, Denis. *Haig's Command: A Reassessment*. London: Penguin, 2001.

Wise, Sydney F. "The Black Day of the German Army: Australians and Canadians at Amiens, August 1918." In *1918, Defining Victory: Proceedings of the Chief of Army's History Conference held at the National Convention Center, Canberra, 29 September 1998*, ed. Peter Dennis and Jeffrey Grey, 1–32. Canberra: Army History Unit, Department of Defence, 2001.

Wood, James. *Militia Myths: Ideas of the Canadian Citizen Soldier, 1896–1921*. Vancouver: UBC Press, 2010.

Worthington, Larry. *Amid the Guns Below: The Story of the Canadian Corps (1914–1919)*. Toronto: McClelland and Stewart, 1965.

Young A.H., and W.A. Kirkwood, eds. *The War Memorial Volume of Trinity College, Toronto*. Toronto: Printers Guild, 1922.

Index

Military Service Act (MSA), about, 26–29; age, 27, 44, 223, 236, 240; cancellation of exemptions, 57; classes, 27, 236–37; Currie's justification for, 215–16; debates on bill, 27–31, 247*n*88; delay in implementation, 30, 31–32, 40, 41–42; divided public support, 29–30, 247*n*90; exemptions, 27, 236–37; implementation after election, 43–44; marital status, 27, 247*n*81; myth of failure of, 5–6, 220, 227–28; non-resident citizens, 46; penalties for non-compliance, 27; postwar amnesty for defaulters, 208–9; postwar reports and official histories, 211, 212. *See also* Borden, Robert,–conscription issue; defaulters; exemption from conscription
–administration: about, 34–35; attestation papers, 10, 44–45, 45(f); casualty form, 44; conscripts under military law, 27; delay on call-ups, 31–32, 41–42; first call-ups (Jan 1918), xi; inability to select branch of service, 35; medical standards for service, 223; Military Service Council, 34; Minister of Justice's mandate, 27; penalties for non-compliance, 27; regimental numbers, 44–45, 225–26; royal proclamation, 36–37, 37(f). *See also* defaulters; exemption from conscription
Military Service Council, 34, 248*n*1
Military Voters Act, 32–33, 248*n*101
Militia Act: dormant clauses, 24–25, 27; voluntary tradition, 12
Militia and Defence, Department of: about, 19; unpreparedness for war, 13–14. *See also* enlistment and recruitment
Mill Switch British Cemetery, 161
Millar, J. MacIntosh, Maj., 112
Millen, L.H., Lieut.-Col., 102
Miller, Ian, 7, 21–22, 38
Miller, L.W., Maj., 144
minorities. *See* race and ethnicity
Mitchell, Coulson, Capt., 165–66, 269*n*8
MM. *See* Military Medal (MM)
Moldavia (troopship), 66
Mons: Battle of (1918), 183, 198–200; libel suit (1928) against Currie, 217–18, 276*nn*51–52

Mons, Pursuit to. *See* Cambrai; Pursuit to Mons, (12–23 October); Pursuit to Mons, Valenciennes (25 October – 2 November); Pursuit to Mons, Valenciennes to Mons (3–11 November)
Montreal: anti-conscription press, 26; exemption records, 249*n*14. *See also* French-Canadians; Quebec
Moorehouse, W.N., Lieut.-Col., 122
Morton, Desmond: on conscripts, 6, 44, 243*n*17; on demobilization, 213; on inadequate training, 53; on knowing one's history, 8, 243*n*21
"Mother's Pet" (Campbell), 20–21
Mott, William Thomas, Pte.: Military Medal, 79, 80(f), 239, 256*n*40
Mount Sorrel, Battle of, 21
Mousseau, Emile, Pte., 168–69
MSA. *See* Military Service Act (MSA)
Murphy, Charles, 30–31
myths about conscripts: about, 6–11, 220–22, 234–35; Currie's influence, 9, 206, 208; historiography, 6, 8–9, 123; insignificant number at battlefront, 4–5, 221, 225–26; MSA as partial success or failure, 5–6, 220, 227–28; poor reception of conscripts, 123; postwar troublemakers, 206–7; records as counter evidence, 9–10, 213, 221, 242*n*1, 244*n*28; Vance on power of myth, 220, 221. *See also* Granatstein, J.L.
–inferiority ("slackers and shirkers"): about, 7, 222–23; Burstall's views, 174; historiography, 243*n*17; patriotism, 64, 68–69; stigma, 222–23. *See also* stigma of conscription
–insufficient training: about, 7, 59, 223–24; actual duration of training, 55–56, 58–59, 223–24, 253*n*39; actual performance, 7; "bunch together" under fire, 114; Burstall on "partial training," 253*n*42; compared to volunteers, 223; Currie on "very little training," 207, 253*n*42; historiography, 243*n*16
–late arrival: about, 4, 123, 224–25; Currie's views, 9, 216–17; first arrivals, 220; news media, 123; speculation on two corps, 224–25

STUDIES IN CANADIAN MILITARY HISTORY

STUDIES IN CANADIAN MILITARY HISTORY
*Published by UBC Press in association
with the Canadian War Museum.*